D0088886

The Stuff Americans Are Made Of has two great virtues: It succeeds in presenting conscious and unconscious springs of action within most of those Americans who lead businesses, and most of those who buy products. Though plenty of Americans don't trace their lineage or their point of view to Plymouth Rock, but instead to Chaco Canyon, to Galway or the Warsaw ghetto, or to Senegal doesn't diminish one whit the utility of knowing that most of us do think of ourselves as Hammond and Morrison do.

Second, its blithe and friendly way of imparting information invites a lively bicker from the reader. It should be read with a red pencil in hand, which says a lot for the authors, because they are interesting.

> Roger C. Kennedy
> Historian and author of *Hidden Cities,*
> Director Emeritus,
> National Museum of American History

A powerful merging of the cultural foundations of American society that explains corporate success, and reinforces the system dynamics structure of a new kind of K-12 education that is beginning to take root across the country.

> Jay W. Forrester
> Founder, System Dynamics,
> Professor of Management, Emeritus,
> Massachusetts Institute of Technology

A thoughtful analysis that gets at the heart of what makes Americans tick.

> Richard J. O'Connor
> Chairman, Lintas/Campbell Ewald

Disney University Professional Development Programs is now offering nationally a two-day training program based on the AQF research. It builds on the information presented in this book and provides participants with three business basics: the role of national culture in performance improvement; tools for personalizing quality and productivity; and a process for aligning people and process. For more information, call (407) 828-5611.

THE STUFF AMERICANS ARE MADE OF

The Seven Cultural Forces
That Define Americans—
A New Framework for Quality,
Productivity and Profitability

JOSH HAMMOND & JAMES MORRISON

Macmillan • USA

To the next generation of
Morrisons, Hammonds, and McCormicks

MACMILLAN
A Simon & Schuster Macmillan Company
1633 Broadway
New York, NY 10019-6785

ISBN 0-02-860829-1

THE STUFF AMERICANS ARE MADE OF is a registered service mark of the American Society for Quality Control (ASQC). The title is also the formal name for a training program marketed exclusively by Disney Professional Development Programs on behalf of ASQC. Permission to use this name as the title of this book has been generously granted by Disney Professional Development Programs.

The following permissions to quote have been granted: throughout the book, excerpts from *Distant Mirrors,* © 1993, Wadsworth, Inc., by permission of the authors, Philip R. DeVita and James D. Armstrong; reproduction of SIMA Map Chart, © 1994, ASQC (Stuff program); excerpt from Russell Baker, "He Filled a Vacuum," October 17, 1995, © 1995, *The New York Times*; excerpt from Orlando Patterson, "Affirmative Action on the Merit System," August 7, 1995, © 1995, The New York Times Company; excerpt from John Heidenry, *Theirs Was the Kingdom,* © 1993, W. W. Norton & Company; excerpts from Fortune writers, © 1994, 1995 Time, Inc. All rights reserved; excerpt from Michael Beckerman, "It's Time to Play Ball, and Stretch and Sing," April 3, 1994, © 1994, The New York Times Company; excerpts from Octavio Paz, *Labyrinth of Solitude,* © 1963, Grove/Atlantic Press; excerpt from Lowell Thomas, *So Long Until Tomorrow,* by permission of Lowell Thomas, Jr.; excerpt from *Digital Audio* (now *CD Review*), April 1985; from *The Twilight of Sovereignty, How the Information Revolution Is Transforming the World* by Walter B. Wriston, © 1992 by Walter B. Wriston reprinted with the permission of Scribner, a division of Simon & Schuster; from *America as a Civilization* by Max Lerner, © 1957 by Max Lerner, copyright renewed 1985 by Max Lerner reprinted with the permission of Simon & Schuster; from *Baseball, An Illustrated History* by Ken Burns, © 1994 by Ken Burns reprinted with the permission of Alfred A. Knopf Publishers; from "Let America Be America Again" by Langston Hughes, reprinted with the permission of Alfred A. Knopf Publishers.

Design by Rachael McBrearty

Manufactured in the United States of America

10 9 8 7 6 5 4 3 2 1

Contents

Acknowledgments

Most book acknowledgments end with a nod to the publishing editor. We begin there because, to paraphrase Duke Ellington, it don't mean a thing, if a book ain't got a good editor. Macmillan's John Michel is that editor. He grasped the concept of our book from his first reading of our proposal. His enthusiasm for our style and approach, plus his guidance, knowledge, wit, and insightful editing, made the process of writing it fun and an important growth experience for us.

At the proposal stage we got some sound, daughterly advice from Kelly Hammond who had done a New York publishing stint, knew the process, and had read a proposal or two. She not only critiqued and helped structure our early drafts, but most important, she became our first cheerleader. The resourcefulness, creativity, and imaginations of our literary agent, Amanda Urban at International Creative Management and her assistant David Roth-Ey, are the stuff that great books are made of.

A vital part of writing and structuring the book was the questioning of and advice from a group of outside readers whom we built into the process from the very beginning. Those who contributed their personal time and professional knowledge included Stephen Yearout of Coopers & Lybrand Consulting (Rosslyn Office); Richard LeVitt at Hewlett-Packard; friend and investment consultant David Ingrim; part-time Southern folklorist Laurin Baker; Doug Park with Worldwide Quality Systems who was always a phone call away; and two colleagues and former credit-card managers, Scott Epscamp and David Hussain, who have started their own financial services business under the great, inventive name of Leapfrog Development in Evanston, Illinois. From the very start, through the scattered files and stacks that almost ate the living room, my wife, Lynn McCormick (Hammond), contributed substantially to the content and editing process, constantly maintaining a nice balance between broad business knowledge and best friendship. Brenda Niemand, who had worked with us from the first days of our research at the American Quality Foundation, came through as always, by providing ideas and editorial support.

Special thanks to Anne Morrison for unflagging patience in the face of a writer's habitual grumpiness.

The dedicated researchers who staff the reference desk at the Penrose Library in Colorado Springs and branches of the Pikes Peak Library District were especially helpful in ferreting out arcane data and verifying an occasional obscure fact. They are book lovers, questers of truth, and keepers of knowledge deserving of praise and respect. Thanks also to David McCullough, Robert M. Baylis, Felicia Rogan, Gerald Dickler, professor and attorney Harry L. Smith who introduced the two of us back in his General Motors speechwriting days, and James B. Taylor and Alan Levenstein for early-on advice and encouragement. Helpful too were George Gumerman, John Holland, and Mike Simmons of The Santa Fe Institute. John Allen was always prompt in returning calls and lending a hand, as were Larry Gustin, Jim Crawford, Ellen Mandenach, Tony Foster, Barry Richmond, Joan Yates, Maryan Baridon, Myron Lowery, Tom McGrath, Bob Sann, Fran Sears, Frederic Rockefeller, and Florence Farr. At Macmillan there were many behind-the-scene folks who worked hard and contributed their talents and skills to bring this book forward. They include the line-editor who fine-tuned everything and got us to fill in those TKs. Estelle Laurence was known to us only as CE somewhere in Arizona, but she was indispensable. Also at Macmillan, thanks to all those who produced and marketed the book, including Jennifer Feldman, Denise Hawkins, Heather Keller, Sharon Heede, designer Rachael McBrearty, and jacket designer Kevin Hanek, who humorously reminded us that the grammatically correct title for the book should be *The Stuff Of Which Americans Are Made.*

There would have been no book without the opportunity that I (Josh) was given by ASQC and its forward-thinking president at the time, Dana Cound, to help create the American Quality Foundation, the first think tank on quality management. It was at the AQF that the original Stuff research was conducted and developed. And there would have been no AQF if Robert Stempel, then president of General Motors, had not agreed to be chairman and tap his executive peers around the country to sit on the board. Bob also gave generously of his time, resources, and leadership in order that we could challenge the status quo conventions at the time. The research for this book, and the training program that bears the same name, was made possible by a challenge grant from General Motors.

Those who conducted and supported some of the studies and those who contributed directly to the research we reference in this book are acknowledged throughout and cited further in the Appendix.

Many thanks for buying the book. As the subtitle of the book claims, we mean it to be a new framework for business performance in America. Therefore, we'd love to hear from you—we need your perspective for our personal and professional development. Besides, we hope there is another book somewhere down the road.

Josh Hammond, New York City
James Morrison, Colorado Springs

Foreword

At Hewlett-Packard (HP), we watch the world with a practice we call scanning. It is the way we see into the *possible* futures, to create new products and services, to update our technologies, and to improve our work processes. In short, scanning helps us keep oriented toward the future so that we remain a vigorous and growing enterprise that returns fair value to our stakeholders. We do our best scanning *en pirouette*—whatever it takes to keep us on our toes. In fact we train all of our managers to create the future by scanning, so that they stay on top of the latest thinking in universities and think tanks, monitor industry developments, and listen closely to customers. We train ourselves to create new opportunities and challenge old assumptions, to understand the implications of the world becoming a smaller place as globalization increases the demand for alertness, flexibility, quicker responses, innovation, and creativity.

Yes, we benchmark other companies. But, scanning is not the same thing. Benchmarking tends to look at practical operational matters. It gives you a snapshot of the present, but it doesn't take you into the future. Benchmarking allows you to catch up, but not always to become a leader. Leaders have advantages; there is a saying that has been around here since the early days, "Only the lead dog gets a change of scenery."

One of the advantages of this process is that it keeps us in touch with the latest in business practices and with consultants and others who are constantly striving to improve the American corporation. This is how we learned about *The Stuff Americans Are Made Of* and the authors' new framework for quality and productivity. Their work is lead-dog stuff. It's not every day that a business book talks as much about the *Mayflower* and the Pilgrims as it does about cycle-time reduction or more about jazz than re-engineering. But it is precisely these kinds of connections to the history and the dynamics of American culture that provides the basis for a new understanding of why business practices work or fail to meet our expectations.

I'm pleased to introduce this book for three reasons. First, it's imperative that we continually seek to know ourselves better as Americans before we presume to understand others; the realities of globalization demand it, business effectiveness requires it, and diversity depends on it. By more deeply knowing our own culture, we can develop a richer appreciation of others. Second, while there may not be room on your shelves for another book on *what* you should be doing to improve your business performance, this one opens new windows to understanding *why* we as Americans do the things we do the way we do them, and simply asks us to be more conscious, deliberate, and judicious in our actions—particularly when we interact with people of other cultures. Third, this book is interdisciplinary in its approach, and it synthesizes a great deal of research in an accessible framework that should resonate with even the most casual business reader. And while I may not agree with all of the authors' conclusions, I believe the issues the authors have raised are worthy of open discussion.

Plenty of Ah-Ha's

Josh Hammond and James Morrison have identified seven macro-cultural forces that define Americans, from the demand for choice and doing the impossible to our country's impatience with time and fixation on what is new. That's four of them. The other three focus on our obsession with bigness, mistakes (the authors use the term *oops*), and our constant need to improvise and fix things. They have challenged us to think beyond our more narrowly focused (micro) corporate cultures and conventional ways of doing things to examine and at least think about the implications of bringing these larger cultural forces into play *within* our company and organizational environments. They use the word *activate* instead of the more conventional word *apply* because they demonstrate that these cultural forces are present whether or not we use them, and by inference, we are shortsighted if we don't.

Like any good book, there are plenty of ah-ha's in *The Stuff Americans Are Made Of*, some good, insightful, and replicable corporate examples that span the spectrum of companies and business practices, and an evocative way to think about ourselves, our neighbors in Mexico and Canada, and our global trading and business partners in diverse cultures around the world. Over the years I have observed that too often, we as Americans have been naive, indifferent, or arrogant about other cultures at the cost of lost business opportunities, failed joint ventures, and personal embarrassment. Clearly, as the authors point out, there is wisdom in *all* cultures. So if this book may make us more world-wise, as well as more American-wise.

In a rapidly changing business environment, especially in the diverse industries that HP serves—from health care to computers to printers to testing and measurement—the competition is more intense today than at any time in history. With the exploding rate of technology driving daily innovations in the marketplace, it is reassuring to know, as the authors document, that cultural forces have been in play from day one, and that these forces have been manifest in the lives and activities of the early Americans and industrial pathfinders and are mirrored today in the innovator down the hall or the entrepreneur across town.

Put "The Seven Cultural Forces" to a Test

We are just beginning the process of examining the implications of this work for our own business. Some of my associates here in Palo Alto had the opportunity to read and critique early drafts of the book. The first thing they did, once they understood the seven forces framework (see page 4), was to see how many are already in play at HP. We discovered that no less than five were immediately apparent to us.

The most conspicuous one for us was #7, the Whatsnew Force. From the first days of HP, when Bill Hewlett and Dave Packard worked out of their garage, their eyes and energies were constantly focused on new technology, new applications, new opportunities, and new ways to meet the constantly changing demands of their customers.

I have a saying that I repeat a lot at HP: *Eat your lunch before someone else does.* By that I mean, each business unit has the responsibility to make its products obsolete before the competition does. At HP we are very proactive about reinventing products and services—activating the Whatsnew Force. How has it worked out? Two-thirds of our revenue comes from products that we have introduced within the past two years. (The authors write more about this force and HP in Chapter 7.)

We also recognized Force #5, the one no one likes to talk about. That's the Oops Force, the failure to do things right the first time, or worse yet, the failure to follow-up promptly, courteously, and efficiently when something has gone wrong. I have a personal practice at HP: I make it a habit to be open—directly through E-mail, telephone, and correspondence—to the pains and concerns of customers *and* employees. This habit keeps me directly connected to the reality of our quality and commitments. It reminds me of the need to be diligent and to follow through on promises and expectations. This openness has been so important to our customers and employees that I have expanded my capacity to respond to these concerns by engaging retired employees, who care passionately about HP, to personally assist me in these matters. An employee in the quality organization, Francesca Rudé, now runs the operation. She is doing such an effective job that in some quarters around here she is known as the Mother Teresa of customer satisfaction.

The force that we didn't understand on the first pass was the Big and More Force, #3. I agree with Ralph Larsen at Johnson & Johnson, who told the authors that J&J does not pursue bigness for bigness' sake, but if bigness is the result of doing your best and being the most responsive to the needs of customers, then bigness is in perspective. (See interview beginning on page 138.) At HP we have 98,400 employees worldwide. Within the bounds of HP's core values, each group is autonomous. They are each free to act, design, respond, create, and determine their own future. In other words, "to *act* big," as the authors point out, taps into this need for bigness, regardless of their size.

One of the most provocative chapters in the book is what you might call the dream chapter. The authors make a case for organizations to dream; they go so far as to encourage us to use the actual word instead of safer but less powerful words, such as strategy, goal, stretch target, task, or job. The result may often be the same, but the intrinsic value in the word dream is something we have not explicitly tapped.

A Timely Contribution

Finally, this book comes at a time when we at HP have a major internal and external effort underway around the q-word, a word that has lost some of its luster in some quarters. I am serving this year (1996) as Chairman of National Quality Month, a twelve-year-old international business education campaign, started and directed in the early years by ASQC and Josh Hammond, one of the authors. This campaign, authorized by a Congressional Resolution and a proclamation by President Reagan, seeks to keep the business community, especially in the U.S., abreast of the latest developments and breakthroughs in quality management. I have agreed to be chairman as part of my effort within HP to keep our quality focus dynamic and effective.

Concurrently, we have launched an initiative to reinvent quality that began to unfold last year. What quality looks like once it has been reinvented has become clear. We call it *Quality: 1 on 1.* Our scanning on this front, led by Richard LeVitt, Director of Corporate Quality, told us that no one in the world has a completely effective quality system that directly benefits customers—in spite of more than fifteen years that American companies (longer in other countries) have been at quality improvement in a deliberate way. We have observed what Robert Pirsig, the author of the classic *Zen and the Art of Motorcycle Maintenance,* calls "stuckness."

For example, we were struck by the similarity of a recent acceptance speech by a Japanese Deming Prize winner with one our joint venture, Yokogawa Hewlett-Packard, gave in 1982 when we won this prestigious award. The speeches were virtually identical. The concepts, tools, and practices described were well-implemented, but exactly the same. Had nothing changed in thirteen years? Is quality thinking frozen in place?

These questions prompted HP to embark on this *Quality: 1 on 1* that goes beyond "walking a mile in our customer's shoes"—we want to run a marathon in their sneakers. We want to be there when they start dreaming (that force again) of running in their first marathon, when they start to practice, when they are thirsty, when they hit the brick wall, when they cross the finish line, when they brag about their personal-best time, when they reminisce about the event and the process they went through, when they start over again for next year's event, when they search for new sneakers or stick with the brand that got them there. We want to be with them every step of the way to help in any way we can. This renewal on our part, both internally and externally, will call for innovation (Force #6), for some dreaming and stretching to the impossible (Force #2), for opening up our internal and external process to more choice (Force #1), and for being ever vigilant to whatsnew (Force #7).

Anthropologists Philip R. DeVita and James D. Armstrong, editors of a collection of essays by non-Americans, entitled *Distant Mirrors: America as a Foreign Culture,* note the following in their introduction:

> *Had Alexis de Tocqueville been American instead of French, his unusually perceptive 1835 observations on American life* [Democracy in America] *would probably have been unremarkable. They are acutely perceptive precisely because he brought to them what no American could: the startling freshness of an outsider's perspective.*

Obviously Josh and Jim are neither French, nor outsiders. But their observations are no less fresh. We serve ourselves well by giving careful consideration to them. Our approach to *Quality: 1 on 1* will make use of some of the knowledge in this book. I encourage you to scan *The Stuff Americans Are Made Of,* to put some of these ideas to a test, to give this new framework a try.

Lew Platt
Chairman of the Board, President, and Chief Executive Officer
Hewlett-Packard

On Your Mark, Get Set, Go

ON YOUR MARK

It's a fact that the average American kid buys fewer Lego building sets than his German counterpart. Why do you suppose this is? Does culture or upbringing have something to do with it? What marketing problems does this present to the toy manufacturer? What are the implications for the rest of us?

Here is what we know: an American kid tears open a Lego box, tosses out the instructions, and proceeds immediately to create something from his (or her)* own imagination. The result has no resemblance to the elaborate and exacting drawings on the box or instruction booklet, it has leftover parts, and it attracts quick praise from the nearest adult: *Wow! Fantastic! How clever of you! Cool, what is it?*

That's not the case with German kids. A German kid opens the box carefully, finds the instruction booklet, *reads it*, and takes great care to follow the instructions: blue pieces here, red pieces there, yellow in this pile. Then, methodically, with exacting reference to the drawings, he or she builds the first object. If there is praise from an adult, it is of a different sort, the kind that simply says, "Well done."

Now here's Lego's marketing problem in America: the American kid takes his initial creation apart, invents something else to his liking, and continues this process until he gets bored and moves on to something else. There is little or no concern for doing it "right." The same Lego kit remains a constant source of invention and creativity—there are no instructions to get in the way, the child can go as far as his imagination and attention will take him. In short, there is little need for another box of Legos.

The German kid also takes his initial creation apart, but there the similarities end. Once the piece is disassembled, he moves systematically through the instruction book to the next challenge. This process continues until all of the possibilities pictured in the instruction booklet are completed. He is now ready for his next kit—the Lego marketer's dream!

No sex-role stereotype is intended here. We will use the masculine and feminine pronouns interchangeably throughout the book. Also, while we use the term "American" throughout to refer to U.S. citizens, we are fully cognizant that the term could also refer to others on the North or South American continents.

Why the difference? Why is the baseball-capped (on backward) American kid hell-bent on doing something with the Lego set the instant he gets it? Not five minutes later, not even ten, but right now! Why does the kid in the lederhosen read the instructions so patiently, deliberately, systematically?

What the Danish toy company Lego discovered in its marketing study is the inescapable power of cultural forces. American and German children are biologically the same (for all practical purposes), but they have already learned completely different ways to survive and get ahead in this world. They have different histories, live in different cultures, and exhibit different patterns of behavior.*

To observe differences among cultures is not to say that one culture is "better" than another; there is wisdom in every culture. For example, Americans tend to act before they think; Germans tend to spend too much time thinking (and questioning) before they act. And in spite of such differences the United States and Germany are two of the three top-performing economies in the world today. (Japan, which is different still, is the third.)

What the Lego example illustrates is how two different sets of cultural forces result in behavior that is uniquely American on the one hand and decidedly German on the other. It is the set of seven cultural forces that influence the behavior of the American Lego kid that is the subject of this book.

If This Were a Box of Legos, We'd Be in a Heap of Trouble

The following is not a set of instructions—otherwise you'd probably toss them as the American kid did with the Lego instructions. Instead, what follows is the minimum orientation you need to read and understand *The Stuff Americans Are Made Of*. In this first section, "On Your Mark," we provide a quick summary of the seven cultural forces, introduce ourselves as authors, and define what we mean by culture. The next part, "Get Set," contains some important background information on the research we've drawn on and identifies the restraining elements for each of the cultural forces. The final section, "Go," provides a more detailed overview of each of the seven cultural forces.

Our goal with the book is to identify the business advantages of tapping into our *national* American culture, with the hope that you, like American kids† with their Legos, will go on to create your own inventions, applications, and possibilities.

At a time when American business is seeking to intensify its competitive advantages globally, our explicit purpose is to make us more aware of who we are as Americans in order to leverage our unique strengths in our dealings with other nations and cultures so that we maximize the pluses as well as minimize the minuses. We want to make us all conscious of these forces that all too often lie fallow in our boardrooms and on our factory floors. We hope this orientation will clearly show you the importance of the case we make for the need to understand and activate the seven cultural forces that define Americans.

Toys change from generation to generation, but the patterns of play and growing up in a given culture remain the same.

†*If this American Lego approach doesn't completely ring true in your experience, you probably belong to the quarter of Americans who claim German heritage, the largest heritage affiliation in the United States, followed by English and Irish. So approximately one in four of us has some cultural connection to order, discipline, and adherence to instruction.*

Of course, like the American kid with his Legos, you can always skip right over all this and get to the overview of the seven cultural forces that begins on page 21.

What, Exactly, Is a Cultural Force?

The focus of this book is national culture. When we talk about national culture we don't mean a cultural stereotype (Brits can't cook, Italians are great lovers, the French are snobs, Americans are slobs) that pigeonholes a group or makes a caricature of a trait. We mean the manifestation of a nation's collective, usually conscious, *cultural forces*. By cultural force we mean the "locked-in" emotional energy and structure of behavior that, in the aggregate, defines, drives, and sustains a group or, in this case, a country in its growth and development. Unlike opinions, generational fads, and management trends, these cultural forces are permanent—they have been with us since Plymouth Rock and they will carry us well into the next millennium. These forces are the glue that keeps us together and the common aspirations that drive us forward. Our preferences and styles and abilities and looks are clearly all over the place, but *our framework is the same*. As Americans, our individual designs may be different but we're all constructed from the same stuff. The same is true for the national culture of Germans or Australians or Koreans.

Curiously, however, Americans seem to deny the existence of a collective culture. It is essential for us to see ourselves as individuals, not necessarily as a group—except when push comes to shove. Anthropologist E. L. Cerroni-Long, an Italian-born Asian scholar, concludes the following from her research:

> *What seems to me uniquely American, is a profound disbelief in systemic social constraints and, in particular, in the reality of an indigenous culture. For years, I have been systematically polling students, acquaintances, and miscellaneous informants on their perceptions of American culture, and I must conclude that denying that an American culture exists seems to be one of the most consistent local [American] cultural traits.**

In this context, it is important to note that the one thing Americans will insist on saying is that they are different. Researchers and marketing people run into this all the time: Nobody wants to be the same. If you talk to Bostonians, they'll say, "We're different." In Atlanta they say the same thing with a different accent. No Texan will admit to being like everyone else, nor any other Westerner for that matter. Folks in Chicago and Fargo, North Dakota, will all say the same thing: "We're different."

It is a marketing mistake to overemphasize the avowed difference, because in fact these Americans are *saying the same thing*. The cultural structure of America is such that it enables us to act, think, and say we are different, when in reality access to the seven cultural forces is the same for the core of Americans.

On the other hand, the need to embrace diversity in business is good because in the process of doing so we identify our differences, and that process resonates within each of us. It gets right to the heart of being an American: *I'm an individual eager to make a difference.* But when emphasizing diversity one can overlook the

---

**"Life and Cultures: The Test of Real Participant Observation,"* by E. L. Cerroni-Long, in a very useful, condensed reference, Distant Mirrors: America as a Foreign Culture, *edited by Philip R. DeVita and James D. Armstrong.*

common bond, the emotional ties, and strong values that make us *e pluribus unum*—out of many, one.*

In this book, we will look in some detail at several American organizations that we feel have reached beyond their own corporate culture and, either knowingly or unknowingly, have tapped into the power of all of the seven cultural forces. We'll hold up these companies—Disney, Federal Express, Ford, Hewlett-Packard, Johnson & Johnson, 3M, Levi Strauss, Allied Signal, Ritz-Carlton Hotels, Milliken—as role models, organizations that have intuitively activated one or more of the seven cultural forces.

This will not be an examination of how they deal with their corporate culture in the conventional business management sense† but how they—consciously or unconsciously—manifest, use, and reinforce the seven cultural forces in the following kinds of business practices:

★ leadership

★ research and development

★ values and alignment

★ product or service deployment

★ improvement processes

★ manufacturing/production

★ personnel management

★ customer service relations

★ advertising, marketing, and retail

★ public relations

★ investor relations

★ community affairs

The Seven Cultural Forces that Define Americans

What is it, then, that defines us as American? What are the cultural forces that make marketing Legos in this country so different from marketing them in Germany? What drives us? What are our unique energy sources? Why are we American, by George?

We have identified seven cultural forces that define us as American. We have assigned each force a symbol for shorthand reference throughout the book. Here are thumbnail sketches of the seven (a summary of the seven forces begins on page 21):

---

*The motto that appears on the Great Seal of the United States.

†The whole subject of culture change in corporations has been well addressed by many. Three of our current favorites are What America Does Right: Lessons from Today's Most Admired Corporate Role Models *by Robert H. Waterman, Jr.;* Built to Last: Successful Habits of Visionary Companies *by James C. Collins and Jerry I. Porras; and* Corporate Culture and Performance *by John P. Kotter and James L. Heskett.*

1. Insistence on CHOICE (☑).

Everyone who came to America in its formative years—and those who continue to come—came here by *choice*.* They came to start a new life in a land where they could choose what, where, and who they want to be. Choice is the dominant force in America.

2. Pursuit of IMPOSSIBLE DREAMS (°◌⌣).

"Impossible" is a misnomer, really, because the genius of Americans is their ability to turn their personal, corporate, and national dreams—the seemingly impossible— into the possible. America is the land where the possibility exists that all dreams can come true. Technology is the great enabler, but the dreams must come first.

3. Obsession with BIG AND MORE (▌).

America is the land of wide-open spaces, rich in enormous natural resources and populated with Paul Bunyans. Because the country is so big physically, it comes naturally to its inhabitants to *think big*. But this force is all about America's obsession with being Number One. And this is the force that sometimes gets us into big trouble, especially when taken to extremes.

4. Impatience with TIME (🕐).

Americans are, in a word, impatient. We are the most time-obsessed culture in the world. Time is money, and we want it—and everything else—*now*. If we don't get it or do it now, somebody else will, and we don't like being second.

5. OOPS! Acceptance of Mistakes (🐞)

Making mistakes is part of how we learn and achieve things. We unconsciously don't do things right the first time because we are not motivated by a desire for perfection. However, we "learn" from our mistakes. This force triggers the emotional payoff that comes through force number six.

There are two exceptions: Native Americans, who were here before the "white man" came, and African-Americans, who were brought here against their will. The fact that they are not here by choice is the crucible of America's pernicious racism.

6. Urge to IMPROVISE (✂).

We value fixing things *more* than doing things right the first time. This enables us to show how human we are and *how good we can be*. The way we fix things—and create breakthroughs—is through improvising. Once the situation is fixed (or almost fixed), we are free to move on to something else, and moving on is a major preoccupation in America.

7. Fixation with WHATSNEW (💾).

As individuals (and even as a nation) we are in a perpetual search for new identities, new ideas, new strategies, and new products, because they provide new *choices*. We have now come full circle. These seven American cultural forces are the focus of this book. Some readers may feel there's an eighth or want to make a substitution or two—which of course is very American, and your *choice*. However, our research and the work of others have clearly identified these seven.

The Interrelationship of the Seven Forces

The relationships between and among the forces may already be obvious to you. For example, if we reduce choices, we limit dreams (and the other way around). Our rush to do things—and to read the instructions only when all else fails—invariably results in an oops or two. Improvising enables us to fix what went wrong and then move on to something else—to whatsnew. Our insistence on being bigger and better helps make our impossible dreams come true.

In addition to the way the forces interact, their overall order is very important to note. The general pattern Americans follow in leveraging these seven forces can be summarized this way:

> *Our freedom of* **choice** *allows us to tackle an "impossible"* **dream** *that is* **bigger** *than anything we've done before; we want to achieve it* **now** *but* **fail** *in our initial attempts; we try again and through some form of* **improvisation** *succeed, only to wonder* **whatsnew** *so that we can start all over and make another* **choice**.

These seven forces, and their interactions, are important whether we are dealing with an improvement process at work, a community renewal effort, a family project, or a personal-development program. They script our endeavors, chart our activities, plot our responses, explain our behaviors, structure our innovations, energize our processes, and, in the end, define us as American. They have major implications for how we handle (or mishandle) the issues of the day—downsizing, changing management, education, affirmative action, prayer in public schools, productivity, speed-to-market, health care, guns, greed, politicians, diets, innovation, teamwork, and the constant need to be valued as an individual.

In the great tradition of American frontiers, these forces represent a new place to explore, conquer, and develop. This frontier is just sitting there waiting for us to explore it, touch it, build on it, play with it, apply it to our business enterprises, our personal relationships, and the improvement of our communities. And meanwhile, you can keep right on doing what you are already doing, except now you will know why some things you do work well and others, in spite of your best intentions, don't. You'll also see how to get unstuck, if indeed you are.

What This Book Is About

When Miles Standish, Priscilla Mullins, John Alden, and William Brewster and his two sons (with the unlikely names of Love and Wrestling) landed near Plymouth Rock on November 11, 1620, our cultural forces dropped anchor, too. Those cultural forces had nothing to do with the particulars, the tools, the what-should-we-do's, but they had everything to do with what made those Pilgrims—and now us—tick. And that is the subject of this book.

This is a book about *why* we do the things we do and *how* to do the things we do better, faster, and cheaper—with higher personal satisfaction. This book answers questions: What drives us? What turns us on? How can companies activate the cultural forces to improve quality, productivity, and profitability? What companies have been successful using these forces?

We also address the issue of change and how Americans feel about it. We debunk the conventional notion that most American workers resist change. The research shows the opposite: Americans like change—provided they can control it. Americans tend to resist change that is imposed on them, forced from the outside, but self-initiated change is welcomed. This is the fundamental underpinning of change in America: It is not something somebody else (parent, teacher, manager, politician) does *to* us, but something we do *for ourselves.* It is tangible, immediate, within our own grasp, something of intrinsic value. Yes, we will conform to imposed change, but not with a willing spirit or an attitude that will result in increased value to the initiator or the coerced. Change—I-can-make-a-difference change—is a theme that runs through the book, and we describe it specifically in Chapters 1, 5, and 6.

Having an understanding of the seven cultural forces helps us to make changes naturally, in our own time and fashion. These forces are available and accessible to everyone; all we have to do is tap into them, activate them. Which is why, throughout this book, we will use the word *activate* where you might expect the word *apply*. Activating the forces means making use of what is already a part of us; it doesn't require the application of new techniques or external know-how.

Go Anywhere, Young Man, Young Woman, Young Child!

Closely tied to Americans' need for personal control is what Max Lerner calls the constant "moving frontier" in America. Frontiers were, and continue to be, a recurring theme in America's development. There was nothing but frontier when we started this experiment more than one thousand years ago (depending on your starting point), and when we've finished exploring the current cyberspace frontier, we'll find another. The frontier theme has run from Plymouth Rock through the Northwest Ordinance,*

---

*An early land law that established federal jurisdiction in the unexplored "old Northwest" territory that America had acquired from Great Britain as a result of the revolution—in the part of the U.S.A. now known as the Midwest (Ohio, Indiana, Illinois, Michigan, and Wisconsin).

A Profile of the Authors

To begin with, we are treading in the footsteps of a pair of illustrious predecessors. Over 150 years ago, a French tourist named Alexis de Tocqueville spent a mere nine months traveling around the eastern part of the new United States trying to fathom the American culture. He got so much of it right that his book is now required (or at least recommended) reading for new members of Congress.

Later, in the nineteenth century, historian Frederick Jackson Turner gained fame as the proponent of his theory that the frontier itself—its abundance of free land, its promise of bounty and generosity—was the seminal element in the formation of the democratic American way that is the foundation of our culture. (Contemporary academics have gone back and forth on Turner's thesis.)

We—the authors—are a *different* pair (of course). We were born at different times in two different countries, have traveled in fifty-seven others, and have collectively lived 123 years. We have learned how business is done by collecting data on 950 management practices in four industries in Japan, Germany, Canada, and the United States. We know which of these practices drive profitability and productivity and which ones (the most popular ones) don't. We have some experience in how the United States is governed, having worked in the U.S. Senate, the executive office of the president, and a state capital or two.

We have researched and delved into the unconscious forces that drive American quality, teamwork, trust, credit card use, boats, and barbecue sauce. We've designed or collaborated on more than fourteen national surveys (with Gallup, the Wirthlin Group, and Peter Hart) and over two hundred focus groups (with *Fortune* magazine, the Annenberg School of Communications at USC, and others). Our stock-in-trade is information, ideas, innovations in thought, and the gathering and communication thereof.

We've used our stuff to advertise soap, elect politicians, stop drug abuse, promote quality initiatives, and win the hands (and hearts) of fair ladies. We've used it to publish novels, make movies, publish magazines, and produce more than fifty how-to booklets and pamphlets. And we have used it to motivate, celebrate, and exacerbate just causes.

We have been subjected to the drone of bean-counting market researchers in meeting rooms cluttered with stale doughnuts and cold coffee, and we have separately and equally come to the same conclusion: Today's statistics are tomorrow's "so what's" because they miss the emotional dimensions of what makes us American.

A statistic never got us out of bed or kept us working into the wee hours of the morning. Here is what has: The knowledge that we could make a difference, could make choices, could make our dreams and other people's dreams come true, could try again and again, with the freedom to improvise and the certainty that we could move on to anything anytime.

That's why we decided to pick up where Tocqueville and others left off. That's why we have built on the works of anthropologist Edward T. Hall, historian Max Lerner, political scientist Howard Zinn, multiculturist Ronald Takaki, market researchers Richard Wirthlin, Dee Allsop, and Clotaire Rapaille,

musicologist Albert Murray, Nobel Prize winner Octavio Paz, culture management consultant Fons Trompenaars, executives Roger Milliken and Horst
Schulze, and people diagnostician Art Miller—to name a few.

Manifest Destiny, right on to JFK's New Frontier, cyberspace, and, lately, the
Republicans' Contract with America. The frontier offers challenge, opportunity, a new
start for individuals and businesses. By nature, Americans seek unfamiliar territory:
The frontier is our nation's narcotic—we're hooked.

Although Horace Greeley is given the credit, it was John Lane Soule, his fellow
editor, who told young men in 1851, "Go West." Today any of us can go anywhere
we want to—it's all a frontier out there.

It's a *frontier in business,* as companies constantly invent new products and services, expand customer relationships, and try new internal processes. It's a *frontier
in government,* as Big has run its course and for the first time since the beginning of
the republic the "counterforces" are on a pell-mell course in the opposite direction.
It's a *frontier in the inner city,* where the future of the average fourteen-year-old kid
is bleak and no one knows how to change the odds. It's a *frontier in the job market,*
as the first full generation of techies makes it into the management and teaching ranks
of business and schools. And it's *a frontier in the meaning of work,* as jobs undergo
their biggest transformation since the industrial revolution, over a hundred years ago.

Our quadrennial national debate about which frontiers we will explore begins
earlier and earlier every four years. This time it seems to have begun in 1994, with
the congressional elections. Now the debate about our future is more about our past—
who we are as a people, where we have been, and what core values and cultural forces
will sustain us well into the next millennium. Because of the subject matter, this
debate will have more personal consequences than any that have preceded it in the
last fifty years.

Let Me Think About It. . . .

—*I don't think about the things I don't think about.*

—*Do you think about the things you do think about?*

This exchange from Clarence Darrow's famous cross-examination of William
Jennings Bryan at the Scopes trial in 1925, caught silver-tongued orator Bryan off
guard and furthered Darrow's reputation. It gets to the heart of the intent of this book:
We do not offer a quick-fix recipe, although Americans persist in their search for one.
Rather we call for reflection, for some thinking about these matters and, like the
American approach to Legos, some experimenting with them and their possibilities.

GET SET

If you are set and need no further backgrounding or direction from us, go for it. Skip
to page 21 and you are on your way—that's where the overview of the seven cultural forces begins. However, just a few words before you skip this section. We consider the information in this section important because it will help you more fully

understand the forces that we write about. Not only will you understand our *set,* but you will gain valuable insight into the limitations of the following kinds of conventional business practices:

★ regular or annual customer satisfaction surveys

★ employee questionnaires

★ 360-degree employee evaluations

★ marketing research

★ process improvement

★ change management

The Three "Givens" of American Culture

1. American Adolescence

In our business performance workshops we have an exercise in which we divide the group in two: One group is assigned a five-minute task of listing the words (adjectives) that describe their improvement process; the other group is given the same amount of time to list words that describe teenagers—our sons, daughters, grandchildren, or next-door neighbor kids.

When the two lists are compared, there is an immediate *aha!* experience. What the participants have discovered is that, as Americans, our approach to improvement is not much different from our behavior as adolescents. As much as we may not like the comparison, Americans are impetuous, unpredictable, boring, inventive, sloppy, full of surprises, stupid, brilliant, destructive, fun, depressed, lacking a respect for time, expansive, and full of hope and endless promise.

The negative characteristics that we see so clearly in American teenagers are painfully evident in how we run the affairs of the nation: **bully politics**—you treated us this way when you were in power, so we are going to treat you the same way; **personality politics**—name calling, negative campaigns, dirty tricks; **"fire-ready-aim" policies**—gays in the military, foreign interventions, health care reform; **blaming others**—the I'm-a-victim syndrome; **rush to action**—from rubber-stamping and repealing legislation to filibustering and pork-barreling. And lest we think all of this applies only to national politics, consider your own internal corporate politics.

We can think of no institution in the United States that is exempt from both the good kind and bad kind of adolescent behavior. In the grand scheme of things, we are, after all, a young-in-years country. And so it has been since Christopher Columbus bullied his way into the Caribbean and others followed suit.

To this point, historian Max Lerner, in *America as a Civilization: Life and Thought in the United States Today,* writes:

> *The sharp change in the American attitude toward Europe came with the world wars. Once it was clear that Europe was no longer the father demanding obedience and exerting his authority but an endangered civilization needing help, America's response changed. It broke through the isolationist sheath [adolescent behavior] to aid Western Europe in two great wars, and afterward it helped to rebuild Europe's economic strength. Yet even here Americans had to dress up their aid in the ideological garment of a struggle against tyranny and authoritarianism. You ended by*

*helping the father you had rebelled against, but you did it by continuing to slay
another potential authority-image.*

No other nation exhibits these dynamics as clearly or as consistently as America.
And we hasten to add, this is not a value judgment, just a statement of fact. By
contrast, France prides itself on reason; England has a reserve and caution we don't
see in the United States; Switzerland maintains its neutrality—an attribute wholly
absent in your basic, red-blooded American; and Japan is patient, respectful of process, careful with time, dedicated to cautious long-term planning. These cultures, by
comparison, are more mature, more adult, if you will.

And to complete the analogy, the world clearly has nations that are still developing—Iraq, Somalia, Bosnia, Cambodia, Colombia, and Cuba come to mind. Age is
not the variable here, the mode or style of a country's behavior is.

2. American Culture Is All About the Search for and Glorification of Individual Identity

We think in individual terms—"What's in it for me?"—and leave group-think to the
Japanese and others. While this individualism fuels the American engine, it also
isolates or fragments us. It has major implications for increasing work productivity
(see Chapters 1 and 5) and enhancing the work of teams (see Chapter 7).

Professor Cerroni-Long, the anthropologist quoted earlier, suggests an explanation for Americans' reluctance to acknowledge a common culture. Writing in
Distant Mirrors: America as a Foreign Culture, she says:

> *In effect, all through my explorations of American culture, I repeatedly found a
> common popular concern with the ideational realm, an attitude almost opposite of
> the Japanese preoccupation with behavioral norms. A great many Americans seem
> to believe that "ideas make the person" and because ideas can and do change,
> people can continuously reinvent themselves. Perhaps because of this belief, the
> idea of American culture as a stable configuration is not commonly accepted,
> and even members of minority groups feel that their identity is a matter of
> "negotiation."*

In response to what we might conclude is "fragmented individualism," it is interesting and helpful to note that Americans are the joiningest nation on the planet. We
have more than two hundred thousand formal associations and countless informal
ones. Out of all of this group activity—the search for individual identity—America
has created a new economic force, a third sector known as the private or independent (nonprofit) sector, which now accounts for more than 10 percent of GNP and
one in every five jobs in America.

3. In God We Trust

This third given of American culture is what Franklin Roosevelt referred to as "the
God stuff." Virtually no one in America questions whose side God is on. There is,
for all practical purposes, a unanimous agreement that God is on our side, so all our
causes, by definition, must be righteous and our actions blessed from on high. What
we don't agree on is how to worship God. There are more than five hundred organized religious groups in America. And while no one questions "In God We Trust"
on our currency, there is consternation, to say the least, about prayer in public schools.

Since one is always well advised to avoid religion, sex, and politics in public discussions, we had best end this quickly—except to note, as other commentators have, that there will always be prayer in public schools, so long as there are tests.

Understanding Cultural Forces

The first part of understanding these seven cultural forces is *not* to focus on what they are and how they work but to discover *where* they are and *how* they got there. Once you understand these basics, it will become more readily apparent why they are important.

As you can see in Snapshot #1, cultural forces are outside of our awareness. They lie buried. Deep. Invisible in that subterranean, little-explored, ancient domain called the unconscious—the stuff Carl Jung and others have written about.

Cultural forces are a form of natural energy. They are manifest only through our behavior. They are not something that we can quantify like a front-page headline or a vintage bottle of wine. But the performance power they can yield when we surface them and bring them to the forefront is very compelling. In tough competitive times or a downsizing environment these are pivotal pockets of power.

Snapshot #1 is a vastly simplified chart that shows four levels of conscious and unconscious behavior in any culture. This graphic representation makes abundantly clear that the *conscious* level of awareness (opinions, what we say and think) is the small tip of the iceberg compared to the vast *unconscious* levels of behavior (biology, culture, individual preferences, what we do).

The Limitations of Opinions

Let's begin with the tip of the iceberg: Opinions. Here is a hypothetical case to help illustrate the things we are conscious of: You think you know the guy who lives two doors down. He has a wife and two kids and drives a Detroit muscle car. Nice guy. He borrows your weed whacker and you use his leaf blower in the fall. It's a routine, no-second-thought transaction.

Your wives swap recipes (is this still politically correct?) and your kids play Little League together. You alternate car-pooling. You have lots in common. He's a yellow-dog Democrat, but you don't hold that against him; your grandfather from Georgia was one, too, but you still had a fondness for him.

Then one time he returns your weed whacker with a played-out cord and no gas—and doesn't say anything. When you discover this, you suddenly don't like him much anymore. That state of mind brings his other quirks and mannerisms to the forefront (ones you have been choosing to ignore), and this nice guy suddenly becomes, in your eyes, a thoughtless boob, an inconsiderate slob. If you are mature about the situation, and not passive-aggressive, you confront him, get an apology, come to terms, and just as suddenly change your mind about liking him again.

That's the conscious mind at work. It's capricious. It flip-flops. It is something we instantly recognize as *opinion*. It is always accessible. We control it. We can change it. Don't be fooled—these variables apply to your customers and employees, which is why simply asking how people feel is tricky business at best and not the most reliable predictor of behavior and true attitudes.

Snapshot #1

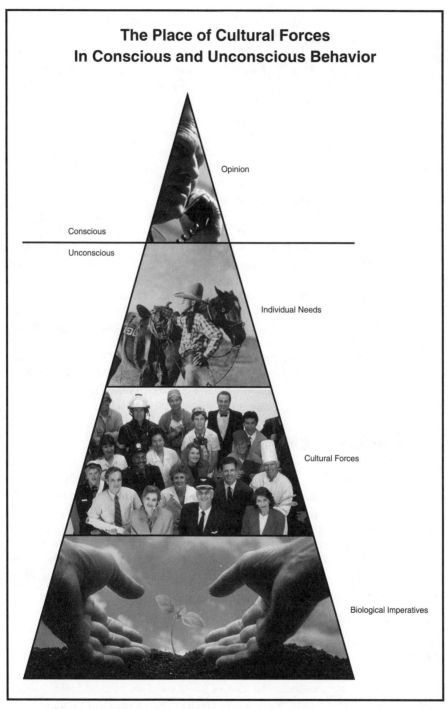

The Place of Cultural Forces
In Conscious and Unconscious Behavior

Opinion

Conscious

Unconscious

Individual Needs

Cultural Forces

Biological Imperatives

Source: Adapted from Archetype Studies, Inc.

Just as individuals have fickle opinions, so do groups, families, teams, corporations, and nations. For example, we saw this dynamic in full play at the national level during the 1994 presidential election. A year before the election President George Bush had a 92 percent national approval rating—the highest ever for any president since we have been tracking these numbers as a nation. A year later, on Election Day, the same George Bush plunged 42 percent and lost to Bill Clinton. Since then, Bill has made it past a 50 percent approval rating only a couple of times, and his almost daily fluctuation may result in a thrill ride being named for him.

The moral here: *Don't count your opinions before they hatch.*

Clearly our opinions change, influenced by our moods, the time of day, our stress level, whether things are going our way, what we think the boss wants to hear, peer pressure, and the headlines in the news.

Opinion is the arena of market researchers, pollsters, politicians, and policy wonks. Opinion polling is a big business. Asking questions is how most corporations find out what their customers want, how their employees feel, what their suppliers think. The problem is, the responses to these questions have a very short shelf life: The answer is a mere glimpse of a moment in time in the past and is subject to immediate change. Worse, these responses are often the right answers to the wrong questions.

It is clear that most of us say one thing and do another, say one thing and mean something else. This discrepancy between what we say and what we feel is why most TQM (total quality management), reengineering, internal process alignment, and other executive-dependent programs fizzle out (see Chapter 5). It's the same problem with dieting, with personal relationships, with politicians. That is why we can't afford to rely just on what people say or intend. Understanding what goes on below the surface of opinions is more important than the moment of the opinion; in fact, it helps process the meanings and changes of the expressed opinions.

The Basics of Biology

What we have just described is some of what goes on above the black line on the pyramid illustration. Now for a look below the line. Here are three levels of stuff we don't think about much and talk about less. It's all outside our awareness.

At the bottom of the pyramid is biology—the domain of the biologist, the family doctor, the naturalist, or the genetic engineer. It's the world of the insects that your child collects, the subject of your gardening magazine, *Scientific American*, or a corporate research lab manual. *Unlike opinions, there are three things about the biology level of the pyramid that have an important bearing on our understanding of the seven cultural forces.*

1. Biological Needs Are Universal

This applies to all creatures large and small. It doesn't matter if you are a bug in Bogotá or a boy in Boise, the sun rises in the east everywhere. "What goes up must come down" is true in the four corners of the earth, and when you cut flesh it bleeds the same color in every culture. The laws of science and the rules of biology do not change from country to country.

2. Biology Is Logical and Ordered

We know from biology, "the logic of life," that there is in nature an exacting order that we must observe to survive. Life begins with breathing and continues in a logical order through the intake of liquids, eating of solid foods, disposing of waste, finding shelter, securing safety, procreating, maintaining order, and evolving as a species. When you or someone else messes with the order, chaos is usually the result.

3. Biological Needs Don't Change

In contrast to the high variability of opinions, biological dynamics are permanent. Yes, there are mutations: Species evolve or adapt over time, the geneticists are messing around with DNA, and there is in-vitro fertilization and other high technology. But these have no immediate impact on the *campo* in Mexico or on a community in Maine. In contrast to opinions, the biological dynamics are, for all practical purposes, reliable.

A Cultural Survival Kit

Tier two of the pyramid is all about group or national culture—the focus of this book. It represents the ways in which groups of people *organize* their existence to address, get at, manage, redefine, extend, or meet their basic biological needs. Fulfilling these biological needs has the same priority for all groups and societies around the world: *to survive as a species.* However, different cultures have evolved quite different ways of meeting basic biological needs; each creates its own unique survival kit. The fact that a society functions and survives is proof that its culture works; there are no "good" or "bad" cultures.

Eating is a clear example of how cultures differ; it illustrates how many radically different ways there are to satisfy the same biological need for sustenance. For instance, what is dinner? In America it is something we *do* around six o'clock, in ten minutes, on one plate, and when we are finished we say, "I'm full," and we go on to *do* something else. In Spain or France, this same biological need is met by a different cultural practice. Dinner there starts three or four hours later, it takes ten to twenty times longer to finish multiple courses, with corresponding plates and utensils, and at its conclusion one would never say, "I'm full." In some cultures people eat with their hands. In others, the men eat first, then the women and children eat what is left over.

All these cultural differences are designed and passed down through generations to meet the same universal need: hunger. The food and packaging may change, but within a given culture the patterns of eating don't change that much over time.

Also, we have observed in America that eating is essentially a fueling process. We count calories, snack on energy bars, and get a sugar rush from decadent double-chocolate cake, in much the same way we deal with gassing up our cars: Fill 'er up with high test. Whether we are refueling our bodies or our vehicles, we don't waste much time at it: The average time it takes to eat a hamburger in the United States is five minutes and eleven seconds. And now there is a drive-through restaurant chain in the Midwest called Hot 'n' Now where the object is to serve the customer in thirty seconds or less as the car drives through *without stopping.*

Unlike opinions and in contrast to biology, there are three things about culture that have an important bearing on our understanding of the forces.

1. Cultural Forces Are Constant

Though not as constant as biology, cultural forces change little, if at all, over time. Cultural forces may manifest themselves differently at different times, there may be some generational variations on the theme, but the underlying structure of the force remains the same. We'll show how they are just as active today as they were at Pilgrim Rock or at the turn of the century. They are constant and consistent, and therein lies their predictive value for thought leaders, executives, marketing directors, ad agency folks, public policy designers, community planners, teachers, and you.

2. Cultural Forces Are Consistent

Every national culture has primary or umbrella forces, those forces that are available to all members of that group or country. Different groups or subcultures may exist under this umbrella and manifest some of the larger groups' forces differently. For example, there are regional cultures (Long Island, the Deep South, the Midwest, etc.), ethnic cultures, corporate cultures, and family cultures in the United States.

Language, or the syntax of language, illustrates our point. No matter where you are in the United States, our grammar is the same: noun before verb; object after verb; adjective before noun. Within that grammatical structure there is room for enormous variety: local or professional vernacular; pronunciations, dialects, cadences; special meanings for words; slang; etc. When you put a Georgia cracker, a Long Island teenager, a Maine (Down East) farmer, and a Texas rancher in the same room, it's the grammar that holds their communications together. And so it is with our cultural forces: They are our common language, they tie us together, they make us American.

3. Cultural Forces Are Emotionally Driven

Like biology, there is a logic to cultural forces, which is expressed primarily through emotions. For example, consider the emotional logic connected with food: eating pork in Iran can cause quite a stir; in another culture *not belching* is the best way to insult your host; and rushing through tea in Japan will not get you invited back. Although there are strong emotions and reactions related to food as it is presented in different cultures, even mightier emotions are connected with territory and religion. The war in the Balkans shows what can happen when cultures collide on such emotionally charged issues. In Chapter 5 we identify and discuss the value of emotions in the American business improvement process. These emotions are quite different from those in Japan or Germany.

The Restraining Elements of Culture

To fully understand cultural forces, it is important to remember this: All cultural forces operate on an axis. Each force is held in check by a restraining element or two within the culture; for every *over*reach in culture there is a reaction. Of course, all cultures have restraining forces. It's just that the American pendulum swings more widely; the range in which each force operates is much broader here than in other countries. Here is a list of the restraining elements that check the excess of each of the seven forces:

Cultural Force	Restraining Element
1. Choice	Prohibition
2. Impossible Dream	Reality
3. Big and More	Small and less
4. Now	Sleeping Giant
5. Oops	Fear of Failure
6. Improvise	Conformance
7. Whatsnew	Tradition

One of the marvelous and essential dynamics of a democratic culture is its ability to maintain an equilibrium, to keep things in balance with restraining elements of our culture. American democracy functions as a near-automatic search for the center, something like a compass point searching for true north.

What is often described as "culture change" is only a shift or movement in our position on the axis, not a change in the forces. There is always movement on the continuum when the restraining elements react to the overreaching force.

An example of the movement of forces along an axis was Prohibition (expressed through the Eighteenth Amendment to the U.S. Constitution). Here was a choice we made to limit choice.

The constitutional prohibition against the manufacture, sale, and transport of alcoholic beverages in the United States was a well-meaning attempt to force the steelworker, coal miner, and assembly-line grubber (always the powerless and poor) to stay sober on payday and bring the money home to his put-upon wife and kids.

The intent was honorable, but the strategy was proved beyond doubt to have been dead wrong. The denial of choice tore at the very seams of the social fabric of the national community. After a brief experiment we chose to repeal the amendment and restore the balance.

What Do We Mean When We Say "Americans"?

We categorically reject the political use of the expression "the American people" to imply *all* Americans, or even a majority of Americans. It is pernicious overreaching that polarizes, exploits, and denigrates the public debate. (This usage, by the way, is nonpartisan: Democrats, Republicans, and independents alike misuse the phrase.)

For example, in the 1994 "historic" vote that changed the control of the U.S. House of Representatives to Republican after forty years of Democratic domination, everyone on the winning side said, "The American people voted for change." The fact of the matter is that only 24 percent of eligible voters voted for the change in Congress in 1994—just short of one-fourth of Americans over the age of eighteen, a long way from a majority and certainly not a statistical basis for laying claim to "the American people," a collective term implying all.

Neither do we mean by "the American people" what the powerful lobbying groups in Washington mean when they promulgate their opinions and positions on legislation in the name of "the American people." Although you wouldn't know it from their press releases, they each represent a *limited* number of us 270-million Americans: e.g., the National Rifle Association, 3.5 million; American Association of Retired Persons, 34 million *over the age of fifty* (representing about half of that

Opening the Door to Understanding Emotions

The most useful way we know to communicate the emotional element in American cultural forces that we write about is a story about doors. The following case profile summarizes a study on how Americans experience security around doors. It was conducted a few years ago by Clotaire Rapaille, a French-born cultural anthropologist and colleague of ours.*

—KNOCK, KNOCK
—WHAT'S THERE?

This is not a knock-knock joke; it's an example of how cultural research can be applied to real business issues in the real world. Pretend that you are the copy-writer at an ad agency. Your client is Simpson Doors in Seattle. They have been making wooden doors—only wooden doors—for a hundred years. Along comes a new door maker boasting about the security of its doors, which are made of steel. Simpson Doors is anxious about the security claims of the new steel-door manufacturer. They want to know if they should start making steel doors and how they can counter their competitor's claims in the meantime.

What do you tell them? Should they diversify their product line and get into the steel-door business? What about their ads? Would you counter the security claims by recommending that Simpson Doors show their doors

★ locked

★ simply closed

★ open

★ off the hinges, pointing out all the strong features and dimensions of the door

Simpson turned to Rapaille, who conducted a study that revealed the surprising answer: It turns out that for Americans security has nothing to do with what a door is made of, but how it is positioned or shown. And the position of the door that communicates security is—counterintuitively—open and viewed from the inside.

Why open? Because as Americans our first experience with a door was when our mothers fed us, bathed and diapered us (those universal biological needs), and took us to our room, put us in our crib (a little cage), and said, "Good night, Mummy loves you" as she closed the door—and in our child's perception disappeared off the face of the earth! (Wow!)

At this stage in the child's experience and perception development there is no awareness that Mother is still present, probably listening in on one of those high-tech monitoring devices. Because the door is closed and Mother is gone, the emotional "imprinting" is insecurity.

The American door experience is not universal; in other countries doors don't carry the same message of insecurity. In Japan, where doors often are

For a discussion of the methodology here, see the Appendix.

literally sliding paper walls, a child sleeps in the same room with the parents. In Germany, what the doors are made of and how they *sound* is of primary consideration—thick doors and walls at work. A solid thud when the Mercedes door is closed communicates security to Germans.

What about subsequent experiences? Put yourself in this situation. Your company is downsizing. Rumors have been on the vine for a few weeks about 10 percent of the workforce being laid off. It's Friday afternoon. Your boss asks you to stop by his or her office on your way home at the end of the day. When you arrive you are invited to "come in and have a seat," but just before you sit down, your boss adds, "Why don't you close the door."

What's the emotional response? Probably identical to that of the child behind the closed bedroom door: insecurity.

Take the work situation one step further. How secure do you feel when top management is making decisions about downsizing, or anything else for that matter, *behind* closed doors? Or legislators are negotiating amendments and the fine print behind closed doors? Not too confident, no doubt.

By the way, Simpson Doors changed its advertising strategy and began showing all doors ajar, whereas before they had been closed (to show off the door, of course). Results? Sales rose 18 percent and they never went into the steel-door business.

While you may have had a different experience with doors as an infant, the significance of this research is that there is an emotional imprint that conditions and drives our behavior. The same is true for the seven cultural forces that define us. The more conscious we are of these energies, the more responsive and sensitive we can be to each other. For businesses this has profound implications.

age group); Christian Coalition, 1.2 million; and countless think tanks that represent a handful of people or no one but themselves. Somewhere along the way their limited-number views are positioned as what *all* Americans want and need.

For our part, we will be diligent to avoid using "the American people" to imply 100 percent. Throughout this book we will simply say "Americans" and by that mean a *substantial majority* of us—well over the minimum 50.1 percent. Where it's particularly relevant, we will quantify the number, especially when the percentages are up in the stratosphere—the 70 and 80 percent range—that we sometimes see in national surveys.*

National Variations

The illustration on the following page shows the variation in the balance between freedom (endless choices) and prohibition (limited choices) that exists among four

*For all practical purposes, when survey numbers get up that high, you're talking about everyone. This is the territory where it is justifiable to say "all" Americans. Even percentages in the 60s give the folks at Gallup, ABC News, and CNN a big lead story.

Keep in mind that the forces we will describe are available to every American. As with the intent of the declaration "all men are created equal," the capacity to activate the seven cultural forces we are writing about is always present for all Americans.

Snapshot #2

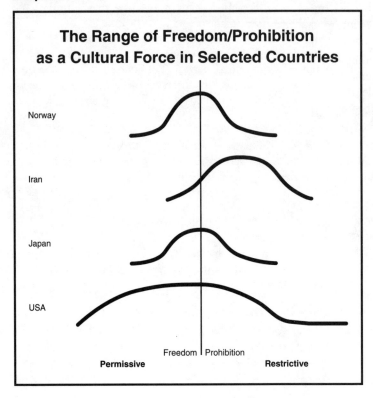

The Range of Freedom/Prohibition as a Cultural Force in Selected Countries

Norway

Iran

Japan

USA

Freedom | Prohibition

Permissive   **Restrictive**

selected countries. Although the curves are approximations, we hope they illustrate how different cultures manage this freedom vs. prohibition axis. For example, America has the widest axis and is the most liberal with respect to freedom. Prohibitions are not as dominant in America as they are in Iran or Japan, where the axes are narrower. Norway has a shorter axis, but more balance between the two.

In the United States there have been periods of extreme expressions on both ends of the axis. This was true in the 1770s, 1860s, 1890s, 1920s, 1950s, 1960s, and 1990s around issues of revolution, abolition (Civil War), prohibition, exhibition, conformance (McCarthy witch-hunts), permissiveness, and the conservatism of the present. What is shown here for the United States is a general distribution at no particular moment in time.

The relevance of this comparison is to remind us of two things. One, all of the seven cultural forces operate on an axis and therefore can manifest themselves differently at different times. This graph shows that in America, or Norway for that matter, a totally permissive society could not function, nor could a totally repressive one. There would be more tolerance for the repressive extreme in Iran and to a lesser degree in Japan. The same could be said for work environments: Totally permissive ones would simply not work. But because Americans choose the freedom side of the axis more often, restrictive work environments inhibit productivity, stifle innovation, and dampen what Fred Smith, chairman of Federal Express, calls "discretionary effort."

The second point about this graph is the power of the restraining element and the need to monitor where on the axis the force is manifesting itself. In this sense, the positioning can help predict behavior and response to a policy change, a new management practice, a new pricing strategy, or a new marketing campaign. For example, if a company has flextime for employees (freedom) and this policy is the most liberal in a particular industry, employees would rebel if the policy were eliminated overnight. Even restrictions on the policy or new management guidelines implying abuse of the policy would meet with resistance.

On the other hand, if a choice or incentive were offered (read freedom of choice) to drop or modify the flextime, a policy change would not meet the same degree of resistance. The same reasoning would apply to consumer choices, pricing strategies, and the design of new products and services. Always, in America, present the options or change in terms of more freedom, being careful to avoid the pitfalls of prohibition.

GO

If you chose not to read through "Get Set," you probably know viscerally why the American kid with her Lego set skips the instructions and invents a creation of her own. However, if you read through the background information, we trust you have a better understanding of our starting point and the assumptions we will make from here on about the seven cultural forces that define Americans.

So, enough already.

GO.

The Magnificent Seven:
An Overview of the Cultural Forces that Define Americans

It's 1959. Ike's in the White House. Wally and the Beaver are on TV every Thursday night. Chevy is the best-selling car in the world, promising a "jet smooth ride." A gallon of ESSO costs twenty-eight cents. Life is good.

Two more stars are added to the American flag: one for Alaska, one for Hawaii. Able and Baker, two monkeys, make a fifteen-minute, three-hundred-mile missile launch at the start of America's space program and land safely off the coast of Antigua. Out in Hollywood a talented young composer, Elmer Bernstein, has just screened the rough cut of a new movie. It will be Bernstein's job to come up with a musical theme to breathe some life into this expensive turkey. He has taken some notes, and the film editor has handed him the timing of a few key scenes. Elmer gets into his convertible, puts the top down, and heads for his piano and home in the hills beneath that big crooked sign.

Bernstein has his work cut out for him. The picture is a shoot 'em up about some American gunslingers who get together and cross the Rio Grande to rid the world of some parasitic banditos. (If this reminds you of the American Army's recent visits to

Grenada, Iraq, Somalia, or Haiti, you can skip the rest of this and jump to the next section.)

Elmer reaches deep into the very marrow of his American bones and comes up with a musical score that soars with majestic grandeur and captures the mythic glory of the American frontier. The name of the picture, of course, is *The Magnificent Seven.* It stars Yul Brynner and his six galloping buddies (Steve McQueen, James Coburn, Charles Bronson, Robert Vaughn, Horst Buchholz, and Brad Dexter—all representing different facets of the American character) who band together to rescue a small Mexican village being terrorized by a Mexican bad guy played by American actor Eli Wallach. Enlivened by the score, which masks its plodding script, the movie stirs the American heart. The picture plays and plays at neighborhood theaters and finally fades, but the Bernstein score will live on.

Cut to 1954: Now it's the Philip Morris cigarette people who have a turkey on their hands. It's a brand of cork filter tips, boxed in white to appeal to ladies. Problem is, the ladies ain't buying. The brand is Marlboro. The challenge of rescuing the brand falls to a frumpy little gent in Chicago named Leo Burnett. He had started out in the Depression as an advertising copywriter, and his touch was so sure that over time he created one of the most respected advertising agencies in the world.

Many a young comer in the ad game had tried to fathom the wellspring of Leo's sure touch. His advertising instincts were habits of the heart of which he probably was not fully aware. In any case, he got the Marlboro assignment and must have thought the brand might be revived by spreading a little old-fashioned fertilizer on it. And who has the most fertilizer in the world? Cowboys. And where is the best cowboy music around? In that Yul Brynner movie.

The next thing America knows, whenever it flips its TV dial to any of the four or five channels then operating, a lantern-jawed cowpoke comes on screen at full gallop, swinging a rope and yelling, "YAHOOOOO!" as Bernstein's music swells to a crescendo and a wrangler's voice-over implores, "Come to where the flavor is. Come to Marlboro country." Then the camera sweeps across the rugged buttes. Cattle bellow. Cowboys light up and inhale deeply. But it is the music and its evocation of a mythic frontier that reaches the American soul. As we like to say in America, the rest is history. Marlboro is now the leading cigarette brand in the world.*

Besides their musical connection, the Grade B movie and the Marlboro ads (not the products necessarily) also share an ability to activate some of our cultural forces. Like many best-selling films, music, commercials, or books in America, they resonate with us because they speak our common language. Our "Magnificent Seven" cultural forces are the foundation of that language.

What follows is a quick overview of each of America's Magnificent Seven. In turn, we will devote a full chapter to each force. We know that as a reader you may want to get to the bottom line *now*, but each of those chapters will provide details on how to activate the forces in business environments, public-policy debates, and personal development. Remember, we will be tracking six primary companies, a nonprofit agency, the drug abuse problem, and a half-dozen or so individuals who exemplify and personify the seven cultural forces that define us.

Incidentally, the last film Yul Brynner made was a public-service commercial announcing that he was dying of lung cancer; he begged his audience to stop smoking.

FORCE #1 Choice ☑

Portuguese anthropologist Francisco Martins Ramos, whose area of special interest is American culture, has a problem: He doesn't know how to operate American bathrooms—the faucets, for starters. Each time he uses an American bathroom the fixtures are different, or so it has been in "20 American homes, hotels, motels, dormitories, bus and train stations, restaurants, and bars."

Writing in "My American Glasses" in *Distant Mirrors: America as a Foreign Culture,* Ramos says:

> *The problem is that the tap mechanisms can be put into action by the pressure of a forefinger on a generally hidden button, by turning a screw that we wouldn't think to turn, by moving an appurtenance considered to be ornamental, or by using a masked hook, a secondary metal arabesque, or an invisible pedal.*

And it's not only the faucets—it's showers, baths, and toilets, too. Ramos says, "It is easy to recognize the embarrassment of a common Portuguese who is forced to make a detailed preliminary study of the sanitary equipment, which the circumstances do not always permit."

As Americans we give faucets no thought. In fact, when we ourselves read about Ramos's quandary we thought he was exaggerating and did some checking of our own: Of ten sinks in our two homes, only three faucets work the same, and they took some getting used to. But until we made the conscious effort to understand Ramos's complaint, we had simply never thought about it before. It seems perfectly natural to us to encounter variety and choice in every part of our lives.

Insistence on Choice

More than any other people, Americans insist on choice. It's in our Constitution, the oldest written one in the world. It is the dominant force in our pursuit of happiness. We can say, feel, think, organize, and do just about anything we choose—just short of the other fella's nose.

Choice is the force that brought Pilgrims to Plymouth Rock, and it is the force that brought all who followed them to America's shores. Little wonder that this force transformed and continues to transform all who come under its sway.

Choice drives American buying habits. Not only is choice formative, it is ubiquitous and mundane. It manifests itself every day at our lunch counters, where tourists, to their consternation, are confronted even with a choice of salad dressings: Thousand Island, blue cheese, ranch, French, lite something or other, vinaigrette, and house—whatever that is. In Europe the salad comes with a dressing of the chef's choosing; the customer is not consulted. And it comes blended in with the ingredients, not on the side the way some of us choose to order it in the United States.

The Consequences of Too Much Choice

Choice is clearly something we can't live without. But of late we have had more choice than ever. Today, we are often faced with a constant, staggering array of choices. Brands eventually begin to merge; product claims are misleading; word of mouth contradicts the marketing campaign; the "new and improved" is stacked next to the older model, brand, or style that seemed just fine the way it was; it's cheaper to buy two, but you only need one.

Like any of the seven cultural forces taken to excess, choice can be overwhelming; indeed it can produce anxiety (and maybe some forms of neurosis). Ironically, this bewilderment is especially prevalent in the proliferation of consumer newsletters and magazines like *Consumer Reports,* which make the choice for us or help narrow the range. Ten years ago there were ten national health newsletters with the basics of health care and prevention. Today there are over forty covering vitamin therapies, herbology, homeopathy, acupuncture, etc. Nevertheless, given the complexities of over-choice, Americans will always come down in favor of more choice rather than less.

A Fighting Word

Choice has always been a charged word in the American language. Pro-*choice* is the name given to one side of one of the most divisive contemporary issues in America: abortion. It is so powerful that the other side started a national counter-campaign: "*Choose* life."

America has fought over choice (the Civil War) and for choice (two world wars). Our interventions in other countries, while also serving America's need to "fix" things, are about ensuring that everyone has a choice—whether they want it or not!

★ Starting in 1985, AT&T embarked on a multimillion-dollar (☑) post-divestiture campaign to get consumers to designate a long-distance telephone carrier—and tagged it "The Right Choice." In the intensified battle with long-distance carriers, the choice theme continues to dominate the AT&T ads. (It shouldn't be long before we have a choice of local carriers as well.)

★ The national debate on health care reform in 1994 hemorrhaged on choice—too much or not enough, depending on which side you were on. HMOs (health maintenance organizations) constantly struggle to accommodate customers who want to *choose* their doctor or bring along the one they know.

★ Though there is little difference between airlines today, to paraphrase Independent presidential candidate Governor George Wallace about the Democrats and Republicans, airlines nevertheless acknowledge that passengers have a choice in airlines when the pilot thanks us for flying with them—this time.

Public Policy by Choice

Public policy-making starts with choice; that is why politics is called the art of compromise—choices have to be made from among the multitude of choices. America's marvelous governmental system of checks and balances keeps the choices in a reasonable perspective. In America we can make choices and then turn right around quickly and make the opposite choice, as we did with Prohibition, for example. Or we can take our time making choices, as we have for the past twenty-five years regarding cigarettes.

Drug abuse (including alcohol and nicotine) is the public policy issue we will track through some of the cultural forces. The choices we've made and continue to make, and the choices we chose not to make, are at the heart of the complexity of drug-abuse prevention.

Most people will concede that the government's war (an unfortunate label) on drugs has been less than victorious. While the DEA (the federal Drug Enforcement

Agency) is busy interdicting known substances, the dope chain is inventing "designer" drugs to fill the void. At the turn of the century we chose heroin to get folks off opium, and in the 1970s we chose another drug (methadone) to get folks off heroin. At home as a nation, we've tried everything except decriminalization, legalization, and the firing squad. And it is generally agreed that crop substitution—the American foreign policy of paying other countries not to grow opium, marijuana, and coca—is a failure.

At the prevention end of things, drug-abuse education programs work when they address the reasons *why* people choose to experiment. Programs that focus on *what* people use don't work. Choice works when we understand the role of choice in the decision-making process. For example, the popular anti-drug-abuse campaign "Just Say No" applies only to the choice at the beginning of the process, not after the onset of experimentation—a fact misunderstood by those who use the slogan for all drug-abuse efforts.*

FORCE #2 Impossible Dreams

America is *the* happening place for dreams. It all started with the Pilgrims and hasn't stopped for one day since. Here our endless choices enable us to dream the impossible and make them come true sooner or later.

This is the land where Barry Goldwater noted that everyone can grow up to be president, except him. There are no limits to what Americans can become, try, fail to do, and then try again. This highly variable American Dream is the ageless magnet for immigrants. It is what prompted Miami doctor Manuel Rico Perez to take out a full-page ad in *The New York Times* on October 14, 1994 (at the height of the latest wave of Cuban emigrants attempting to boat to America), to call our attention to a young Cuban girl held at the Guantánamo naval base, who had just learned to play "The Star-Spangled Banner" on her only worldly possession: a violin.

The Business of Dreaming

Times have changed since Walt Disney said, "I could never convince the financiers that Disneyland was feasible, because dreams offer too little collateral." Dreams now have a tangible, bankable business application—just ask the people at Disneyland or Disney World today, or the guys who just left Disney to form DreamWorks SKG, who are teaming up with the founders of Microsoft to make all of the fantasies and daydreams about interactive media a reality.

Corporate vision statements today are beginning to tap the intrinsic power of dreams. Perhaps businessmen have learned something from the visionary Martin Luther King, Jr., about inspiring followers. King, remember, had a dream—not a strategic plan, that corporate document that often lays flat and is not deployed throughout an organization in a manner that can energize a workforce. A flawed plan that can inspire will outperform a perfect plan with no passion. Levi Strauss & Co. provides one case in point through their Aspirations program that we outline in Chapter 2.

The best way for American companies to activate this Dream Force is to spell out seemingly impossible tasks and to challenge workers with stretch goals or ideal states,

*For a fuller discussion of the drug-abuse problem see Chapter 1.

like the kind CEO Jack Welch is trying at General Electric, the company "that brings good things to light":

> ... a company where people come to work every day in a rush to try something they woke up thinking about the night before. We want them to go home from work wanting to talk about what they did that day, rather than trying to forget about it. We want factories where the whistle blows and everyone wonders where the time went, and someone suddenly wonders aloud why we need a whistle. We want a company where people find a better way, every day, of doing things; and where by shaping their own work experience, they make their lives better and your company best.

Welch's dream for GE appeared in the company's (normally staid) annual report to stockholders, Wall Street analysts, and potential investors. That's a good place to let the world know that you are serious about reaching for the stars. There is nothing like a financial analyst to keep your feet to the promise of your fire.

How Dreams Materialize

Americans don't just sit around dreaming, they invent the necessary technology to *make* their dreams come true. Big dreams = big technology. In an extension of the chicken-or-the-egg quandary, it is sometimes hard to know which comes first, the dream or the technology. What is clear is that we can't make dreams come true without some kind of technology. First and foremost, it is *the* answer. Whether it was taming or building the nation, fixing education, increasing productivity, fighting drug abuse, preventing illnesses, meeting the increasing demands of customers, or competing in the global marketplace, technology is the first consideration and often the only one. Americans put great faith in technology—they worship it.

At the turn of the century our impossible dreams were the fuel for our industrial engine. We invented the technology to make them all possible: the steamboat; the sewing machine; the steel plow; the harvester; the transcontinental railroad (which created the need for steel rails and drove the invention of the Bessemer furnace); the telegraph and cornucopia of goodies from the mind of Edison; precision tools (which made possible interchangeable parts, assembly-line production, and the related principle of automation); and on and on.

Business Dreams in Action

Our research suggests that the people of Levi Strauss are working the hardest at making their dreams or aspirations come true. A staff of over forty people work the process on a daily basis. This is serious business. They have a set of principles and objectives that focus on the needs of the individual that often go beyond the product and service perimeters of the company. In the following powerful words, Levi's CEO, Robert Haas, often reminds himself and his employees, "You don't work *for* Levi's, you work for yourselves. You just happen to work *at* Levi's."

Other companies have found their own way to make this highly charged cultural force work for them. Here are some of the few we will review throughout the book:

★ In Chapter 2 we will detail how the Ritz-Carlton Hotels, winner of the 1992 Malcolm Baldrige National Quality Award, ties its personal and business strategy into a statement of their dream: *Ladies and Gentlemen* (the employees) *serving Ladies and Gentlemen* (the hotel guests).

★ At Motorola, if you have an idea that doesn't promise a tenfold improvement, don't bother mentioning it. Such "impossible" challenges are called stretch goals (perhaps a little more palatable than the word *dream* but possessing the same emotional energy), and people love them.

★ Johnson & Johnson has a credo (see page 143) that serves not only as their dream statement but their management bible. It is what guided them through the tough Tylenol-tampering-poisoning days in the early eighties and set a benchmark example for how companies should manage a crisis.

FORCE #3 Big & More

Big is a big word in America. We like things big. Very Big. The bigger the better. If we can't have something bigger, we'll settle for more, that way we eventually get bigger by having more.

Big and more is another way of saying that Americans are obsessed with being Number One. We recently saw a Bentley with a bumper sticker that said, "Whoever ends up with the most toys wins."

America is dotted with big stores—superstores we call them now—because big has lost some of its punch in retailing. Stores like Home Depot are up to five acres big with more than fifty thousand separate items in them. On your way home you can stop by a Barnes & Noble, a super-bookstore chain, and choose from sixty thousand titles in the smaller stores to one hundred and seventy-five thousand in the bigger ones. We have no idea how many toys there are in the super Toys "R" Us; maybe your kid or grandchild knows.

Americans love big—it gives us more choice, that first cultural force. It even enables our dreams to be big, that second force. But big is not always welcome. For example, there's the case of the city parents of Burlington, Vermont, who, fearing the consequences to their (small) beloved downtown merchants, are making the entry of a big Wal-Mart quite unwelcome.

When Franklin D. Roosevelt was in the White House, the nation was dotted with thousands of one-room schoolhouses where one teacher would educate all eight grades. Of course, she had the help of older kids teaching younger ones, and in that way both groups learned. Then it occurred to school boards throughout the country that if the Ford Motor Company could make cars cheaper with a production line, why not do the same to educate kids. This gave rise to the central school. Kids were bussed in from all over the place to attend big schools. Thousands of kids in big schools. Big classes. Big learning. Big success.

Then came big administrations. Big budgets. Big unions. Big drop in test scores. Big dropout rates. Big lobbies. And big studies about what went wrong. Now there are big plans about getting away from big.

The Trouble with Big and More

Big and more served us well at the turn of the century. During the industrial revolution, big and more technology transformed America into a big power in the world.

But in the waning years of the same century, this force could spell big trouble ahead. Consider these randomly selected big national problems:

★ The savings-and-loan fiasco, which we may never stop paying for

★ The federal deficit, which in the summer of 1995 amounted to $57,690 for each man, woman, and child in America and was growing at the rate of 157 bucks a day

★ Skyrocketing health care costs, which make up a greater percentage of the GNP than that of any other nation in the world (and they're going higher every year)

★ Runaway high school dropout rates, with more kids dropping out of school each day than the number of soldiers killed at Pearl Harbor

★ The drug-abuse problem, which costs us all $237.6 billion a year and has American businesses suffering a 25 to 33 percent reduction in productivity because of it

For most of us, big and more is not a problem. We have ways of dealing with the opportunities and challenges of big and more in our own work environments and in our personal lives. In Chapter 3, where we talk more about this force, we will provide an important insight into the value of letting small units within our operations *act* big. There is a lot of business advantage to being a big fish in a small pond!

FORCE #4 Now ⏱

Jets owner Leon Hess dismissed coach Pete Carroll after one season because, he said, "I'm eighty years old and I want results now." Another football coaching legend, George Allen of the Washington Redskins, coined the quintessential American expression: "The future is now." You can be watching TV at two in the morning in a big American city and a local mattress commercial will implore you to come down *now* for the deal of a lifetime—not in the morning at sunup, but now.

This *now* imperative is what one researcher refers to as "animal time." Animals in the wild live in the moment—there is no future. This explains, for example, the frenzied behavior of animals that seemingly kill and devour their supper in one motion.

Anthropologist Edward T. Hall says that America is the most time-obsessed and time-compartmentalized culture in the world. We break time down into small formal units of time—such as one minute, five minutes, ten minutes, fifteen minutes, half an hour, and an hour—units that are meaningless in most other cultures. Of course in our speech we talk about split seconds, nanoseconds, and even say, "Give me a second," or something took "forever" when we really mean a few minutes or more.

Unlike other cultures, Americans live in the present/future. Tomorrow is too late and fast is not soon enough. All of these time dimensions have major implications for change management, public-policy expectations, all types of scheduling, child rearing, interpersonal communications, and more.

Jeremy Rifkin, in his insightful book *Time Wars: The Primary Conflict in Human History,* points out that the computer "works in a time frame in which the nanosecond [one billionth of a second] is the primary temporal measure." (Yet how often do we sit impatiently in front of the screen, frustrated that it isn't faster still?)

But the time force is a powerful concept in business—not the Just-in-Time stuff we got from the Japanese (initially an inventory control system), but the competitive juices that come from beating someone to the starter's gate and finish line, especially when satisfying customers is the prize.

Just a few years ago the law required credit card companies to respond within thirty days to a customer's request to increase his or her credit limit. MBNA America, the fourth-largest issuer of credit cards, was the industry leader at the time, responding in around ten days. One day a customer called and asked for a credit increase while he was in the store (imagine that then!). MBNA made an exception and the customer got what he wanted (MBNA has a policy that the customer is always right!). Anyway, this led the charismatic Charlie Cawley, the president, to ask why this couldn't be done for everyone. MBNA went from ten days to two hours, and now they and everyone else do it routinely in under an hour—or instantly. And as the time force ticks, most of us are getting credit line increases without even asking for them!

American companies are faulted for not having twenty-five-year strategic plans or (real) one-year operational plans, when the Japanese excel at both. Americans are criticized for short-term thinking (really short-term *acting*). But there is nothing wrong with short-term acting if we can perform better and get more sustainable results. In this regard, the research we managed while at the American Quality Foundation, a think tank on quality management, shows that breaking a traditional, year-long business process down into two- or three-month intervals will bring companies bigger results in a shorter period of time. Ernst & Young, a Big Six accounting firm, proved it. In its Richmond, Virginia, office they increased the amount of new billable tax consulting hours *threefold* over prior efforts by abandoning conventional time frames and setting shorter time intervals to get the job done. We'll show the reader how to do it as well—not *now,* however, but later, in Chapter 4.

FORCE #5 Oops 👓

It is no coincidence that the movie *Rocky* won the Oscar for best picture in 1976—our bicentennial year. It beat out *Taxi Driver, All the President's Men, Bound for Glory*, and *Network. Rocky*, after all, is the quintessential American movie.

The script follows what we call the American Oops Script. It contains the elements, habits of mind, and behavioral proclivities that we Americans invariably follow and repeat over and over and over again. The basic sequence is:

★ We take on an impossible task

★ We are unprepared to attain our goal immediately

★ We discover we are underdogs

★ We are goaded on by the odds against us

★ We fail the first time but try again

★ We get caught up in the process (no pain, no gain)

★ We triumph in the end and celebrate

★ We move on to something else impossible (often to repeat the process again).

Remember the story of Rocky Balboa, the small-time punk boxer who is totally unprepared when given the chance to go up against the champ? He doesn't train, gets knocked silly, and doesn't do it right the first time. We get to see the bloody knuckles, the busted nose, and feel the pain. Then with some after-the-fact training, he tries again. This time there's a different—triumphant—ending (even though he loses to the champion, he went the distance).

Life Mimics Movies

Remarkably, but not surprisingly, Sylvester Stallone's personal life follows the American Oops Script as well—in many respects *Rocky* is autobiographical.

Stallone was born in New York, his parents divorced when he was fifteen, and he moved to Philadelphia, where he was in and out of trouble and ended up in a special school for young men with learning disabilities and adjustment problems. He couldn't make it into an American college and ended up studying in Switzerland, but never graduated.

Back in the States he worked at low-paying jobs, from cleaning lion's cages to working in a deli. During this time he did manage to get some bit parts in movies but no major roles. Unable to get a break in the movies, he decided to write one instead, with himself in the lead role—his impossible dream. Nothing worked until he saw a potential movie in the real-life fifteen-round world heavyweight championship fight between Muhammad Ali and Chuck Wepner, who went the distance with Ali but lost on a technical knockout.

The details and travails of getting the movie made repeat the American Oops Script. Suffice it to say that in the end United Artists let him star in his movie at scale wages. He also agreed to accept twenty thousand dollars for the screenplay, the minimum Writers Guild fee, plus 10 percent of the profits.*

Americans Don't Do Things Right the First Time

This same American Oops Script—the real version or the Memorex—is repeated over and over in our history, novels, movies, political scenarios, in the development of our corporations, and even in our personal lives. President Clinton is known as the Comeback Kid, and Congressman Newt Gingrich made it to Congress on his third try. Abraham Lincoln had at least a dozen failures in business and politics before he made it to the White House.

We all have a personal or business American Oops Script or two under our belts. When America was shocked into World War II through the surprise attack at Pearl Harbor, the American Oops Script kicked right in. As a nation we would have to wait four years before we could celebrate and move on to something else. It was none other than Winston Churchill who said, "You can count on Americans to do things right, after they have tried everything else." We are certain that he had more than just the war in mind.

Americans don't do things right the first time, in spite of all of management's exhortations. In fact, research indicates that unconsciously we don't do things right the first time because perfection, or the pursuit of perfection, represents a dead end

Rocky went on to gross $200 million worldwide.

to Americans; it means there is no place to go. Moreover, we place a higher value on fixing things than on doing them right. Fixing something enables Americans to show that we are human, and once we have fixed it, we can move on to something else. As our colleague Clotaire Rapaille says, "If Rocky had done it right the first time, there would be no movie."

Our goal in our work endeavors, as well in as our personal activities, is modest: to get it to work, whatever the "it" is. When it works, we're satisfied and we're ready to move on to something else.

FORCE #6 Improvise ✂

Just before the turn of the century some New York swells thought the United States could stand a little more culture, so they hired composer Antonin Dvořák, bringing him over from Europe to run the National Conservatory of Music. While here, he was to compose a symphony or two, which would serve as the basis for the missing culture.

After a stint of high-society living in New York, he spent a summer in Spillville, Iowa, where he caught one of Buffalo Bill's "Wild West" shows, mixed with hard-drinking Czech-Americans, attended the Chicago Centennial Exhibition, and saw a traveling Indian medicine show, among other things. He wrote his *New World Symphony* and the pastoral *American Suite* for piano, drawing heavily for content on these experiences and on America's Negro spirituals and Native American chants. Musicologist Michael Beckerman even says Dvořák's *New World* score was directly inspired by Longfellow's *Song of Hiawatha.* Dvořák didn't change American culture; American music changed him. What he did for his New York benefactors and the rest of us was to serve as the first European classical musician to urge Americans to value their own musical roots.

It was at this time that a new American musical form was emerging from our saloons and riverboats. This indigenous music required not only a mastering of the form but an appreciation of the spirit of the whole. As our own American Duke, Duke Ellington, said repeatedly, "It don't mean a thing if it ain't got that swing."

What was new? What was non-European about jazz? In a word, *improvisation.* What was novel in American music was not only its unique idiom but its structure, within which each player could take a solo turn at improvising. In jazz, participation was totally collegial, just a bunch of guys or gals who wanted and knew how to play together using a few simple rules.

In classical (European) music every player is given an exact script on tempo, entry, mood, tone, etc. It is hierarchical. In the words of Wynton Marsalis, "You can't stand up in the middle of a Beethoven concerto and say, 'I hear a B flat here.'"

Jazz is genuinely American. It could not have been created anyplace else in the world. It is a vibrant example of the American predisposition to improvise, especially when the alternative is hierarchy. It is play, first and foremost. And that is the source of its joy.

We will use jazz as a metaphor to help us understand improvisation and its more organized counterpart, innovation. In Chapter 6 (see pages 232–64) we will show how this "invented-here" music form is the real song of America, with a structure applicable to everything we do. In jazz, failing to hit the high note from time to time won't get you kicked out of the group, but failing to pay attention is grounds for immediate dismissal. What a different message from the faddish-but-failed management imperative of "Do it right the first time!"

For those readers who don't relate to jazz, we will give other examples of how the structure and elements of improvisation operate in such contexts as the work of film crews (often composed of total strangers) and the lives of resourceful people like Harry Hopkins, who, dying of cancer, saved England when he ran the Lend-Lease program by phone from a card table in a White House bedroom.

Americans love to improvise. This is the force that Americans rely on day in and day out to get a stalled engine started, to save a flood victim, to talk their way out of a jam, to soothe an angry customer, to play basketball, to repair an emergency room patient, and to make us laugh at the "Comedy Center."

FORCE #7: Whatsnew 💾

Sideburns, hula hoops, tail fins, body-piercing, New Deals, Manifest Destiny, Elvis, Elvis sightings, Contract with America, Newt today, gone tomorrow. The American fixation on whatsnew is more than generational fads or fashion frolics. It is the energy that has kept us reinventing ourselves since Plymouth Rock.

Americans are in a perpetual search for new potential identities. We are never satisfied with who or what we are. This characteristic explains typical American Doris Eaton Travis, a brand-new Phi Beta Kappa college graduate at eighty-five. It explains why papermaker, commercial fisherman, heavy-duty mechanic, biologist, solid-waste manager Royce W. Perkins ran for state representative in Maine. It's why Jimmy Carter published a book of poetry. It's why Grandma Moses said, "If I hadn't taken up painting, I would have raised chickens." And it explains why Richard Nixon said that the career he would have chosen over politics, if it had been available to him at the time, was rap singer.

Among other things, whatsnew, or our quest for a new potential identity, has major implications for how we reward people at work. In most companies, rewards and recognitions are delayed and look to the past. They are usually a tombstone—you know, those walnut plaques that some of us hang on the wall—*behind* us on our wall graveyards. They say very little about the future, where we want to go. New potential identities can make a big difference at home or at work. We'll show how in Chapter 7. In the meantime, here are some interesting examples of this force in action:

★ There's no doubt that any product or service that is presently stationary can be put on and/or delivered on wheels. Really! Chicago has probably the first, but not the last, fitness center on wheels. It gets only eight miles to the gallon, but the North Shore One on One van features a StairMaster, treadmill, weights, color TV, VCR, and personal trainer.

★ Greyhound's slogan used to be "Go Greyhound and leave the driving to us." Within the next decade, we may just sit in a car, press the gas pedal (if it still has one), and leave the driving to infrared and magnetic sensors, microwave radar, and satellite navigation. The Pentagon is already contributing; its global positioning system, via satellite, can help travelers find the nearest restaurants, service stations, and other necessities in and around selected cities. There is a whole institute at Texas A&M, the Texas Transportation Institute, that is devoted to finding applications of existing space technology and inventing more.

★ The online-services industry is for this generation what Henry Ford's production-line system was for the industrial revolution—more through faster, bigger, improvise, and whatsnew! Never mind the oopses or taking it back to the shop for repair; we can't let mistakes stand in our way. There is an online service that can even tell us *daily* where the "bugs and turkeys" are.

There you have it: The Magnificent Seven. As you learned about each one, was your reaction typical of most Americans—first "Wow!" and then "But I knew that!"? We hope so. As we've pointed out earlier, these forces are so much a part of our beings that we should be comfortable with their influence on us. So, bringing these seven cultural forces to the forefront of our consciousness is the *way to go*, the key to a higher level of business performance in America. This book will show how that is possible; how the seven cultural forces that define Americans can work together to enable us to achieve the dream of Langston Hughes.

> *O, let America be America again—*
> *The land that never has been yet—*
> *And yet must be—*
> *The land where every man is free.*

Chapter 1

Anything You Want
America's Insistence on Choice

It doesn't matter whether you are selling mutual funds or machine tools, chewing gum or cars, you'd better give Americans a choice or they won't even honor you with a change of mind. If you try to deny or limit choice it can destroy your enterprise or your initiative, whether your trade is plumbing or politics.

Choice is the First Force in America. It is formative and formidable. Overwhelming at times. We can't escape the power of choice in dealing with money markets, consumer preference, fashion fads, public policy, or rebellious teenagers who won't pick up their rooms. Our Constitution, the oldest written constitution in the world, guarantees each American choice in speech, choice in what is written, choice of religion, choice in association, choice even in choosing or not choosing a weapon. Finally, and most important, there is choice in how we are governed, and by whom.

In an Orwellian sense, the Choice Force is "more equal" than the other forces we write about because it drives our inner gyroscope. Psychiatrist Rollo May writing in *Freedom and Destiny* says this about choice: ". . . each of us experiences himself as *real* in the moment of choice. . . . When one asserts 'I can' or 'I choose' or 'I will' one feels one's own significance." To feel one's own significance amid a multitude of 250 million is why we insist on choice.

This chapter outlines how the Choice Force came to be so dominant. We describe how it can be activated to increase productivity, restore the value and dignity of work, enhance training and development, and more effectively manage our employee relationships. Because of the girth of choice, we have chosen to narrow the focus of our exploration to these people-related issues. If we can provide some new insight into this basic component of business, then we will have suggested something about its application to customers, suppliers, process reengineering, marketing, and new product and service development. We also show how the Choice Force plays out in the design of public policy, and what must be done to keep choice active in *all* our business endeavors, from Washington to Wall Street, from plants to playgrounds.

Meet Marvin and Mabel

We have chosen to start this chapter by introducing you to two fellow travelers to remind you of the pervasiveness of choice and how ingrained it has become in our everyday lives. They could have been your neighbors or co-workers, any pair in America. But they happen to be Marvin and Mabel. Ride along with James Morrison as he met them briefly in the summer of 1995:

> *It's a clear day and I'm roaring down an empty two-lane highway under a brilliant sky. All around me is one of the most spectacular landscapes in the world—the high, flat plains of South Park, Colorado, a breathtaking emptiness surrounded by snow-capped Rockies.*
>
> *A few cattle, some buffalo, and herds of shy pronghorn antelope graze in the distance. A beeline black tape of two-lane macadam bisects it, so you can go flat out at ninety or ninety-five without much chance of seeing flashing colored lights.*
>
> *Then it happened—it always happens in the tourist season. Coming up over Wilkerson Pass at an altitude of 9,507 feet and snaking down toward Cripple Creek and Divide, with Pikes Peak in the near distance, you ease 'er down to forty or so behind a twenty-car string held up by a motorized mansion monopolizing the asphalt, indifferent to the seething impatience behind it. On a hairpin turn, way ahead, we get a glimpse of the thirty-five-foot Winnebago, towing an '87 red Ford Escort, plodding along at the pace of a tired donkey.*
>
> *In what seems like a century later the line of cars are all stopped at that traffic light where there's a turn to the gambling parlors of Cripple Creek. But just before breaking away and zooming for home I see that the Winnebago whale has pulled over for gas. I can't resist doing some on-the-road research.*
>
> *It's important in America to be "friendly." I say "howdy," and after a few offhand remarks about the rig, I'm on board the Marv and Mabel land yacht, which has a satellite dish that can bring down seventy-eight channels of color TV, a Carrier 500 BTU air conditioner, four folding vinyl-stripped tubular aluminum lawn chairs strapped to the back with bungee cords, and a 1200-watt Sharp micro-wave oven with a revolving glass dish to make sure baking potatoes get done evenly. They also have a propane refrigerator and a four-burner gas stove with oven, and double queen-sized beds in case they ever have grandchildren on board. Mabel refers to Marvin as Marvin, and Marvin refers to Mabel as "She."*
>
> *Marvin likes being on the road after all those years at John Deere (the yellow and green tractor folks). They locked up the house and left Moline five weeks ago, took a northern route through Sioux City, across by Bismarck, then on to Missoula, Spokane, and down to Pullman, where She has a daughter by her first who is married to a fellow who is in construction. With that Social Security check and the income bargained by the UAW, the two of them have a steady income of just under $35,000, which is plenty to get by on.*

Marvin's Choices

Marvin's life, just like the rest of us, is made up of an endless succession of choices. He is not a prisoner of class. He is neither royalty nor a commoner. He's part of the great American consumer choice class. And consume he does. His is a heritage that from the beginning has been based on the freedom to choose—to make choices about work, family, where to live, how to live, how to sojourn on this planet. This *range* of choices does not exist in other cultures: It is uniquely American.

Marvin's first big choice happened when he got angry with a stubborn math teacher his junior year in high school, which happened to coincide with not making third base on the varsity baseball team: He decided not to go back for his senior year. He was seventeen and knew everything and the war was on and the Navy was looking for warm bodies.

The Navy did two things for Marv. It took off some rough edges and taught him how to run a drill press, metal lathe, and a milling machine. This led to a job in the Livonia plant for Miller Tool and Die, where he met Eunice, who was a timekeeper. They were married and blissfully happy until Marvin found out about Arnie. Realizing the impossibility of working alongside Arnie and Eunice for the rest of his life, he chose to quit Miller, sue for divorce, and head for better moments in Moline.

But while Marv was paying for gas, she said something to me that made Marvin's choices about his life that much more dramatic. She said it without a trace of envy or wistfulness, scorn, or pride. It was about Marvin's little brother back in Detroit. She said sometimes you see his picture in magazines. Works for Chrysler and flies around in one of those company jets. Has a big house and the country club and company cars. Marvin says he wouldn't want to be bothered with all that. He and Marvin talk off and on, but not much.

She cut her story short when Marvin came back carrying a Pepsi for her and an orange drink for himself. They climbed on board, waved good-bye, and headed into the sunset as though this had been a scripted end to some TV documentary on consumer choice in America.

By Choice, By Golly

Because a Winnebago may not be the way we choose to go, we might dismiss Marvin as interesting but not relevant. However, beyond the choices he has made about the trinkets in his wagon and his lifestyle on the road, two-thirds of us who have been married in the United States share a divorce experience with him. Each day, more kids make the same choice he made about dropping out of high school than the total number of service personnel who were killed at Pearl Harbor. And unlike him, these hapless kids cannot choose to join the Navy, a diminished choice in the post-Cold War era of today. The one choice most Americans have over Marvin is that we have chosen to pick up our stakes and move lock, stock, barrels, and all that junk in the garage, attic, and basement an average of eleven times in our lifetime, beating out Marvin by a half-dozen moves or more.

Finally, maybe like us, Marvin and Mabel don't have a clue that they are driven by seven cultural forces. Their antecedents, way back, were from Bavaria, Ireland, Wales, and Sweden—all of which interest them not in the least. The thing that they share with the rest of us is that all of our ancestors came from someplace else—and this is important—by choice!

Sure, you will find some Irish and English who take their "caravans" (their word for "Winnebago") off to the shore for a "holiday" (their word for vacation). And in the deserts of Saudi Arabia families like to drive their Cadillacs out into the desert for an evening, and there in the silence of the shifting sands, drink Pepsi, tell stories, and praise Allah. But in no other nation do ordinary folks have the options or live by the choices that Marv and Mabel demand and take for granted.

The choices we make about the cars we drive, places we go, people we marry, where we work, why we work, how we work, and how we choose to live our lives follow no particular pattern. Demographers, sociologists, and market researchers have some general idea and never let up trying to tie it all down. This is important information that facilitates product and service marketing and enables us to target advertising better. But it doesn't explain *why* Americans insist on choice.

No Choice in the Matter: "Lock-in"

"Lock-in" is a simple-sounding expression for a complex theory about how certain things, in our case the seven cultural forces, prevail over other options that may have competed at the outset but now have no comparable weight, power, or presence.

Lock-in occurs when initial events of seemingly little importance have large and long-term consequences measured by increasing returns and feedback.* For example, Detroit is the automotive capital of the world, not because it is the best place to design and build cars, but because out of the literally hundreds of automobile manufacturers in the early days of the industry, the entrepreneurial talents that were behind Ford and General Motors happened to live in the vicinity of Detroit. They chose to do business in their hometown. Their early-on success created increasing returns, so the capital, engineering, and marketing talent flowed to them. This convergence of talent, technology, and resources accelerated the process to the point that Detroit became the only sensible place to make cars—simply because that's where all the car-making brains, bucks, and brawn were located.

The lock-in theory also explains why VHS beat out Beta, why New York City is the financial capital of the United States, why movies are made in Hollywood, and why computers come from Silicon Valley.

One of our favorite examples of lock-in can be found in two out of three homes in America and in virtually every company and organization in the world. It's QWERTY, the left-to-right arrangement of six letters on the keyboard of computers and typewriters. It's not the most efficient layout of a keyboard, but it's been "locked in" since 1873.

The QWERTY layout came about because the early typists were typing too fast and jamming the keys. To slow them down, an engineer named Christopher Scholes made a keyboard layout that put the letters Q-W-E-R-T-Y in the upper left, out of the way.

It had the desired effect: it slowed down the typists. Then the Remington Sewing Machine people started mass-producing typewriters with the new board, which meant that more typists learned the new layout, which induced other typewriter companies to use the same layout, which reinforced the acceptance and dominance of the layout. So QWERTY it is—to this day.

Choices: From the Pilgrims to the Present

All organizations have histories. Only a notable few use those histories to focus their decision-making process, inspire their employees, and guide their business

---

This theory comes by way of Stanford's Brian Arthur, from an article of his in the American Economics Review, *"Competing Technologies, Increasing Returns, and Lock-In by Historical Events."*

operations.* By history, we don't mean what happened in 1492 or that in 1887 Robert Wood Johnson invented the precursor to the Band-Aid. We mean the context, texture, sinews, choices, debates, options, and luck (or lack of luck) of a people, group, organization, or nation. We mean the connective tissues that make sense out of the choices of the past. We mean the experiences we bring to the futures we plan.

It is generally very difficult to get an American to focus on history. As a culture we are so future-oriented that we have little regard for the past. Only in America do people say, "Yesterday is history." This attitude stands in stark contrast to the rest of the world. For example, a couple of years ago, England's Oxford University turned down an American gift to establish a chair on American History, because we didn't have enough yet.

Two of the seven cultural forces help us understand why Americans have this attitude toward history: We are impatient with time (🕐) and fixated on whatsnew (🖳). So trying to get Americans to sit still (or read on) for a little history is always a challenge. However, in keeping with the premise of this chapter we have decided to put the Choice Force to work and give you a choice about how to finish reading it.

1. **Start in with some history** (how the seven cultural forces came into play in the formative years of our country).

2. **Skip to page 45** (how choice and the other forces apply to an individual).

3. **Skip to the "bottom line"** (the direct application of the forces to business, starting on page 46).

READER'S CHOICE #1: SOME HISTORY

Even the history lesson begins with a choice of answers. The question is when did the American experiment begin? James W. Loewen, a professor of sociology at the University of Vermont and author of *Lies My Teacher Told Me: Everything Your American History Textbook Got Wrong,* gives us more choices than one would expect. When he asked several hundred college students when America was first settled, the consensus answer was 1620. They didn't choose 1526, when some African slaves were left in South Carolina by the Spaniards, who abandoned a settlement attempt there. They didn't choose 1607, when the British settled in Jamestown (now Virginia) or 1614, when the Dutch settled Albany (New York). And, of course, Native Americans make a strong case for none of these.

We agree with Loewen, who concluded, "no matter." Loewen calls Plymouth Rock the *mythic* origin of America, so we too have chosen 1620 as the moment in time that the forces were forged.

As destiny would have it, England prevailed in the conquest of the eastern shore of the American continent. Had one of the other contestants won, either Spain or France, America would be a far different country today. English would be our second language, our national anthem would be easier to sing, Prince would have had to change his name, we'd be eating baguettes instead of bagels, and we'd be predominantly Catholic.

The Walt Disney Company and Johnson & Johnson are two such companies that we will write about throughout this book.

England prevailed in large measure because private English venture capitalists, impelled by vivid fantasies of quick riches, were determined to settle and establish a civilization in the far-off land. They put their money on the Pilgrims, who chose to come to the New World seeking religious freedom under "divine guidance." A smart choice back then, because the Pilgrims were driven by a religious fervor that is almost inconceivable today. Their belief was the epicenter of their very narrow lives.

At this point, it is important to set aside the sentimental histories we remember from sixth grade and think of the Pilgrims at Plymouth as America's first economic model; remember, their venture had been organized as a joint stock company financed by London merchants. It was to run for seven years and proceeds were to be deposited in a common fund that would pay for the bare necessities for the settlers. After that, profits were to be split between the venture capitalists ("*undertakers*" they were called) and the settlers.

What the Pilgrims established in Plymouth was a primitive form of communism, in that all of the settlers tried to work together farming the common fields. It was even less successful than the system put in place by Lenin and it was soon abandoned, replaced by individual ownership. Thus capitalism was born in America. This, by the way, was the first and last time in recorded history that an economic system was established under conditions that were both democratic and, out of bare necessity, improvisational.

Plymouth became what professor of engineering John Holland calls a complex adaptive economic and social system.* It modeled America. It had cast aside, by choice and necessity, the habits of a feudal English hierarchy. Changing circumstances required the settlers to create a new form of governance, while providing for food, shelter, and common defense—all at the same time.

The business plan called for the Pilgrims to go fishing. There were ships aplenty plying the banks of the New England shore, piling up profits taking salted cod back to England, but these Pilgrim farmers could never quite get the knack of the sea. They turned to farming for survival, and fur trading for profit. While mimicking the Native Americans, they improvised (✂) and applied new technology to expand their trade. Then, in a now disquieting part of our history, they killed their mentors, appropriated the land, and used these exploits to fuel their divine mission.†

By 1627 the Pilgrims had restructured their deal with their London investors, who agreed to sell their interest. The debt was finally paid off in 1648, and the Pilgrims were on their own—which was just the way they had wanted it all along.

---

*Dr. John Holland teaches at the University of Michigan and is a fellow at the Santa Fe Institute, an interdisciplinary think tank. Some of the work at the institute inquires into what it calls "complex adaptive systems," an examination of the common behavior of such differing organizations as ant colonies, international alliances, and world economies. Holland and his colleagues describe the characteristics of such systems as they emerge over time: Perpetual Novelty, Resilience, Emergence of the Aggregate, Formation of Individuality, Internal Models, Non Zero Sum, and Exploration Tradeoff. These are interdisciplinary terminologies; however, they appear to closely parallel some aspects of what we have called the seven cultural forces.

†In addition to the Loewen book that we have referenced, Ronald Takaki's book A Different Mirror: A History of Multicultural America is well worth reading. Both books should be part of any company's library and curriculum on diversity training.

The Pilgrim experience gave birth to the seven cultural forces. But why and how is it that these forces persisted for 375 years, are still going strong to this day, and will continue to dominate us as long as there are Americans?

Because they worked and they got locked-in.

How Choice Got Locked-in

The primary choice the Pilgrims made was rooted in a history of religious intolerance in their native England. James the First (of the King James Version of the Bible) was head of the Church of England. He declared that religious dissent and civil sedition were inseparable—a threat to the monarchy and punishable by death. In response, a group of dissenters formed quietly to "purify" England's Church and rid it of pomp, ritual, and the corrupt vestiges of Catholic Rome. The purifiers called themselves Puritans.

It was under these circumstances that one obscure little congregation in the remote village of Scrooby refused to play along at all. This pious congregation called themselves Separatists and broke away completely from the Church of England. It was a pivotal moment that would turn out to be one of the most momentous decisions in history. It set in motion a sequence of hard choices that ultimately forced these Separatists, in 1609, to flee into exile.

Their place of refuge was Leiden, Holland, a beautiful city in the midst of its golden age. It was the center of trade, manufacture, crafts, and art, and had at that moment the greatest universities in Europe. It was Rembrandt's hometown.

In the Holland of that day, children went to schools supported by the state. Most folks could read and write; they were conversant with math and knew other languages. And in terms of the rights of the common man, they were two centuries ahead of the rest of the world. Thus the Puritans were free to worship as they wished in Leiden.

William Bradford, who would grow up to play a pivotal role in the early days of our country, was an impressionable nineteen-year-old upon arrival in Holland. The twelve years he lived in Leiden's enlightened environment were a formative experience for the future governor of the Plymouth Colony.

America's First Spin Doctors

The Puritans had spent more than a decade in Holland before the storm clouds began gathering again. There was a real threat that Holland's truce with Spain was coming to an end and that Spanish/Catholic rule would return to Holland, and with it intolerance and oppression for nonbelievers. The Puritans' greatest worry was that they might again come under the power of an established religion. They were also concerned that their children would abandon the faith and take up Dutch ways.

Finally, these yeomen, who were born to the soil, had not stopped yearning for the land—to own it, possess it, work it, treasure it—always with the possibility of creating a utopian community. There was some talk of returning to English soil—but that was no real choice. Meanwhile, back in England, Captain John Smith, whose vivid *Map of Virginia* depicted a wondrous New World, glossed over its obstacles and problems and gave America a spin that would make today's spin doctors blush.

The Dutch were trying to lure the Puritans to a trading post in the New Netherlands. But in the end, having sold their homes, they made their destined choice. In Bradford's words from his *Plymouth Plantation* chronicles:

So they lefte that goodly and pleasante citie, which had been their resting place near 12 years; but they knew they were pilgrims, and looked not much on those things, but lift up their eyes to the heavens, their dearest cuntrie, and quieted their spirits.

Pilgrims Choose Virginia

The year was 1620. Altogether there were 104 souls (50 men, the rest women and children) aboard the *Mayflower* when it departed for Virginia. Yes, they were chartered to sail and settle in Virginia.

Now keep this in mind: Virginia in those days was most of what we know as the states of Maryland and New Jersey, right up to the Hudson River, not the sliver of land that today is tucked in between Maryland and North Carolina. Still the Pilgrims missed it. By three hundred or so miles, and they ended up landing at what is now Plymouth Rock.

But before they landed, with no time to waste (🕒), they had to make some big choices (☑) about governance, order, process, and priorities. Off course (🔁),* they were out of their jurisdiction and headed to uncharted land. With no legal charter, they improvised (✂). The result was the Mayflower Compact (🖥). *Here, then, are five of the seven forces already in play as the Pilgrims set foot on American soil for the first time.*

The now famous Compact resolved a crisis aboard ship—a mutiny was brewing— just before they landed. About half the *Mayflower* settlers were fleeing from religious persecution. The rest were quite ordinary folk, merely looking for a better life. So, as the good ship approached the Cape Cod shore, a dispute arose between the Pilgrim "Saints" and the so-called "Strangers" about whether or not to land at the Plymouth site, which was not plan A, and about how the new colony should be governed.

The resolution of the dispute between Saints and Strangers[†] was the first agreement for self-government put in force in America. It successfully reconciled the "we and them" into a cooperative body that would submit to "just and equall Lawes." It was, George F. Willison notes, "for its day an extraordinary document, a remarkable statement of revolutionary new principles, an important milestone in our long, hard, and often bloody ascent from feudalism, from that degrading aristocratic system of power and privilege for the few which had held Europe in irons for centuries."

This mistake business may have all been started by Columbus. He "discovered" America by mistake, and a German mapmaker working in France gave America its name by mistake, having concluded that Amerigo Vespucci discovered the New World. The only good thing is that he used Vespucci's first name.

[†]*Also the title of an insightful book about these formative times by George F. Willison, to whom we are indebted for these insights and references.*

Finally, the document assured that everyone (women excluded)* would have a choice, a say in who would govern, a pattern that continued throughout the life of the colony. It was a flickering flame of freedom that refused to die, even after the little colony was subsumed by the more ambitious Massachusetts Bay Colony ten years later.

Winthrop's Choices

Certainly the news about the problems and opportunities in New England was not lost on an aristocrat back home named John Winthrop. His appraisal of the possibilities in the colonies coincided with plague, inflation, depression, and oppression in England, and by 1629 he and family were ready to pack it in and shove off. Winthrop was wealthy, educated at Cambridge, a father of seven, a man who had lived handsomely, with servants and tenants. He was also a rigidly inflexible Puritan.

Winthrop's settlement would be a bold theocracy governed by severe Christian standards, set by Winthrop himself. But Winthrop had an advantage over Bradford, because he ran the pilot program. Plymouth was the prototype. Winthrop would improve on that. He would avoid the mistakes of Plymouth, which he believed to be too small (▮) and lacking in vision (°⟨⟩), *two new cultural forces that would be locked-in, and combined with the five from Plymouth, bringing to seven the cultural forces that define Americans.*

There was one other thing about John Winthrop: he was a lawyer. He would leave nothing to chance, and he would take care of Number One. And he would think big. Where the Pilgrims sailed in one ship, Winthrop would take four. Where the Pilgrims took a hundred people, Winthrop would take five hundred. Where the Pilgrims sailed around till they found a likely landing spot, Winthrop would choose in advance the mouth of the Charles River, already carefully explored and mapped by John Smith. Where the Pilgrims came with "Saints and Strangers," Winthrop would have only Saints. And he would tell 'em what to believe, and punish anyone believing otherwise.

Winthrop's Boston and suburbs would, within a few short years, eclipse Plymouth in population, trade, and the reach of its spread. It would master the fishing and ship-building industries and become successful in agriculture.

But there were significant differences between the two colonies. The Pilgrims were Separatists, who were making a complete break with the established church. Winthrop was not only a Puritan but an aristocrat, and he brought the thoughts and trappings of his ruling aristocracy with him to the New World. He would establish the same rules of governance and the same kind of autocratic theocracy he was fleeing. He would deny choice and it would backfire, but not before the notorious witch-hunts of Salem had taken their toll.

In John Winthrop's Boston, political power and adherence to religious orthodoxy were intertwined. Five (5!)-hour sermons were *de rigueur*. Massachusetts Bay was a colony founded on an abhorrence of democracy and religious tolerance and on a contempt for separation of church and state. Its political structure was not unlike that of the Soviet Union in our own time in that only party members had the right to vote,

---

*It would take three hundred years to correct this oversight and give women the right to choose their form of government. The Nineteenth Amendment to the Constitution passed in 1920.

but acceptance into the party was gained by passing rigorous tests of orthodoxy. And the rulers imposed discipline from the top, directing every function of society, including work, worship, business, literature, and morals.

Making Other Choices

Folks who didn't like things Winthrop's way had a choice: love it or leave it. Since the Choice Force was still evolving, many created a third alternative: they improvised, started something else, did their own thing.

One who was forced to leave it and do his own thing was Roger Williams (the reverend) who was booted out of Boston in the middle of winter for offensive preaching. He walked south through the wilderness, eventually founding Providence and Rhode Island, a haven for nonconformists.

Others dissenters followed suit. Some like Thomas Hooker and his congregation left Boston and set up in Hartford. All these choices, the forced ones and the voluntary ones, were acorns of democracy that were being scattered and sown. It would take years for them to take root and flourish, but once planted they were locked-in.

Choice and the Development of the American Economy

By 1641 some fifty thousand settlers had reached the American shores. There arose an unusual economic paradox. Wages in America were high, which was of course a powerful inducement to European workers. At the same time, with cheap lands readily available, the high wage scale made it possible to provide . . . what else? Choice! Thus a wage earner with a couple of good years in earnings saved could strike out on his own and become his own master.

In any case, there was too much work to do, and too few to do it. Skilled artisans and craftsmen were always in short supply, and a youngster wishing to enter a trade could become an apprentice, and had the choice of becoming a tanner, candlemaker, blacksmith, courier, carpenter, cooper, bricklayer, wheelwright, glazier, you name it.

In the seventeenth and eighteenth centuries it was a given that the government should regulate business. Adam Smith and his *Wealth of Nations*—"the whole laissez-faire concept"—would not appear until the time of the American Revolution. In the meantime, mercantilism was the accepted operating system. It was a system intended to increase the value of exports and thus augment the economic power of the state. And the colonies, for the most part, found this to be an acceptable arrangement.

The Navigation Acts assured a ready market for American exports and encouraged American shipbuilding. The growing of tobacco was forbidden in England, giving the colonies a virtual monopoly in the English tobacco market. And of course American merchantmen on the high seas were always under the protection of the Royal Navy. That was the good news.

The bad news arrived in the form of the British government's attempts to control manufacturing (read denial of choice), in which restrictions were placed on the manufacture of any products that would be competitive with British manufacture. The colonies were forbidden to export woolen goods by a 1699 act, but the kicker came when the Brits passed laws imposing fines and imprisonment upon persons with textile knowledge imigrating to colonies or shipping tools used in the manufacture of textiles.

The results of this intervention can be seen today at the Slater Mill Historic Site in Pawtucket, Rhode Island. With the enactment of this law, young Samuel Slater, working as an apprentice for a textile mill in England, simply recast himself as a bricklayer and sailed for America, having committed to memory every working piece of the Arkwright textile machine. After he made a deal with Moses Brown of Providence, who had been experimenting with the development of a cotton mill for some time, the textile industry in America was on its way. It was an eighteenth-century example of industrial espionage, brain drain, and the enormous value of intellectual property. Within a short time America had surpassed England in the production of woven cloth. Choice in America was not to be denied.

An Explosion of Choice

By throwing off the shackles of the British Crown and forming the United States of America, we became free to exploit even greater possibilities. The vast plains to the West were an open invitation. The lure of free or cheap land proved irresistible to those who thirsted for freedom and opportunity. If life in a mill or small town seemed stifling, there was always the romantic choice of greener pastures just over the next rise. Or across the river, or out there somewhere. It was a time when the choices that heretofore seemed unimaginable to newly arrived immigrants were suddenly within the grasp of everyone.

Then came the steam machines.

It was in 1807 that a boat, derided as Fulton's Folly, chugged up the Hudson belching smoke and astounding the silk-hatted and hoop-skirted folks on shore. The steam machines kicked off a revolution of a kind that had not happened since Gutenberg invented movable type and made literacy possible for ordinary folk. The steam machines multiplied the ingenuity and the muscle of men and ushered in advances in technology that once again multiplied American choices.

The march toward an industrial society was interrupted by the terrible War Between the States. It was the beginning of the end of America as a nation of farmers. By the last years of the century railroads had crisscrossed the continent, and the dominant industries were steel, petroleum products, processed foods, fuels, metal, and communications. The economic transformation was fueled by abundant resources, fast transportation, continental marketing, a favorable social and legal climate, an ebullient burst of technological breakthroughs, and entre-preneurial boldness.

Americans had choices beyond the wildest imagination.

The Engines That Could . . . And Did

The railroad was among the first big engines of change. It not only connected the cities and commerce centers on America's two ocean boundaries, it connected the small dairy with metropolitan markets. It drove the steel industry, coal mining, the telegraph, electrification. It could haul most anything anywhere, fast and cheap. It brought oranges from Florida, beef from Kansas, and put a whole new offering of choices on America's dinner tables. From the Sears, Roebuck catalog a farm kid could order a catcher's mitt on a Thursday from the warehouse in Chicago and have it delivered Parcel Post, RFD, in time for the Sunday game ten days hence.

Because of the industrial revolution and the telecommunication age on its heels, today's choices are practically endless: There are a dozen different catalogs that cram the mailbox each day; the telephone companies have run out of the 7.71 million possible combinations of 800 numbers because of consumer demand for immediate access to more choices (telephone companies are beginning to offer a new prefix—888); and there are at least a half-dozen choices on how to get your choice delivered to you overnight—by eight, ten-thirty, or three in the afternoon—just another choice we take for granted.

READER'S CHOICE #2: THE INDIVIDUAL

From time to time throughout the book we will go beyond history or a company case to show you how the seven cultural forces are manifest in an individual. Seeing the forces in human terms may help us personalize them. We'll start with Ben.

Dr. Franklin was nothing less than a scrivening, politicking, philosophizing, innovating, moneymaking, chance taking, networking, team playing, perambulating epitome of all seven cultural forces rolled into one. To put the character of Franklin in today's context, he was Ted Turner, Peter Ueberroth, Warren Christopher, Steven Jobs, David McCullough, Russell Baker, Red Adaire, Dave Barry, and Teddy Roosevelt under one hat.

1. **CHOICE:** The choices he made, beginning as a kid, made the man. After only a few years of formal education, his father made him apprentice with his older brother. But Ben chose to educate himself; he read everything he could get his hands on. His popularity as a writer began when he chose to start writing under the assumed name of Silence Dogood. He chose to leave Boston for Philadephia to pursue his writing and inventive curiosity about the things around him. Others would choose him to be one of the drafters of the *Declaration of Independence.*

2. **IMPOSSIBLE DREAMS:** Ben was a visionary who realized what were impossible dreams for his time, such as founding the Philadelphia library, hospital, fire company, insurance company, militia, philosophical society, college, plus encouraging the paving and lighting of city streets.

3. **BIG AND MORE:** Franklin worked tirelessly for a bigger and better Philadelphia. Later, as a skilled diplomat in France during the American Revolution, he worked toward uniting the colonies to form a bigger, freer, and better United States.

4. **NOW:** He worked twelve-hour days (the norm when he was starting out) so that he could retire from business in his forties; he did neither and didn't waste a minute in the process. Much of the popularity of his aphorisms was due to his rewrites, which made them shorter, snappier, and more adaptive to early American readers. A popular one we are all familiar with from *Poor Richard's Almanack* is, "There are no Gains, without Pains," shortened even more to "no pain, no gain." And one that gets to the title of our book, "But dost thou love Life, then do not squander Time, for that's the Stuff Life is made of."

5. **OOPS:** At one time he was a slave owner, but recognizing the horror of that institution, he soon became an advocate of abolition.

6. **IMPROVISE:** He was a consummate improviser and inventor. Credit him with the first bifocals, the Franklin stove, the capacitor or electric storage battery, lightning rods, and an electric motor. He also invented a two-faced clock. It took ten minutes to figure out the correct time. Somehow it never caught on.

7. **WHATSNEW:** His fascination with whatsnew is manifested in his endless inventions, some of which we listed. Above all he was a publisher of newspapers, writer of books, and editor of his popular *Poor Richard's Almanack,* which he published in three editions, one for New England, one for the middle colonies, and one for the Southern colonies. Whatsnew was his stock-in-trade.

On top of all that, he was a delightful dinner companion and fully attuned to the world around him. How could you live in Philadelphia and not know Ben Franklin? He was the original American joiner and was into everything. Finally, as a team player, he was a member of the greatest team in the history of the republic. He was behind the locked doors of that Constitutional Convention, and he was one of the authors in that body of the Great Compromise, which resolved the dispute over representation between large and small states by establishing two houses of Congress.

READER'S CHOICE #3: THE BOTTOM LINE

You can't run a business without choice—that's the top and bottom line. There is no part of a business, or running a family or country for that matter, that can be closed off to choice—unless we *choose* to close out choice.

The most fundamental choice in a start-up or ongoing business, the one that can make or break it more than any other, is whom the company chooses to work with and how they will choose to work together. Who will the company's partners be? What labor force is available? How will the business recruit and train? How will it manage its employees? Who will lead? Who will manage? What are the company's values? How will it reward and compensate? How will it inspire peak performance? How will it build trust?

A Booz-Allen study a few years back identified the number one concern of CEOs as the development of a plan for sustained growth and profitability. The number one strategy for implementing the plan was the full utilization of the company's employees. And the number one roadblock, as the CEOs saw it, was their inability to motivate or change the employees.

These findings clearly express a bias for changing people rather than systems. We lean the other way. We strongly recommend that CEOs and other executives create environments and change systems that free people *to do* what they are ready, willing, and able to do right now. In Chapter 2 we show how two companies create these ideal environments, one a manufacturing company, the other a service company (Levi Strauss and Ritz-Carlton Hotels).

Through the balance of this chapter and throughout the book we will devote considerable time and space to the people side of business and how to leverage the seven cultural forces in that area. For example, because teams are the dominant way companies have chosen to organize people at work, we spend some considerable time (see pages 265–301), exploring how the seven cultural forces impact team performance (it's not what you think). We'll also look into how to apply the forces to the whole area of compensation, rewards, and employee retention, other major concerns for companies. We'll cover some new tools and technology as well as describe some simple practices that we feel match the seven forces and that are already working for some companies.

Since most of the initial choices we make about the people we hire are based on a résumé, we have chosen to start there. How Americans write résumés compared to other countries says a lot about culture and business priorities.

Judging People by Their Résumés

Job résumés in Germany are different from American résumés in one fundamental respect. German résumés begin with education, specifically referencing secondary schools. This is true for all job applicants, regardless of age and prior job experience. In America, education is usually listed last, if at all. Except for those who are just starting out in the job market, no one even mentions the secondary school they attended. The more job experience one has, the more the education gets buried, unless one has some Latin *lauds* to brag about.

In Germany, as in a lot of countries, the national education system is tied quite closely to vocational training and job preparation. The type and name of the secondary school in Germany serves much the same function as the type and name of business schools in America—a shorthand for job screening. Just as American companies make judgments about applicants based on the business or graduate school attended, so German companies make assumptions about applicants based on the primary and secondary schools attended.

Once a person is hired, we know of no industry or company in either country that has *complete* knowledge of this employee and updates that knowledge on a continuous basis. Some companies, like MBNA America, the Wilmington-based credit card company, and U.S. Healthcare, the HMO giant headquartered outside Philadelphia, use a *daily* tracking model to keep regular tabs on what all employees are doing as a group, but no company that we are aware of has such a system for individuals. The only exception is baseball, which uses such a system on an individual basis.*

Typecasting: Judging People by Their Cover

Besides judging people by their one-pagers, most large corporations and many smaller ones use one or more of the numerous personnel assessment tools— Performax, Strong-Campbell, Minnesota Multiphasic Personality Inventory, Thematic Apperception Test, Myers-Briggs—that are widely available to help measure and quantify the type of people they want to hire, promote, and assign to teams. Myers-Briggs is perhaps the most widely recognized. However, continuing discoveries from brain research that are providing new insights into how we as individuals receive, store, process, and use information is fueling the development and testing of additional tools and technology.

---

*Baseball coaches, managers, trainers, and executives know how well each player performs under myriad variables, including artificial or natural turf, early or late innings, runners in scoring position, day or night games, type of pitches, and speed on the bases. The list is endless, but the point is that baseball, unlike other sports and all other business enterprises, takes the time to know the complete and total performance profile of each player. Baseball is a powerful metaphor for American business and we write more about it later on in the book (see pages 99–104).

While we don't pretend to be experts in this area, we generally reject all of these assessment tools, or stated more positively, we accept them all as a *limited piece* of the complex puzzle that describes who we are as individuals. To paraphrase Abraham Lincoln, they all seem to get part of you right some of the time, but not all of you right at any time. As a piece of the puzzle they can be helpful; as a typecasting process they can be disastrous.

Our first experience taking these kinds of tests was fun—how can you go wrong with a test that has no right or wrong answers? But often the process, which gave us a choice between two extreme options, did not meet our style or preference. We wanted a third option that more accurately reflected our experience, but none was available. These tests don't work that way: you don't get the opportunity to say, "Yes, but . . . ." It didn't take long for the dread factor to set in—when we discovered how some of these tests were being used. And some of the analysis was way off or downright wrong.

Although they all claim to deal in preferences, the result is that the individual gets boxed in. Rather than facilitating growth, they inhibit development. As psychological tools they are regularly misinterpreted and misused, causing more harm than good. In spite of the preambles and disclaimers, these kinds of tests are invariably used by employers to identify probabilities, predispositions, and aptitudes. They are often employed to screen out applicants or to find "the right type." They all tend to view people management as an open system where people can be taught, managed, and directed according to their psychological makeup.

Are There Alternatives?

In the process of developing THE STUFF AMERICANS ARE MADE OF training program, an alternative assessment tool was happily discovered. It is the System for Identifying Motivated Abilities (SIMA®* in the acronym world), and it has none of the characteristics of the other tests in the genre.

This system was developed by Art Miller, along with his associates at People Management, Inc. The one thing you will *never* hear Art and his group talk about is how to change people.[†] Rather they talk about fit: how to match personal motivation (read competence) to job function; how to enhance job performance; how to configure interdependent teams; how to find the key to personal productivity in a sea of organization lemmings; how to have happy and contented workers producing beyond the norms of corporate rigor mortis.

We provide a quick overview of this self-assessment process for two reasons. One, it uniquely fits the needs we have as Americans to *feel* that we are different, that we are individuals, not some part of an indistinguishable glob out there somewhere, or a downsized dot.

SIMA allows management to tap the intrinsic values and skills of an individual. It facilitates diversity—if by diversity you mean more than race, gender, or age— by identifying the psychographics of how people function and how they express themselves.

---

*SIMA® is a registered trademark of People Management, Inc.

†A paradigm shift if there ever was one.

The second reason we provide this overview is that SIMA fits the seven cultural forces with remarkable convergence, and it adds an ennobling* dimension the others lack. When the folks at Disney, who have some of the most sophisticated personnel systems in American business, said, "yes" to the SIMA approach, we knew we were on to something.

The end product of the SIMA process is a personal MAP[†] (Motivated Ability Pattern) that is unique to the individual. This process describes *who you are*—based on *what you have done in your past that you think you did well and that turned you on*, not on how you choose to answer multiple-choice questions that someone else thinks get at the soul of who you are. The MAP doesn't deal in probabilities and it can't predict specific performance or outcomes. It is task- or job-related, not norm- or type-related. It sees the whole person, not just the parts. It is about abilities, not aptitudes or preferences (it turns out that preferences can change). Abilities have a permanence to them that is reassuring—I have the skills now to make a contribution, and I don't need to learn any particular new skill or change my approach to do what needs to be done.

Personal Eureka

One of the real bonuses of SIMA is that you are the one who identifies your own "motivated abilities." We cannot overstate how powerful it is to make this discovery by yourself. It is *your* revelation: you made the choices through a guided activity of telling others what you have accomplished in the past, and you analyzed *only that self-generated data* for the result. See Snapshot #3. In the process of adapting SIMA for the Stuff training program, Disney University's Professional Development Programs added a unique activity that effectively captures the synthesis of the individual's motivated abilities; it is a picture frame which each person personalizes by adding the appropriate icons that say *this is who I am*. This process provides an immediate (☺) result, a complete profile, with Polaroid, of what, why, and how that individual learns, improves, relates to supervisors, supervises, and works on a team.

The MAP process works like this (in a simplified version): Each participant, at the end of the process, will select corresponding icons for each of the ten profile categories (i.e., "Payoff," "Subject Matter," "Circumstances," "I learn by . . ." etc.) from the choices in the forty-eight subcategories (see Snapshot #3). For example, choices for "Payoff" are Personal Performance, Impact or Effect, Personal Power, Achieving a Goal, and Engaging a Process. For example, Dave Camous, University Relationships Manager at Hewlett-Packard Company (Colorado Springs) created the MAP in Snapshot #4.[†] Camous's payoff is having an impact on others or making a

Here is a case when the acronym helps rather than obscures communication. Since Americans are constantly on the move, the notion of a personal abilities MAP, to keep track of where you are going and to determine whether you are on course, is eminently helpful.

†*Camous was exposed to the MAP process through* THE STUFF AMERICANS ARE MADE OF *training program (described in more detail in Chapter 7 and the appendix). He had this to say about his experience: "I am not trying to be dramatic, but it would not be an overstatement to say that my participation in the* Stuff *program was a transforming event for me. It validated the behaviors that had made me successful previously, but which corporate America, in many subtle ways, often tries to discourage. It provided me with clearly defined situational characteristics that will define my future successes. The MAP experience is a principal catalyst for change in my life."*

difference in people or things. In the category of how people learn, the subcategories are by trying, by tinkering or doing, by reading or studying, by watching or observing, by memorizing, by asking, and by conferring with others. Camous learns by trying first, and then conferring with others.

Snapshot #3

MAP Chart

Name: _____

SUBJECT MATTER
- ☐ Data
- ☐ Things
- ☐ Senses
- ☐ People
- ☐ Ideas

CIRCUMSTANCES
- ☐ Visibility
- ☐ Different
- ☐ Structure
- ☐ Measured
- ☐ Difficult

RELATIONSHIPS
Working with others
- ☐ Individual Contributor
- ☐ Influencer
- ☐ Overseer

Working with supervisor
- ☐ Hands off
- ☐ Collaborative
- ☐ Supportive

ABILITIES
I learn by
- ☐ Reading
- ☐ Observing
- ☐ Trying
- ☐ Memorizing
- ☐ Asking
- ☐ Conferring/Discussing

I evaluate by
- ☐ Analyzing
- ☐ Empathizing
- ☐ Weighing pros and cons
- ☐ Calculating
- ☐ Comparing
- ☐ Assessing worth

I prepare by
- ☐ Organizing
- ☐ Practicing
- ☐ Picturing
- ☐ Setting goals
- ☐ Strategizing

I take action by
- ☐ Nurturing
- ☐ Creating/innovating
- ☐ Developing
- ☐ Physically doing
- ☐ Producing
- ☐ Maintaining
- ☐ Operating
- ☐ Overseeing

I influence by
- ☐ Bargaining
- ☐ Getting others involved
- ☐ Motivating
- ☐ Conversing
- ☐ Counseling
- ☐ Teaching
- ☐ Writing
- ☐ Suggesting
- ☐ Persuading
- ☐ Performing

PAYOFF
- ☐ Personal Performance
- ☐ Impact or Effect
- ☐ Personal Power
- ☐ Achieving a Goal
- ☐ Engaging in a Process

Snapshot #4

MY MOTIVATED ABILITIES PATTERN℠

ME

PAYOFF

IMPACT OR EFFECT

SUBJECT MATTER

PEOPLE

IDEAS

CIRCUMSTANCES

DIFFERENT

DIFFICULT

RELATIONSHIPS WITH OTHERS

OVERSEER

RELATIONSHIPS WITH SUPERVISORS

HANDS OFF

I LEARN BY

TRYING

CONFERRING/ DISCUSSING

I EVALUATE BY

WEIGHING PROS AND CONS

ASSESSING WORTH

I PREPARE BY

SETTING GOALS

STRATEGIZING

I TAKE ACTION BY

DEVELOPING

OVERSEEING OTHERS

I INFLUENCE BY

MOTIVATING

PERSUADING

Why Can't We Choose How to Learn?

Regardless of how we get hired or the outcome of those personnel tests, we have little or no choice in the training we receive. Orientation and training are not something employees get to vote on; they have no choice in the matter. Unfortunately, too many companies think they don't have much choice either. Wrong!

The annual amount of money American corporations spend on training is conservatively estimated to be $50 billion. In our equally conservative judgment, 40 to 75 percent of it is wasted, depending on the industry.* With the innovations that are taking place in some training facilities, plus inventions like the SIMA process, companies now have choices, and training dollars are being spent more effectively.

Most corporations choose to do the bulk of their training at the beginning of the employment process, when the individual knows the least about the product or service and is the most afraid, or inhibited, to ask or seek clarification about what is being taught and why. According to Kathleen Ryan and Daniel Oestreich in their hard-hitting but largely ignored book, *Driving Fear Out of the Workplace,* 70 percent of employees, practically three out of every four, are afraid to speak up at work. Our guess is that this is more true at the beginning of the work process, when one is still tentative, still checking out the ropes and finding out "how things get done around here." The failure to speak up has an immediate and direct bearing on work performance, quality, productivity, and job satisfaction.

We know from the International Quality Study† that while Americans tend to concentrate training at the beginning of the work/hire process, the Japanese train continuously. German companies fall somewhere in the middle, relying more on the preexisting, high level of education and training of the new employee as the Japanese do, but tending, as the Americans do, to concentrate training earlier in the work process rather than continuously.

Japanese also value regular meetings as a way of continuous learning and education, and they have a high level of overall employee involvement. Germans place little reliance on regular meetings as a way to engage and educate employees. Although meetings in America are becoming a more frequent way to get employees together on quality improvement, most continue to feel they are a waste of time, so too often little if any learning is taking place.

As Snapshot #5 shows, in the auto industry Japanese companies have a much higher number of employees participating in regularly scheduled quality meetings than do those in other countries. The Japanese report that 62 percent of their employees participate in these meetings. This level and consistency in participation over time clearly suggest the value the Japanese attach to this type of learning.

---

*Some of our adviser/experts put the figure at 80 percent.

†The International Quality Study® was a joint study between the American Quality Foundation and Ernst & Young conducted from 1990 through 1992. Co-author, Josh Hammond, served as the project director for AQF. Because of the comprehensive nature of the IQS, it will be referenced from time to time throughout the book. IQS was the first major study to examine the quality management practices on a cross-industry, cross-cultural basis, over three time periods (past, present, and projected practice). It gathered and analyzed data on over 650 companies in four countries—Canada, Germany, Japan, and the United States—within four industries—automotive, banking, computers, and health care. Six reports were issued on the study and they are available from Quality Press at ASQC in Milwaukee, Wisconsin. To order the reports call 1-800-248-1946 or 414-272-8575.

Snapshot #5

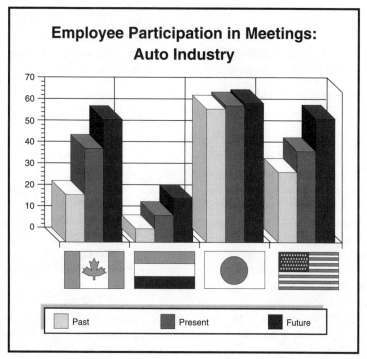

Employee Participation in Meetings: Auto Industry

Past Present Future

Source: IQS

U.S. companies have less than half of their employees involved in these meetings, reporting 42 percent for current (1990) levels of participation,* and the German companies virtually ignore the practice.

In general, once some initial training or orientation takes place in an American company, continuing education is often viewed by employees as something that gets in the way, something that interferes with work. This attitude also reflects on the value employees place on the content of the training and its relevance to their needs. If employees believe the training they receive is useless, they are probably right in that this sentiment is likely to be self-fulfilling at the very least. That is why the SIMA employee differentiation, or segmentation, can make a major contribution to how a company does its training.

Just as market segmentation is used to increase the effectiveness and impact of advertising and sales, so employee segmentation can increase the effectiveness and impact of training by matching the training to an employee's preferred style of learning. What could be more sensible than giving people a choice about how they learn. A segmented approach is a win-win: the individual grows, the company profits.

*The IQS found that American companies, ever optimistic and hopeful of the future, say they will do more of everything better in the future. While this optimism is consistent with the seven forces, it should not be relied on as something American companies will in fact do. The projections of the Japanese, with their longer planning and operational cycles, tend not to change, as one would expect. When the Japanese do signal a change, the expectations for that change to occur are very high.

What we know from SIMA is that there are six primary ways people choose to learn. Until now, a breakdown on the percentage of people who learn one way or the other has been hard to come by. In the list below, the numbers in parentheses reflect the percentage of 1,234 managers and employees from twenty different companies who favor a given learning style. The figures are drawn from a recent representative SIMA database analysis prepared especially for us:*

1. Studying, reading (25 percent)
2. Observing (20 percent)
3. Listening, asking (6 percent)
4. Trying (30 percent)
5. Memorizing (2 percent)
6. Participating (5 percent)

Now ask yourself which category do you prefer? Then ask yourself if your company has provided you with this choice or were you forced to "learn" a different way? If there is a match for you, what about the others in the company? Does your training department provide alternative ways to cover the same material? How do they go about matching the learning styles?

Listening/asking is the most popular way of training. However, check out that low percentage of employees who favor this approach and remember that this is the most common way people are taught in companies. We couldn't get over that figure when we saw it; only 6 people out of every 100 prefer to learn this way. In other words, if you have 8,000 employees and train them all using a conventional lecture approach, only 480 employees get the maximum benefit.

Trying is the number one preference employees have for how to learn. This preference ties in with the Improvise Force we write about in Chapter 6—Americans love to *do* things. "Let me at 'em" could easily be our national motto. But when it comes to training, trying is usually left to the actual job with few opportunities to try things during the training itself. The exception, of course, is training around equipment, repair, and technical processes. Obviously, some industries, such as the airline industry and the military, use simulation, the best form of trying out; others simply use exercises or role-playing, where applicable. By contrast, many in the service industries complain that role-playing is often too general or too contrived to have any real benefit or value.

Studying/reading is the second most popular choice for how people would prefer to learn. But when it comes to training, this is an approach that companies usually expect workers to do on their own time (there are no study halls in corporations). At a time when employees increasingly are making choices about balance in their lives, companies should not assume that those textbooks in the tote bag get looked at overnight or on the weekends. Nor should companies expect homework. Homework can't be the only choice—for Pedro's sake. Finally, this is a group that learns by wide-ranging reading, not just the required syllabus reading. Studying, as it is understood here, also implies individual pacing and self-discovery, not only the scheduled training-center hours before or after dinner at the training retreat.

Figures do not total 100 percent because not all participants completed this category of the SIMA.

Observing, the third most popular way to learn, is often overlooked. Most instructors assume that telling and trying cover most people. However, clearly one in five has a need to see others trying, or to watch demonstrations. This serves multiple functions, not the least of which is building some self-confidence that we will not be made to look foolish or be otherwise embarrassed. It also enables us to process the information that has been learned and see its direct application.

Until an organization begins to segment the learning styles of its employees and to match learning styles with teaching styles, the training resources will continue to miss their mark widely. No wonder we don't expect much from training; no wonder it is viewed as a necessary evil. At the risk of being transparent, the SIMA approach can help change all that—explosively.

Don't Patriotize Me

Companies may have their way with employees, but not customers, at least not in this country. And we all like it that way—it's the way that Roger Williams and William Bradford set things up (the stuff we wrote about in the history part of this chapter that you may have chosen to skip). It's what got locked-in.

This national insistence on choice provides major marketing challenges to American businesses. The range of choice and the reasons American buy things are so broad that many American businesses often wish it were otherwise.

One choice that plays havoc in America, but not in other cultures is patriotism. Surprisingly, Americans are not jingoistic about products made in America. Japanese, on the other hand, have a strong preference for Japanese products. Germans also have a general preference for things German, and again, the patriotic undercurrent is strong. Regardless of price, Japanese buy Japanese cars, Germans buy German cars, but Americans shop around, as Detroit discovered much to its dismay in the 1970s.

Studies consistently show that Americans are as patriotic, if not more so, than the next nation, but in general don't go for the patriotic pitch to choose a product. That appeal works only for some, usually older, less-educated consumers with *less* disposable income. Although this group represents 43 percent of all consumers, it is not exactly the market you want to target. (See Snapshot #6). And this is an aging market segment.

The Crafted with Pride campaign that was launched in the mid-eighties to help save a beleaguered textile industry did manage to show, through controlled marketing studies, that apparel displaying a "Made in the USA" label or claim resulted in a 10 percent increase in sales over items that did not display such things.

However, these were low-ticket items and often the choice was driven by price. The European advantage in the U.S. market was styling. Euro-styling is a big choice for Americans in clothes, cars, chairs, china, and crystal.

The American buyer who favors and prefers imports is younger, better educated, and most importantly has a higher level of disposable income. This group represents one in every four consumers. This is the key market to target.

The decision to buy foreign is not an anti-American statement, rather it is a statement about quality or the lack thereof. The consumer choice patterns shown above did not form overnight. American businesses, across the board, chose to emphasize productivity and short-term profits instead of quality and long-term loyalty. American business did not lose out to a lack of patriotism, but to a dearth of quality.

Snapshot #6

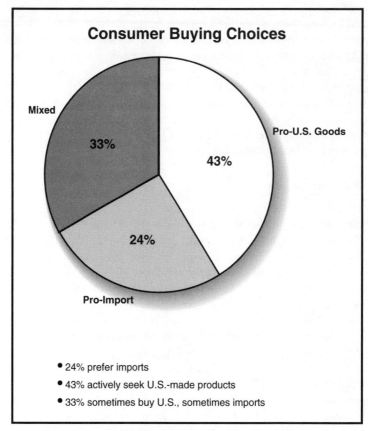

Consumer Buying Choices

Mixed
33%

Pro-U.S. Goods
43%

24%

Pro-Import

- 24% prefer imports
- 43% actively seek U.S.-made products
- 33% sometimes buy U.S., sometimes imports

Source: Peter D. Hart Research Associates, Inc., 1991

Dealer's Choice vs. Customer's Choice

For car dealers these are the best of times and the worst of times—most of this the result of their own doing or not doing. Buying a car is an emotional experience for most Americans. Some of us look forward to the haggling over price, others just bring our checkbook. Saturn says it is a different car company, and it is. Not only does it make its cars differently, but it sells them differently. No haggling for starters: One price for everyone. When you come to look, there is a special room where you can, at your leisure, review the literature on the company's cars and those of the competition. Why? To keep you there, to show you the company cares, to make it easier for you, and the most important reason, to establish a relationship with you.

Why every car dealer doesn't provide this kind of choice—for that matter, why other General Motors companies don't adopt the same approach—is no doubt wrapped up in tradition, the right to haggle, and the desire to let dealers do their own thing. That's fine if you get what you want, but that's not always the case.

Most consumers don't get the exact car they want: it would mean waiting too long (🕑). Dealers know that and use the Now Force to sell something they already have on the showroom floor or "in the back." They make more money if they can move stock—the dealers' objective—rather than get the customer exactly what he wants—the customer's objective. Using the Now Force (the impatience of the consumer), dealers usually win—they are trained to sell that way.

Some rare dealers see you as a potential $250,000 customer—ten cars over the next thirty years—and treat you that way. Others, more typically, see you as a quick commission and quota bait. Whichever, these are conscious choices that car dealers (as well as other retail salespeople) make every time a customer walks through the door or dials in.

Any Choice, So Long as It Is Black

Henry Ford is often quoted as telling customers that they could have any color car they wanted, so long as it was black. That's a joke now, of course. It gets a laugh when you are giving a lecture or workshop on customer satisfaction and the power of choice that consumers insist on.

Back then it was no joke.

Henry started out making his cars in green and red. Folks had a choice. Since his Model T car was the first choice or alternative to the horse and buggy, buyers lined up so fast that Henry soon had a backlog of ten thousand orders. In those days that was a bigger problem than it would be today. When Ford started out, the plant could make only two cars a day; so, not counting any new buyers, these orders amounted to about a thirteen-year backlog.

Now, Americans will wait a little bit, but not a lot—they want it Now (🕑). So Henry needed to do something about that backlog or he'd lose his line to one of the other hundreds of carmakers.

Henry figured out one way to speed things up: black paint. It dries faster, as one of Henry's paint pioneers found out, and the rest is (Ford) history.

What Henry Ford did with his Model T was to give ordinary Americans a choice they could afford; they could either keep their horse and buggy or, for around three hundred bucks, tool around in a "Tin Lizzie." The goal of his early life was to drive the car's cost down. As Robert J. Shook writes in *Turnaround,* his history of the Ford Motor Company, Henry once exclaimed, "Every time I reduce the charge for our car by one dollar, I get a thousand new buyers." Take your pick.

This pricing strategy gave Ford market share, but profits were lean and the shareholders were disgruntled. The Dodge brothers (only later makers of the Dodge), who were stockholders with a large minority interest, sued Ford and won. In one of the biggest financial transactions in history, Henry chose to pay out $105 million to outside stockholders to give the Ford family 100 percent ownership.

Now in complete control, Ford chose to stay with the Model T even as sales began to slip. This at a time when the motoring public was becoming more sophisticated and had other choices. Durant's Chevrolet was becoming popular, and just a few years later General Motors, under the management of the venerable Alfred P. Sloan, offered a choice of five different cars in five different price categories.

Ford was also unwilling to relinquish power or introduce professional management, and this intransigence, combined with the sheer size of his organization, eventually proved to be the company's undoing. The stubborn personality of old Mr. Ford molded the Ford corporate culture. Even after the grandson, young Henry Ford, took over, brought in professional management and ushered in subsequent years of prosperity, many of the old habits of mind persisted. By the end of the 1970s, Ford Motor Company was losing money by the truckload, and many a Wall Street analyst saw it heading for certain bankruptcy.

What happened was that Ford, along with the other American car manufacturers, made the mistake of ignoring the Choice Force. At the outset in the 1970s Americans had a simple choice: They could buy a big expensive American-made car with quality problems that the manufacturers didn't care to hear about, or they could buy a smaller Japanese-made car that was inexpensive, had few problems, got good gas mileage, and was sold by dealers who cared about the customer. Then the oil embargo hit, compounding the situation, and Ford's market share went into the toilet.

It was then, at one of the lowest points in Ford's long history, that top management made the decisions that would, before the end of the 1980s, make Ford the world's most profitable car company ever, with earnings of $5.3 billion: They made "quality job #1" and they made the Taurus. It was these two events that made buying a Ford once again a viable choice for car buyers.

Either/Or Thinking

Did you ever wake up in the morning and have a great, original thought about something, formulate it in your mind, rehearse it a time or two, and then burst forth with it at some meeting, only to discover that this great "discovery" has been out there for some time? "Either/or thinking" is one of those ideas for us. It deals with how we think of choices and the limits we place on the choices we make at work, with our families, and in how we run the country. We thought it was our special discovery.

As a result of some additional research for this book we were given a copy of *Built to Last* by James C. Collins and Jerry I. Porras, published in 1994. There on page 43, with a yin/yang symbol, was our idea under a different name. They call "either/or thinking" the "tyranny of the or" and "the genius of the and." They do a good job of it *and* the rest of the book is important reading as well. (Coincidentally, they cover some of the same companies we profile,* but from a visionary and strategic perspective.)

We have been using the expression "either/or thinking" in many of our workshops over the past fifteen years or so. We ask a group to make a list of *eithers* and *ors*. The list usually consists of things we have to do a certain way or choices we have to make between one option and the other—things like on-time or high-quality, short-term results or long-term results, change the process this way or that way, tell the customer this or that, control or decentralize.

When we get to this point in the exercise, we ask someone in the group to come up and scratch out the words *either* and *or* at the top of the corresponding list and substitute the word *and*. The response, like applause at a Broadway play, makes us feel as if we really earned a day's pay this time around.

As we mentioned at the beginning of the book, Americans tend to take things to extremes, which is why we appear to have this addiction to either/or thinking. Either my way or your way is clearly a choice, but not a satisfactory or effective one. Why can't *both* be a choice or *and* be another choice. Obviously, it can. It is much more

Ford, Hewlett-Packard, Johnson & Johnson, 3M.

powerful to say: "What are *all* of our choices here?" "What are the *different ways* we can go about this?" "Let's give them (the customer, supplier, employee, shareholder, taxpayer, child) the choice."

Choice and Public Policy

Curiously, Americans tolerate limited choice when it comes to electing others to make choices for us. Yes, the political party process, in theory, is open to endless choices, but in the final analysis, most of us choose to let the choices come down to two, neither of which any of us really like.

It has always been that way: the names of the parties have changed a little, but basically there have always been just two. There is usually no serious room for a third choice (indeed, we make it nearly impossible for third parties to qualify). So we are basically stuck with the choice we make or let others make on our behalf. It is no surprise then, that this dualism carries over into public policy.

Sometimes the focus is on specific issues with polar wrenching choices: slavery, voting rights, health care reform, welfare reform, crime prevention. Sometimes the choices diverge more on strategy than goals, issues like drug-abuse prevention, school reform, environmental concerns, tax reform, government regulations.

Sometimes public policy choices come down to the profound difference one letter makes. As Father Theodore Hesburgh, former president of Notre Dame University, said to us while back, "I am struck by the fact that there is only one letter difference between the word quality and equality." As a member of the 1968 National Advisory Commission on Civil Disorders (the Kerner Commission), Hesburgh contributed to a report on racism in America that could have been issued in 1995, or yesterday for that matter. The commission warned, "Our nation is moving toward two societies, one black, one white—separate and unequal." It is disheartening to remind ourselves that the commission report blamed police racism, repression, and neglect of the economic and educational needs of African-Americans.

Author and columnist Russell Baker, commenting on the so-called Million Man March at the nation's Capitol on October 16, 1995, wrote in *The New York Times*:

> *The portrait of a nation in trouble is etched in the statistics on black unemployment rates, black school dropouts, rising imprisonment of young blacks and killings of black youngsters by black youngsters. When a large portion of a nation's youth is being thrown away, or hustled into prisons, or lowered into graves, it takes a remarkable capacity for indifference to say that, well, it's a pity, but it's not our problem, it's a problem for the black community, black churches, black neighborhood leaders. It is hard to see how a multiracial nation can avoid damage if its leaders refuse to deal with its gravest problems on grounds that they are distinctively problems of race.*

Choice and Consequences

The history of racial discrimination in America is more than a scar on the American character, it's an open festering wound as choices are still being made that exacerbate the problems of race in America. Howard Zinn's books, especially *A People's History of the United States,* and Ronald Takaki's eye-opener, *A Different Mirror: A History of Multicultural America,* chronicle the discrimination and decimation that tarnish the land and tear the heart. No minority groups were exempt, from the first Americans who were here from the start, right on through the multiple waves of Irish, Japanese, Chinese, Mexican, and others who continue to migrate to America.

In 1635 a ship docked in what is now Baltimore. The transfer of a special "cargo" of thirty slaves set in motion a series of choices that this nation has yet to recover from. While Americans did not invent the institution of slavery, America exploited it for personal gain and the sins of the first abusers have been visited on all subsequent generations. Concurrent with the exploitation and abuse of slaves (property as the first slave owners choose to rationalize them) the vision of a new hope for all Americans was being planted.

After more than 150 years of dabbling in democracy and trying to accommodate the old order, an American constitution was forged out of hard choices. The first of those choices, which nearly torpedoed the attempt, was the choice of the first three words of the Constitution, three words that gave the choices—the authority to govern—to "We the People" instead of "we the states." Then within the next twelve words to set the primary objective for this new way to govern: "to form a *more perfect union.*"

This admission of imperfection in the Preamble of our Constitution is America's saving grace. It has taken too long for that union to "more perfect" itself and, damn it, we have a long way to go! But the choices to abandon property as a condition for voting, to emancipate the slaves, to enact the Fourteenth Amendment (due process and equal protection), to enfranchise women, and to enact the civil rights legislation of 1964–65 moved us inextricably toward more perfection of the union. In the words of historian Clarence L. ver Steeg, writing in *An American Primer,*

> *In accordance with the Preamble, therefore, the people as currently conceived continually animate anew the Constitution and the objects of government it enunciates. This is true even though the theoretical equality implied by the source of authority is not fulfilled in its exercise, because of special interests which are reflected in the unequal financial power and social organization of those who live under the Constitution, a fact clearly recognized by the framers. Unfortunately, the source of constitutional authority is too frequently confused with the empirical operation of the government under that authority.*

Earlier, infant America made a choice to declare its independence from others through bravado and its dependence on each other through equality. These words set in motion choices that imbue us to this day. Historian Henry Steele Commager, also writing in *An American Primer,* said this principle of equality "worked like a ferment in American society." He poignantly adds, "Each successive generation, none more guiltily than our own, has felt called upon to square the reality with principle."

Squaring the Reality

Because of the appropriate concern within business to address and accommodate the issues of diversity in the workplace, this chapter would not be complete without a perspective on a public policy matter aimed at squaring the reality—affirmative action. Of everything that has been written about this public policy issue, an op-ed piece by Harvard sociology professor Orlando Patterson in *The New York Times* caught our attention. He wrote:

For years Americans have complained about government programs for the disadvantaged that do not work. Now, however, we are on the verge of dismantling affirmative action, the one policy that, for all its imperfections, has made a major difference in the lives of women and minority groups and has helped us achieve the constitutional commitment to the ideal of equality and fairness. In utilitarian terms, it is hard to find a program that has brought so much gain to so many at so little cost.

Patterson then goes on to agonize about why affirmative action has become the focus of contention. He cites a National Opinion Research Center survey that reports that while 70 percent of white Americans *say* that whites are being hurt by this policy, only a paltry 7 percent claim to have experienced some form of reverse discrimination and only a "minuscule" number have any *real* grievance. When compared with the hard data that describes the pervasiveness of issues such as abortion, drug abuse, crime, or joblessness, the frequency of reverse discrimination is inconsequential.

He concludes that the cause of the consternation can be traced not to personal experience but to political leaders who have chosen to exploit reverse discrimination for political advantage and to the press for pandering to sensational appetites. From our perspective, the issue is not affirmative action per se, but the obligation to continue "to square the reality."

Professor Patterson also made this observation which seems to us a strong affirmation of the "stuff" concepts:

What brought me around to support affirmative action after some strong initial reservations was not only its effectiveness as a strategy for reducing inequality, but [based on the University of California experience, the site of Governor Wilson's showdown on affirmative action] also its possibilities for cross-pollinating our multi-ethnic communities. In the process, it could promote that precious, overreaching national culture—the envy of the world—which I call ecumenical America.

The stand-off on affirmative action today is an example of what results from either/or thinking. We should demand more choices in policy making. Patterson proposes a ten-year extension of affirmative action. This would give all of us the opportunity to judge the policy on a different basis and would provide the present beneficiaries with alternatives—of their own choosing. At the very least we ought to make an honest effort to salvage a policy that is being blamed for fixing a problem.

Another choice is one proposed by Russell Baker; it gets back to the founding principle of equality—and all that *stuff*. In the same *New York Times* editorial referenced above, Baker says:

Maybe it is tired old racist thinking to keep talking about a "black community" complete with "black leaders." Maybe it makes more sense nowadays to drop all that separatist language and say, "There's nobody here but us Americans."

Defining the Problem

The fundamental objective with regard to any public policy issue, or for product or service positioning for that matter, is to be the first to define the problem or the position. Whoever defines, or more precisely, frames the problem first controls the debate and formulates the policy. For example, hijacking was framed as a *security* issue by the government, drug use was framed as a *privacy* issue by individuals, so we tolerate searches at airports in the name of security but protest searches related to drugs because of privacy. Gangs are framed as a right-to-assemble issue, vaccinations as a national health issue, so we let gangs roam at will, but will not admit a kid to school without a vaccination card.

So how we choose to frame the problem determines the solution. Nowhere is that more clear than in the ambiguity and complexity of the nation's drug-abuse problems. Having the use of drugs—all kinds of drugs including licit and illicit drugs—defined as a privacy issue is at the heart of the problem. Until the problem is defined differently, don't expect alternatives to the mess we have now. Regrettably, don't expect much change in the problem either.

Strung Out on the Problem

The Japanese have a saying: Fix the problem, not the blame. Americans do the opposite. Although we are a fix-it society (see Chapter 6), when we can't fix something, we crank blame into high gear in the misguided notion that blaming is a form of fixing.

The drug-abuse problem may have more blames than there are psychoactive substances. Every group has managed to blame another group for the prevalence of illegal drug use in America. (Blaming is not a prerequisite for effective public policy, it is a choice the blamers make.)

We chose the drug-abuse problem as a social issue we would examine from time to time in this book because it is a serious problem for society, an expensive problem for business,* a wrenching problem for families, and a life-threatening problem for the individual who chooses to use drugs. It is also a public policy issue that thrives on the seven cultural forces. We also chose it because we have some special knowledge about it; it has been a significant part of the Hammond side† of the writing team for many years.

We can think of no other public policy issue where personal choice is so pervasive: the decision to *not* use drugs, to experiment with drugs, to continue to use drugs, to get strung out on drugs, to resort to crime to support a drug habit, to seek treatment, and to stick to treatment is in the final analysis all about personal choice.

Although it is common to separate legal drugs from illegal drugs, medicine from recreational drugs, alcohol from other drugs, we feel that those distinctions compound the public policy problems, confuse the public, foster duplicity, and undermine public education. So throughout this book when we use the term drug use we mean

---

*The drug-abuse problem in business is discussed in greater detail in Chapter 3.

†As a Senate aide in the late sixties I crafted some of the first treatment legislation and developed the National Coordinating Council on Drug Abuse Education, the largest private consortium (120-plus education, professional, scientific, pharmaceutical, business, social, and religious organizations) on drug education in the early seventies—the height of the first broad public awareness of the drug-abuse problem. I directed the communications efforts of the drug-abuse office at the White House under Presidents Nixon and Ford and served as the first director of communications for the National Institute on Drug Abuse in the Department of Health, Education and Welfare, as it was known then. In the late seventies I worked for California Governor Jerry Brown on several innovative advertising programs on drug and alcohol abuse prevention. Finally, as president of the Public Advertising Center, I developed the "Just Say No" to drugs campaign later popularized by Nancy Reagan.

to specifically include them all; from time to time we will mention a particular group by name to make a more specific point.

Policy Pills and Politicians

Some public policy choices with regard to the drug problem have simply not been tried, or more accurately, have not been tried since the current drug-abuse problem surfaced in the late sixties and early seventies. These polices include criminalization of all non–physician prescribed drug use, legalization of all drugs, decriminalization, regulation, and prohibition. At one time in our history *all* drugs were legal and *none* were regulated. Now we have a hodgepodge at best: some drugs are legal some of the time for some people, but not legal all of the time for everyone. And in no case is that more conspicuous, ambiguous, duplicitous, and unctuous than the current efforts to sort of control, possibly regulate, maybe, the smoking of tobacco, but exempting chewing it.

On the worn-down heels of the first Surgeon General's report in 1964 alerting the nation to the dangers of tobacco use, President Richard Nixon signed a bill banning TV advertising of cigarettes in 1970. Many expected the cigarette smoking problem would go away—after all, TV advertising was to blame for recruiting new users and keeping the old users hooked. What we forget is that *anti*-smoking TV ads were also taken off the air. So what, you may query?

Research from places like the Annenberg School of Communications shows that complex, value-ladened issues like this are resolved best when both sides of the story are presented and the intended target for the message gets to *choose* one offering or the other. As a nation we'd be better off with an equal number of pro- and anti-smoking ads running in prime time. The consumer public would then have a choice and whichever option was chosen, it would be more informed—and more effective—than it is now. So all the arbitrary banning of cigarettes did was simply eliminate choice and compound the problem.

Now the tobacco companies and advertising agencies, anxious at first because they were set in their marketing ways, were forced to invent other advertising venues, courtesy government policy. The anti-smoking group chose not to pursue those venues, leaving them to the vicissitudes of the offending vendor. Therefore, only one choice was presented to the public through print advertising, event advertising, sport sponsorships, and a splashy TV who-could-object sponsorship of the bicentennial celebration of the Bill of Rights by the tobacco industry.

Today, smoking is banned on TV, except in those reruns of *Casablanca*. Ironically, chewing the same substance, as ball players do on TV, is not banned—they are even allowed to spit or drool on camera!—a classic case of duplicity which complicates all the choices even more.

Another complexity is that the full consequences of eliminating the choices of where adults can smoke cigarettes have not been fully measured or assessed. Already, nonsmokers are complaining (at least in New York, where everyone chooses to complain about everything) that smokers are getting fresh-air breaks while they don't. There is a certain mystique and come-on among the defiant smokers who stand outside the revolving corporate doors on Sixth or on Madison Avenue for the morning and afternoon puff break. (Is there a segmented market here?)

Smoking parlors and smoking clubs are springing up all over. And cigars are the "in" drug, with business executives, radio and television personalities, politicians, and the President of the United States leading the smoke parade. With puffers like this, normalizing relations with Cuba can't be too far off—and then those Cohibas, *hecho a mano,* won't need to be smuggled in at fancy prices.

Prohibition is not a choice—never was.

Whenever we reduce choices we exacerbate the problem. That is why, in some respects, the case for a change in the laws or enforcement of existing illegal drug use is so pervasive. It is our hope that conscious awareness of the seven cultural forces will give us a broader range of choices in dealing with these issues. Americans, as we write in Chapter 6, are great improvisers—it is one of the seven forces. Why not apply some of the improvising force to the drug-use problem in America? Why not fund innovative ways of dealing with the various stages of drug use? Why not experiment with the experimenters?

It was this kind of thinking that led Hammond to create the "Just Say No" approach to drug experimentation. This choice-based approach, adapted in 1978, provided the research basis for the still popular "Say No" campaign that Nancy Reagan touted in the eighties. However, it is also an example of how failing to understand the Choice Force has undermined a program that had a lot of initial promise, and probably still has if we got it back on track.

Taking the Choice Out of "Just Say No"

Hammond was not part of the Nancy Reagan effort, though he watched it from the sidelines. Hammond took the cigarette smoking research done at the University of Minnesota, and independently validated at the University of Houston, and applied its findings and recommendations to marijuana smoking, thereby establishing the credibility of the initial "Just Say No" campaign.

However, this work sat in the shelf in the Carter administration for two years, going nowhere. Someone dusted it off for Nancy Reagan, or she independently came up with the idea on her own, as some have claimed. "Just Say No" has since been applied to all drugs, rape prevention, and trivial applications like "Just Say No" to Realtors and politicians. And in all of these applications the slogan has been used to promote abstinence, a goal it never espoused.

As we saw the campaign unfold, we noticed that three important elements of the strategy got lost in the translation. The success of the original research was predicated on three key variables:

1. A segmented target strategy. The strategy was limited to twelve- to fourteen-year-olds—period. This is what advertising people call market segmentation—it is what makes product and service advertising effective. But government can't get that concept into its thinking. Somehow all kids are "youth" and all teenagers are the same. So a target message was universally applied.

This kind of thinking presents serious missed opportunities because the twelve- to fourteen-year-old age group, like all age groups, has special, identifiable developmental needs that must be met. Erik Erikson and Gail Sheehy, in particular, write about these developmental needs.

In the case of the twelve- to fourteen-year-old age group, one of the needs is to begin to assert one's independence from parents and other authority figures and to find, albeit tentatively, one's own place in the world. Until the age of twelve, most kids have parents and other adults making choices for them.* Now that they are in this magical (or mystical) transition period to adulthood, they want to begin the process of defining themselves—on their own terms—and making choices for themselves.

It is tough for a parent to let go at this stage and to trust the kid to continue to make the right choices. Parents confuse the process with the outcome. How a kid chooses to say no should not be confused with the fact that he or she is in fact saying no. Pink hair, pierced noses, and torn jeans are not signs of drug abuse, as convenient as that thought might be for some.

2. An alternative strategy. The "Just Say No" strategy was effective because it was an alternative (read choice) to two more conventional strategies that are still highly favored by policy makers and adults. These two strategies are scare-the-hell-out-of-'em-with-whatever-it-takes (usually exaggerated distortions about drug effects and long-term consequences) and educate them with the facts (always a highly selective process, by definition).

The Now Force (Chapter 4) explains why the scare approach doesn't work—we all live for today. The future, as in the long-term consequences of drug use, simply does not exist. The second approach, education, overlooks the anti-intellectual conditioning in America. So you can say and spell *tetrahydrocannabinol;* but *blow,* one of the street names for pot, sounds so cool—let's check it out!

What this suggests is a drug Catch-22 for policy makers and parents. Saying No works only in an environment where there is a real choice—something to "Say No" to. But of course the objective of the existing public policy is to have environments where no real choice exists.

3. Delay experimentation. The purpose of the "Just Say No" strategy is not necessarily to prevent drug experimentation but to delay the *onset* of experimentation— a more realistic public policy objective than total abstinence. The longer a kid waits to experiment with drugs, the less likely he or she is to continue to use the drug. That was the good news in the research: the twelve- to fourteen-year-old group that was taught to say no delayed their experimentation with cigarettes for up to two years over the other two groups—the scare 'em and the educate 'em groups. If you were given a choice between your kid's trying cigarettes, or any drug for that matter, at the age of twelve or fourteen versus sixteen or older, pick the latter—at that age the reasons for experimentation are different, the body and mind are more mature, and the kid is a little wiser and not as vulnerable.

That was the objective of the "Just Say No" strategy—a point completely missed in the wholesale adoption of this approach. Abstinence was never the objective of the program. However, the longer a kid delays experimentation with drugs, the less likely he or she is to continue to use drugs, if and when the kid chooses to experiment. So the goal was to delay the experimentation, not abstinence.

The best prevention is giving kids choices before this formative age so that when they reach this age the decision-making process is second nature. What kind of choices? Small, initially inconsequential choices like: "Do you want to do your homework now and then go out and play, or play now and then do your homework?" "You can take the trash out before dinner or after dinner, you choose." "You choose what you want to wear, but it's going to be hot out today."

We have no illusions that the "Just Say No" strategy will get back on track. We do hope that all public policy matters with respect to drug use will be examined in light of the power of choice in America. Unless we change the definition of the problem, presently defined as a privacy issue, expect no change in the incidence and prevalence of drug use and abuse in America.

Volunteer Fixers

While Americans don't always do things right at the front end, as we have already mentioned, we are great fixers. Therein lies a great hope for the drug-abuse problem: the return on investment for treatment (fixing) is now well established; the cost-effectiveness of treatment is now well documented; and community- and school-based education programs are innovating, searching, trying, and working at it.

While there is no magic pill for the drug-abuse problem, there are a multitude of organizations, at both the national and community level, that have as their mission, fixing the problem. None are more effective than AA, Alcoholics Anonymous, founded in 1935 by Bill Wilson, an unemployed New York stockbroker with a severe drinking problem, and Dr. Bob Smith, an alcoholic surgeon in Akron, Ohio. Today there are over 1.5 million people in 76,000 AA groups around the country and in 114 nations around the world. It has also given rise to a host of associated groups that provide choices to spouses and children of alcoholics. And the AA model, in one form or another, provides the elements of the formula for successful treatment, intervention, and prevention of drug abuse. These choice-based models are indispensable to drug-abuse prevention and treatment.

Choosing to Do Good

Why Do We Volunteer?

Fundamentally, because we choose to do so. It makes us feel good; we can make a difference in other people's lives and in the process validate the good in ourselves. This choice is second nature to us, part of our heritage as Americans. It is what Max Lerner said Franklin Roosevelt referred to as the "God stuff." And as we noted at the beginning of this chapter, God and the God stuff landed full force at Plymouth Rock and got locked-in along with the seven cultural forces that define us.

In his book *America as a Civilization*, Lerner says, the "American religious tradition is at once deeply individualist, anti-authoritarian, concerned with sin and salvation, yet secular and rationalist in its life goals." He adds, "America owes much of the effectiveness of its democracy, as well as much of its dynamism, to this strain in its religious experience."

Unseen are the volunteer services that provide choices every day for the 80 million Americans whose dreams are unfulfilled, unmet, and, really, in the final analysis, unchallenged. That is what volunteering is about: Give choice to the unchallenged (☑); provide opportunities to do the impossible and personalize the dream (∘⌣); expect big results (❙); act now (🕒); and improvise like crazy (✂)—in other words, about activating the cultural forces.

Choice Fake Sheet*

This is the task of writing a business book that authors hate the most, but the part of a book many readers immediately scan. Writers feel, and we are no exception, that chapters are already a summary of what he or she knows and the task of deciding what to exclude has been tough enough without the added obligation of an MTV version. Besides, a summary of a summary seems impossible at this point. Then our editor, John Michel, played gotcha and reminded us that Americans like the challenge of the impossible—the cultural force we write about in the next chapter. So here goes, for you and for John.

We began by saying that it doesn't matter whether you are selling mutual funds or machine tools, chewing gum or cars, you'd better give Americans a choice or they won't even honor you with a change of mind. If you try to deny or limit choice, it can destroy your enterprise or your initiative, whether your trade is plumbing or politics.

★ The Choice Force gets "locked-in" at Plymouth Rock and defines us today. Choice is *the* formative and formidable force in America. It got *locked-in* when the Pilgrims landed at Plymouth Rock and it has defined us ever since. (See page 40). It is the only one guaranteed in writing (in our Constitution). While choice can be overwhelming at times, we can't escape the power of choice in dealing with money markets, consumer products, fashion fads, public policy, or rebellious teenagers who won't clean up their rooms. Like typical American consumers Marvin and Mable in their Winnebego, we have a range of choices as consumers that simply does not exist in other countries. Ironically, and in contrast to other industrial countries, Americans make those choices on the basis of *personal preference* with little regard for patriotic appeals (see page 55).

★ Consumers demand choice, real choice. Few companies have understood the power of choice as clearly as the Ford Motor Company has from its inception. Founder Henry Ford, equipped with a revolutionary production idea, was a man in search of a product that turned out to be the car. He revolutionized manufacturing and democratized the machine in the process: Ford's approach to mass production made a car affordable and within reach of the common man. Today, Ford has the number one best-selling car in America, a car that connects with the choice-conscious consumer. Nevertheless, all American car dealers are trained to manipulate the buyer's ideal choice and "make a deal" for something else that is sitting "out back." Because of the power of the Now Force (Chapter 4), consumers usually oblige.

A fake sheet is to a jazz musician what Cliffs Notes are to a student: the bare minimum you need to get by. So if you have to sum this up for your boss or make a presentation on it at your company, we'll do our best at the end of each chapter to summarize things for you. We say more about jazz and fake sheets as a metaphor for American management in Chapter 6.

★ Employees, as well, function better through choice. Consumer marketing companies, like Ford, are conscious about choice when it comes to the ultimate consumer and they have elaborate processes and systems for managing those choices. However, when it comes to *internal* choices about employees and work processes, most American executives and managers close down the choices. "That's-the-way-we've-always-done-things-around-here" thinking limits productivity, inhibits quality production, and handicaps employees. Failure to deal effectively with the people side of productivity and performance accounts for up to 70 percent of the failure associated with reengineering. Confirming these earlier observations about reengineering, a 1995 Arthur D. Little study conducted by the Opinion Research Corporation found that 79 percent of executives say that growth is inhibited by their "difficulty in hiring and retaining talent." The MAP, or individual Motivated Abilities Pattern outlined in this chapter, is a more complete way for companies to find better job fits and thereby retain employees who are more productive (see page 48).

★ Activating the Choice Force, as we have outlined, can have profound impact on work processes and productivity. For example, most companies waste up to 80 percent of their training and personnel development costs and time because the method of training does not match the way people learn. Only 6 percent of employees say they learn by listening—being lectured at—but that is the most prevalent way workers are taught. By contrast 30 percent say they learn by trying, 25 percent by reading on their own, and 20 percent by observing—choices that are rarely available to employees through traditional corporate training programs. That means a minimum return on your training investment because the choice of how to teach or instruct does not match learning styles of approximately three-fourths of all employees (see page 52).

★ Choice defines public policy: Reduce it at great risk. The power of choice is also limited in the public policy arena. Either/or thinking has severely limited public policy options that can restrict, handicap, or cripple businesses. Whoever defines the problem first tends to control the debate. Therefore, public policy issues related to complex social problems like drug abuse, with a severe toll on business, often get unresolved or the debate is sidetracked and unresolved (see page 58).

★ Ban "either/or" thinking; make choice explicit. Choice needs to become part of the *conscious and deliberate* way of running a business—and a country. First, everyone needs to abandon "either/or" thinking. Effective policy making, as well as efficient management, can accommodate both, if we put our mind and practice to it. Second, no CEO speech, no corporate policy, no new work process or procedure, no manufacturing or marketing plan, no consumer offering, no public policy issue should attempt to bypass or short-change choice. Each step of the process should be screened for the presence of choice, explicitly expressed or implicitly implied. It has the power to unleash the imagination of a hamstrung work force, stimulate growth, foster creativity, enhance personal self-worth, fulfill dreams, or realize the things we hold to be self-evident.

Real choice builds and binds. It fosters respect and enhances loyalty. Choice guarantees engagement—the precondition for sustaining performance.

Chapter 2

The Impossible Dream
America's "I.D."

Dreams are the lifeblood of America.

America's great thinkers and writers have all understood this. Carl Sandburg said, "The republic is a dream. Nothing happens unless first a dream." Dr. Martin Luther King, Jr. acted on this fact when he led a march on Washington for jobs and freedom. On August 28, 1963, he said, in a way that still stirs the heart of America: "I have a dream that one day this nation will rise up and live out the true meaning of its creed . . . I have a dream today." And Henry David Thoreau instructs, "If you build castles in the air, your work need not be lost, that is where they should be. Now put a foundation under them."

These then are the dynamics of dreams in America today: They come first, they need vigilance, and they need a foundation in order to materialize.

In this chapter we will write about corporations like The Walt Disney Company, The Ritz-Carlton Hotel Company, and Levi Strauss & Co. who have perfected management processes for doing the impossible. We'll provide a model and a high-performance definition for dreams, even though the word itself might make us squirm or wince when we think of business tactics, satisfying customers, and increasing shareholder value. And we'll worship at the American altar of technology to see how dreams materialize. On the way, we'll remind ourselves about the power of this force in igniting the spirit (soul, heart, mind, eyes, ears, mouth, backs, hands, fingers, and feet) of America. And we'll remind ourselves that behind every large or small company in America and every struggle or progress we've made as a nation, there is an American dreamer.

The fundamentals of dreams in America are easy to forget. But it was dreams and dreamers that got us to this point. Before there was AT&T, there was Alexander Graham Bell, dreamer. Before there was Boeing, there was Orville and Wilbur Wright. Before there was an NAACP there was W. E. Walling and W. E. B. Du Bois. The list goes on and on: before NASA, Robert Goddard; before John Deere & Company, Cyrus McCormick; before CNN, Ted Turner; before Microsoft, Bill Gates and Paul Allen; and before Macmillan Books, Stephen Day.*

*A near literate locksmith from Cambridge, Massachusetts, who printed the first full-length book in America in 1640, and in the words of J. North Conway, author of American Literacy, "unlocked the door to America's preeminence in publishing."

Dreams have ignited everything you see out your window, down the street, or across the plain. They shape things not yet imagined. They inspired the Pilgrims and engulfed the framers of the Declaration of Independence. They kept the pioneers on track and rocketed us to the moon. They make corporations and energize workers. They make millionaires and fools. They forged and feed democracy. They built the greatest nation on earth. And they continue to fuel the engines of change.

At a personal level, dreams are the reason eleven Romanian stowaways sealed themselves in a metal container and came to America as cargo on a 43,000-ton freighter. They were simply following in the wake of twenty other Romanians who had tried an identical scheme several months earlier in 1994. At the other end of the spectrum, dreams are what brought together movie giant Steven Spielberg with Jeffrey Katzenberg (former head of the Disney movie studio), and David Geffen (a billionaire record business executive) to form a new company they call DreamWorks, SKG. Their dreams are so big that Paul Allen, co-founder of Microscoft, invested $500 million of his money to be part of whatever materializes.

The Magic of Dreaming

The big DC-10 Caledonian jetliner from England (no *Mayflower* this time) touches down in Orlando, and after rolling to a stop at the terminal gate the door swings open with an onrush of sodden Florida heat. The Hockney family steps off with expectations that have been building for years.

Ian Hockney is a cabdriver from Bradford, England and, as he says, he's bringing the "Missus and the three pups" over to Disney World for "a bit of a break in the routine, ya know. A bloody holiday that I hope they'll never forget, by God! Costing me an arm and a leg." Their destination is not America, but what America has come to represent to many foreigners—Disney World, the realization of one man's dream.

The Hockney "pups" and the Missus will swelter all day in the Florida sun, ride the horse-drawn streetcar as it clip-clops up Main Street, eat cotton candy, popcorn, and Hershey bars. They'll feel guilty if they don't drop the wrappers in the ubiquitous trash cans. There, without the Hockneys knowing it, the wrappers will be sucked into a pneumatically propelled aluminum tube to be blown at sixty miles an hour inside a twenty-seven-acre tunnel beneath the Magic Kingdom to the place where all Hershey wrappers go when their wrapping days are done.

Meanwhile the Hockneys will go ga-ga over Mickey, Minnie, and Mary Poppins, and the Hockney stomachs will churn on the whoopsy-doo rides. At the end of each day a string of silver monorail coaches will noiselessly carry them from the bright lights and the Magic Kingdom across tropical fairways, over gullies, and beside lakes, finally zooming right into the third floor of their massive air-conditioned A-frame hotel where they will collapse into a sleep like they never had before.

How Dreams Materialize

Looking at the Disney theme parks in California, Florida, Japan, and now France (not to mention those approximations at Busch Gardens and Seven Flags), it's hard to imagine why bankers and backers in the early fifties would balk at financing a theme park envisioned by Walt Disney. But at the time, the words "amusement park" conjured up visions of a low-down, Coney Island, honky-tonk, hoochie-coochie, freak show, rickety-sky-rides, greasy-food, rollicking-sailor, hurdy-gurdy confine whose carny denizens had a "let's fleece the suckers" mind-set—in other words, a nightmare.

By contrast, Walt's was a dream. Perhaps it reached back to childhood. According to Charles Solomon in his *History of Animation,* Walt Disney and his friend Rudy Ising were in one of the best amusement parks in Kansas City when Walt, out of the blue, said, "One of these days I'm going to build an amusement park, and it's going to be clean!"

Like all impossible dreams, his took a while to materialize, and by the end of World War II Disney was world-famous, rich, and restless, which manifested itself in playful ways. He had a miniature steam railroad that ran around the perimeter of his Carolwood estate in Holmby Hills, California, and to stave off boredom and generate ideas he used to get up early, don striped overalls and an engineer's cap, and slip behind the controls of the *Carolwood Pacific.*

In the late forties, Disney had acquired eleven acres across the street from his Burbank studio with the intention of constructing what he wanted to call Mickey Mouse Park, but the Burbank City Council was not amused. One councilman declared, "We don't want the carny atmosphere in Burbank." And that was the end of that dream detail.

It was then that Walt engaged the Stanford Research Institute for advice. They located an alternate site for what he now wanted to call Disneylandia. It was a 160-acre orange grove near Anaheim which had the advantage of being close to an about-to-be-built-freeway.

At this point Disney put together a secret creative team of what he considered to be the most talented art directors to design and lay out his Disneylandia. Out of this came an exquisite five-foot scale working model of the park, which he took to New York to show to ABC-TV's Leonard Goldenson. Goldenson, as the head of the third-ranked network, was desperate to have Disney's film library for ABC programming. Ironically, however, he could not convince ABC to invest in Disneylandia.

NBC's president, David Sarnoff, dismissed Walt out of hand, saying, "Television will never be a medium of entertainment." (This was the early days of television.) CBS equivocated and Walt finally went back to Goldenson.*

A deal was finally struck with ABC, but the impetus came from a Dallas banker who also owned a theater chain and understood the power of the Disney imagination. He came through with a $5 million commitment and Walt Disney's impossible dream got the most basic of technologies—money. Meanwhile, Leonard Goldenson, pointing out that Disneylandia would be too closely identified with *Fantasia*, a box office failure, talked him into changing the name to Disneyland.

Construction moved ahead at a frantic pace, and all the while the Disneyland television weekly series was bringing news of the park to everyone's attention. The show was a blatant promotion of the yet-to-be-opened theme park, but America loved it.

When the big opening night finally arrived on July 17, 1955, much of the park was still under construction (oops). No matter, the show must go on. And it did. And it was a disaster (oops, again). Instead of the fifteen thousand invited guests, an equal number of gate-crashers broke in. Then, with live television covering the events, ladies' high heels got stuck in the hot asphalt on Main Street. Then Walt exploded

Ironically, it was the reverse strategy that prompted the Disney/Capital Cities ABC deal made in 1995.

with four-letter expletives over an open mike, and it went downhill from there. But America forgives. And America adores a comeback.

The comeback became official on a night in February 1957 when Walt received the Milestone Award at a banquet at the Beverly Hilton Hotel. Lowell Thomas was master of ceremonies and read a telegram from President Eisenhower: "Your genius as a creator of folklore has long been recognized by leaders in every field of human endeavor, including that most discerning body of critics, the children of this land and all lands." Later, Pat Boone and Gene Kelly sang, "When You Wish Upon a Star," as a tearful Walt Disney disappeared between the drapes behind the podium.

Behind the Drapes

Behind the scenes at Disneyland and Disney World—at any Disney theme park—is an astonishing group of 1,200 or so engineers, artists, architects, designers, technologists, craftsmen and jacks-of-all-trades whose job it is to make sure that the dreams of Ian Hockney, the missus, and their three pups all come true. They are called "Imagineers"* at Disney and it is their job to do the seemingly impossible.

Everything you've seen and experienced at a Disney theme park, including everything you don't see, is the work of an Imagineer, most likely a team of Imagineers. They are the makers of the endless dreams that create the magic of Disney.

Marty Sklar, president of Walt Disney Imagineering, talked with us about the early days with Walt and what Imagineering is all about today. He started by telling us that back in 1952 Walt had this notion that he could simply hire an outside firm to build his park and do his bidding. So he turned for some help to his friend and neighbor, Welton Becket, a well-known architect in Los Angeles.

Becket listened to what Walt wanted to accomplish and then gave him some of the best advice he ever got, a strategy that has served the company well ever since: Train your own people to do what you want to do, so they can know how you work and how you think.

So Walt took people out of the motion picture industry, art directors and designers, people who had worked with him on various projects over the years, and created an internal organization that has designed and created everything for every Disney park worldwide.

In order to be an Imagineer, you must meet two sets of criteria. First, you must have the necessary engineering, architecture, or design skills. Second, you must have imagination, and in Sklar's words, "be willing to take a chance."

Like everything else about Imagineers, this risk-taking criteria comes from Walt himself. Sklar recalls an article Walt wrote for a book called *Words to Live By*. The article, titled "Take a Chance," was all about doing something that you've never done before. Walt ended it by expressing the hope that he, and we by inference, "would never get too old to march in a parade and to try something new."

Sklar said, "Walt Disney was really the epitome of this attitude. He didn't like to repeat himself. I remember when he made a speech to a group of theater owners and he told them about the time, in the mid-1930s, when he made a sequel to 'The Three Little Pigs' because theater exhibitors were clamoring for more. Walt asked anyone who could remember the sequel to raise his or her hand. Of course, no one did.

Imagine someone asking you what your profession is and you say, "I'm an Imagineer!"

The sequel just bombed and he never made another one. He believed that every time he went up to bat, the only way to really hit a grand slam home run was to try and come up with something new each time. That's the tradition that we live with here."

Which Comes First, the Dream or the Technology

There is no chicken-or-egg riddle at Disney: Dreams come before technology; technology is merely the great enabler. Sklar says, "There are all kinds of ideas and things we dream about accomplishing, but then we have to figure out how they can really work. In our business the big challenge is how we handle the millions of people who visit the Disney parks. We have a unique challenge; we have to design a single attraction to be able to handle thousands of people an hour on a ride system or whatever it happens to be. That's a huge challenge—it influences everything that we do. So technology is really the great enabler for accomplishing our objectives."

Although Disney invents new technologies and holds many patents, they are constantly on the lookout for innovative ways to combine existing technologies. The purpose of the technology and the search for new combinations is to enable the Imagineer to "tell the story of an attraction." "Everything we do," Sklar says, "is an attempt to tell a story, whether it's a ride system, a show, a facade of a building, a street. They all contribute to the story we are trying to tell."

A case in point was *The Twilight Zone Tower of Terror*™, which opened in 1995 at Disney-MGM Studios in Walt Disney World. When it was done, it wasn't really done. Somebody came along after millions of dollars had been spent and said, "This is a two screamer, we have got to get this thing up to a five screamer!" By revisiting the story that *Tower of Terror* needed to tell, someone was able to come up with a $25,000 idea that, at the end of the day, got the tower to a "five screamer." This inventing, fixing, collaborating, improving, perfecting process is an everyday occurrence at Disney.

Who gets final say on the creative result? Sklar proudly says, "We have a lot of talented people here. A lot of them grew up with Walt or Disneyland as their inspiration. In fact, that's one of the interesting stories about our place. A lot of our key Imagineers had their first job at Disneyland, whether it was selling ice cream or parking cars. So they learned the business and understood, from the beginning, the standards we needed to reach and maintain. Today, there are a variety of people who make those decisions, and eventually they are brought to my attention, and then ultimately to Michael Eisner's. He loves the creative process and really is the final arbiter of the attractions and parks we open."

Sklar sees attitude and teamwork as the real magic in the process. "Technology is important," he says, "but the attitude that you bring to things is the key part. In our case, we really relish the success of the team. We often say that when we finish a project there are so many hands that touch it, we have no idea who did what. The important thing is that we did it together—that's what matters. At the same time, it's also important to be able to say, 'I had an important part to play.' "

Worshiping Technology?

We expect someone out there to try to make a case for technology as a cultural force. After all, they will say, technology has played a major role in getting us this far and nothing but technology looms and blooms on the horizon. Besides, they'll continue, ample evidence abounds that Americans worship at the altar of technology and high priests of American technology are anointed practically every day. What other country would pass a bill mandating a V chip (technology) in new televisions to regulate what kids cannot see because parents can't do it on their own!?

But as Marty Sklar pointed out, technology is really just an enabler. It increases choice (☑), makes dreams come true (🐚), leads to big and more (▮), speeds up delivery and reduces waiting time (🕘), not a day passes that there is not a technology oops or two or three (🐝) and it's a key element in our ability to improvise (✂). By definition, of course, technology creates whatsnew (💾).

In their book, *Incredibly American: Releasing the Heart of Quality,* authors Marilyn Zuckerman and Lew Hatala discuss the role of technology in quality improvement. They are equally concerned with the emotional or human side of improvement and how leadership factors into the performance equation, and what trade-offs, if any, need to be made between people and technology. It appears as if technology is a solution in search of a problem.

The Zuckerman/Hatala view of technology and the priority it is given in business is as follows (the primary emotional or human response is noted in the parenthesis):

1. Technology (great!)

2. Plans (even better!)

3. Leadership (now we can't lose!)

4. Emotions (huh?)

Note that technology leads the parade and virtually dictates what follows. Even leadership is technology dependent. Why make bold choices about television programming when technology (the V-chip) can do it for you? Why teach kids math, when icon cash registers can simplify the process? With technology in front, who cares about how people feel about it? Better get used to the endless technology-driven options when you dial a retail service (or wholesale, for that matter).

Corroborating the experiences and processes that Marty Sklar and his fellow Imagineers at Disney follow, Zuckerman/Hatala show that the following reordering of priorities is more effective:

1. Leadership (great!)

2. Emotions (of course!)

3. Plans (now we know what to do!)

4. Technology (let's do it!)

Not only is technology in proper perspective, but the emotional dimension of work, that Disney understands so well, is acknowledged early on and supports the process rather than drags it down. We write more about this emotional dimension of performance improvement in Chapter 5.

Is a Dream by Any Other Name Still a Dream?

When we talk about impossible dreams, invariably someone says, "Don't you really mean possible dreams?" Yes and no. In the end the American goal is to make the impossible possible.

Of course, there is only one way to make a dream a reality: hard work. One great dreamer, President John F. Kennedy, understood this implicitly. Most of us are familiar with his moon-mission statement, the half with the dream stuff in it; we forget the second part where dreams meet the road:

> But there is no sense in agreeing or desiring that the United States take an affirmative position in outer space, unless we are prepared to do the work and bear the burdens to make it successful.

Work makes dreams come true, even the simplest of dreams. Captain John Smith's foundational charge to Americans put the simplest of dreams in the simplest of terms: "if you don't work, you don't eat." As Kathleen Deveny, staff reporter for *The Wall Street Journal,* notes, while today the value of the work ethic is often strained between employers and their workers, "immigrants still believe in the redemptive power of work."

Although the Dream Force is locked-in in America, unlike any other country in the world, we get a blood transfusion from the million or so immigrants who legally come here each year. Two, by way of example that Deveny describes, are Tung Choy, housekeeper at the Four Seasons in New York, and Ivan de la Brena. Choy's dream is modest by most standards: He wants to make it up to the room-service department where there are tips, thereby enabling him to better provide for his two daughters, whom he is planning to put through college. Ivan de la Brena, night manager at the Riverside Sunoco gas station in Westport, Connecticut, is another one. He's working to save money for a house and one day expects to own his own business. You can bet he will—just as millions have before him.

The word "possible" doesn't carry the same punch as *impossible,* the "never-done-before" and "I-can-be-*anything*-I-want-to-be-yes-I-can." Imagine if these were the lyrics that Joe Darion wrote for "The Quest" (a.k.a "The Impossible Dream"), the memorable theme song from the Broadway hit musical, *Man of La Mancha:*

> To chart the corporate plan,
> To fight a beatable foe,
> To bear the bearable details,
> To run where the wimps want to go.

And how about this for a quest?

> This is my job,
> To follow the plan,
> To eke out some profit,
> Wherever I can . . .

Not very exciting, is it? Not even Mitch Leigh's majestic score could have rescued these Frederick Taylor-ish lyrics. Had these been the words, there would have been no musical, no song to sing.

A High-Performance Definition of Dream

Throughout this book and especially in Chapters 6 and 7 we will introduce you to what we call "high-performance definitions" of conventional business terms. These high-performance definitions are not a business writer's device. They are real tools

Mitch's Magical Music

When we caught up with Mitch Leigh he was sipping a calvados on the sun-splashed terrace of his Riviera lair above Miramar, overlooking the Mediterranean, just minutes away from the pleasures of Monte Carlo. The name of his villa is *Le Rêve Impossible* (French for *The Impossible Dream*, of course). It has been thirty years since his long-running Broadway hit *Man of La Mancha* left New York for the American heartland. It is still playing out there somewhere.

Mitch is about to close his Riviera home and pack up the wife and kids and get back to his New York studio. The next time we hear about him will no doubt be for a symphony that he is composing for a synthesizer—another dream. But this dream is not daunting for Mitch: he's a dreamer from the slums of New York's Lower East Side who made it to Yale and learned his trade from Paul Hindemith, the distinguished twentieth-century composer and teacher.

This is how Mitch described "The Impossible Dream" to James Morrison:

JM: *What went on in your head when you wrote "The Impossible Dream"? What inspired . . .*

ML: I wish I could make it more romantic than it really was. There was a lyric that was handed to me that was, you know, three thousand miles long, and it had to be cut down 'cause no song could stand that. It was hard because it was a pretty good lyric and it was saying some pretty important philosophical things. So I had to both mold the lyric and write the tune to get to the most salient points.

I was really solving a problem for a dramatic moment. The man is finally faced with the fact he's being ridiculed by these people who know he's crazy. They don't doubt it. They know he's crazy. The people who run the inn know the guy is nuts. And this girl. She can't imagine, can't figure out why she gives a hoot, you know? Why?—that's the moment—why do I care about this crazy guy? She asks, "Why do you do this?" And he tells her in this song why he does this.

You have to dream. If you don't dream it's all over too quickly. No matter how virtuous you are in life, you will die. So it's the impossible dream . . . the . . . the . . . the . . . [etc.]" "and . . . and . . . and . . . [etc.]" What you have to do is try. And that's the point. You have to try. And that's what this thing is all about. It's impossible. You cannot get immortality. It doesn't come with the job.

JM: *How about the moment when you put down the notes to the tune?*

ML: Oh, I don't know how they came to me. They came out of my scrotum.

to help in understanding the power of cultural forces and the untapped energy that can be activated—as long as we have the will to do so.*

The first of these words is dream (see Snapshot #7). The conventional column lists some of the meanings this word generates in a general business context. It is the way the word is generally understood and commonly used in most businesses. The high-performance definition identifies some of the emotional dimensions of the word that are less common in bigger businesses, but are often operational in many entrepreneurial companies or start-up ventures.

In general, the high-performance definitions are meanings that resonate with Americans, but lie just under the surface of their awareness.

Snapshot #7

Dreams Conventional vs. High-Performance Meaning	
Conventional	*High-Performance*
pie-in-the-sky	down to earth
waste of time	necessary
vague	tangible
impractical	inspiring
private	shared
individual activity	group activity
results in complacency	gets you going
for creative types	for everyone

It is not our intention to insist that you use only the word "dream," but to point out the power of the word. Clearly there are other words in use throughout companies that get at the same intent. There is no common definition for these words—one company's mission is another company's vision, one group's goal is another group's target.

In the final analysis, let's agree to judge the power of the word by the outcome of the effort. For our part, we'll use the word dream more often than not (we see these words on a continuum—see Snapshot #8). The cultural force, after all, is impossible dream, not strategic plan.

Dreaming of Zero Defects

Dreams are a conundrum for business—and they go to one of the challenges of this book: how to take a force that we acknowledge in the culture at large and bring the same dynamics into our boardrooms and factory floors as a way to energize every employee from chairman to cashier, from founder to foreman.

*All of these definitions are based on the research behind the book. See Appendix. Some are based on a collaboration between us and the quality department at AT&T in 1991; we have updated them and added the notion of high performance to the new definition.

Snapshot #8

Continuum of High-Performance Words

high	impossible dream
	dream
	aspiration
	vision
	mission
	stretch target
	stretch goal
	excellence
	target
	goal
	strategic plan
	plan
low	job

Why does business acknowledge the power of dreams at home and on the ball field, in plays and at the movies, in classrooms and in a research lab or two, but deny them at work? Some of us may say, "This is a dream come true," about a project breakthrough or an impossible goal that has been met, yet we won't put the word in our value statements, in our business plans, or train our people how to dream or how to use the power of the impossible.

In 1994 Robert J. Eaton, chairman of Chrysler, told *The Wall Street Journal*'s staff reporter Douglas Lavin, "Internally, we don't use the word vision. I believe in quantifiable short-term results—things we can all relate too—as opposed to some esoteric thing no one can quantify." And this came on the heels of incoming IBM CEO Louis Gerstner, who took over a company on the skids with the comment that "The last thing IBM needs right now is vision."

No doubt Tom Watson, who built IBM, and Lee Iacocca, who saved Chrysler, would take exception. Take the ability to dream away from an American and you have on your hands a disengaged child, a disinterested student, a less-productive worker, a handicapped executive.

One quantifiable strategy that executives like Eaton no doubt like is zero defects. This manufacturing strategy idea was birthed in America in and around the early 1950s. It was conceived by Phil Crosby, known in some circles as the evangelist of the quality movement. At the time he was with ITT and the U.S. military was one of its prime customers. The goal was 100 percent perfect parts. As a consequence it became a military procurement requirement of sorts and still lingers there in some form. But Crosby's dream, that this would become the mantra of business, never materialized.

There was one major defect in Crosby's cause: Zero defects are not the stuff Americans are made of. The end goal is desirable and necessary, but Americans don't dream of perfection nor are they inspired by it. At an unconscious level, perfection represents death to an American, the end of the line, no place to go.

The Pursuit of Perfection

Phil Crosby's dream of zero defects is dead in America; it never caught on. However, it is alive and well in Japan where a cultural force is the pursuit of perfection. There they have ZD clubs, ZD hats, ZD T-shirts, ZD pens and paraphernalia, ZD notepads, and in a throwback to our Sunday School days, ZD pins that you wear on your lapel. For each year you meet your ZD goals, you get another addition to the pin. So you will see Japanese workers with a string of ZDs. You'll see ZD charts on factory walls with those bright red lines going down.

Unlike Americans, Japanese are motivated by the search for perfection. That's what bonsai is all about—growing the perfect miniature tree, arranging the perfect garden (sometimes just with rocks), clipping one leaf at a time to keep things growing perfectly. Hedge clippers and weed whackers are not the things that Japanese gardeners are made of. Another example of perfection in Japan is *kanji*, the Japanese form of writing. This is an art form, something one perfects—Americans are lucky to get their children to scribble *between* the lines, let alone end up with a legible script. When they grow up to become doctors, only the trained pharmacist can read the handwriting.

Continuous improvement is a Japanese idea—the goal is perfection. It is one of those imported ideas that doesn't resonate with Americans. Yes, executives and managers *say* the word and the plan calls for those kinds of results, but the benchmark companies in America don't brag about continuous improvement—it's the breakthrough stuff they show off and others seek to replicate. Industrial tourism (making the benchmarking rounds across the world) is not about learning to twinkle the stars, but to discover the secrets of the universe, the breakthrough thinking, not the process improvement.

Snapshot #9 is from the formative research done by AT&T on what quality means to Americans. This is our representation of the research. It shows the differences between the Japanese path to perfection and the American boulevard approach. Japanese keep the specific goal in mind and strive for perfection. Americans are all over the place and need short-term impossibilities to get the job done. Once the "impossible goal" is within range, Americans tend to lose interest and need another goal to spur them on—we are not good finishers, which is why a new target is necessary.

So rather than striving for perfection inherent in a single goal, Americans resonate more to a series of stretch goals, each one incrementally further out than the next one. Americans simply want to make things work, not to be perfect or to reach a point of perfect. So the ideal model is keep the target *moving* so that your employees are engaged—avoid establishing a *fixed* goal that is the be-all and end-all.

Americans usually fall victim to "we're-almost-there" thinking. In many of our minds, almost being there or knowing that we can be there does not energize us as it does the Japanese. At this point in the process we are already thinking, whatsnew—the seventh cultural force we write about on pages 265–301. So as we approach the goal, we perform better if the goal is reset just a little higher, just a little further out of reach, so that the juices flow again—but just enough to almost get us there again. The business implication is to keep moving the target, keep setting it higher, tap the breakthrough energy rather than prodding on the continuous improvement trail.

A vivid example of the differences between Japanese and American cultural attitudes can be seen in the advertising copy for products from each country: *The*

Snapshot #9

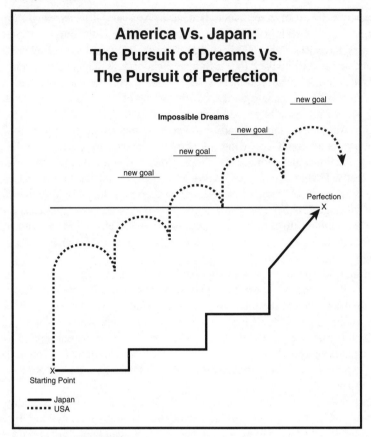

America Vs. Japan:
The Pursuit of Dreams Vs.
The Pursuit of Perfection

Source: Adapted from AT&T.

Relentless Pursuit of Perfection for Lexus vs. *Start Doing Extraordinary Things* for Texas Instruments; or *See, Hear and Feel the Difference* for NEC vs. *Just Do It* for Nike.

Incidentally, the Germans end up somewhere in the middle. They are standard-driven. The standards are high with an emphasis on precision and engineering. Like the Japanese they achieve those standards through a gradual process at the beginning, ensuring that everything is in place and all questions have been clarified. Unlike the Americans, there is no need for breakthrough thinking, especially once the standards have been set or met. For example, the Germans set the standards for beer over 450 years ago and they have not changed since. German product ads also reinforce this dedication to perfection. For example, *Precision Thinking* for Siemens or *The Ultimate Driving Machine* for BMW.

Each of these approaches—pursuit of perfection in Japan, meeting standards in Germany, and breakthrough thinking in the United States—is an example of how culture imbues the work process in different countries. The key to competitiveness for each country is to stick to your cultural knitting. For Americans, it is the challenge of the impossible.*

Getting to Jerusalem

Consider the following analogy. As you read it, think about how you motivate those around you—at home, in your communities, at work. Think about what you need to get the job done. Do you ever ask yourself, "Why do they want me to do this? What is this all about?" Do you ever get an answer?

> *Bob,*
> *I want you to buy a horse.*
>
> *Rita,*
> *I want you to buy a horse*
> so that you can learn to ride it.
>
> *Calvin, I want you to buy a horse*
> *so that you can learn to ride it*
> because I want you to lead the cavalry.
>
> *Jerry, I want you to buy a horse*
> *so that you can learn to ride it*
> *because I want you to lead the cavalry*
> so that we can free Jerusalem.
>
> *Christina, I want you to buy a horse*
> *so that you can learn to ride it*
> *because I want you to lead the cavalry*
> *so that we can free Jerusalem*
> by the end of the year and
> save the world for Christianity.[†]

In our workshops, when we take this basic story and go through the sequence, we can feel the electricity in the room. Sometimes we single out one individual and walk her through the levels, stopping at each stage to get reactions to the increasing levels of knowledge and understanding of the mission. Sometimes we do a similar process with five different people. Invariably, we take this basic story and apply it to the specific mission of the group we are coaching. Then the whole thing really sings!

None of us likes to think of our organizations, job descriptions, team efforts, or management styles as being at the buy-a-horse level or learn-to-ride stage. If asked, we'd all *say* we are at saving-the-world level. However, in our research, we have

---

There is a delightful short video "Quality and Culture" that contrasts these cultural differences. It was produced by Josh Hammond and Dave Pool, one of the video-magicians at Disney World. It is available from ASQC at 1-800-248-1946 or 414-272-8575.

[†]*Don't let the reference to Jerusalem or Christianity, or the political correctness of the fictional names of the employees get in the way of the point we are trying to make. This metaphor is adapted from a similar story we first heard from Clotaire Rapaille.*

noted that nothing could be further from reality. Most companies operate or manage on the buy-a-horse or maybe lead-the-cavalry level—employees are simply told what to do with no understanding of why.

Having declared that, we have also observed that every company has some people or levels of management functioning with Jerusalem in mind. We find most CEOs, strategic planners, and senior executives at the Christina level—that's their job. Depending on the levels of management there may be some Calvin enclaves and Jerry groups around. But somehow there is no awareness of the power that would come from sending Bob out to buy some technology that he needs to learn to master so that he can lead a group to develop a new product by the end of the year that will position the company as the global leader.

In short, everyone buying horses should do so with saving the world in mind. Dream the whole dream, don't just ask that the sheets be turned down.

Remember that the high-performance definition of dream is a group activity. So the next time there is a new process, training activity, new market opportunity, or a new technology that you want to introduce at your company or community program, go through the buy-a-horse exercise. It might look something like this:

> *Design Group A, we want you take this training program*
> *So that you can master a new technology,*
> *So that you can head up a division wide research effort,*
> *So that we can achieve a product breakthrough,*
> *By the end of the year and*
> *Help find a cure for cancer.*

The most important part of this exercise is establishing a connection between the initial steps of the program and the ultimate mission. The more "save the world" dimensions you can put into the mission, the better. The more you can combine an impossible dimension with an emotional appeal, the more effective the process. The ultimate appeal should be based on broad intrinsic values or merit, rather than some extrinsic value. Missions like saving the environment, expanding educational opportunity, or building a better community have more intrinsic appeal than building the biggest plant, making more money, or increasing productivity. While a bigger plant may enable you to hire more people and thereby better the community, those goals are not explicit. Better to put "building the biggest plant" at the cavalry level and end up with a better community as the goal than have the construction of a building as the objective.

Engaging the Bobs

Our corporate Jerusalem strategies are our best-kept secrets. They are our best untapped source of energy, and when connected to each employee's job function, result in substantial increases in productivity and profitability. We discovered this power in the data gathered for the IQS, referred to in Chapter 1.

The analysis of the data on over nine hundred separate management practices revealed that there were only three universally beneficial practices. What a surprise that was!

A universally beneficial practice means that it doesn't matter what country you are in or the business you run, your size or level of sophistication, an increase in any of these three management practices results in increased productivity, profitability, and customer-perceived quality.* The three universal practices are:

1. Use of the process improvement tools (i.e., cycle-time reduction, value-added analysis, cause-and-effect diagrams)

2. Supplier certification programs (i.e., programs that align production standards and service processes with the next-in-line customer)

3. Deploying or communicating the strategic business plans (Note that this is not about having a strategic plan—all companies have some kind of overall business plan and corporate strategy—but simply about what you do, or don't do, with the one you've got.)

The data on how American companies *fail* to take full advantage of the power of the third of these three management practice were staggering. On average in the American companies we studied,[†] less than one-third of middle management "fully understands" their company's strategic plan and only 85 percent of senior management does. We were amazed at the low level for middle management and very surprised that for senior executives the number was anything less than 100 percent. Given these figures, there was no surprise when the data showed that only 18 percent of frontline workers understood the plan. However, the figures on the percent of board members who fully understood the strategic plan, 22 percent (!) had to be double- and triple-checked.

By contrast, the Japanese did a much better job of deploying their plans throughout the organization. More than twice as many middle managers, 68 percent, fully understood their strategic plans.

For the purposes of understanding cultural differences, it is important to remind ourselves that Japan has a more reflective and collective way of doing things. By contrast, the American approach is highly individualized, occasionally an enclave approach. Because of this individualized approach, Americans miss the power that comes from a fully engaged workforce, from knowing that the company is headed to Jerusalem instead of Juneau. It is remarkable that we produce the way we do with one substantially beneficial management practice in the drawer. Imagine if we could change that!

The key to the higher awareness of the strategic plan in Japanese companies is not a function of deployment after the fact, but engagement at all levels of the organization *during the process of creating the plan*. Japanese companies ask middle managers to participate in the creation of the plan. In order to do that the middle managers talk to and exchange ideas with the frontline workers. Already parts of the plan, though not final, are being communicated—and understood.

Middle managers then formulate some plan or strategy and communicate it to the next level—another degree of understanding is achieved. When the plan is completed, deployment simply builds on the foundation that was established during the creation of the process.

---

*Determined by a profitability measure of return-on-assets, a productivity measure of value-added per employee, and quality measure based on an index of customer-perceived quality.

†Over 180 large, medium, and small American companies in 1991.

The Japanese also have the advantage of thinking in longer strategic terms; ten- and twenty-year plans are not uncommon. By contrast, Americans may have the attitude that since we are either going to change the plan soon (see pages 265–301) or *not* stick to the plan anyway, there is no sense in communicating it. There is something to be said for that attitude, but we know that there are certain core values and operating principles that are the foundation of any effective strategic plan. Those should be communicated and reinforced on a regular basis.

When we discuss this research with companies, some say that their plan is sensitive, that there is a secret that the competition may discover. Of course, this assumes that the competition is sitting around waiting to respond to *your* plan and they don't have one of their own (that they aren't telling anyone about either). It also assumes that Americans like to mimic and copy other company strategies. Even assuming there is some truth to that, the real secret or competitive advantage, as one leader of the we-share-all strategy, Milliken & Company, points out, is not in the plan, but in how the plan is executed.

Finally, with respect to this cross-cultural study of management practices, deploying the strategic plan does not mean a passive or limited communications approach, such as an article in the monthly employee publication on page three when someone gets around to writing it, a summary form for managers only, a paragraph in the annual report, or a passing reference to it in the employee orientation program. It means just the opposite—assertive, inventive, personalized, and visible marketing of the plan to all stakeholders. For role models, we have two case studies to follow in this chapter and Allied Signal's case study in Chapter 4. Also, check out Southwest Airlines' 1994 annual report for a good example of a compelling visual model.

This could mean chats with the chairman in round-robin meetings at plants, facilities, or other natural units of the company; personalized letters to the employees (mailed to their home); an electronic watercooler meeting with an executive or interactive E-mail of some kind; a video explaining the strategic plan in graphic or dramatized format; or any other invention that says the following: *This is important, pay attention, engage, execute—we are all in this together, your personal contribution is important.**

Corporate Dream Statement

Most companies have vision statements or mission statements. The words vision and mission have their own high perch in business, but in our opinion, they are a rung or two below Dream. You can see it in the words that are used or in the lack of urgency in the time line—if there is one. A vision statement might be "we are going to be the premier company in the exploration of space." A dream statement is precisely what John Kennedy laid before the nation when he said that we were going to put a man on the moon (a clear destination) within ten years (a precise time frame) and not just leave him there, but bring him back safely (the criteria to measure success).

Dream phrases create tensions. They send a chill up the spine, and when the truth be told, a doubt through the mind. But they energize, invigorate, and egg us on. Even substituting the word "dream" for "vision" or "impossible" for "goal" can ignite the power of a Dream. And although this power is not necessarily in the use of these

*See our High-Performance Values Ladder on page 209 for a message model.

Fielding Dreams

In an Interlude that follows this chapter, we write about baseball as a metaphor for American management. But these forces, in this case the Dream Force, have a profound impact on our nonbusiness lives as well. Nowhere is this more evident than in the lives of kids (and grown-ups) who dream of some day making it to the big leagues in their favorite sport, winning a gold medal at the Olympics, or often just hoping (and praying) to make the team.

Both of us have a bias towards baseball and the dreams that baseball players are made of. And in the fall of each year as World Series time rolls around, I (Morrison) usually get Birdie Tebbetts on the phone. Eva and Lizzy Ryan were sisters, which made Birdie and me first cousins. As a waif I used to haunt Yankee Stadium to watch my very own cousin battle the immortals Gehrig, DiMaggio, and Berra. I like to hear the old All-Star catcher's forecast on likely winners and also-rans, whether he's going to be at any of the games, and I talk about maybe joining him for one or two.

But today I asked Tebbetts if he remembered a pitcher named Lou Brissie. "Sure. A big fella. Wore a cast aluminum brace on his leg."

Then he starts telling the story of opening day, 1948, at Boston's Fenway Park. That had been more than two years since the end of World War II. On the mound for Connie Mack's Philadelphia Athletics is this newcomer named Brissie. For the first six innings it was going well for him. Then Boston's right fielder Ted Williams comes to the plate, digging in nervously with a mind for a belt-high fastball that he can park in the bleachers.

Almost fifty years later Tebbetts recalls Brissie having a better-than-average fastball which is the pitch Brissie is about to deliver as he goes into a full windup. All six feet–four inches of Brissie bend into the throw to release the white blur spinning toward the plate. Williams's bat slams it back like a cannon shot smack into the aluminum-clad leg of Lou Brissie, where it caroms off with a resounding clang heard throughout the ballpark.

The crowd falls silent. Brissie is down.

Williams, after touching first base turns and races for the mound and the fallen Brissie. Legendary Williams kneeling beside rookie Brissie looks down and asks anxiously, "Are you all right?"

Brissie rubbing his aluminum leg brace replies, "Why didn't you pull the damn ball!" They had a laugh and play resumed.

That was on an April day in 1948.

But on a December day in 1944, Corporal Lou Brissie was along the front in Italy's Po Valley with his platoon as they cautiously approached the German line. Out of nowhere a shell from a German 88 exploded within a few feet of them. Although Brissie was closest to the hit, in a freak of war he took most of its impact in his left leg while eleven of his buddies further away were struck higher in their bodies and killed outright. Brissie crawled to a nearby stream and passed out. He'd been given up for dead until a few hours later when a passing medic noticed a quivering sign of life and dragged him back to an aid station.

continued

Within days Brissie had been moved to an Army hospital near Naples where an Army surgeon told him the leg would have to be amputated. Corporal Brissie, said, "You can't do that. I'm a ball player! You'll have to find another way."

The other way turned out to be massive doses of a new wonder drug called penicillin. Soon Brissie was well enough to be put aboard a C54 transport and flown by way of Casablanca to New York's Mitchell Field and then on to Finney General Hospital in Thomasville, Georgia.

There they surgically removed metal and bone chips and told him to be mindful of his limitations, stop dreaming about getting back to baseball, and start thinking about other things he could do. Then they sent him on to an Army hospital in Alabama where he met up with surgeon Al Suraci. The reconstructive surgery plan called for twenty-five operations. Lou had had enough after twenty-three and headed home to North Augusta, South Carolina.

There he staggered around on crutches, all the while burning inside with his impossible dream. So he started his own recovery program, walking a little each day. Walking farther, and farther. Not running.

As he said fifty years later:

I don't really . . . . I can't really recall thinking about going back to baseball. The biggest question in my mind was how am I going to do what I want to do with what I have. It was more a question of "how" rather than "if." No, I never thought about "if." No sir, Mr. Connie Mack had written me and told me when I was well to let him know and he would give me a chance to see if I could play. So I knew that for a fact, because he had told me.

Little by little Brissie's bum leg gained strength and he began to throw. The more he threw, the harder he threw until two years and a lot of pain later, Lou Brissie started pitching for the A's minor league Savannah club in 1947.

The following spring, Mr. Mack, true to his word, brought Lou Brissie up to the majors and made him a starting pitcher on that opening day in Fenway Park. The pains and infections in the aftermath of that blast in Italy did not go away, but Lou Brissie went on to make the All-Star Team in 1949. After winning forty-four major league games, he retired from baseball in 1951.

Looking back on a time long, long ago, Brissie said something that made me stop and consider. He said, "In my heart I just believed . . . . It was an honor for me to be out there with those guys . . . . " And he stopped. I start thinking that Lou is talking about himself on the mound among all those graceful gents, in white flannel suits, on the green grass, in the sunlit stadiums of a bygone day.

He continued, "It was a real honor. I tell you that I was very, very fortunate." And then, where his memories and his heart reside, it all became very clear. "I was spared when a lot of them weren't."

words (rather it is where the sights are set), the result is invariably different when you say or think the impossible.

Regardless of what we call our objectives, the process should inspire employees, managers, suppliers, customers, and any other stakeholders. It should result in higher productivity, a more satisfied workforce, and a fuller sense of purpose and value.

In our workshops we talk about the need to visualize a statement in order to be able to see it, not just read it. We even get artists involved or bring scissors, paste, and a lot of pictures to help the process. Seeing what each word depicts is much more insightful than just picking the right words.

Could you see your company adopting the following dream statement?

To make every person's experience with your product or service the best experience of their life.

How would you picture this? Would you be comfortable with it? What words would you modify? Most instead of every? Satisfied instead of best? Over the course of the life of the product or service instead of the person's entire life? Or to date instead of entire life?

Can you imagine adopting this in your company? Can you imagine any company or group that would? There is one group we have heard say this, the folks at Disney World. Their objective is: "To make every person's experience at Disney World the happiest day of their life."

How many of us can honestly claim that we would not have said: "To *help* make *most* people's experience at Disney World the *best* day of their *vacation*." What a difference four words make!

Ladies and Gentlemen Serving Ladies and Gentlemen

The Ritz-Carlton Hotel Company, winner of the 1992 Malcolm Baldrige National Quality Award and one of the best hotel groups in the world, is one of a handful of companies that we have seen actively embrace the Impossible Dream Force in a formal and serious business way. They have no "Bobs" in their company who buy only horses—they are all Jerusalem-bound "Christinas," out to make your experience at the hotel the most memorable you have ever had.

After tracking customer satisfaction—as most companies do—and keeping those numbers relatively high and constant, they have moved on to measuring "Memorable Experiences"—a big dream-step up the traditional customer satisfaction ladder. All of this comes naturally to them (although they work hard at achieving it) because they have a huge call to action; they see themselves as "ladies and gentlemen" serving their guests, whom they see also as "ladies and gentlemen."

Here is how this works at the corporate level. There is an overall mission (the dream term they use) statement. Each hotel then interprets or applies that mission to its own operations. In turn, each department or division of the hotel extrapolates the mission statement to its special functions and responsibilities. Finally, each employee is encouraged to write, in his own words, how his work—from cook to concierge—contributes to the aspirations of the entire organization.

Here is how this works at one hotel. The following are actual mission statements. We have italicized certain words and phrases to emphasize the dream aspects of their statements. These are dream words, impossible achievements, stretch-stretch goals, beyond-vision words. They are the kinds of words that the Dream Force is made of. These excerpts are from the actual mission statements of Ritz-Carlton. Each level of the hotel has one; we've selected three, one from corporate, one from a department, and one from an individual from the Ritz-Carlton in Manhattan, where there are 231 other hotels competing with them. But you wouldn't know it from what follows.

Mission Statement (excerpts): The Ritz-Carlton Hotel Company

The Ritz-Carlton Hotel Company will be regarded as the quality and market leader of the hotel industry worldwide . . . we will consistently provide all customers with their ultimate expectation, a memorable experience and exceptional value. Every employee will be empowered to provide immediate corrective action should customer problems occur . . . Our restaurants and lounges will be the first choice of the local community and will be patronized on a regular basis . . . We will strive to meet individual needs because our success depends on the satisfaction, effort and commitment of each employee.

Mission Statement (excerpts): House Keeping Department (New York City)

The House Keeping Department will meet the unexpressed wishes *of our guests by preparing and releasing rooms prior to check in time. . . . To give* uncompromising *lateral service to all departments. . . . We will maintain the highest level of cleanliness both in the front of the house and the* heart *of the house. This will ensure a* positive experience for our employees *and our guests who will* always *enjoy a warm, relaxed yet refined ambiance.*

Mission Statement: Thomas Ramirez

I, Thomas Ramirez, will hold upright, *all that I deem important for a full life: honesty, compassion, knowledge and faith. Through my commitment to hard work, I will establish myself as a leader in the culinary* world *and do my best to* anticipate the correct moves *within the industry. I will share* any *knowledge I have obtained with* any one *who requests this of me. I will appreciate the different cultures around me, understanding their value and* tremendous worth. *I will* never lose compassion f*or my fellowman and will* always *tell the truth, no matter how* difficult this may be.

Thomas Ramirez is chief tourant (a roundsman in the kitchen) at Fantino, a restaurant in the Ritz-Carlton Hotel, New York. He knows what headquarters in Atlanta expects of him and what each intervening level of the company expects of him. He is a gentleman serving ladies and gentlemen and proud to oblige.

These statements are not laminated on a plaque or nailed to a wall, they are personal and accessible, often in back pockets or posted over kitchen sinks. And the hotel's credo card, which captures all the themes and principles described above, can be found literally within reach of every employee. Not that they need reminding, but for bragging rights, in case anyone asks.

A Word About Stretch Goals

On the twenty-fifth anniversary of our landing on the moon, Eugene Cernan, the most recent (note we didn't say last) American to walk on the moon in December of 1972, said, "We don't have a space program today. We've got a series of space events. We need a goal out there in the future we can all get our arms around." NASA director Daniel Goldin said, "My worst fantasy is that people are going to be celebrating Apollo as a high-water mark in what the human mind and spirit can do."

Cernan no doubt had President Kennedy's moon goal in mind when he made his observation about what the space challenges are today.* As we said earlier, impossible dream carries the emotional wallop, but stretch goals† also can get the job done. And it would seem that stretch goals are more commonly accepted inside corporations. Who are we to interfere with success?

Shawn Tully, writing for *Fortune* calls them stretch *targets*. He says, "Stretch targets reflect a major shift in the thinking of top management. Executives are recognizing that incremental goals, however worthy, invite managers and workers to perform the same comfortable processes a little better each year. The all-too-frequent result: mediocrity."

Tully says, stretch targets are "often the one subject that can turn a harried, taciturn boss into an impassioned chatterbox." He adds that Boeing CEO Frank Shrontz "rhapsodizes" their value by noting, "We're doing things we didn't think were possible." Tully, in his research, independently came to the same conclusions that we have made throughout this chapter. He says it this way, with our corresponding comments in brackets:

> *Honesty* [see our Levi Strauss story] *is the best management practice. To instill the sense of urgency necessary for radical change* [see Chapter 4 and our case study on Allied Signal], *a CEO must level with employees, explaining in clear, convincing terms why the company must either change or fall on hard times* [review our Bob-to-Jerusalem metaphor and revisit Ford Motor Company case study in the preceding chapter]. *The goals must ring true* [the Ritz-Carlton Hotel case study]: *imposed arbitrary objectives is the quickest way to turn employees off* [see Levi Strauss again]. *A stretch target, such as halving the time needed to produce a mainstay product, must derive unambiguously from the corporate goals* [see 3M case study in Chapter 7, the case studies in this chapter, and Allied Signal story in Chapter 4].

Thinking back on our "Bob-buy-a-horse" metaphor, Tully advocates benchmarking as a way to convince managers and employees that "it can be done." He adds that benchmarking has a conversion factor: "It is a potent psychological tool to enlist them [the employees] in the crusade." Where have you heard that earlier in this chapter?

Just Show It

Enough words. Show me some stuff.

In the next chapter, we'll show how a division of Johnson & Johnson uses the Big and More Force to do the seemingly impossible—making daily disposable contact lenses with higher quality than the permanent ones. We'll show in Chapter 4 (the Now Force) how Allied Signal does the impossible, training eighty-five thousand employees worldwide in eighteen months when others, considered the best in the business, take twice as long. In Chapter 5 (the Oops Force), we'll show how Johnson & Johnson did the "impossible" to turn around a major catastrophe, not of their own

---

*One stretch leads to another, that's the nature of the Dream Force.

†James C. Collins and Jerry I. Porras, in Built to Last: Successful Habits of Visionary Companies, call these "big, hairy audacious goals."

making. In Chapter 7 (the Whatsnew Force), we'll show how a public school system is reinventing itself at a time when turning them around is seemingly impossible.

What follows in this chapter is how a company has chosen to run all of its operations, especially those that focus on the employees, by aspiring to more than they are, to all they can be. There is a big dreamer behind this one.

The dreamer is Robert D. Haas, the great-great-grandnephew of Levi Strauss, founder of the San Francisco–based Levi Strauss & Co., which was founded in 1850.

In 1987, Bob Haas came up with the business equivalent of a cross between Dr. Martin Luther King's dream speech and Moses' tablets (see Snapshot #10 for the text of the Aspirations Statement). As we did with the Ritz-Carlton statements, we have added our own emphasis in italics to identify the kinds of words that typify the Dream Force.

Haas is dead serious about every word in the statement. He crafted it in 1987, took a year to process what this would mean in practical management terms, and then started training everyone in 1989. He now has a department of forty people who make it their business to train, facilitate, and monitor the use and integration of the Aspirations Statement in everything they do. This is a living document, one anyone can use to run interference for him when he feels a need to challenge a directive or even the tone of the person who is delivering the directive.

We caught up with Diane Woods, Vice President of Consulting Services in Human Resources at Levi Strauss. She took a drop in grade and pay to come to Levi Strauss from a buttoned-down utilities company in New Jersey where she constantly had to "battle uphill to be perceived as a valuable contributor." Woods found the environment and attitude at Levi Strauss was completely the opposite: "There is no swimming upstream here, everyone in the company is headed in the same direction, guided by the Aspirations Statement."

A Lifelong Quest

We asked Woods why it is called an Aspirations Statement and not something else. She responded, "Because we know that we will never get there. It is something we aspire to. It is the ideal. It is a lifelong quest." (Remember that sentiment from *The Man of La Mancha*? Here are the lyrics in action.) In reviewing the Aspirations Statement, we noticed something that we had never seen before—a leadership script, the spelling out of specific behaviors that are expected. One of those behaviors is that executives are required to talk to people about their own vulnerabilities, failings, and mistakes. Why? In Haas's words, "It demystifies senior management and removes the stigma traditionally associated with taking risks."

Woods has been present on numerous occasions when an executive has in fact done this. What's the effect? Woods says, "The notion that an executive is vulnerable, is self-aware, and is capable of learning in public, allows the rest of us the opportunity not to hide our mistakes, not to hide our flaws, and also take the opportunity to share with others the things we've learned. Sharing of learning, sharing of vulnerability multiplies by the number of ears that are listening."

We'll revisit Levi Strauss and the Aspirations Statement when we discuss other forces throughout the book, especially around the Now Force in Chapter 4 and around the Oops Force in Chapter 5. But before we move on, a word about whether the Aspirations Statement is making any kind of difference, or whether this is just soft-stuff that plays by the Bay.

Snapshot #10

Aspirations Statement (excerpts)

We want a company that our people are proud of and committed to, where all employees have an opportunity to contribute, learn, grow and advance based on merit, not politics *or background. We want our people to* feel respected, treated fairly, listened to *and involved. Above all, we want* satisfaction from accomplishments and friendships, balanced personal and professional lives, *and to have* fun *in our endeavors.*

What Type of Leadership Is Necessary to Make Our Aspirations a Reality?

New Behaviors: *Leadership that* exemplifies directness, openness *to influence, commitment to the success of others,* willingness to acknowledge our own contributions to problems, *personal accountability. We all want a company that our people are proud of and committed to, where all employees have an opportunity to contribute, learn, grow and advance teamwork and trust. Not only must we model these behaviors but we must* coach others *to adopt them.*

Diversity: *Leadership that values a diverse workforce (age, sex, ethnic group, etc.) at all levels of the organization,* diversity of experience, and diversity of perspectives. *We have committed to taking full advantage of the* rich backgrounds and abilities of all our people *and to promote a greater diversity in positions of influence.* Differing points of view will be sought; *diversity will be valued and honesty rewarded,* not suppressed.

Communications: *Leadership that is clear about Company, unit, and* individual goals *and performance. People must know what is expected of them and receive* timely, honest feedback *on their performance* and career aspirations.

Empowerment: *Leadership that* increases the authority and responsibility *of those closest to our products and customers. By* actively pushing responsibility, *trust and recognition into the organization we can* harness and release the capabilities of all our people.

The *Harvard Business Review* asked Haas if it wasn't "disingenuous to be championing values like empowerment in an environment where workers worry about losing their jobs." Haas replied, "There is an apparent contradiction but not a real one, because our most basic value is honesty. If we have too much capacity, it's a problem that affects the entire company. Sometimes, the only solution is to close a plant, and if we don't have the guts to face that decision, then we risk hurting a lot of people—not just those in one plant. We need to be honest about that." Some would say this is an impossible way to run a company. But they are demonstrating, on a daily practical business level, how it can be done.

Levi Strauss works hard to manage by the Aspirations Statement. For example, potential displacement issues are surfaced, faced, and understood by all parties *before* any decisions are made about technology that might result in the need to lay people off or close a plant. If there is displacement, the Aspirations Statement *guides the process*: Workers get more notice than the law requires, medical benefits are extended, and often support of community organizations continues through the company's philanthropic programs. It may sound like quite a dream, but clearly it's not impossible. Levi's is doing it!

From Companies to Individuals: The Benefits of Impossible

What if you don't work for a Levi Strauss or a Ritz-Carlton hotel? What if you are in a small business and have to make things happen on your own? How can one activate the Dream Force on a smaller scale? Here is one example.

Kim Hammond, daughter of one of the authors, works at Forsyth Fabrics, Inc., a textile warehouse, drapery, and upholstery fabric store in Atlanta. Kim is one of five who specializes in window treatments, giving her a chance to bring her art and painting skills into play. If Paul Simon sings about 50 ways to leave your lover, Kim says there are 500 ways to dress your window. If they don't have what you want, they'll make it 501 ways. There isn't anything they can't do.

One of the things they do especially well is custom design finials, those fancy things at the end of the curtain rod. They make finials and the hardware that goes with them. Like carpentry, they are supposed to measure twice and cast once. Like carpentry, they sometime misread the measure or mess up the casting.

To the point, they discovered on one occasion, with two hours to go before the customer was expecting the new living room drapes to be hung for the open-house party he was throwing that evening, that the brackets didn't fit. Kim got a call from Bob, the head of the workroom, telling her that they would need to cancel the installation because "It's not going to work."

"Bob, who's doing the installation? Is Russ doing it?" Kim asked.

"Well . . ."

"Put Russ on," Kim directed in that voice people get when they are desperate and start improvising.

Russ came on the line and he had already talked to Bob, so he had the party line down pat.

"We can't do it. I've been looking at it and it can't be done," said Russ.

"You can do it. *We* have to do it. You create magic, Russ. You can do it. We have to do it," Kim said earnestly.

"It's impossible," Russ said. "It will not work. It's impossible."

Without pressing the point, Kim set the challenge. "I'll call you back in twenty minutes. See what you can do."

About fifteen minutes later, just before Kim would have had to give the bad news to the customer, an excited Russ called. "I got it! I figured out how to rig it. I can make it work!" he exclaimed. Then quite literally the curtains went up and the open house went on.

Next day the customer, who knew nothing of the behind-the-scenes response to the impossible, walked into the store, found Kim, and bragged about how perfect things were, how everyone noticed the curtains and the finials, what a successful evening it was. He then said, "Let's do the rest of the house."

Kim closed the loop. She immediately called Bob and Russ and told them that there would be two thousand dollars more work coming their way. "And thanks again, guys. I knew you could do it."

What Kim was able to do was use the challenge of doing something impossible to motivate Russ to give it one more try—actually to reach back into the most improvising recesses of his mind and imagination to make it all possible.

Models to LEAP By

Numerous models already exist for start-up enterprises, problem solving, brainstorming, creativity, breakthrough thinking, and processing opportunities. Your corporate training department, no doubt, has its favorite. Not all of these models work for dream fulfillment, so we have included one of our own. We call it LEAP because it creates an image that joins the seven cultural forces and connects dreams to doable actions and concrete processes that already exist.

The LEAP model stands for:

L Where do you want to land?

E What currently exists?

A What are the necessary actions?

P What processes will be engaged?

Where do you want to *land?* Dreaming, stretch goals, making things happen—whatever you want to call them—begins with a destination in mind. No destination, no dreams. The destination can either be a specific target or a general place you want to get to. For example, the new Interhemispheric Bering Strait Tunnel & Railroad Group wants to build an intercontinental railroad between the United States and Russia. President Kennedy wanted us to land on the moon. In the summer of 1995, we, the authors, wanted to land the finished manuscript of this book by fall (it seemed impossible at the time). Ford Motor Company wants to be the number one car maker in the world by the year 2000.

The other way to *land* your dream or hit your stretch-target (we are starting to soften up on insisting that "dream" can be the only operative word) is to set a general destination or place to *land*. For example, 3M, a company renowned for its product innovation, has as its landing point, 30 percent of its annual revenue (about $5 billion) coming from products that have been introduced within the past four years. At Motorola, management doesn't much care what workers decide to work on, they just insist that it result in a tenfold (!) performance change.

What currently *exists?* In other words, what is there to build on? What is the reality? Building sand castles at low tide with the hope of making them last the night is an impossible dream, but one that will be washed away. Stretch goals are one thing, a reality check is quite another matter. If there is no reality at the starting point, there is no hope for the finish line.

There are two general approaches here as well. One extends a process or technology that exists—in other words, more of the same, as impossible as that might be.

Where It All Started

Every third weekend in May, in the gold-rush town of Angels Camp, in the foothills of the Sierra Nevada Mountains, *Rana catesbelana* enthusiasts gather to carry on a sixty-eight-year-old American tradition.

It began on September 18, 1865. Readers of the New York *Saturday Press* no doubt convulsed with laughter when they read a story called, "The Celebrated Jumping Frog of Calaveras County," written by some unknown who called himself Mark Twain. It was the story of Jim Smiley, a jumpin' frog named Dan'l Webster, some Bowery Boys, and a forty-dollar "resk," as Twain called it, on which of two frogs could jump the farthest. The loser did not know that his frog had been force-fed a fistful of buckshot. (Perhaps the origin of the aphorism "get the lead out.")

It turned out Mark Twain's (a.k.a. Samuel Clemens) story about the leaping frog was a leap forward for him as well—his dream of making it to the big time. Until his nonleaping frog story broke, he was a ne'er-do-well journalist knocking about the country trying to figure out what to do with his life. With the acclaim that followed this story he found his calling. Twenty years later he wrote what turned out to be perhaps *the* American classic. Of that book, Ernest Hemingway said, American literature "begins with *Huckleberry Finn.*"

Like a lot of things in America, this *Rana catesbelana*-frog thing has gone global—the Jumping Frog Jubilee is now an international event with entries from countries like China, South Africa, Germany, and Mexico.* The first winner was "Pride of San Joaquin" at 3 feet 9 inches back in 1928. The current world record—are you ready?—was set by "Rosie the Ribiter" in 1986 with a leap of 21 feet 5 3/4 inches. The "trainer" was Lee Giudici of Santa Clara, California.

From the imagination of Mark Twain and the commercialization in Calaveras County, we bring you back to the serious business of this Dream Force and how you can activate it within your organization. Clearly the folks at the Chamber of Commerce in Calaveras County saw a way to put themselves on the map—the mission of any local chamber worth its local business dues. Calaveras County, population 33,000, figures to bring in $1.7 million each spring.

The other approach builds something new or starts from scratch, based on certain principles of science, engineering, or certain expectations about human behavior.

For example, George Koumal, president of Engineering Technology International, dreamed up the idea of a "chunnel" under the Bering Strait, in part because there was one in the works to connect England and France. The reality of the English Channel tunnel makes the Interhemispheric Bering Strait Tunnel & Railroad Group's dream a possible reality.

Starting from scratch, with no precedent, is tougher, no question about it. The Pilgrims and democracy are the best case. Some ideas had been floating around, there

For entry forms and competition rules and tips write Calaveras County Fair, Jumping Frog Jubilee, P. O. Box 96, Angels Camp, CA 95222 or call (209) 736-2561 and ask for Tawny Tesconi.

were some principles to carry over from England and elsewhere, but no nation had tried this one before. One of the most remarkable things about democracy is that it is a constantly evolving idea, a perpetual stretch goal, the impossible ideal that we still keep working at, with a breakthrough here and a breakthrough there. The Wright brothers and other inventors had no precedent, just certain principles and laws of nature they were testing or harnessing, yet their dreams materialized.

What *actions* are necessary? Here is where dreams can get stuck. Why? Because we tend to do things the same way we have always done them. Dreams simply don't materialize when we do things the same old way. So the objective of this critical third step in the model is to explore *all* the possibilities, examine *all* the options, even dream up new ways to make it happen. It is essential to begin with *all* the options in mind *and* on paper. Write them all down—the goofy ones and the more traditional ones.

Sometimes a new slant on an existing process will do the trick.* We call this improvising; it is one of the seven cultural forces that defines us and we write about it in Chapter 6. Americans love to improvise. (Remember, necessity is the mother of invention.) Improvising is closely connected to the Dream Force and making things a reality. Thomas Edison tried a thousand different approaches before he could shed any light on what he was doing.

The Interhemispheric Bering Strait Tunnel & Railroad Group has engineers like Koumal figuring out how to build the fifty-mile tunnel under the Bering Strait and thinking through the logistics of building the five thousand miles of railroad needed to connect Alaska and Russia through the Chukchi Peninsula. Others are busy raising the estimated $40 billion and attending to other details.

3M, now an established and respected global corporation,† takes the unusual action of requiring its engineers and designers to use 15 percent of their time to think up new products and innovations in order to fill the product end of their business goal. The Ford Motor Company abandoned the usual local way of making cars around the world in 1994 when it designed a uniform platform for all its cars worldwide— something that has never been done in the history of automobile manufacturing.

What *process* will be engaged? It is our observation that most other models go soft at this point. They create general "ways forward" or vague "paths to take" that sound right, but then seem to float off into space, unconnected to reality. These "next steps" are not sufficiently grounded in real business practices and established procedures. That is why our model has the word process, not path or plan or proposition.

By process we mean a tested business way of getting something done, an acceptable existing practice or procedure for implementing an idea. Process suggests completeness and implies doing work for someone else that adds value or produces results. In other words, it is not busy work.

Path implies that you can blaze your own trail or go your own way. That is not what we mean. Dreams often collapse on execution: the proposal is too fancy, the

---

*A fabulous book for stimulating these kinds of ideas is A Wack on the Side of the Head, by Roger Van Oech.

†They didn't start out that way. See Chapter 5 where we discuss the Oops Force. It's a miracle, actually a set of miracles, that got 3M off the ground.

business assumptions are not thoroughly researched, the revenue forecast is too optimistic, or the time line is unrealistic.

Connecting the dream to an established process ensures a greater likelihood that it will be accepted and acted on, especially in a larger company. Entrepreneurs often bypass these processes with disastrous consequences. For impossible goals to be met and for dreams to materialize, they need to be tethered to appropriate processes.

In some cases, like Allied Signal, which we write about in Chapter 4, companies are taking traditional ways of doing things and changing the processes themselves, in effect treating the change process as an impossible dream. At Allied Signal, cycle time, the length of time it takes to go from product conception to customer, is being radically reengineered to cut the time in half. So, in this case, the process itself was subjected to the LEAP-type model thinking.

3M again. We show in Chapter 7 how the processes they used enabled them to make a "quantum leap" in the design and manufacture of an ordinary household item like the scouring pad. Concurrent engineering has been around for a while (it used to be sequential engineering, the step-by-step process of product or service design). 3M doesn't call it this, but what they do sure looks like concurrent innovation.

So LEAP.

Dream Fake Sheet

We began this chapter with a powerful observation by Carl Sandburg: "Nothing happens, unless first a dream." We then showed how powerful the word itself is and provided a high-performance definition for dreams that companies should tap into. By example, we showed what the Ritz-Carlton Hotels and Levi Strauss & Company are doing to activate the Dream Force. Above all, we've shown that the ability to make dreams come true is the real force in America. Anybody can dream, but America has institutionalized the dream process and created a national environment where anything is possible. From the first Pilgrims to new immigrants each day, America is the only place on earth where people come to fulfill their dreams.

★ The word dream is a powerful, but underused business term. Conventionally, business sees dreams as something intangible, a waste of time, a private activity that leads to complacency. However, the high-performance definition that we outlined (see page 77) brings a practical and tangible definition to dreams that does just the opposite: it can get us focused, energized, and up and going. Dreams can engage us for a longer time than less emotionally charged terms.

★ Use whatever term works. The business key to the Dream Force is not necessarily in the use of the word, but in embracing the energy that Americans instinctively have for doing the impossible. If words like vision, mission, stretch target, and even lesser terms like goal, plan, or job, can be used to generate and sustain high performance, use them. The objective is to engage people in a process that enables them to max out for the cause, whatever the cause may be, and feel good for having made the commitment.

★ The search for perfection is not a motivator. Unlike the Japanese, Americans have a utilitarian approach to a task. The objective is to get it to work, preferably immediately, rather than to set out in an endless quest for incremental improvements that lead to perfection somewhere on down the road. Staid goals bore Americans, and the zero-defects movement that was invented by an American is only alive and well in Japan (see page 79).

★ Engage everyone in understanding the total mission. Usually one of the best-kept secrets in an American company is its strategic plan. Created in isolation from the rank and file, it rarely becomes a tool for harnessing everyone's energy and sense of purpose. In American business, strategic plans or operational strategies are usually meted out on a need-to-know basis, with top executives usually keeping the plan to themselves. Yet, according to an international study, it is one of only three universal management practices that can directly boost quality, productivity, and profitability in any company, regardless of size or industry (see page 83). To paraphrase the prophet Isaiah, without a shared vision the company may perish.

Two companies, the Ritz-Carlton Hotels and Levi Strauss, are held up as role models for how to activate the Dream Force. Ritz-Carlton uses the more pedestrian term "mission," but employs other powerful words to engage each level of the organization in carrying out the goals of the company. Levi Strauss uses the term "aspirations" to engage each of its employees in the creation of its work process, procedures, management practices, and everyday business decisions (see pages 88 and 91).

★ Put your dreams to work. Dreams don't materialize on their own. Because of the intrinsic motivation for breakthrough thinking—and action—we provide a LEAP performance model to help you actualize your big ideas or dreams. The model (see page 93) is a four-step plan for bringing a dream out of the sky and making it work for you. There are many similar models, but this one adds a step that is often missing in the others: Linkage to an existing process that is acceptable in your company or has worked for you in the past. Most models fail to connect to business reality; this model ends or brings you to this fact of dream-making.

Dreams have intrinsic value to Americans. They engage us in what is possible, in the future, where our security lies and our hopes materialize. For business they are an endless gold mine, the Midas touch.

> *The dreamer dies, but never dies the dream,*
> *Though Death shall call the whirlwind to his aid,*
> *Enlist men's passions, trick their hearts with hate,*
> *Still shall the Vision live. Say nevermore*
> *That dreams are fragile things. What else endures*
> *Of all this broken world save only dreams.*
>
> Dana Burnet
> "Who Dreams Shall Live"

Interlude

The American Game

Sports metaphors are usually messy things. They start off with the right intention, but sooner or later someone will poke so many holes in your favorite one that you wish you had never started in the first place. Nonetheless, it seems as if everyone has one or two. They are particularly popular with American business*men*. Increasingly, American businesswomen will talk about quarterbacking a team, full-court presses, and throwing someone a curve, but we think it is safe to say that it is not the second language it is to men.

Sports metaphors are completely loathsome to European business folks, but that doesn't stop Americans from using them in speeches (lectures they are called over there), negotiations, and consultations. They go over like punting on first down. Besides, when we make reference to football outside of England, Europeans are thinking of a game played with a round white ball with hexagonal black patches. And while the Japanese get the drift of baseball, they play the game altogether differently, having adapted our rules to fit their culture. More about that in a bit.

Nevertheless, baseball is the one game that explains what America is all about. For example, it is more likely that a professional baseball player will be self-taught, illiterate, or a mere high school graduate than college-educated. Unlike the other major sports, the audiences come in all ages, shapes, and sizes. Regardless of the level of literacy or athletic ability, a fan can quote and instantly update the most complicated and intricate set of statistics that fluctuate from day to day.

Here is why this languid game, so full of ritual and tedium, resonates explosively with the most profound emotions in the American psyche: It is the only team sport where the *person* scores, not the object. And, profoundly for Americans, you come *home* to score.*

The baseball metaphor dominates everyday speech, unlike any other sport: *your turn at bat, don't throw me a curve, who's on first, safe at home, it's time to play*

In football, basketball, hockey, soccer, tennis, etc., the object scores. In baseball, you don't run across home plate with the ball in your hand. In other sports you defend the home territory and "invade" the opponents' turf.

hard ball, etc. In some cases it even provides a shorthand way to communicate a change in public policy, as in the *three strikes and you're out.*

The baseball metaphor offers American business important insights into a management style that resonates with Americans and summarizes much of what we have said in this book, particularly in Chapters 5 and 6, where we talk about how we make mistakes, learn from them, and improve. The metaphor is almost endless. Following are some of the major ones; you'll no doubt think of a few more.

★ You don't have to do it right the first time. In fact, employees (players) get multiple chances to do it right.

★ Everyone on the starting team gets numerous chances to make a difference, to win the game, to be a hero.

★ The team is there for defensive purposes; the offense comes from individuals.

★ All infields are the same dimension, addressing the need for standardization, precision, measurement, conformance. All outfields are different, addressing the need for variation, vagueness, and a range of self-expression.

★ Home runs, the coveted part of the offense, occur only in the part of the field where variation exists.

★ Trainers and coaches are strategically placed on the field to advise *during* the game and provide immediate feedback to the players (employees).

★ Each manager knows the individual strengths and weaknesses of each player and uses that information to the team's competitive advantage.

★ The game is played every day.

★ You never give up: There is always the bottom of the ninth when the *home* team gets to bat last.

★ And for everyone, fans and players alike (especially for the Boston Red Sox and the Chicago Cubs), there is always *next year!*

At the Old Ball Game

Baseball is the most written-about sport in the world. As of September 1995, 12,992 books had been written or contained baseball stories, countless (no one knows) movies have been made, one nine-part (inning) popular TV documentary, and more than a dozen magazines. There is even a Society for American Baseball Research with 63,000 dues-paying members.* One journal, called *Nine*, is devoted to "the history and social policy perspectives" of the game. A recent issue had these thought-provoking entries: "Nine Principles of Successful Affirmative Action," "The Religion of Baseball: Psychology Perspectives," and "When Technology and Culture Collide: The Advance of Night Baseball." But best of all, and unlike any other sport, baseball even has its own song! Who doesn't know, or has never heard, at least the chorus to "Take Me Out to the Ball Game"?

For thirty-five dollars a year you can join SABR and get in on the game. Write to P.O. Box 93183, Cleveland, OH 44101 or call 216-575-0500. Membership includes a subscription to National Pastime, written by members, and Baseball Research Journal, the serious business of SABR.

Besuboru

If American baseball players are a romping fraternity of free-spirited, free-spitting, free-spending adolescents on a beer-bust in the park, it is also true that Japanese besuboru (as they would say) players are chivalric, self-effacing, self-sacrificing Shinto monks. If an American baseball hero is likened to a lone gunslinger come to Dodge City to tidy things up, in Japan the baseball hero is the slugger who looks at a fat pitch and lays down a sacrifice bunt.

Robert Whiting, author of *You Gotta Have Wa*, tells how the Japanese have adapted our baseball to their culture. In short, their game mirrors their culture: it is more civil than ours. The word "wa" means harmony.

The Japanese game is not exactly the game we know. It is nine men moving in stylized formation, laying out quadratic equations on equilateral triangles. It's a game adapted to the rules of an ancient culture that was formed on tiny islands so crowded with cheek-to-jowl humanity that suppression of impulse became the only means of maintaining civility. As one Japanese baseball great expressed it, "The real man in Japan is the one who keeps his feelings to himself, so as not to disturb the harmony of others." (His name isn't Steinbrenner-san.)

Consider some differences:

Where the majors start spring practice in March, with a few hours in the Florida sun, the Japanese start theirs in January, with all-day workouts, and into-the-night lectures. Where Americans curtail workouts on hot summer days to conserve energy, the Japanese step up training in the heat in the belief that extra work helps beat the heat.

Attention is paid in Japan to opposing players' blood type in the belief that it is a predictor of behavior on the field. For instance, a type-A blood type is thought to indicate an inclination to be easily intimidated.

In America at the end of the season most ballplayers head for the golf links or go north to hunt deer. In Japan, they head for training camp and twelve-hour-a-day workouts and a 10 P.M. curfew.

Japanese managers stress training with the slogan "Practice until you die!" Japanese pitchers throw hard every day, unlike American pitchers, who stay on a four-day rotation. However, Whiting says that the training pays off: Japanese ballplayers make fewer errors and are more precise bunters, bunting three times as often as Americans.

Whiting reports that when the professional players union was established in Japan in 1986, the union head quickly declared, "We will never strike like the Americans do. It wouldn't be fair to the fans."

Take me out to the ball game,
Take me out with the crowd,
Buy me some peanuts and
Cracker Jack,
I don't care if I never get back;

Let me root, root, root for the
Home team,
If they don't win, it's a shame;
For it's one, two, three strikes,
You're out, at the old ball game.

It's more than a song really, it's another national anthem. "Take Me Out to the Ball Game," written in 1908 by Jack Norworth with music by Albert Von Tilzer, was around for years before Congress adopted the one we sing before the game starts.

We all know the chorus to the baseball anthem, but most don't know that it's a song about Katie Casey, who, to put it bluntly, was a baseball nut, or as Norworth's lyrics put it, "baseball mad, had the fever, had it bad." Her nameless boyfriend wants to take her to the show, but she says no and tells him "what you can do," thereby setting up the chorus we know.

Michael Beckerman, music history teacher at the University of California, Santa Barbara, has a theory about why the song is an anthem. He suggests that it may have survived because the style "perfectly fits America's vision of baseball," since it belongs to a popular subgenre of so-called "Gay Nineties" songs that include "Daisy Bell" ("Bicycle Built for Two") and "East Side, West Side." But it's the composition, the "clever composition" in Beckerman's words, that may have more to do with it. He describes them this way:

The chorus begins with a joyous octave leap, a metaphorical spring, up to "me." Then a kind of relaxed pentatonic inflection spills down to "ball game." The leap is repeated with "Take me," and the line hovers on "crowd," but this time it dissolves into a whining demand for "peanuts" and "Cracker Jack" with a self-mockingly pathetic move to a minor chord. Note how childishly spoiled is "I don't care if I never get back," with the accent uproariously on "never." The words "Root, root, root" replace "Take me out" when the opening is repeated, a kind of hooting cheer. Then the grandest touch: the onomatopoeic conclusion, "For it's one, two, three strikes, you're out, at the old ball game," sound for all the world like the whoosh of futile swings at low curveballs in the summer dirt. Finally, the words, "ball game," which dominate the first line with a downward leap, end it with stretched-out (may it never end!) upward steps.

Management Metaphors

The person who has made a management "science" out of sports and business is Robert W. Keidel, a senior consultant to the Wharton Center for Applied Research and author of several books, including *Game Plans: Sports Strategies for Business and Corporate Players*. In Snapshot #11 we greatly oversimplify his work to help drive home several of his observations and a few of ours.

Baseball, as we have outlined, is a pastoral, bygone, nostalgic sport of individuals playing on a team. In Keidel's words, it is about "autonomy" and "decentralization." It is quite applicable to the sales and marketing function in a company. It is ambivalent about time—in conflict with the Now Force—because there is always the bottom of the ninth for last-minute heroics—not in conflict with the Now Force.

Above all, baseball is about individual performance and personal contribution.

Snapshot #11

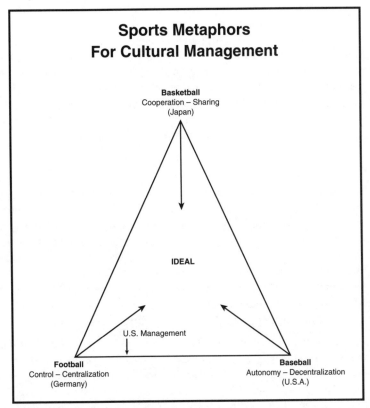

Source: Adapted from Robert Keidel Associates

Football is a centralized control game with specialty teams—one for offense, one for defense, and multiple teams for special occasions and opportunities. It is representative of the management style we see in manufacturing or mass production. Football tends to be managed from a more global perspective with plays often called by one individual who "sees" the whole field.

The game is played on a standardized field, marked off in precise yard-by-yard measures; no deviations are permissible. There is a lot of grunt work that goes unrecognized by the average player, who tends to concentrate his attention on the *progress of the object,* rather than the play of the team. Only a few designated players get to invade the "enemy's" territory to score a bunch of points at one time. Tie games are permissible and the game is played with strict time limitations.

In football, a great deal of preparation goes into the development of a game plan that is usually closely adhered to, regardless of the score in the game. The preset game plan is most often viewed as a simple matter of proper execution in order to win the game—regardless of what the other team does. (Any changes usually occur at half-time when the game plan can be adjusted.)

In general, the football metaphor represents the management style of the Germans, with adherence to standards and measurements, focused team discipline, and sophisticated approach to the game of business.

Basketball is played by fewer players in a smaller venue. As Keidel would point out, it is more a finesse game of cooperation and sharing. The players are more homogeneous. Each player is required to play all over the field on both offense and defense and master all of the basics of the game—run, dribble, pass, block, and shoot. Although there is a general game plan, it is immediately adapted to what the other team has to offer. It is more reflective of an R&D function in business and mirrors the Japanese approach to competition and personnel management with their intense cross-functional training and high adaptability. During time-outs, the entire team huddles off the playing field in a quasi-circle, reminiscent of Japan's quality circle approach to business production, which was a dismal failure in America.

Batter Up

In the final analysis, football is the closest metaphor to the way American businesses are run today. But baseball is American culture. It's tethered to the seven forces. Above all, this evocative game—now full of adversity and avarice like society itself—comes down to individuals who played the game and to the memories that all of us have of them.

Ken Burns, the genius behind the monumental PBS TV documentary *Baseball*, which was four years in the making, said of that experience, "We were hardly prepared for the complex emotions the game summoned up." In the preface to the companion book for this popular PBS TV series, Burns commented:

> We quickly developed an abiding conviction that the game of baseball offered a unique prism through which one could see refracted much more than the history of games won and lost, teams rising and falling, rookies arriving and veterans saying farewell. The story of baseball is also the story of race in America; of immigration and assimilation; of the struggle between labor and management; of popular culture and advertising; of myth and the nature of heroes; villains, and buffoons; of the role of women and class and wealth in our society. The game is a repository of age-old American verities, of standards against which we continually measure ourselves, and yet at the same time a mirror of the present moment in our modern culture—including all of our most contemporary failings.

Now as Willie Mays might call out, "Say hey, it's your turn at bat!"

For you, it could be early in the game and you know you'll get a couple of more times up before it's over. Or it could be late in the game and this could be your last at bat. As Yogi Berra would remind us, "It gets late early out there."

You could be in a hitting slump with nothing connecting at work or at home, missing your deadlines, seemingly striking out at every turn, not following through on your commitments, simply not keeping your eye on the ball, or just sour about the way things are going out there. Or, you could be on a roll, connecting on every opportunity, sacrificing when necessary, putting it over the fence when you have to.

None other than Walt Whitman said in 1848, "I see great things in baseball. It's our game—the American game."

Chapter 3

Big, Bigger, Bust
America's Obsession with Big and More

We don't have a definition for *big*. By its very nature big can hardly be defined: One person's big is another person's small; today's big is tomorrow's puny. In the American language, the words *big* and *more* are closer to nouns than adjectives, goals rather than modifiers. In a big land like ours, we don't have the constraints of Japan, where small is big. With our natural bounty (which we sometimes squander in a big way) we don't worry about other nations that don't have the resources or technology to leverage those gifts of nature.

But having identified Big and More as the third of the seven cultural forces that define Americans, we will show you how it has been used and abused. We'll provide you with five ways to leverage this force, and provide an American model for business performance that some of us are already using, unaware of its power. We'll also provide some ideas about balance and the business advantage of small, or thinking big about small.

Big and More is a force that was formative in the early days of the republic and it defines much of what we are today, from big discount warehouse stores to megamergers and instant millionaires. Throughout our history, in fact, bigness has played a significant role in defining business and culture.*

The Big and More Force is the most complex of the seven. It has three facets: Big; More; and the obsession with being number one, which are sometimes interchangeable, and often inseparable. The force is both constructive and destructive. It enriches and entraps, it builds up and brings down, it increases options and decreases choices, it offers security and invites abuse. Unchecked, it is the one force that can threaten the American way of life. It requires due diligence to make sure the ends

---

Kenneth C. Davis, in his best-selling book Don't Know Much About History: Everything You Need to Know About American History but Never Learned, *devotes a good part of the text to the influence of Big in America. Two of his eight chapters pay particular homage to the Big Force in America. These chapter headings are: "When Monopoly Wasn't a Game: The Growing Empire from Wild West to World War I" and "Boom to Bust to Big Boom: From the Jazz Age and Great Depression to Hiroshima."*

don't justify the means. Big and More plays right off the Dream Force (covered in the previous chapter) and it is fueled by the Now Force (next chapter).

In this country, Big and More is always happening all around us. We see it in the constant megamergers of corporate America in banking and telecommunications. But one of the most interesting examples of this force at work is in retail.

Three Acres of Home Improvement

The Grand Opening was on Thursday. By Saturday morning a feeding frenzy was on. A tidal wave of cars from all points was endlessly converging on a vast parking lot that was overflowing onto adjacent lawns, spilling into walkways, blocking loading areas, and ignoring all sense of suburban civility. The destination was a new Home Depot three miles from Morrison's house in Colorado Springs.

This was Home Depot #364 in the United States and the second one in Colorado. It's a three-acre, roofed-over temple to the homesteading, nest-feathering, green-gardening, cement-pouring, fence-building, home-improving, "please-Ethel-I'd-rather-do-it-myself," plastic-wielding citizens of the U.S. It's crammed with over fifty thousand different kinds of homey nifties for comfort, convenience, and cosseting. It is *big,* and it has *more* of everything than one could imagine.

The building has been designed with one way to get in and two ways to get out. On the congested way in, the first thing customers face is a sign-up table inviting each and every one to embrace and bond with a Home Depot credit card. Once inside you have a choice of directions in which to proceed, but why bother. Dead ahead lies an irresistible ambush.

If you've always wanted to replace a toilet bowl but didn't know how, this is your Harvard, and the tuition is free. Because right up there on the wall is a display that explains the five simple steps leading to a royal flush. The display also shows the parts and tools required. And if you have any doubts about undertaking the operation, there's a highly trained and knowledgeable associate in an orange apron standing by who just can't wait to tell you more than you want to know.

Going left we ran into Ken, who like all of the associates is wearing the orange carpenter's apron. Ken is the kitchen-cabinet-layout virtuoso. When I asked about a layout, Ken said, "If you come back with all of the measurements, I can set 'em right up here in the computer and with a little pointin' and a little clickin' I can give you a printout floor plan in less than two minutes that'll be within a cat's whisker of how much it will cost for a brand-new remodeled kitchen, you betcha."

Before I pose my next question, Ken is telling the lady next to me that she can have the Moen two-handled hi-spot kitchen faucet with spray for just $109 plus tax and that it carries a limited lifetime warranty. And, he adds, in case she hadn't noticed it on every page of the mailing piece that went to every home in this city of three hundred thousand, "We buy big, so you save big."

Big Competition

Home Depot started in 1978 with three stores in Atlanta, and now it has over 350 and plans to double that by 1998. As the company grew, its sales went from $50 million in 1981 to over $12 billion in 1994, with most of that growth coming in the past five years. That's Big and More any way you figure it.

Of course, it is the insatiable appetite for Big and More that brings Americans to Home Depot in the first place. Like the Price Clubs, Barnes & Noble superstores, and the other mega-retailers, Home Depot not only represents the Big and More Force, but the people who operate the chain understand it and they use it in their retailing. They know that Big and More is a fundamental part of the American psyche, that American consumers respond to it favorably, and that their customers are more likely to make purchases when they are surrounded by this force.

Take the lighting fixtures department as an example. It's a low-hung forest the length of a catcher's throw from home plate to second, and about as wide. Hanging like a thick canopy, or thatch, are chandeliers and two-tone tole lamps, brass, swivels, fixtures beaded and beveled with shades, indirects, dangling ceiling-fan–lighting combos, carriage lamps in choices and choices of choices and sizes, not to mention the fluorescents, the incandescents, and the high-intensity halogens. And if that is insufficient, there are recessed and pinpoint lamps galore. All are presided over by a couple of smiling associates in orange aprons answering dumb questions, willingly crawling the recesses to deliver the hard-thought choice into the waiting hands of eager customers who in the meantime have changed their minds.

To the right of this is the aisle leading to the local Brazilian rain forest. It's now the end of August, and Wal-Mart and Kmart have long since shut down their gardening enclaves and moved in the leaf compactors, rakes, mulchers, and the getting-ready-for-winter doodads. The florists are showing mums and awaiting pumpkins, squash, and tied bunches of bittersweet, but not Home Depot. They are displaying a half acre of botanical green-growth, and the place is jammed with humanity, as though it were the first day of spring.

On my way home I wondered what the draw was at Home Depot. Why the frenzy? I thought about Schoch's, a local legend micro–hardware store like no other in the United States. A gentle lady runs it on a side street. It's been there since the First World War, and everything for sale is dumped in piles on top of the counters. You want those rubber rings for your Ball canning jars? Home Depot doesn't sell them and Schoch's does. However, you have to ask Mrs. Schoch where to look for them. Just don't bother her when she's getting one of those doillywhoppers for the top of your forty-year-old pressure cooker. She also has wicks for your kerosene lamp and other things that Home Depot doesn't have. But she doesn't have orange-aproned associates and she's getting on in years.

I drove by Crissey-Fowler, the oldest established hardware store of the seven "Lumber-Retail" stores in the area, which has been trading for 121 years. They provide a wide range of products and services and they are also big. But they close on Saturday at 1 P.M., and they are never open on Sunday. And they are not big like Home Depot: *big* big; big in every way; big in a way that makes you want to shop; big in a way that makes you think to yourself, "I *need* that" or, "I really should install a new shower body. I'm sure I could do that myself with all of these tools and materials."

It may not surprise you then that Home Depot doesn't worry about stores like Crissey-Fowler or Schoch's. This is a $124 billion, fast-growing business, and it is number one in its field.

The advantage to being number one is that you don't have to look over your shoulder; you can concentrate on what lies ahead. The disadvantage is that you and your strategy are in full view. The competitive advantages you have created for today will soon be the givens for everyone else (the Whatsnew Force at work in business). The challenge is continuous development, renewal, inventiveness, and acute awareness of the Big and More Force in American life.

How to Get Bigger

It is clear in this business, and it's true in any business, that you don't get bigger sitting around worrying about the other guy. There are three general strategies for growth, two are popular, the third is the new kid on the block:

1. Acquire from outside
2. Grow from inside
3. Redefine the business

The first way to get bigger is to acquire more. Home Depot has taken that popular business approach, acquiring nine Bowater Home Centers in 1984, three Modell's Shoppers World stores in 1988, and seven Waban stores in 1993. Big problems are usually associated with acquisitions, and the Bowater acquisitions caused Home Depot's earnings to "dip" in 1985 for the first time in its short history.

The second approach to bigger is more of the same: duplicating, triplicating, quadruplicating what works. This approach has been part of the magic for Home Depot, which began with three original stores in 1979, adding four in 1980, four the next year, two the next, nine in 1983, and six more in 1984. By the time the nineties rolled in, Home Depot was tripling its pace, adding twenty-five stores in 1990, thirty in 1991, and forty in 1992.

The third approach is redefining the business by creating new marketing strategies, introducing new products and services, or inventing new stores. Home Depot is doing all three. Early on, "low day-in day-out pricing" was introduced, thereby eliminating the standard retail practice of special sales events that are both costly and time consuming to mount and manage. In 1995, Home Depot introduced Right at Home, a product line of coordinated home furnishings, including textiles, wall coverings, floor tile, and those multiple-choice lighting fixtures described earlier (☑ 🖫).

Then, in 1994, Home Depot opened its first Expo Design Centers (❘) in San Diego and Atlanta, offering upscale interior designed products and services. And in 1995, Quincy, Illinois, was the site of the first CrossRoads store (🖫), which offers professional building and home-improvement supplies as well as farming and ranching supplies (☑).

With the success of these pioneer stores, Home Depot is bound to duplicate the new formats and services as a growth plan in the coming years. In the meantime, Bernard Marcus and Arthur Blank, who started Home Depot when they were let go by Handy Dan Home Improvement Centers in a corporate buyout, are no doubt thinking of still more new store configurations (❘ 🖫). As the saying goes, only the lead dog gets a change of scenery.

Writing Selling the Book on Big

Anyone familiar with the Upper West Side of Manhattan should notice a glaring omission in the sidebar litany of big offerings—especially book readers: the four-story 66th Street Barnes & Noble *super*store.

How Big Is Big?—Part 1

In America, from the minute you are born, people want to know how big you are. There are big skies in Montana, fifty-two-ounce steaks in Kansas, and big plans in Washington.

Both authors have lived in the Big Apple; Hammond still does. New Yorkers are jaded when folks talk about Big and More. This is such a big place that if someone tells you that you are one in a million, there are still eight more people just like you.

Within a few blocks of where Hammond lives on the Upper West Side, there are fifteen, count 'em, fifteen movie theaters (one with the big eight-story-high IMAX 3-D screen billed as the next adventure in movies); a concert hall; two opera houses, one of which is also a ballet theater; one jazz joint; two live-stage-show theaters; five coffee spots (with more on the way); four gyms; three highly-rated restaurants (where small-portion *nouvelle cuisine* is out and big American farmland portions are in); seventeen more run-of-the-mill (by New York standards) restaurants; a half-dozen convenience stores with one open twenty-four hours a day; a music store (with 90,000 compact discs, 20,000 videos, and 15,000 laser discs to choose from); six different banks you can get money from round the clock; and two or three of everything else one needs to survive in a big city.

Just around the corner you can buy the Bible in any one of sixty-eight languages from the American Bible Society and take it to the biggest city-center park in the United States, which is literally a stone's-throw away.

One block past the Bible store, near Columbus Circle, is the old Paramount building being converted by Donald Trump into a luxury residence and hotel. In full stride with the Big and More Force, the construction site claims, in blazing bold letters, that it is "The most important new address in the world . . . the ultimate in luxury." Only in New York, only Donald Trump. But people will line up to live there, and the Big and More Force will have had a lot to do with it.

As of this writing there are 268 Barnes & Noble superstores, all of which use the Big and More Force much the way Home Depot does, with much the same results. These superstores dwarf most hometown libraries, the way Broadway shows dwarf high school plays. There are anywhere from 60,000 to 175,000 titles in each superstore—and remember, they have multiple copies of many of those titles on the shelves and boxes more in their warehouses. You can spend the day there in pleasant surroundings, attractive wood features, antique-style chairs, reading tables, and a cappuccino bar—and that's the point. People come, browse, stay, and then buy in this big, library-like atmosphere.

All this is what Leonard Riggio began dreaming about as a bookstore sales clerk working his way through night school at New York University. Bored with studying engineering, at the age of twenty-four he borrowed five thousand dollars to open a college bookstore of his own in Greenwich Village called the Student Book Exchange NYC. That was in 1965.

A few years later he bought other college bookstores. Then a few more years later (by now it's 1971) he paid $1.2 million for a one-hundred-year-old, big, money-losing bookstore called Barnes & Noble. With another acquisition in 1979, Marboro Books, Riggio's company went into the mail-order and publishing business.

Then—and this is the way Big and More Force really works—Riggio started eyeing the 754 B. Dalton mall bookstores. He teamed up with Dutch retailer Vendex International to buy them for $275 million. Like others we'll meet in this chapter, Riggio more than doubled his outlets and inventory overnight—the ultimate expression of Big and More.

The idea for superstores came from Bookstop, the first book superstore chain in the country, which got started in 1982. Barnes & Noble acquired it in 1990 and used that company's big idea to get bigger in size and bigger in marketing strategy.

Barnes & Noble is not slowing its expansion: By the end of 1995, it will have 352 superstores and plans on more than 200 additional stores over the next three years. However, bookstores in malls were big back when malls were big; malls aren't that big anymore, so it is no surprise that Barnes & Noble's mall business is a drag on the company's sales. Business at the superstores is up 12.6 percent in fiscal 1995, but down 2.3 percent in the mall stores. So it is closing the once-big-idea mall stores about as fast as it is opening the other ones. What's working is the big superstore idea, making Barnes & Noble the number one bookseller in the United States as well as the fastest-growing.

The Power of Big: Five Leverage Points

We've already started to peel the onion of Big and More with the examples of Home Depot and Barnes & Noble. In many ways these companies are not unlike the other seven-force companies we have been writing about in this book—"big" companies all: Disney, FedEx, Ford, Johnson & Johnson, Hewlett-Packard, and 3M. One thing in particular that all of these companies share is the leverage power of being big. There are five principal leverage points that can be exploited with size:

1. Economy of scale

2. Risk tolerance

3. Source of employee motivation

4. More customer choice

5. Room for small

1. Economy of Scale

Home Depot and Barnes & Noble use this built-in advantage of Big and More: Barnes & Noble is able to discount all *New York Times* bestsellers by 35 percent while Home Depot even uses it as a marketing come-on: "We buy big so that you can save big."

You won't catch the upscale Ritz-Carlton Hotels using that approach, but it was this precise leverage of Big and More that made the sale of 49 percent of its stock to bigger Marriott Hotels such an attractive deal. Ritz benefits from the big leverage Marriott has on suppliers from soaps and laundry to fish and chips.

The danger with this leverage point is that once the discounting begins, it is hard to discontinue. Thus, these economies of scale are often the only margin of profitability.

2. Risk Tolerance

It's obvious that a bigger company can take more risks than a smaller one. Big gives you some cushion for those so-called, calculated risks,* it lets you experiment and take chances that have big rewards.

Kevin Helliker's front-page August 25, 1995, story in *The Wall Street Journal* about Wal-Mart puts a human face on this risk-taking dimension of Big and More. Big Wal-Mart was willing to take a chance on Michael Quinn, a twenty-four-year-old college dropout, who is now running the Wal-Mart store in Greenville, Mississippi. After starting off as a part-time clerk and bathroom cleaner while in high school, Quinn dropped out of college at nineteen and became a full-time assistant manager. Now, five years later, he runs a business that generates $22 million a year and manages two hundred associates. He puts in big hours, sometimes up to eighty hours a week, and he has moved seven times in the last eight years. But his big efforts have paid off for himself and others; in a store he managed in Ferriday, Louisiana, he "reduced inventory losses to 0.82 percent of sales from 3.2 percent for an annual savings of $150,000." He raised the store's profit margin above 5 percent, which resulted in a profit-sharing check for his employees, who had gone without one for years. And, as Helliker notes, he's making about $75,000 "in a town where luxury apartments rent for $350 a month."

3. Source of Employee Motivation

The Big and More Force as a source of motivation for employees was a nice surprise discovery for us during our research. We found this one at Disney, one of the companies cited in the first Tom Peters and Robert Waterman book, *In Search of Excellence.* Since then Disney executives in Orlando talk about excellence and the pursuit of excellence—and they believe in it. But excellence is not one of the seven cultural forces: Americans are not motivated by the search for perfection, because it is not something that can be achieved immediately. Besides, perfection implies a dead end for Americans, no place to go. (We'll explain more about America's avoidance of perfection in Chapter 5.)

What we noticed in our interviews at Disney is that the real source for motivation of its employees was the opportunity to do something bigger! Implicit in their way of doing things, bigger means the opportunity to do something better, but not necessarily to perfection. In example after example, it was obvious to us, and it became clear to them, that the energy source for employees was simply the opportunity to do something again—only bigger this time.

4. More Customer Choice

This is about more than just variety of goods and services. With the financial security of big, companies can afford to offer customers entirely new approaches to their

---

*On taking "calculated risks," we have always been fond of a refrain from Dana Cound, author of Quality Through Leadership, "Show me your calculations."

business. Barnes & Noble did this with the superstore concept. RCA did it in the 1940s with television. Although television had been invented and was proven to be a workable concept, no one got into the business at first. This was because no one wanted to broadcast signals until there were televisions in homes to receive them and no one wanted to manufacture TV sets until there were signals! RCA was a big conglomerate that not only manufactured electronic components (such as radios), but owned NBC as well (at the time a radio broadcaster). This allowed them to start both processes at once and be the first to offer television to the nation.

5. Room for Small

An obvious one with a surprise twist. The discovery here was not that Schoch's hardware store will survive in the shadow of Home Depot or that microbreweries have found a niche in a big suds market or that a small work group is more nimble and responsive than a big centralized department. The surprise is that when small is given the chance to *act* big, it performs better.

Case in point, Hewlett-Packard: This diversified manufacturing and service company of eighty-seven thousand employees is big by most industry standards. It has twelve major product and service divisions around the world. But they are broken down into sixty-two smaller units that range into various sizes. Size is not the issue, however, because they all get to act big. That means create their own mission statements, define their own business, establish their own policies, invent their own processes, manage as they see fit, and change when they wish—everything the big boys get to do in Palo Alto.

The only condition is they must pledge to do business in keeping with HP's high ethical standards and they must meet certain financial goals. Everything else is a big call for a smaller group.

How We Got So Big

How did we become so enthralled with bigness? Just as happened with choice and dreams, America's love affair with largeness was locked-in early on, and it has continued to reassert itself throughout our history. So, to understand why we love big is to understand how we got big.*

America was always the land of plenty, of big chances and big opportunities. Thomas Jefferson was probably the first to get the Big and More Force going in new America. In 1803 he made a quick deal with Napoleon that nearly doubled the size of our landscape overnight. This deal, known as the Louisiana Purchase, stretched the young American nation from the west bank of the Mississippi to the Rockies.

Jefferson's brash purchase set off one of the first big battles between the executive branch of government and Congress, one that persists to this day. The issue is the constitutional requirement that the President seek the *advice and consent* of Congress with respect to treaties and related foreign affairs. The Iran-contra scandal of the late 1980s was nothing compared to the mess that Jefferson created. But times

---

*If you drive an hour outside of Paris you can be speaking another language in another country, with different customs, different food, and different manners. On the other hand, if you beeline it from New York, you can leave your passport home and cover over three thousand miles while staying in the same country, eating at the same McDonald's, and waking up in the same Holiday Inn for six consecutive days.

were different then and Jefferson was able to finesse his way through uncharted waters.

As expected, there is always an explanation, a rationale, and an excuse but rarely a clear plan (see the Oops Force that we discuss in Chapter 5). Here was Jefferson's dilemma: At the time of his inauguration the western border of the United States ended at the Mississippi. The vital port of New Orleans was controlled by Spain. Upland American farmers were blocked from exporting their products by way of the rugged Appalachian Mountains to the East.

However, farmers and merchants had become accustomed to floating their goods down the Ohio River and other tributaries of the Mississippi, to the port of New Orleans for shipment abroad. By an arrangement with Spain called the "right of deposit," farmers were allowed to drop their flour, tobacco, pork, bacon, furs, lard, feathers, cider, butter, cheese, hemp, potatoes, salt, whiskey, and beeswax at the port for export without paying Spanish customs duties.

Enter Napoleon.

The French ruler forced a weakened Spain to cede Louisiana to France, and the Spanish governor promptly suspended the right of deposit. Jefferson was horrified, realizing the possibility that the French army might soon be at America's back door. The British offered to conquer the territory on America's behalf, but Jefferson didn't want the British army nearby anymore than he wanted the French.

Jefferson's response was to send his friend James Monroe to France with congressional authority to spend $2 million to buy New Orleans. However, Napoleon, in need of cash (as usual) and realizing the difficulty of defending Louisiana against the British, made a surprising offer to sell the whole Louisiana Territory, comprising the present states of Louisiana, Arkansas, Oklahoma, Missouri, both Dakotas, Iowa, Nebraska, Kansas, Minnesota, Colorado, Wyoming, and Montana. The asking price: $15 million—$13 million more than Congress had authorized.

This was an offer that Monroe could not refuse—the whole enchilada going for four cents an acre. To put this deal in perspective, the annual income for the federal government at the time was just under $8 million. Even so, the deal was struck and a treaty signed without the advice or consent of Congress.*

Even though there was no CNN in those days, word got back quickly to the United States that the big deal had been signed, sealed, and was about to be delivered by Monroe. Criticism and a constitutional confrontation preceded Monroe on his way home but the treaty was finally ratified by the members of Congress, who saw the value of Big and More. Overnight the size of the United States doubled.

The Big Fix

Big has something of an addictive dimension to it: soon you need another injection of bigness. For a heroin addict the need for a fix occurs every four to six hours; for America it seems to be every twenty or thirty years. Twenty-six years after the Louisiana Purchase, which doubled our size, Andrew Jackson acted on America's need for more.

Napoleon was not willing to take Jefferson's check, but he was willing to take one drawn on Barings Bank, which took 60 percent of the American note and laid off the rest on a Dutch bank. Barings, of course, is the same bank that twenty-eight-year-old Nicholas Leeson brought down on February 21, 1995, in one of the most spectacular debacles in modern financial history.

The election of Andrew Jackson was significant because, coming from Tennessee, he was a Westerner, whereas all presidents before him were Easterners, somewhat aristocratic by American standards. Jackson was also "westward" thinking. He wanted to annex Texas and he hated the British, Indians, and bankers—in that order.

He cleared the way for the settling of land in the East and ordered that all Indians be moved across the Mississippi to the West. It was ethnic cleansing of the first order—not a part of American history we like to be reminded of these days, but that's what we call it when some other nation does it.

The Big Domino Effect

What Americans learned to fear about the Communists in Europe and Asia in the fifties through the eighties, we had already perfected in the nineteenth century. The force of Big and More spurred the drive to acquire Texas through a war with Mexico, and then through a westward domino chain of events, California and the Oregon Territory all became part of the United States.

The Civil War did not halt the quest for Big and More. At its height, in 1862, the Homestead Act was passed. It was an open invitation for ordinary folks to own a place of their own. By the terms of the law, any adult citizen could claim 160 acres of the surveyed public domain, and after five years of continuous residence, a settler could get final title upon filing a few papers and paying a small fee.

The problem was that wresting a living out of 160 acres of raw prairie was totally unrealistic, since farming the land would require a capital outlay for machinery to work the stubborn sod. Finding or developing an adequate water supply was also an expensive proposition. A mere 160 acres could not produce enough to justify such a capital outlay.

To put it into today's perspective, look out the window of your airliner as you fly over Kansas, Nebraska, and Colorado and note those great circular patterns on the ground below. Those green patches are the result of immense irrigation machines that pump water to the thirsty plains from deep wells drawing off a vast underground lake called the Ogalalla Aquifer. That takes big money today, to say nothing of what it might have cost in the last century.

The result was that vast stretches of choice land were claimed by "dummy entries" that were fronted by farmhands and cowboys for their bosses or powerful operators. By 1900 half a billion acres had been disposed of, yet only 16 percent of these acres went to the little guys for whom they were intended.

North to Alaska

The next big buy, at two cents an acre, was 586,400 square miles of wilderness known as Seward's Icebox: Alaska. It was twice the size of the big state of Texas. Eighty-two years later it would become the forty-ninth state of the Union.

At the end of the Spanish-American War in 1898, the United States claimed the Philippines, Puerto Rico, and Guam. The occupation of the Philippines was viewed as a strategic advantage until it was necessary to send in Marines to put down rebellions. It was with great relief that the United States gave the Philippines independence on July 4, 1946.

Acquisition and domino effects are not limited to countries. "Growing big for self-protection" is as common a business practice as it is a political process. We know of

America the Big

Cultural forces pack an emotional as well as financial wallop. To Americans, the Big and More Force has mythical proportions that transcend the dictionary definitions. Big and More touches the very depths of the American soul and reaches deep into America's collective subconscious. Emotionally, this was probably best expressed by Katharine Lee Bates.

On the twenty-second of July in 1893, Katharine Lee Bates, a teacher at Wellesley College, near Boston, traveled by rail to Colorado Springs to teach some summer courses at The Colorado College. Young Katharine joined a party of picnickers who climbed aboard an old prairie schooner and started up the winding dirt road to the summit of Pikes Peak.

Today you can make the drive to the 14,010-foot summit in air-conditioned splendor, but when Ms. Bates made the trip the horses had to stop halfway up and everyone had to change to a mule-drawn buggy. Either way, the trip is worth it. As she later wrote, "An erect and decorous group, we stood at last on that Gate-of-Heaven summit, hallowed by the worship of perished races, and gazed in wordless rapture over the far expanse of mountain ranges and sea-like sweep of plain. It was then and there that the opening lines of 'America the Beautiful' sprang into being. . . . It is my impression that I wrote out the entire song on my return that evening to Colorado Springs."

Now, Ms. Bates had no disk jockey plugging her song. No radio. No Marine Band playing in the gazebo in the city park on the Fourth of July. The lady put the song away for a couple of years and then allowed a church publication called *The Congregationalist* to publish the lyrics. It gradually took hold upon the affections of the public. In 1926, in the early days of radio, a contest was held to find a musical setting for the words. The version that got "locked-in" and stirs our souls is by Samuel A. Ward:

> *O beautiful for spacious skies[BIG]*
> *For amber waves of grain[MORE]*
> *For purple mountain majesties[BIG]*
> *Above the fruited plain![MORE]*
> *America! America!*
> *God shed his Grace on thee[VERY BIG]*
> *And crown thy good with brotherhood[MORE]*
> *From sea to shining sea![VERY BIG]*

no industry or company that has said, "Enough is enough, no more customers for us, no more deals, close the doors, we're big enough as is."

The Fuel for the Force

What fueled America's historical obsession with Big and More? What sustained this dynamic over 350 years? What will sustain it in the future? What drives your need to be number one? What factors will you need to maintain in order to keep on top of the heap?

Max Lerner, in *America As a Civilization,* captures the historical roots of the staying power of this force. He says, "Never in history has a civilization risen to world power in so short a span." Lerner identifies the following three developments as those that uniquely converged on America to fuel this phenomenon:

1. The moving, unexplored frontier—space, room to grow
2. The constant motion of the American economy,
   which he calls the "moving technology" revolution
3. The fresh energy and motion in the idea of democracy itself

Countries like Canada, Russia, Brazil, and Australia all had comparable vast land masses like the United States, but none had the three converging factors in play. Consequently, these other countries didn't develop the way the United States did. Lerner says:

With [the following] clue we can understand [the development] of the American character. Self-reliance, courage, alertness, obstinate endurance, friendliness, a democratic informality, are traits that emerged from the continuous cycles of land settlement. A sharp and shrewd aggressiveness, a willingness to take chances, an organizing capacity, a genius with machines, a sense of bigness and of power, an assumption of destiny, are traits that emerged from industrialism and the capital markets of the metropolis.

Now it seems to us that these same fuels persist today for virtually every American organization. When all three are present and in sync, a company can prosper and grow. When one is tinkered with, diminished, or dropped, trouble ensues. Here is the contemporary application of Lerner's thesis to American business today:

Lerner's Thesis	Business Application
1. Moving frontiers	Increasing market share
2. Moving technology	New product development
3. Moving democracy	Engaging workers, empowerment

1. Moving Frontiers: Increasing Market Share

We all have frontiers, unexplored areas, unconquered space in our organizations, be they untested waters with our customers or heights to scale with our employees, be they increased market share, development of assets, corporate growth, mergers, acquisitions, personnel training and development, new product or service configurations—all the things that get us big, more, or closer to number one.

Take the example of beer. Miller, Stroh's, and Heileman's, the runners-up to Budweiser, decided that the most economical way to keep pace was to buy up smaller breweries and add to one's share. Stroh's bought Schlitz, Schaeffer's, Goebels, and Old Milwaukee; Miller bought out Miller Lite; and Heileman added Carlings, Tuborg, and Blatz. In other words, get bigger or die. Over time this kept the lion at bay, but now as if in response to an aversion to bigness, there is a proliferation of micro-breweries—six hundred and counting.* We cannot imagine any of these breweries capping the bottle at a fixed number; they have been growing at the rate of 50 percent a year for the past five years. Because this growth provides choice (☑), the Big and More Force will result in more breweries, more mergers, and more suds.

Whether it's microbreweries, microchips, or microbionics, the big bucks to make the mergers and acquisitions possible have to come from somewhere. Mergers are back, if they were ever out of favor. No industry is exempt from Big and More—too many territories (market share) to conquer, too many frontiers (product and service innovation) to tame.

This is especially true of the banking industry where seemingly everyone was merging in 1995 to lay claim to some form of being the biggest bank. Citibank and Bank of America, currently number one and number two, respectively, are not apt to give up their rankings.[†] Would you? None of these banks can rely on Americans to save more as a way to build assets,[‡] and borrowing and interest rates are not reliable as a long-term building strategy, thereby leaving acquisitions as the one certain way to get bigger. The repeal of the 1934 Glass-Steagall Act, which keeps banking and securities businesses separate, continues to gain momentum. The changes proposed would create huge interstate and international financial services companies. The attraction is the big pension funds, mutual funds, and money markets that have, you guessed it, gotten bigger. You can bank on big changes here.

2. Moving Technology: New Product Development

Lerner's "moving technology" revolution has not diminished: We are all affected by the continuous evolution of technology. It is as essential to business today as it was a century or more ago. The technology is different, but the role it plays is not. The challenge today is appropriate technology, technology transfer, and fuller utilization of technology. As we saw in the preceding chapter, technologies make dreams come true. The fact that Americans are on the leading edge (the Whatsnew Force, Chapter 7) of most new technologies is part of that fuel. Here's an especially good example of moving technology at work at Vistakon, Johnson & Johnson's contact lens division.

Technology, of course, has changed the way we see and are seen. Although today there is an endless choice of colors, shapes, and styles of glasses and lenses, the real developments are in contact lenses. The concept of contact lenses were first recorded by none other than Leonardo da Vinci. But the idea sat around for three hundred years when in 1823, an English astronomer discovered that vision could be corrected by placing a lens directly on the cornea. More than one hundred years would pass

---

For some perspective on the suds business, there is the saying that Anheuser-Busch spills more beer in a single day than all of the microbreweries make in a year!

†*As we were reviewing this chapter, Chase Manhattan Bank and Chemical Bank announced a merger in August 1995 that made the combined entity number one. There is no staying on top of the Big and More Force!*

‡*The Big and More Force has not impacted individual savings accounts or strategies for Americans. We have the lowest per capita savings rate of all the industrial nations in the world. This has been a perennial concern for policy analysts and futurists, but it hasn't gotten bad enough (big in the wrong direction) for anyone to provide options or choices. The urge to spend, the Now Force we write about in the next chapter, dominates Big and More when it comes to personal savings.*

Finding and Keeping a Sense of Proportion

The biggest surprise nonfiction best-seller in 1987 was written by an obscure Yale professor named Paul Kennedy. The book was called *The Rise and Fall of Great Powers*. It was about the possibility of the United States running the risk of "imperial overstretch" and consequent decline, as happened to seventeenth-century Spain and the nineteenth-century British Empire.

As Kennedy says, "Precisely because a top-heavy military establishment may slow down the rate of economic growth and lead to a decline in the nation's share of world manufacturing output, and therefore wealth, and therefore power, the whole issue becomes one of the balancing of the short-term security afforded by the large defense forces against the longer-term security of rising production and income."

This book was written well before the fall of the Soviet empire, but it proves the point. The maintenance of a top-heavy military establishment was of course one of the contributing factors of the ungluing of the U.S.S.R.

A 1995 book by Ronald Steel brings the dialogue up-to-date. His work, called *Temptations of a Superpower*, points out that the current U.S. military budget of $253 billion "is down fractionally from the previous year, but is still 85 percent of the average cold war level," making it "as large as that of all the other nations of the world combined." Little wonder that Europe and Japan under America's military umbrella are able to "concentrate on productivity, market penetration, wealth and innovation: the kind of power that matters most in today's world."

How much of this military expenditure is driven by need and how much by misguided political opportunism must be examined on a case-by-case basis. However, the big lesson to be learned is that the persuasive argument that big is always better and more is always safer carries with it the historical precedence of ultimate decline.

By the end of the Cold War, not only had big defense industries come to lean on the government as a customer, but so had many communities become dependent on the infusion of spending from local military bases. The decisions to close surplus military installations were politically impossible to make. Only a neutral "commission" could get to the heart of the matter through a process we call a "legislative bypass" that got the vested politicians off the hook.

The commission process was not a tidy operation; bypasses never are. The commission only recommended; the President and Congress had veto power, or, as we have learned in the first round, tinkering power. Now, in successive rounds, the process appears to be working as intended.

before the first hard (plastic) lenses were introduced in 1939; soft lens technology followed within thirty-two years. And, as frequently happens with the concept of moving technology, the time lapse between subsequent breakthroughs shortened considerably. In half the time it took to get from hard lenses to soft, technology was developed to mass produce disposable lenses. In 1987, Johnson & Johnson's Vistakon division introduced the first disposable contact lenses. Today, thanks to yet another advanced technology at J&J, you can buy a pair, toss them out when you go to bed, and put on a new pair in the morning.

Back in 1983, J&J had the foresight (no pun intended) to buy the rights to a new Danish technology that produced disposable lenses cheaply. Within a few years, J&J was ready to test-market a disposable lens under the name of Acuvue. The concept of a *daily* disposable seemed like an impossible idea at the time: If just one percent of the 45 million contact wearers in the world were to switch to a daily disposable lens, more than 325 million lenses would have to be made to supply each with up to 730 lenses per person per year. J&J's Stabilized Soft Molding technology, used to manufacture Acuvue and Surevue, could not do the job initially. So J&J invested more than four years and $150 million to improve the technology. Known as MAXIMIZE technology, it takes mass lens production into a new dimension: *All* phases of production have been fully automated, including the compounding of hydrogel (soft lens material) and precision, computerized inspection of the finished product. The result is not only a technology that is equal to the task of manufacturing low-cost lenses, but the product is also of higher quality!

Bernard Walsh is Company Group Chairman for J&J's Vistakon franchise. In 1987 Walsh was running a tiny corner of the contact lens market, grossing $20 million. Today, the contact lens business is one of the fastest growing franchises of J&J with over $650 million in revenue, the largest contact lens company in the world. His staff has grown sixfold, from around 400 in 1987 to over 2,500 in 1995.

However, we didn't get the sense from Walsh, when we talked to him, that ranking and revenue were his major sources of pride—as phenomenal as his track record is. Rather, it was staying out front of the moving technology and exploring new frontiers. Vistakon, through Walsh's leadership, is committed to not increasing the price of disposable lenses into the foreseeable future. That means that its self-imposed profit margins have to come from increased efficiencies in technology and further technological breakthroughs. Managing, really un-managing (getting out of the way, coaching, facilitating), a bunch of young scientists, engineers, inventors, and process wizards is Walsh's real source of pride. He talks with enthusiasm about the entrepreneurial spirit of the company, teamwork, fixation (his word) with objectives. Walsh says, "What made this work was a single focus: Everyone understood the objective and worked toward a single end with no conflicting priorities, and no business to defend." In other words, he tapped into the promise and benefits of the technology frontier.

Walsh will do anything to preserve what he calls the "nimbleness" of his company. Unknowingly, Vistakon and Walsh are the embodiment of Lerner's thesis. Walsh says, "We must guard against getting big, adding layers of management, fear of failure, and testing things to death." In other words, explore the frontiers, stay on top of technology, and engage your people.

3. Moving Democracy: Engaging Workers, Empowerment

Now the third element: Democracy. You might ask, what does democracy have to do with running an organization? Are you seriously asking, or just making sure we know the answer?

We learned about the power and impact of Lerner's third thesis from Roger Milliken, the venerable chairman of Milliken & Company. He makes clear that his business is run as a democracy; everyone gets to participate, but only the chairman gets to vote. That distinction is important. Democracy, as it is applied to running a business, is not about voting (the visible dimension of democracy) but the free exchange of ideas, participation in the process of thinking those ideas through, and the personal responsibility and accountability for carrying them out on an agreed upon—at least clearly understood—set of guiding principles and rules (the hidden dimensions of democracy).*

The process leading up to the eventual vote (board, executive, manager, or supervisor approval) is more important than the vote itself. Properly done, as you probably know from how things are done in your organization, the final vote by the committee or board is usually a foregone conclusion. Why? Not because people voted, but because people participated.

Choice, the first force we wrote about in Chapter 1, is the bloodline of an effectively run enterprise. Where choices rule, companies thrive. Where options are limited, companies stagnate and stumble.

"The Curse of Bigness"

America's progression toward bigness was not without its detractors. One in particular was Louis D. Brandeis, one of the best legal minds this country has ever produced. Graduating from Harvard Law School with "the most brilliant record" of any student in its history, he would go on to survive a bitterly contested nomination to become the first Jewish member of the United States Supreme Court. There he would serve with distinction for twenty-three years. But it's what Louis D. Brandeis did in the intervening years that concerns us here.

In the late 1890s and early 1900s Brandeis had built a reputation as "the people's lawyer" by championing the public interest. He had taken on the transportation industries in New England, the public utilities in Boston, and the garment industry in New York, among others. The industries were different, but the theme was the same: the cause *and* conditions of the working men and women of the day.

These were the early days of the union movement in America. Some union officials had just bombed the antilabor *Los Angeles Times* and twenty people had been killed. In the words of historian Alpheus Thomas Mason, "The use of violence had shocked America's sensibilities."[†]

In the aftermath of the bombing, many sought to explain what had gone wrong and why workingmen had resorted to violence. After a series of essays published by *Survey* magazine, Brandeis was among those who petitioned President William Howard Taft to create the Federal Commission on Industrial Relations. Brandeis was invited to chair it but declined. Instead he wrote a series of ten articles for *Harper's Weekly*, later published as a book under the title *Other People's Money*. The eighth essay in the series, to use Mason's description, "bore the searing title with which Brandeis' name is closely linked—'The Curse of Bigness.'"

---

*Russell L. Aekoff, chairman of the Institute for Interactive Management and professor emeritus of the Wharton School has written a thought-provoking book on this topic and its implications for change management, The Democratic Corporation.

†Alpheus Thomas Mason, "Louis D. Brandeis: Curse of Bigness," An American Primer.

On January 23, 1915, in testimony before the Industrial Relations Commission, Brandeis expanded on "the curse." Following are selected portions of his testimony:*

We have the situation of [a generic or typical large] employer so potent, so well-organized, with such concentrated forces and with such extraordinary powers of reserve and the ability to endure against strikes and other efforts of a union, that the relatively loosely organized masses of even strong unions are unable to cope with the situation. We are dealing here with a question, not of motive, but of condition.

The position of the ordinary worker is exactly the reverse. The individual employee has no effective voice or vote.

. . . When a great financial power has developed—when there exists these powerful organizations, which can successfully summon forces from all parts of the country, which can afford to use tremendous amounts of money in any conflict to carry out what they deem to be their business principle, and can also afford to suffer large losses—you have necessarily a condition of inequality between the two contending forces. . . . There develops within the State a state so powerful that the ordinary social and industrial forces existing are insufficient to cope with it.

Size may become such a danger in its results to the community that the community may have to set limits. A large part of our protective legislation consists of prohibiting things which we find are dangerous, according to common experience. Concentration of power has been shown to be dangerous in a democracy, even though that power may be used beneficently. For instance, on our public highways we put a limit on the size of an autotruck, no matter how well it is run. It may have the most skillful and considerate driver, but its mere size may make it something which the community can not tolerate, in view of the other uses of the highway and the danger inherent in its occupation to so large an extent by a single vehicle.

Mason reports that no specific legislation came out of the commission hearings, "yet Brandeis' contributions have long endured. . . . Certain of Brandeis' ideas were translated into Franklin D. Roosevelt's New Deal. Others have been challenged as obsolete; still others seem radical [eighty] years later."

Mason notes that the "collapse of 1929 confirmed Brandeis' forecast. . . . The war Brandeis declared on the 'money trust' in 1913 was finally won with the passage of the Banking Act of 1933, requiring national and member banks to divest themselves of their securities affiliates."

On the heels of this history and given what we know about the power of Big and More in America, it is perhaps time to get out the shoe box or to hold on to our wallets at the very least. Banks are now getting back into the securities business.

Building the Biggest Company in the World

About the time Louis Brandeis was worrying about the social costs of bigness, another man was putting together the foundations of what would become the largest company

*Full text source is "Testimony before the U.S. Commission on Industrial Relations, January 23, 1915," Senate Documents, 64th Cong. 1st Sess., 1915–1916, XXVI, Commission on Industrial Relations Report and Testimony, VIII, 7658-76, passim. More conveniently, we discovered, are the excerpts in An American Primer, *a wonderful collection of important historical US documents.*

Other People's Curses

The headline in *Fortune*'s July 24, 1995, "NewsTrends" page read, "CHARLOTTE'S BATTLING BANKERS ARE SCORING BIG."

It was less about banking, however, and more about a personal rivalry between Hugh McColl (NationsBank First Union) and Edward Crutchfield (NationsBank), two CEOs that run a parade of "top that" acquisitions, as the article phrased it. They have bought 105 banks between them, with no end in sight. McColl's bank has the taller building and was ranked the sixth largest bank in the United States in the summer of 1995. The other bank (see how contagious this force is?), though ranked number four, had the shorter building.

When Crutchfield put up a forty-two-story tower that the locals called "the juke box," banker McColl answered with a sixty-story tower known locally as the "Taj McColl." But Crutchfield was feeling far from beaten: He made plans for a three-story building outside of town that he claimed would have two million square feet—more square footage than New York City's World Trade Center!

In fact, Crutchfield had raised the ante on McColl in banking terms as well: He had just paid $5.4 billion for New Jersey's First Fidelity, making it the largest bank merger in history.* This kind of *mano-a-mano* business management usually gets a follow-up sooner or later. It was sooner: Just one month later Hugh McColl was on the cover of *Fortune* in tall grass, dressed in hunting fatigues, complete with rifle and a caption that said, "Hugh McColl started the hunt. NOW he's aiming to make NationsBank No. 1." The inside photo caption continued, "McColl's reputation as a skin-you-alive deal maker makes other big bankers sweat."

Oops! (See second footnote, page 117).

in the world. William Crapo (Billy) Durant brought to life more big-ticket American brand names than any man before or since, from all the name plates that make up GM today to AC Spark Plugs, Frigidaire, and Delco. He gave a job to the brilliant young engineer Walter Chrysler, who eventually quit Billy to go out on his own.

Across town in Detroit, another man was also putting together one of the largest automobile companies. But Henry Ford was more interested in building cars than companies. Ford was a cranky tinkerer who handcrafted a car, started to make and sell it in quantity, failed, and tried again* with a company called Detroit Automobile Company. He was about to fail once more when a man named Henry Leland bought it out and changed the name to Cadillac, a company that Durant would later acquire as part of his strategy to make GM #1. On his third try, Ford created the company we know today as the builder of the Tin Lizzie, Taurus, and all the models in between.

These two rivals put faces on the force of Big and More as few other Americans would in this century. William was older than Henry, middle-aged, and a very successful builder of Durant-Dort buggies in Flint, Michigan. He knew the buggy

*This is the Oops Force we write about in Chapter 5.

business, and his buggies were designed to be what he called "self-sellers." At forty-two he was a millionaire, at a time when millionaire was as rich as it got.

Former newsman Lawrence Gustin recounts all of this in his stunning biography, *Billy Durant, Creator of General Motors*, which ought to be required reading at any B school. According to Gustin, Durant got started in the auto business when another car maker by the name of Dave Buick couldn't get rid of the forty cars that he'd built. Buick couldn't give them away, but he was a car man, not a salesman. It was pretty well known around town that Dave was about to go under, and that's when some good citizens turned to Durant.

Although he was no friend of the automobile, being a buggy man, Durant agreed to take a look—in that way that folks who don't know anything about cars take a look. He took one for a drive. Up hill and down, through the streams and muddy roads, backyards and barnyards, until at the end of a cold November day a deal was cut—no cash, Buick stock in exchange for Durant-Dort Carriage Company stock.

With the New York Auto Show coming up in a few weeks, Durant decided to show a Buick. Durant was a consummate salesman and New York was the place to start. No one knows how he did it,* but he came back from the show with orders for 1,108 new Buicks. Billy Durant was on his way.

Durant's Advantage

By 1908, Buick was turning out 8,820 cars a year, outbuilding Ford by almost two to one. But it was not only Durant's superb salesmanship that kept Buick ahead of the pack, he was able to link the publicity fallout from his automobile racing victories to his sales business—starting a practice that continues to this day. Durant had the luck of hiring two Swiss/French brothers as part of his racing team. Louis Chevrolet was the better race driver, so his brother Arthur became Durant's chauffeur.

Meanwhile, Oldsmobile, the most famous name tag in the country at the time, was slipping in sales and getting in trouble. Using the acquisition strategy we outlined at the beginning of this chapter, Durant decided to get bigger by buying companies. As in the case of Buick, it was a deal based on stock swaps and the formation of a holding company in which all would share. (That holding company would eventually emerge as General Motors Company.)

At the same time Durant was forming GM he came across a French bike rider in Boston who seemed to have a novel idea for spark plugs. Albert Champion was invited to set up in Flint, and eventually A.C. (for Albert Champion) Spark Plugs became a GM subsidiary. Durant said, "I figured if I could acquire a few more companies . . . I would have control of the greatest industry in this country. A great opportunity, no time to lose, I must get busy."

The Big and More Force Never Seems to Stop

Unchecked, the Big and More Force takes on a life of its own and that can be ruinous. Some think this is what is happening in today's computer industry, and that it is

---

The Motivated Abilities stuff we introduced in Chapter 1 is one of several places to begin if you want to identify those who, like Durant, are gifted salespeople. Too many of us have Dave Buicks around, folks who can make them, but can't sell them.

likely to hit the end of its ability to invent itself. While we watch that one unfold, we can look back at the automotive industry and see if there are any lessons to be learned about how to manage Big and More.

Gustin reports that one of the first companies Durant went after was the Oakland Motor Car Company, built in a small town thirty miles south of Flint. Oakland's Model K was a powerful four-cylinder car that in 1908 had won hill climbs all over the country but the company had recently fallen on hard times. After some initial wrangling the Oakland people accepted Durant's offer of a stock swap, and Oakland became the third arrow in the GM quiver. But Durant never liked the name Oakland, so he changed it to the name of the town in which it was built: Pontiac.

More

Durant didn't stop with Pontiac and although the GM board at first balked at Durant's bid to buy Cadillac, they came around a few months later and agreed to an even higher price, amounting to $4.75 million. Big in those days. But Cadillac's earnings returned the entire purchase price in just fourteen months.

More

By the end of 1909 Durant had bought thirty-one auto parts companies.

More

Same year, 1909, the GM board authorized Durant to purchase Ford if financing could be arranged. The price was set at $8 million. Durant sought the $2 million needed up front from National City Bank (now Citicorp). A few days later the bank called long distance to inform Durant that the loan would *not* be made, because it was felt unwise to sponsor an automobile venture—this being an untested business and all. A few years later Ford's earnings were at $35 million per year and Ford was the number one carmaker in America.

Bust

In no time GM was in trouble. Cash flow was part of the problem, but the bigger problem was that nobody knew how much flow or how much cash. The panic of 1910 was on, and within months GM stock had plunged from about one hundred to twenty-five dollars a share. Bankers, creditors, and suppliers soon forced GM's hand, and by the end of 1910 Durant was out.

(In Chapter 5 we will describe the Oops Force and its built-in comeback mechanisms, and in Chapter 7 we will write about the Whatsnew Force. Durant manifested both forces when he turned to racecar driver Louis Chevrolet as he was heading to Europe for a vacation and said, "I need a car, Louis. I need to have you build me a car, Louis. An entirely new kind of car. You build it, and we'll call it the Chevrolet.")

Henry Has a Better Idea

Meanwhile Henry Ford had a different way to get to big: Make an affordable car so that the common man can afford one. In other words, get to big through more. Rather than use Durant's acquisition strategy, Ford was determined to design a car, freeze the design, and evolve an assembly system that would provide economies of scale—the other advantage of Big and More. While Olds had been mass-producing cars since the turn of the century, and Leland had introduced the idea of interchangeable parts in the Cadillac, Ford was determined to integrate his company vertically through internal growth, and try anything that would increase production and drive down prices.*

By means of trial and error Ford evolved the moving assembly line. By 1912 he was able to produce 82,388 cars. The breakthrough came in 1913 when production soared to 189,088, and by 1916 Ford turned out 585,388 Tin Lizzies. But instead of a big price, the Model T that cost $850 in 1908 was going for less than $360 eight years later. With these twin strategies of vertical integration and the moving assembly line he was able to overtake General Motors. For a while.

Back for More

Back from Europe, Billy Durant went to see what Louis Chevrolet had built. He was disappointed. He was also irritated by Louis's cigarette smoking and suggested to him that gentlemen should smoke only cigars. A spat ensued, and Louis walked away, having sold his car and his name.

Durant soon came up with a car he could believe in and dubbed it the Chevrolet Baby Grand. It was a hit! Chevy would soon gain on Ford's cheap Model T, which was losing favor with increasingly sophisticated buyers.

Consequently, Chevy's stock was selling like hotcakes. By offering shareholders of GM the chance to trade their GM stock for Chevrolet stock, Durant soon had enough GM stock that he was able to regain control of General Motors. It didn't last. He could build a big empire, but he couldn't run one.

During an economic turndown in 1920, Durant was once again out of a job. Enter Alfred P. Sloan, his principles of modern management, and unimagined growth. Following World War II Sloan expanded General Motors to an international company of gargantuan proportions. His management methods served it well and GM was invincible until the Germans and the Japanese came up with a big idea that American carmakers missed altogether: Small cars.

This is a rather hurried overview of American automobile manufacturing; however, it is not our intent to diagnose the decline of so complex an industry in these pages. Others have already done that well. But, hopefully, in examining certain historical events through the prism of cultural forces we can illuminate the continuing power of these forces, so that they might be used effectively, not haphazardly or unknowingly. Thus both General Motors and Ford show an approach to Big and More strikingly similar to Home Depot. However, Home Depot appears to be more diligent about reinventing and redefining its industry than were GM or Ford. It is also true that the mega-retailer is not likely to face any foreign competition or surprise entries into the marketplace comparable to a Volkswagen or Honda. But undoubtedly the most important key to Home Depot's future success will be its ability to manage the very thing that brought customers to it in the first place: Its size.

Note that each car company took a different strategy trying to outguess the other. Home Depot combined all three approaches.

Ford Wants to Be Number One Again!?

Once you have been number one it is hard to remain number two. So Henry must wink in his grave when he hears current Ford chairman Alex Trotman talk of *and* plan for being the number one carmaker in the world. GM is still in first place, having built 1.7 million more vehicles than Ford in 1994. However, with Ford grabbing seven percentage points* in market share from GM and foreign automakers, Ford is within striking distance (⚭).

Trotman says being number one would obviously be a morale booster for employees, but Wall Street analysts debate the merits of the strategy (sometimes "strategy" is more accurately called an obsession—this is part of the Big and More Force). Wall Street would rather see more profitability, which is too often sacrificed in the rush for market share. But Ford is not the "either/or" thinker that we described in Chapter 1. Trotman has already proven he can do both.

To help keep the focus of top management on the goal, Trotman has required that his top eighty managers put their money where their mouths are: They must own Ford shares at least equal in value to their annual salary. Meanwhile out on the golf course, Trotman's immediate predecessor, Harold (Red) Poling, told *Business Week*'s Keith Naughton on August 14, 1995, that while he was calling the strategies from 1990 to 1993, being number one was "never" on the agenda. Poling's concern is the issue we raised in the preceding chapter: "Impossible goals" need to have an attainable dimension in order to make business sense. Poling, speaking of the Trotman goal, said, "If you set an objective so far away, people can't visualize it and have difficulty attaining it."[†]

Flying Dutchman

It's not just Ford that wants to be number one, we all do. Whether it's a strategy in business, the avowed (or unavowed) purpose of sports, parental inducement to make straight As in school, or anybody's top-ten list (a synonym for making it in America), it is very American to think and behave in number one terms. It's what drives the Big and More Force.

In fact, the obsession with being number one is so firmly ingrained in the minds of American business people that we usually aren't even aware of it. We aren't aware that anything short of striving for this position is an option. The point was driven home to a group of U.S. executives by Frank Schaper, director of product development marketing for KLM, the Dutch airline. Schaper presented an entertaining and insightful paper entitled "Service Decathlon"™ at a 1995 *Fortune* magazine business conference. The theme of Schaper's paper was the highly competitive airline wars on transoceanic flights.

Service Decathlon is also the name for KLM's business strategy to improve its competitive standing in the airline service business. Schaper's proposition is that, like

---

This represents a big number–$25 billion in sales. Ford's domestic market share in 1994 was 26.5 percent in the United States compared to GM's 32.3 percent. Ford barely trails GM in Europe, 12 percent vs. 13.3 percent.

[†]*GM's 1.7 million car production lead over Ford in 1994 means that Ford would need to make enough cars to reach from New York to San Francisco when parked end-to-end. Maybe that's what Poling means by "so far away."*

NICE GUYS FINISH BIG

It happened to a friend of mine (Morrison) when we were both maybe 13 years old. I was waiting forever outside Tom's house for him to come out so we could go swimming. When he finally came out I asked him what took him so long?

"We got company."

"Who?"

"Some old guy. A friend of my folks. He owns a big company and he wanted to talk to me."

"What did he say?"

"He asked me what I wanted to do when I got out of college."

"What did you tell him?"

"I told him I wanted to make money."

"What did he say?"

"He said, think big!"

The Tom in this story is Thomas S. Murphy, the former chairman of Capital Cities/ABC. The "old guy" friend of his folks was Thomas J. Watson, Sr., the founder of IBM—Big Blue.

It all happened so fast: One day we were kids, then in and out of a war, and suddenly we were bachelors in our twenties. Murphy did a few years on the fast track at Texaco, while I was flying first class around the world making movies of the wonders of the planet with Lowell Thomas and the boys of *Cinerama* (see Chapter 5). We thought then that the career the other chose was insane.

Then Tom had lunch with Frank Smith, a bantamweight dynamo who had been in broadcasting since there was such a thing. At the time, Smith was Lowell Thomas's business manager. He was a great salesman, deal maker, visionary, and synergist. He talked Murphy into quitting his sure thing, fast-track Texaco sinecure in New York City to manage a low-powered, money-losing, seldom-watched UHF television station upstate in Albany that Thomas had just acquired. (Murphy, of course, is a great salesman, and as they say of salesmen there is nobody easier to sell than another salesman.)

So Murphy moved into the offices of WROW, an unpainted ramshackle Victorian house beside the Hudson River outside of Albany. One of the first things Murphy did was to paint the front of the Victorian (there wasn't enough in the budget to do the whole thing). I was certain the man was out of his mind and would probably never return to civilization.

The years swept past in a blur and as often happens with old friends, we lost touch. Then one day I opened the paper and read the headlines telling of the merger of the Wall Street darling Capital Cities Broadcasting with the giant ABC network. It was the biggest deal of its day, and when I dropped Murph a note reminding him of his chat so many years before with the senior Tom Watson, he was astonished that I'd remembered.

When Murphy co-engineered the $19 billion Capital Cities/ABC/Disney merger in the summer of 1995, again the biggest deal of its day, I began to think of it in the light of the seven forces: First Murph chose(☑) an impossible dream(⚬☁), getting into the quintessential whatsnew business of his day(🖥), and then it grew into one of the largest conglomerates in the industry(❗).

continued

Probably for old times' sake, Tom Murphy graciously assented to an interview for inclusion in this book. After some banter, I said that I wanted to get his personal take on the seven forces, especially on Big and More, so we got on with it.

JM: *How much of that "think big" advice from Watson stuck? When you come in here every day do you have a conscious strategy to make this place bigger and more bigger?*

TM: I think the whole orientation has always been to do the best job I could for the stockholders while obviously being fair to my employees. You do that by putting out the best news product and the best entertainment product that you can. I never had any long-term visions. I never operated under them. I don't know where I'm going to be five years from now. As a matter of fact, recently when I made a deal with Michael Eisner, he said, "Tom, what're your five-year, long-term projections? I said, "I don't have any!" He said, "You don't have any?" And I said, "No."

It [broadcasting] is not a capital-intensive business. You don't have to have plans for building plants and things like that to pay out, with long-term projections. We just operate on a year-to-year basis. So I never had a vision that we were going to be the biggest of anything. Never. It just happened that way.

JM: *In the process of working this way, what were the choices that you had to make? What were the decisions you had to take in order to maintain or effect your preeminence? Was it just a day-to-day gut thing?*

TM: When I started there were only three networks, then suddenly there were five, and now you can get fifty or sixty channels. We hired the best people possible. We ran a decentralized operation. It just fit my personality, I guess. I always had the benefit of having Dan Burke as my partner. We would give a great deal of authority to our people. We would give them a ticket to the horse race by giving them options. And the fact is, we've been a pretty good business. Certainly, over the forty years plus that I've been in the television business, it's been a terrific business. Now, the network business aspect has never had nearly the margins as the station business. There's still a lot of competition, but it's a driving force on the network affiliated stations, so it's very important. . . . I never thought about making Capital Cities as getting bigger and bigger. It just worked out that way. We were limited in the number of television stations we could own, so the only way to get bigger and bigger was to buy a bigger station and sell a smaller one. We could only have five VHF television stations. When the [Federal Communications] Commission allowed us to go to twelve that's when I had a chance to make a deal with Leonard Goldenson at ABC.

JM: *Disney has a formal process for dealing with mistakes [Chapter 5]. Do you have something similar here?*

TM: We are not in the same kind of business. We're not putting on shows like they do. Everything we have is in the can, by and large, except the news. We operate on a very thin scale. Before we ever made the deal with ABC we didn't have a public relations director, we didn't have a legal officer attached to the company! When we needed people, we went outside. We just had our financial people. We had thirty-five people.

JM: *That's all?*

TM: That's all. Of course, we have more now. But with Disney, I think we make a great combination. Don't you, by and large?

JM: *Well, it's a curious thing. One of the things we are looking at in the book, is what happens when things get too big, like General Motors and IBM. They got so big they became unmanageable.*

TM: Well, that's impossible with us, because you've got two smart guys handling it now. Eisner is running it here and he's terrific. I don't see them fooling around with our business, much. We don't operate anything we don't make money on, except for our overseas stuff which we're doing some investing in for the future. We are in allied fields so you can see some savings in some staff operations. They have 70,000 people; we only have about 19,000. That's a lot of people.

JM: *I worked for big companies for a number of years. I was always appalled at the top-heavy layers and layers.*

TM: That's bad . . . . that's what happens when you're that big and powerful for that long. Disney hasn't been that big for that long. Well you give them another ten years and they can get that way. But, I wouldn't think so as long as Michael is there. He's a tiger. Tough. Creative. High energy.

JM: *When you say "tiger" and "tough," you mean . . .*

TM: He's a highly competitive animal. Fiercely competitive.

JM: *Are you competitive?*

TM: Oh yeah. But I don't think I'm tough. People say I'm tough, but I don't think I'm tough. Maybe other people have different opinions.

JM: *When are you leaving?*

TM: Oh, about next January [1996], sometime.

JM: *What are you going to do?*

TM: Probably nothing. I'm the chairman of the hospital board. I'm on several boards. On the Texaco board, and on the Disney board. I'm seventy-one.

JM: *That means you can ski for free now!*

And the conversation veered toward old-time stuff and memories: pranks, peccadilloes, characters that once loomed large, and girlfriends who moved in and out of our lives. Something told me it was time to go, and I stood, but Tom was anxious to show and tell, bringing some photos down from the shelf. We walked to the door and paused by the big fading black-and-white picture of the ram-shackle Victorian mansion in Albany where it all started. Murph pointed to the window where his office had been some 40 years before. We smiled and I left.

the track and field decathlon, where anyone entering the event must perform all ten events in order to compete, so airlines must do the same.

The objective of the decathlon is not to come in first in every event—impossible to do in the sporting event and no doubt impossible to do in business competition—but to accumulate the most points in order to win. It is okay to be second in one event, even third or fourth, so long as you get enough total points in the end.

These ten "events" are things that the customer determines constitute service, and depending on how well the airline performs in each event, it also determines whether or not the customer chooses to fly the carrier again. Now if you have flown business class on a variety of carriers from the United States to Europe, you'll know that Virgin Atlantic is the current decathlon-service winner. It starts with the free limousine service to the airport, includes a massage or manicure on board, a very comfortable seat, and a multiple-channel video player at your personal command.

Who is second? There is a lot of room for more than one airline to stake some claim to being second. A lot of money is going into being second or holding on to second as a starting point to try to be number one. Why have most airlines added personal videos and multiple channels? As Schaper points out, the decathlon is an event where you compete event by event for the total number of points. In-flight entertainment gets high points from customers. From a business point of view, if you are trailing in a particular service feature, you do what athletes do: study the competition, imitate or modify the technique, and practice, practice, practice.

As Schaper wrapped up his presentation, he stunned the audience of American executives when he said, in a straightforward Dutch manner, that KLM's short-term business goal was to be number three. Until that moment, the audience was wrapped up in his highly effective presentation.

It was a good thing Schaper revealed his company's business strategy toward the end of his presentation. Otherwise, he almost certainly would have lost his American audience. What can anyone possibly learn from a company that wants to be number three? How very American to think that a company other than number one has nothing to offer!

The first question in the Q&A session was obviously, "why number three?" Schaper was prepared for a detailed answer—he knew Americans, he had worked here briefly. Not surprisingly, it boiled down to Dutch culture. The Dutch, along with the rest of the world, are not obsessed with being number one. They are just as dedicated and disciplined in achieving their business goals and being profitable as American companies are, but being number one as the motivation or mantra for achieving those goals is the furthest thing from a Dutchman's business practices. Incidentally, Frank Schaper's paper was ranked number one, unanimously, by the American audience.

Governing through Big and More

One area in which we are sure no one wants to claim the number one spot is problems. But Big and More all too often brings along big problems and more of them. This seems to be especially true when the government is involved. Yet as we discussed in Chapter 1, our government—elected officials, public policy makers, or anyone else involved in designing new legislation and government regulations—will benefit every bit as much as business people from tapping into America's forces.

How Big Is Big?—Part 2
or
"Just how much is a trillion dollars?"

The unprecedented six-day shut down of the Federal government in the Fall of 1995 was over a complex and contentious (at times juvenile) debate about how to reduce the federal deficit, now pushing five trillion dollars, and balance the budget. The Republicans were committed to doing it in seven years and President Clinton, depending on when you asked him, was advocating ten years. Clearly both options meant big cuts in spending in order to get the budget balanced, something we had not done since the Miracle Mets won the World Series in 1969.

Most of the political debate was focused on cutting the other guy's favorite programs while managing to make yours look like the salvation of Amerikind. Numbers and percentages and figures—never two alike—were bandied about with no regard for meaning or measure. Cuts were really decreases in increases. And the easiest way to make the cut or the increase sound bigger than the other gal's was to add up the total expenditure for ten years so that it could be expressed in the tens of billions instead of hundreds of millions.

But when the numbers get into the thousands of billions—the trillions— most of us begin to wonder just what that number really means. How much is a trillion, anyway? How can we relate this number to anything in our experience?

When the Federal deficit first hit one trillion dollars back in Ronald Reagan's day, (yes, the end of Ronald Reagan's second term), Boyce Rensberger of *The Washington Post* pictured what this gargantuan sum of money amounts to. His calculations visualized the Big and More Force so effectively that we have chosen to share them and our adaptations with you.

A trillion dollars can be written as the number 1 followed by twelve zeros: 1,000,000,000,000—or as a million millions or a thousand billions. But numbers don't really give a feel for the true size of a trillion dollars. What you can or can't do with it is often a more illustrative measure. For example, if you could spend one dollar a second, it would take you almost 12 days to spend a million dollars; it would take you almost half a lifetime, 31.7 years, to spend a billion; and you would need an incomprehensive 31,700 years to spend a trillion!

Here's another way of looking at it. If you got paid one dollar for each word you read in the *Post* and faithfully read every nonadvertising word for a year, you'd make a tidy $29.2 million. But to make a trillion bucks, you and generations and generations of your grandchildren would have to keep the string going *every day* for 34,247 years.

To top things off, Rensberger described this enormous sum in this way: "If you packed $1 trillion, in the form of $1 bills, into average-size, 50-foot-long railroad boxcars, you could get about $63.5 million into each boxcar. A train carrying $1 trillion would have 15,743 boxcars and be 167 miles long, not counting all the locomotives you would need to pull it . . . If the trillion-dollar train pulled into Washington [where else?] . . . the caboose would still be farther away than Philadelphia, roughly around Trenton, New Jersey." With the deficit at $4.9 trillion in 1995 that would put that caboose somewhere near Chicago— and getting longer every day.

Thus we will continue throughout the book to examine the effects of each cultural force on a variety of public policy issues. In the first chapter we looked at drug abuse (unfortunately the U.S. can almost certainly take the number one spot here) from the perspective of choice; we will return to it shortly from a corporate viewpoint and through the lens of Big and More. But first let's turn to another area in which we can (unfortunately) lay claim to the top spot, one that is guaranteed to cause every American's blood pressure to rise: the high cost of health care.

America's High Blood Pressure

The biggest supplier to General Motors is not steel, plastic, rubber, glass, or textiles. It's health care. It is a big cost of business for General Motors and a major cost for small and mid-size companies all across America. Together we spend more on healthcare proportionately than any nation in the world; in other words, we're number one.

Few recent public policy problems in America have been as big and contentious as health. Politicians, writing prescriptions without a license, helped make it so. President Clinton, with no small help from the First Lady (there is that number one thing again), managed in 1994 to create a labyrinth that made you sick just looking at it, thanks in part to a big advertising campaign on behalf of "*them* the people."

This proposed cure was so convoluted that the name of the architect for the plan, Ira Magaziner, is now used derisively as a verb meaning to screw something up in a big way. To "Magaziner" something is to propose a cure worse than the disease.

But Magaziner, Hillary Clinton, and the cadre of consultants were right in step with the best American tradition of big thinking, big action, big prescriptions, big remedies for what literally ails America.

How did we get this prescription? Believe it or not, this is not a new phenomenon, as convenient as that kind of thinking may be to some. Like the forces we write about, this also has its roots in the formative days of the Republic. It turns out that we have a doctor's signature on the Declaration of Independence, with the unwitting name of Dr. Rush. Doctor Benjamin Rush became an early-on advocate of aggressive medical practice, which fit the mood and tempo of the times, got locked-in, and continues to this day.

The good doctor Rush made the rounds in influential medical circles long before the revolution. Medical historians agree that his influence lasted for decades in the formative years of American medicine. He abhorred the "undue reliance upon the powers of nature" for healing—the French way. To this day, the American medical establishment considers homeopathy, which includes the practice of smaller doses of medications, a "fringe" medicine. But in France, over six thousand doctors prescribe such treatments; half of them do so exclusively.

Historian Martin S. Pernick explains the origins of Big and More in American medicine this way:

> Rush promoted his therapies in part by convincing practitioners and patients alike that they were heroic, bold, courageous, manly and patriotic. Americans were tougher than Europeans; American diseases were correspondingly tougher than mild European diseases; to cure Americans would require uniquely powerful doses administered by heroic American physicians.

Comparative Medicine

Naturally, we were curious if this big approach to medicine was uniquely American or not. After all, an earache is an earache in any language, and high blood pressure is a problem in any country. Or is it?

Our discoveries startled us. For example, in terms of infant mortality and life expectancy it doesn't much matter if you are English, French, German, or American. We all run out of time, more or less at the same time. But in terms of how we spend our time and money on medicine, operations, and efforts to extend life, there are vast—we mean astonishingly vast—differences in philosophy, process, and prescription. Not surprisingly, the practice of medicine in America is largely driven by Big and More. Let's look at some examples.

One big problem in America is high blood pressure. Over fifty million Americans have it, down significantly from where it used to be, but still a big health problem. Since 1972 the Federal Government has sponsored and led a National High Blood Pressure Education Program to the tune of hundreds of millions of dollars when all is said and calculated. In the early years the treatment was focused on taking a pill (of course), in fact, lots of pills. As researchers began to understand the causes of high blood pressure, the education program began to focus on prevention through changes in lifestyle: Excess body weight, too much sodium in the diet, and excess drinking, combined with a lack of physical exercise was causing most of the problem in the first place. A clear case of Big and More in personal lifestyle manifesting itself in a big national health problem that exceeds $20 billion in treatment and hospitalization.

As the much-publicized news about high blood pressure became known in the last decade, many of us might have assumed that this was a problem afflicting all humans, or at least all those in affluent Western societies like our own. This is not the case. In Germany, for example, high blood pressure is not even a recognized illness: *Low* blood pressure is! Blood pressure is but one example, of course, and others abound. For an overview of some other cultural differences in health and medicine, see Snapshot #12.

Another case of Big and More in American medicine was described by *The New York Times* reporter Kurt Eichenwald in a three-part series, titled, "Mismanaged Care: The Perils of Dialysis." An American on dialysis is twice as likely to die in a given year as a patient in France, Germany, or Japan. In fact, 23.6 percent of dialysis patients die each year in America, compared to 11 percent in France, 10 percent in Germany, and 9.7 percent in Japan. Eichenwald's investigation found "an industry that uses equipment and procedures that cut costs and raise profits, often at the expense of patients' health." For example, older equipment that distributes solution to many patients at the same time is still in use, even though these machines are considered dangerous today.

Another practice, rooted in the Big and More approach to medicine (as well as the Now Force), which contributes to the 44,000 plus deaths per year in America from dialysis failure is rushing patients through treatment. In other words, keeping them on dialysis for too little time. This, despite the fact that studies document that the longer the dialysis, the lower the death rate. In the United States about ten hours a week are spent in treatment, compared with twelve and fourteen hours in France and Japan, respectively.

Snapshot #12

Culture Cures

★ American doctors perform six times as many cardiac bypass operations per capita as English doctors do.

★ Hysterectomies, the second most common major operation in the U.S., is rarely performed in France.

★ In the U.S., surgery to enlarge the breast is done twice as often as surgery to reduce them. Breast *reductions* are three to four times more common in France than breast enlargement.

★ Most French patients believe their migraines are caused by a liver malfunction; the Germans blame the heart; and the Americans blame whoever or whatever is convenient.

★ West Germans use six times the amount of heart drugs per capita as do the French and English.

★ Spa and spa referrals are an integral part of French and German medical practice. Not so in England, and there are no medical spas, as such, in the U.S.

★ West Germans see doctors an average of 12 times a year, compared to 5.4 for the English, 5.2 for the French, 4.7 for the Americans.

★ Americans treat the heart as a pump, suggesting that the body is really a machine. The Germans see the heart as an organ "that has a life of its own."

★ British doctors do less of everything. The average doctor visit is about six minutes, compared to fifteen to twenty minutes in France and the U.S.

Although the data are not as clear on a third practice that contributes to these higher morbidity rates in America, it is evident that the American practice of ignoring the instructions from the manufacturer, "SINGLE USE ONLY," leads to multiple re-use of disposable equipment (e.g., dialyzers and blood lines). This practice is forbidden in Japan and frowned upon elsewhere in the world, but it is thriving in America.

Culture on the Couch

At about the same time that Eichenwald and his associates were uncovering the abuses in the big dialysis business, the *American Journal of Psychiatry* published guidelines in November 1995 designed to make psychiatrists conscious of the cultural dimensions of illness and to urge them to consider cultural variations in illness as part of their treatment or therapy. American psychiatrists were put on notice to recognize and properly treat illness such as *amok* (brooding followed by a violent outburst), *brain fog* ("brain tiredness," a mental and physical reaction to the challenges of schooling), *pibloktoq* (physical and verbal violence for up to thirty minutes, followed by convulsions and short coma), and *taijin kyofusho* (a dread that one will do something to embarrass others). These are all culturally framed disorders not found in America, but common in Malaysia, West Africa, Eskimo communities, and Japan respectively. The closest thing in American culture to *taijin kyofusho* is social phobia that shifts the focus from others to you. Social phobia is a result of projected fear that others will criticize you rather than your being the cause or source of the problem.

These vast cultural differences in psychiatry can be seen through the following example. A patient who was listless, rambling about "my soul not being with me anymore" and unable to function properly, appeared psychotic and bound for an American diagnosis and treatment for severe depression. But the patient was from Ecuador and, instead, was diagnosed with *susto* syndrome, which is known throughout Latin America. It turned out that the patient's uncle had died unexpectedly and she had not had a chance to grieve properly. Dr. Juan Mezzich, a psychiatrist at the Mount Sinai School of Medicine in Manhattan, treated the woman and shaped the diagnosis and treatment to fit the culture; the patient was fine after simulating a wake that enabled her to properly grieve for her uncle.

Daniel Goleman, who reported on these guidelines for *The New York Times,** sees this new movement in the field of psychiatry as a good thing. He reports that "virtually every convention for psychotherapists now offers a workshop on how culture affects psychiatric problems." It is hoped that this same awareness will spread to hospitals, clinics, and other institutions in America.

The Diagnosis That Serves No Cure

To some drug abuse (prevention and treatment) is part of the health care problem. To others it is a separate problem—big in its own right. Clearly the illegal aspects and moral sanctions against drug *use* sets the problem apart. But regardless of its definition, drug use and abuse is a big problem that affects both individual businesses and the country as a whole.

However America looks at illicit drug use, much of the rest of the world sees it as "the American disease." Increasingly each country has to face its own version of the American disease, but today America seems to be at the top of the ladder of drug abuse. In some cultures, some drugs have a religious or cultural context that mitigate against their misuse. Others have harsh and arbitrary enforcement policies that prevent most abuse. Most of these safeguards and conditions do not exist in America.

Since the turn of the century, America has struggled to develop a coherent drug abuse policy, to no avail.[†] The problem has only gotten bigger and more complex with successive generations. Today the drug abuse problem is complicated even more by the spread of AIDS through intravenous drug use, the availability of "crack" (the smokable form of cocaine), selective racial enforcement of drug laws, and America's obsession, in our culture at large, to find a pill for every ill.

When it comes to big problems, especially big health problems like drug abuse, Americans like to create commissions, task forces, and think tanks to study the problem and conduct surveys to see how big the problem really is. Then there is a very

---

*"Making Room on the Couch For Culture," The New York Times, *December 5, 1995.*

[†]*For the best history of drug abuse in America, read David Musto's classic,* The American Disease: Origins of Narcotic Control.

brief period when the results of the studies and surveys are open to public dialogue or diatribe—depending on whether or not you like the numbers. Normally, no one likes the numbers except the researchers who usually give you confidence intervals of 95 percent with a sampling error of plus or minus three or four percentage points—the fine print in survey work. So getting excited about a three-point jump or drop in your favorite statistic—a big number in survey terms—might simply fall within that sampling error.

If the problem doesn't go away on its own once it has been quantified or quarreled over, we generally take a rest—about a year or two—and study it again. Most health surveys don't show any significant change in less than two years and many remain relatively constant over a long period of time. That's the case with alcohol, drugs, and cigarettes. One skeptic of the government action on cigarettes (after twenty-five years of research) said, "Cigarettes are the leading cause of statistics."

Yet, the problem rages on while the studies are shelved. Nowhere is this more obvious than the drug abuse scourge in America. The numbers that follow in the next several pages have been around in one form or another since the early '70s when the drug abuse survey business kicked into high gear.* The variation from survey to survey and from year to year has had virtually no consequence on public policy. So quantification is not the sine qua non for action.

Our authority and source for these numbers is Dr. Robert L. DuPont, President of the Institute for Behavior and Health and author of *The Selfish Brain: What We Have Learned About Addiction and What You Can Do About It* (American Psychiatric Press, Spring 1996). He was the first director of the National Institute on Drug Abuse, part of the U.S. Department of Health and Human Services, and the second director (drug czar) of the White House Office for Drug Abuse Prevention under President Ford and President Carter.[†]

How big is the drug abuse problem?

Drug addiction is the number one preventable health problem in America. It is the number one issue of concern to young people in America and has been for years. Four out of ten American families are directly affected by addiction and one in every four deaths in the United States is caused by alcohol, tobacco, or illicit drugs.

In 1990, the last year for which these costs were estimated, illegal drug use cost us $67 billion a year, what DuPont calls "an involuntary addiction tax" that is paid by each of us. This big price tag includes all treatment, law enforcement, and social cost, as well as the cost to industry in terms of lost productivity. On top of this, add $72 billion for tobacco and $98.6 billion for alcohol for a grand total of $237.6 billion—about four thousand boxcars stacked with one dollar bills, stretching more than forty miles, if we used the trillion dollar images we reported on earlier. These are not static numbers; they have gotten bigger in the past five years.

---

*U.S. Department of Health and Human Services has conducted two national surveys on drug use on a regular basis since 1975. One, popularly known as the National High School Student Survey, interviews 50,000 students on all types of drug use and frequency of use. The other survey is the National Household Survey on Drug Abuse, first conducted in 1971.

[†]Josh Hammond worked for DuPont in both government agencies as Director of Communications and Public Affairs.

There are about 500,000 heroin addicts in America, an estimate that has remained relatively constant for the past twenty years or so. Each heroin addict spends about $24,600 a year on his habit—ironically, a little less than it would cost to house the addict in prison, if he or she were doing time for a drug-related crime.

Cocaine is next on the list with twenty-three million who have tried it. It is known as the "rich man's" drug (as Woody Allen once said, "Cocaine is God's way of telling you that you make too much money"), and the average cocaine user spends about $9,200 a year for the habit.

In some books, the statistics go on endlessly, page after page after page. One wonders "to what end?" What value is there in knowing the numbers if nothing is done about it? While we may demur about the drug abuse problem at the national level, we can't deny it at the workplace. That responsibility is yours, not a politician's or pollster's.

Practically three-fourths of current drug abusers are employed. To be precise, 70 percent of current drug abusers are employed. DuPont says, "There is growing evidence that the use of illegal drugs now rivals alcoholism in its devastating effects on workplace safety, performance, and morale."

Drug-using workers, compared to non-drug-using workers are:

★ three to four times as likely to have an accident on the job

★ four to six times as likely to have an off-the-job accident

★ two to three times as likely to be absent from work

★ three times as likely to file medical claims

★ five times as likely to file a workman's compensation claim

★ and 25 to 33 percent less productive

In more direct terms, the January 4, 1987, crash of an Amtrak and a Conrail train in Essex, Maryland, took sixteen people's lives, injured one hundred seventy others, and exceeded $100 million in liability costs. There is no estimate for the cost to either company for the attendant employee costs associated with the clean-up, litigation, public relations, and related activities. The drug use of the engineer, who ran through three warning signals on the high-speed corridor between Washington, D.C., and New York and caused the accident, could have been detected and the accident prevented.

That's only one case. Consider this: DuPont reports that of the employed cocaine users who call the National Cocaine Hotline (1-800-Cocaine):

★ 74 percent use drugs at work

★ 64 percent easily obtain drugs at work

★ 44 percent sell drugs at work

★ 20 percent have been involved in an accident at work

★ 18 percent have stolen money from co-workers for drugs

Clearly drug abuse is also a big problem for business. But business is able to take steps in dealing with drug use in the workplace that the government, so far, has chosen not to take. For example, compulsory testing for drug use is often a condition for employment. New forms of drug screening, such as hair follicle analysis, not only detect the use of drugs over a longer period of time (one month), but they are less invasive of personal space than the more conventional urine analysis that can only detects drug use within the past forty-eight hours.

Ironically, government-imposed vaccinations are compulsory—and accepted—for school attendance to protect against certain diseases and illnesses, but screening for drug possession and use is not. Until the problem is redefined (see our discussion of the problem of definition in public policy in Chapter 1), this problem is going to simply continue to get bigger and bigger with greater consequences for all of us further down the road.

The Big Prescription at Johnson & Johnson

Did you ever notice how big problems have a way of creating big industries to ostensibly make the problem smaller, but somehow never do? The growth in the problem is invariably stated as a function of the "disease" rather than a consequence of the diagnosis. The recent debates on health care are not about the size of the problem as a whole, but simply about the size of the role that the federal government plays. No one has calculated, or seems to care about the eventual cumulative size of fifty state solutions. We'll deal with that (⬩) problem later.

To search for some understanding of how Big and More can be managed more effectively, we turned to the private sector where accountability is more immediate and stockholders get to "vote" as often as they choose. For comparative purposes, we decided to stay in the health care arena to see how corporate America manages Big and More. Here is what we learned at the world's biggest health care products giant, Johnson & Johnson.

J&J was founded in 1885 when three brothers, Robert Wood Johnson, James Wood Johnson, and Edward Mead Johnson formed a partnership to make the first ready-to-use surgical dressings to help reduce the infection and disease that caused such high mortality rates among postoperative surgery patients. Within two years they had hired fourteen people and incorporated as Johnson & Johnson. Today they are the world's largest and most comprehensive manufacturer of health care products with over 81,000 employees in one hundred sixty-eight operating companies in fifty-three countries making products and providing services in thirty-three major lines of business from pharmacuticals and surgical devices to personal hygiene products and the daily disposable contact lenses mentioned earlier. In 1994, with $15.73 billion in sales, J&J's earnings reached the $2 billion mark for the first time, with earnings per share up nearly 14 percent to a record $3.12.

Expect those numbers to be bigger in 1995 and continue to grow because this is a big company that doesn't rest on last year's laurels. Ralph Larsen, chairman and CEO at J&J sees to that. Larsen also is the guardian of the decentralization philosophy at J&J, the company's prescription for Big and More. Since the early 1930s, J&J has operated on the assumption that big is really a group of smaller self-governing units that are easier to manage, quicker to react to changing market conditions, and faster to respond to new business opportunities.

Since J&J has become a model for how to make decentralization work, Josh Hammond visited with Ralph Larsen to get a closer look at the Big and More Force in action.

JH: *How important is big to you?*

RL: We are not trying to be big. We have never, ever, in any strategic document that I am aware of, ever established size or bigness as critical. What we have said is we want to be the best health care company, to be the most competitive health care company. If being big is the result of being the best, that's wonderful. But we don't chase size for size sake. Size is tough to manage and we just never pursued that as a strategic objective.

JH: *Why is size hard to manage?*

RL: We are not good as a function of being big, we are big as a function of being good. I think there is an important point there. Size has a way of bringing bureaucracy in, of accelerating the need for control, and control leads to bureaucracy, bureaucracy leads to smothering, slowing down. So I think size is as big a problem as it is an advantage.

JH: *You don't tell your companies how big they should be. Are there things you do tell them they have to do?*

RL: Our companies develop their own strategic plans, develop their own growth plans, develop their own internal targets for growth. We do not have corporate targets that are then rolled back down into the operating units. They have asked for that many times and they want to know what the target is. But when they come to us for strategic direction, we turn them right around and say what do you think? We don't provide answers here. We question and challenge but we do not micromanage the operating companies. We throw the problems right back in their lap.

JH: *How do you run big or I should say, how do you run best?*

RL: There are three principles that are important to long-term vitality and the continued growth and success of this corporation. One is that we maintain decentralization and all that involves. Now decentralization means different things at different points in time, but the basic thrust of decentralization is to push responsibility down the line, run the corporation from the bottom up rather than the top down. For example, in recent years we have tended to move to shared services where every operating company doesn't do all the things that it used to do. Some people said, "Ah, you're centralizing." We say no we are not centralizing, we are taking a look at the world around us and we are saying look, it just doesn't make sense to have thirty domestic companies buying chemicals from thirty different purchase orders, that's crazy. It makes more sense to buy that as an organization. So we buy common packaging materials, negotiate common contracts with paper and chemical companies and things that all our companies use.

What we haven't centralized is knowledge-based functions that give us our superiority. Sales and marketing and the things that are really the heart blood of the organization—those we keep decentralized.

The second principle is to manage the business for the long term with common sense. Anybody can turn in short-term profits by bilking the business. That's not acceptable. Any idiot can do that. On the other hand, if someone says I am building for the long term and throws tons of money at crazy projects, we say no, you have to deliver reasonable short-term results that meet the practical needs of the corporation. So that's what we watch for. We are alert for managements that may be curtailing research spending in order to turn in quarterly profits.

And then the third thing that we tell our people is we want you to run your business according to the ethics and principles of the Credo. That really is the glue that holds this whole place together.

Our managements know that they can introduce a new product that fails and they can engage in risky research. We accept failure and understand that taking risks involves failure. Building businesses means invariably that most of what you do probably isn't going to work. But you know some of it will and that's what will build the business.

The one thing we will not stand for is where you cut corners or you violate the ethical principles of the Credo. We are not perfect, we make mistakes, and people sometimes do things that you wish they would not do, things happen that should not happen. But we are very tough when it comes to the ethical standards and if we see somebody who just doesn't share our values, they are gone and we will not stand for it.

JH: *Do you have a process or system for learning from your mistakes?*

RL: It's a very informal process. You know, I think there is a lot of shared learning that goes on, but it's done more informally. Although we are a big company, we are a small company in the sense that there isn't anything that happens around here that doesn't move on the grapevine. We have a tremendously effective informal grapevine in this corporation. I mean it's unbelievable! For example, I just spent a day at Neutrogena and I will guarantee you within forty-eight hours what I said out there, the comments that I made, will have permeated throughout the entire organization. So I deliberately will say provocative things or challenging things because I know that it's going to get around. So there is an informal network.

What we try not to do is embarrass people or hold them up to ridicule. The person who made a mistake feels badly enough about it and we don't want to point them out. People feel terrible enough about it, so we are not going to hold them up to ridicule. On the other hand when the hurt wears off and the sensitivity wears off, we go to school on that.

One of the central realities of decentralization is you have to be willing to tolerate ambiguity, some reasonable chaos within the organization. Decentralization is an arrogantly disorderly process. It is both complex and ambiguous. And so in order to manage around here, in order to function effectively within Johnson & Johnson, I think you have to have a higher than normal degree of tolerance and coping ability to deal with ambiguity and complexity. If you have a high need for command and control then you can't function within this corporation. We are inherently disorganized.

JH: *Is this part of your personal nature or do you have to work at it?*

RL: I have to work at it. I tend to be very orderly. In my personal life and the way I think and the way I do things I tend to be very buttoned-up. I like things organized. I'm most comfortable in that. But I have learned that in order to maximize the effectiveness of this large organization, you have to be willing to let people do their thing. It may not be the way I would do it and it may kill me to watch some of them do it, but you have to let go, you just have to do that. What I have learned is that when you do that you release enormous energy within the company. So I may not sleep all that well because I can't control everything and things happen that I worry about, and yet I can't meddle, I can't go in and fix it, I can't go in and tell them what to do. So for me it is much more stressful to deal in this kind of environment than if everything came up to my office and I approved it all.

JH: *I imagine that you have some big customers out there who half of your companies service. How is that coordinated?*

RL: Well, that's a good example of where the world has changed. If you go back five or ten years we might have had ten or twelve of our operating companies calling on a specific customer. Then the trade began to change where the customers could do more centralized buying, where information technology allowed them to accumulate much more in the way of data and information on products and in sales. Then our customers began to have a need for talking to one person at Johnson & Johnson rather than ten or twelve. So we have had to make changes in the way we approach our customers. Most recently we have formed Johnson & Johnson Health Care Systems, in a sense an umbrella marketing sales organization, to address this change.

JH: *If a customer has a problem, how is it now resolved?*

RL: We do whatever the customer wants. In some cases the customer will say give me one phone number and one name. We say fine. Now this person may have to talk to thirteen people within Johnson & Johnson to resolve the problem, but the customer makes one phone call. Other customers say, now wait a minute, I've been dealing with your company for thirty years, I know my way around, I want it just the way it is. And so if I have a problem with baby products I'll call my friend so and so. That's wonderful, whatever you want. We try to make it as easy as possible to do business with Johnson & Johnson. We are not where we want to be in that regard but we don't want to tell the customer about our problems. The customer should not have to worry about our communication lines or our organizational structure. We want to make it so easy to do business with Johnson & Johnson that the customer will not think about doing business with somebody else.

JH: *Shifting a little bit now. I don't know this with a lot of certainty but there are companies like Corning, Xerox, and Motorola who, as part of their global strategy, say there is a Xerox way, there is a Corning way, there is a Motorola way and it doesn't matter if you're in Illinois or France or Singapore, you're in a Corning plant, you're in a Xerox facility. There are other companies like HP that have more culturally adaptive styles without a single management approach. Are you in either of those camps or are you in the middle somewhere?*

RL: No, I don't think there is a Johnson & Johnson way. I mean our companies around the world are very different, depending upon where they are and so forth. Our management styles around the world range from very authoritarian to very, very participative. Some have moved aggressively to teams throughout the company and others remain very command- and control-oriented. So there is a wide spectrum in terms of management style for Johnson & Johnson.

Having said that, there is a sameness to them; you would see similarities. It would be very clean. The quality would just scream at you. Respect for employees, the working conditions would jump out at you. Respect for the community and the environment would jump out at you. That's the part that would be the same. And

The Johnson & Johnson Credo

Our Credo

We believe our first responsibility is to the doctors, nurses, and patients, to mothers and fathers and all others who use our products and services. In meeting their needs everything we do must be of high quality. We must constantly strive to reduce our costs in order to maintain reasonable prices. Customers' orders must be serviced promptly and accurately. Our suppliers and distributors must have an opportunity to make a fair profit.

We are responsible to our employees, the men and women who work with us throughout the world. Everyone must be considered as an individual. We must respect their dignity and recognize their merit. They must have a sense of security in their jobs. Compensation must be fair and adequate, and working conditions clean, orderly and safe. We must be mindful of ways to help our employees fulfill their family responsibilities. Employees must feel free to make suggestions and complaints. There must be equal opportunity for employment, development and advancement for those qualified. We must provide competent management, and their actions must be just and ethical.

We are responsible to the communities in which we live and work and to the world community as well. We must be good citizens—support good works and charities and bear our fair share of taxes. We must encourage civic improvements and better health and education. We must maintain in good order the property we are privileged to use, protecting the environment and natural resources.

Our final responsibility is to our stockholders. Business must make a sound profit. We must experiment with new ideas. Research must be carried on, innovative programs developed and mistakes paid for. New equipment must be purchased, new facilities provided and new products launched. Reserves must be created to provide for adverse times. When we operate according to these principles, the stockholders should realize a fair return.

Johnson & Johnson

those are Credo-based. So there is a common bond but it's Credo-based. The Credo is a very powerful force in this corporation, I don't care where you go.

At a recent four-day worldwide management meeting in Orlando, we spent a day and a half of those four days talking about the Credo and the importance of the Credo. It was a very powerful day-and-a-half session. So more than 25 percent of the meeting was invested in talking about the Credo and how important it is and how we often fall short of it and the standards—and there we did give examples, we cleared everybody out of the room, all the outsiders, we turned off the television cameras and the recording devices and it was just a heart-to-heart talk.

JH: *You led this heart-to-heart?*

RL: Yes. I talked about the things that bothered me. The changing world. How it [the Credo] was the one constant. You know it wasn't because I thought we had some big problem, but I believed that in order for this company to continue to be successful in the years ahead as we get bigger and bigger you really have to work at maintaining values and standards. The bigger you get, the harder job that is. We were hiring people, we were changing people, new people come and join us as we acquire companies. I spend more time on this issue than anything else. And it's not, it's not out of any terrible concern with something that's happened. It's like in a family or in any organized community, if you don't work at maintaining your value system, you are going to lose it. If you don't talk about it, you're going to lose it. If you don't live it, you're going to lose it. To me the ethical foundation of this corporation is not in the big decisions, it's in the thousands of small decisions that are made by all of our people every day.

JH: *What's an example of something that would worry you?*

RL: Our ability to maintain what this corporation is all about, to maintain the high ethical standards of the corporation as we get bigger and bigger is a major concern. That's my first responsibility, it's my primary responsibility. You've got to perpetuate it all the time. I think you have got to work at it . . . I think you've got to work at it.

A New Design for Bigness

Just when we thought that the routine megamergers of the 1980s were behind us, 1995 surfaced as a particularly big year for bigness, a harbinger of things to come. Practically every industry had a run at bigness through mergers or acquisitions: entertainment (led by Disney-ABC and Time-Warner–Turner mergers), financial services (topped by the Chemical and Chase merger that made them the number one bank in the U.S.), utilities (PECO and Union Electric), transportation (Union Pacific and Burlington Northern), consumer goods (Kimberly-Clark buys Scott Paper), and health care mergers of every sort, from drugmakers and managed-care networks to insurance and hospitals.

With all this external, visible bigness, more and more companies in 1995 continued to move to an internal business strategy of fewer and fewer suppliers. The paring down of suppliers, which can often run into the tens of thousands at big companies, has resulted in fierce competition for preferred-supplier designations.

Although fewer suppliers spells bigger suppliers, companies expect lower cost and higher quality as a result of their ability to focus and manage these suppliers better.

While many of the mergers of the 1980s were financially driven, often hostile takeovers and leveraged buyouts, this latest wave of bigness is more strategic, more designed. The goals are to acquire and control distribution channels, invest in new technology, merge product design, gain market dominance, reduce costs, among other strategic business objectives. Not to be overlooked in the new race for bigness is the emergence of global enterprises and so-called megacorporate states where there will be fewer global firms in certain economic sectors. As all this takes shape in the years ahead, American business wants to emerge with this primal force intact and be number one worldwide.

In the race for global bigness, our competitive advantage is the force we write about next in Chapter 4: Now time. America's sense of pace, it's urgency and impatience with time—unlike other cultures—may just be the fuel the bigness design needs in order to work.

Big and More Fake Sheet

The Big and More Force is the most complex of the cultural forces. It has three facets: Big, More, and the obsession with being number one, which are usually interchangeable, but often inseparable. This force is both constructive and destructive. It enriches and entraps, it builds up and brings down, it increases options and decreases choices, it offers security and invites abuse. Unchecked, it is the one force that can threaten the American way of life. It requires due diligence to make sure the ends don't justify the means.

★ The three ways to get big are: Acquire externally, grow internally, or redefine the business. Companies like Home Depot and Barnes & Noble are role models for how to activate the Big and More Force. Both have successfully used a combination of the mergers and/or acquisitions, rapid internal expansion, and redefining their business as a way to become the dominant players in their industry (see page 106–110).

★ There are five key advantages to Big and More. Any business that leverages this force is able to: (1) achieve an *economy of scale* in its goods and services that in turn can be passed along to the consumer through lower prices; (2) support a higher *tolerance for risk* in its product and service innovations, personnel management practices, and in its related growth strategies; (3) increase *employee motivation* by enabling workers to tap into the challenge of doing things bigger and better the next time; (4) *broaden consumer choice* through product and service diversity; (5) accommodate and make *room for small* by encouraging business units, teams, work groups, and others to act big in spite of their size (see page 110).

★ Historian Max Lerner says that America grew big as a nation because of the convergence of three big ideas that were constantly in motion: the unexplored frontier; the emergence of rapidly changing technology; and democracy as a way to govern. Since these work so well for America, they can work equally as well for American business. Companies should explore frontiers of innovation and new services; continue to explore the application of technology; and engage workers in process (see page 116).

★ If you aren't big, act big. Companies like Hewlett-Packard and Johnson & Johnson are big by most business definitions, yet they are highly decentralized, with a lot of authority and autonomy going to smaller business units. Enabling these business units to *act* big, though in fact they may not be big in their own right, is a powerful way to tap into this cultural force.

Americans are obsessed with being number one with no regard for second place. Yet, big for bigness' sake, has little value for American business.

Chapter 4

The Future is Now
American Time

Someone once said that a company like FedEx could not have been invented in any other country but the United States. What he meant to say is that only Americans put off important matters until the last minute and then look up at the clock at 5 P.M. and, in shock, decide that these charts, that contract, or the diamond tiara has to be in Los Angeles first thing tomorrow morning, without fail, or the world will come to an end.

Time is a universal force, but in America we have defined, segmented, standardized, systematized, and segregated it more than any other culture in the world. In contrast to other countries, Americans live in the present future. For us, time is NOW. We have little interest in the past (yesterday is history) and we generally have no interest in the future—that long-range stuff that is five or ten years down the road. Rather we think in immediate terms and act accordingly.

Nothing can wait. The Now Force drives our bias for action, that tendency to plunge in without first testing the waters, or even learning how to swim; it accounts for our impatience with planning; it is responsible for the fact that we make mistakes. It is manifest in every aspect of our behavior.

The Now Force does not allow time to replenish—it is constantly accelerating things. We shot buffalo faster than they could reproduce, poisoned streams faster than they could cleanse themselves, cut forests faster than trees could grow, and spent borrowed money faster than it could be replaced by an expanding economy.

In keeping with our need to do things quickly, to get to the point, to cut to the chase, Americans want things relatively simple and straightforward. We are always angling for a shortcut, not only in complicated business dealings but in everyday routines. For example, when acquaintances, colleagues, or friends meet, Americans are quick to shake hands (short and businesslike) while other cultures spend time greeting one another: The French take time for multiple kisses on the cheeks; the Japanese make the appropriate number and style of bows; Mexicans enjoy a leisurely *abraso* that often involves a hug, handshake, and repeated patting on the shoulders.

We also seek to take shortcuts in our speech: Witness the ubiquitous acronym. If you live in the city of New York, it's N.Y.C.; in Los Angeles (having lost its original Spanish pronunciation), it's L.A.; and the folks in San Francisco are fighting an uphill battle to keep the rest of the world from saying "Frisco." Federal Express becomes FedEx, and the University of California at Berkeley is simply Cal locally and Cal-Berkeley elsewhere. If there is a ten- or twelve-step program, we will want to know the most important three. If your name is Joseph, I'll call you Joe—without even asking permission.

In the world of business there are also countless reminders of how prevalent the Now Force is. Businesses have Just-in-Time (applied to suppliers, inventory control, and delivery processes), Moments-of-Truth (for customer interface), time management (for office and individual efficiency), process simplification (for speeding up the manufacturing or delivery process), etc.

Once we have grasped the impact of the Now Force, the implications for how to work with it instead of against it become obvious. If immediacy is important to Americans, then feedback must be quick and to the point. Since we don't look back, there is little value in an awards dinner that recognizes an achievement that is six months old. Because we can't focus on distant goals, it makes sense to break projects down into stages that allow us to finish sooner. As you'll see, there are some good examples of companies that are already using the Now Force to good advantage.

In this chapter we will examine how two companies, Allied Signal and FedEx, have harnessed the time force and made it an ally in their efforts to dramatically increase quality, productivity, and profitability. We'll look at some formal systems for organizing time and compare U.S. time to three other cultures. A profile of *Reader's Digest* will remind us of how a product can be in sync with the time constraints a culture imposes on itself. We'll identify the ideal amount of time that a plurality of Americans consider optimum before things should change and how Ernst & Young and Milliken & Company have applied short time frames to business performance. And we'll show how most companies have so cluttered work processes that most of us are "wasting our time" doing things that shouldn't be done, could be done better by someone else, or that we were not hired or trained to do.

Our interest here is in time as a force and how the activation of this force can enhance productivity, improve quality, energize the American workforce, and restore the value and meaning of work. In other words, how does the American definition of time become an asset to a company, not a liability?

The Total Quality Speed Company

On July 1, 1991, the day that Larry Bossidy became the CEO of Allied Signal, Inc., he was greeted by a company forecast predicting a negative cash flow of $435 million by the end of the year and $336 million in 1992. Debt was 42 percent of capital and employee morale was at rock bottom. *One year later,* Allied Signal had a positive cash flow of $255 million, a turnaround of $831 million from the day Bossidy walked into his Morristown, New Jersey office. Sales went from $11.83 billion in 1991 to $12.04 billion in 1992. Earnings per share did a total reversal, rising from minus $2.00 to plus $3.80 over the same period of time. And the company's stock went from just over $14 to $46 by 1995.

Allied Signal's businesses are the rather moribund aerospace industry, automotive, and selected engineering and materials industries, all known as "mature" businesses with not a whole lot of wiggle room. So how did this all change? Activating the Now Force, that's how.

We talked with James Sierk, senior vice president of quality and productivity, to get the inside-out story. In the interview that follows, we learned the five key secrets to activating the Now Force:

1. Make *speed* a corporate value.
2. Train everyone in understanding and using speed.
3. Get rid of non-value-added work.
4. Practice the elevator speeches.
5. Hire a CEO who personifies speed.

JS: The story of Allied Signal is very much a story of a corporate revival. It's very much driven by the vision and energy of a new CEO, Larry Bossidy. Prior to him, Allied Signal was a very average company. We had average financials; the street thought we were average; the customers thought we were average; and the employees actually thought we were a little below average. The company had taken an employee attitude survey prior to Larry's coming aboard and the results were so bad that we promptly shoved them in a desk drawer and never looked at them again. Of course, the employee problem didn't go away that way.

When Larry came aboard, one of the first things we did was sit down for a few days and map out the vision for the company. We did not have one before, so we laid out the values of the company and set the framework for what really needed to change.

Prior to 1991 we were sixty-five independent business units, each with its own name. So we had to have a vision on how important it is to be one company. Everyone has those vision things on the wall. Ours is simple; it's to be a premier company, to be successful in everything we do. The values looked like everybody else's too, you know, integrity, focus on customers, people, teamwork, performance, and innovation. However, there is one major difference: We have speed as a value. We focus on speed for competitive advantage. We simplify processes and compress cycle times.

JH: *What do you mean by speed?*

JS: To a lot of people speed means doing the *same thing* faster. When you combine speed with stretch goals, something interesting happens: You have to change your processes. You know anybody can get 10 percent better just by moving a little faster and tightening the belt a little bit. To meet a stretch goal you have to change a process: that was a foundation for change that Larry Bossidy brought from the very beginning.

JH: *What is an example?*

JS: One stretch goal was a 6 percent increase in productivity a year. We also wanted to increase our operating profit from 4.7 percent in 1991 to 9 percent in 1994. And we wanted to practically double our return on equity from 10.5 percent to 18 percent by 1994. Productivity for us means the annual difference between all revenue divided by all cost. Measures are important, as you know. If you don't have goals and measures, you never know where you are. And unless you have a good measurement system, people won't understand what's necessary to meet the stretch goals.

JH: *How did you achieve that?*

JS: We did a lot of training very quickly. We didn't have much of a training organization prior to 1991. Back in the late eighties we saved a lot of money one year by laying everybody off that had "trainer" in their name. So when we started the change effort we didn't have a large professional cadre of trainers. What we did was to build them internally. Now we've got probably three thousand part-time trainers in the company.

JH: *Was the medium also the message?*

JS: Yes. We trained about nintey-five thousand people around the world in eighteen months through a four-day course starting with basically zero resources. Coopers & Lybrand* helped us in this and I think if you talk to Steve Yearout and the other folks in Coopers they will say they were just absolutely amazed at how a company can start a massive effort like that and complete it within such a short period of time.

JH: *Did you find people naturally gravitating to the notion of speed or was there resistance?*

JS: When we first set speed up as a value, I think people took one look at it and said, oh, that's nice, sure, we'll do things faster. The first reaction was okay, I'll just do the same thing faster. There is the fatal flaw. You are doomed to failure when that happens. A company that embarks upon using speed as the underlying value for corporate revival can't just say do things faster, people—it has to be a lot more than that.

What you really have to do is to improve the process. That's where people resist change. They have always done things a certain way; now they have to do things faster. So people have to first understand that processes have to change and then second that they have the ability to change those processes. But you have to give people the necessary skills, tools, and techniques to change their process.

What TQS is.	*What TQS is not.*
Cycle-time reduction	Working longer hours
Focus on core business processes	Working harder
Increases in speed eliminate waste	Applying more resources
Enhancements of customer satisfaction	Hurrying
Improved business results—quickly	

Source: Coopers & Lybrand

JH: *How did you do that?*

JS: Again, we did that through training. We trained people in speed. In fact the initiative was called TQS, Total Quality Speed. We trained probably a third of the company, about thirty to thirty-five thousand people, in TQS. They learned how to

---

Coopers & Lybrand is one of the Big Six accounting and management consulting firms. They are specialists in change management consulting. C&L has established Centers of Excellence for Change Management and Total Quality Management. T. Wood Parker headed up the Allied Signal relationship. C&L is headquartered in Arlington, Virginia.

map processes, they learned differentiation, value-added and non-value-added work. As a result we changed the major processes in every one of our businesses.

JH: *How did you decide to do it in eighteen months or did it just happen to happen in eighteen months?*

JS: Well there is a personal story here. You know I came from Xerox. And at Xerox we did this [train a comparable number of employees] in about three years. So I proposed a plan that would take about three years. Larry's reaction was instantaneous; he said that's too slow. And so with his encouragement we put a plan together to do it in eighteen months.

JH: *What do you mean with "his encouragement"? That's an interesting choice of words. I think you are being soft here.*

JS: Actually, it was a pretty strong directive. Look, Larry is the most impatient man in the world. You know by his own behavior and also by the directive he gives you that he is looking for speed in everything that he does. So when I laid out the proposal to do this in three years, his response was well, why can't you do it in a year? I convinced him that I could do it in eighteen months.

JH: *Was there any resistance?*

JS: We had some management resistance at Xerox, but at Allied Signal there was no resistance, no open resistance. I'm sure there are some managers in their own hearts that said this is stupid, but Larry made things clear at the very beginning of our process.

JH: *How do you know that this emphasis on speed works?*

JS: Well the good thing about having speed as a measure is that you know quickly if you're successful or not.

JH: *What modifications have you made, if any, to the price-quality-schedule trade-off?**

JS: First, we understand that prices don't increase, they just decrease. The day of corporate margins improving by increasing prices a percent or two a year has long passed. We expect from our suppliers and our customers expect of us, decent prices *and* increased quality. Senior management understands that we get higher prices through higher quality.

Second, one of the major reasons why companies go slowly is because they have quality problems. If you have to stop and rework material, and if you get bad parts from suppliers and you have to reorder them or rework them, that slows you down. And if you are creating defects on an assembly line, it slows you down. So one of the major activities that we have right now is directly linked to speed: increasing the quality of our products. Our goal this year [1995] is to reduce defects by 50 percent, thereby increasing quality. We are well on the way to achieving it.

This is the production notion that only two of these can work together. For example, if you want to control costs and produce higher quality, schedule might suffer. Or, if you want high quality and must stay on schedule, costs may increase. Or, if you want to control costs and stay on schedule, quality may be diminished.

JH: *That's great. You used the word "revival" at the beginning and then you have used it a couple of times throughout. Is that a conscious use of that word? Is that your word? Is it Bossidy's word?*

JS: Do we have a PR campaign within the company that uses the word "revival"? The answer is no. Josh, it just sort of naturally pops up. Seriously.

JH: *That's great!*

JS: This is interesting because it isn't just revival, if you will. In English, the word "revival" has an interesting religious connotation, doesn't it? At a revival you have enthusiasm, it's rebirth, it's all of those emotional things that go around with positive change. It doesn't translate incidentally in other languages. But in English it just sort of naturally pops up in our conversation. And you know, you have to have informed zealots as you go through this process.

JH: *My father was a preacher, so I know that revivals have a high emotional component that reengineering doesn't have. What's your take on this?*

JS: We don't use the re-word [reengineering]. TQS, total quality speed, is our word, because we want this to be under the same total quality umbrella. All the changes we make are interrelated. We want to make sure people know that.

JH: *What are you working on now?*

JS: We are training everybody in identifying and getting rid of non-value-added work.

JH: *Before you get too far into this, and for my frame of reference, what percentage of work would you guess is non-value-added? We're trying to get a handle on that.*

JS: Josh, it's an enormous amount. Most people, when they map out their process for the first time, look at it and say, oh my God, real work is only being done 10 percent of the elapsed time. People understand that once they go through the technical layout of their process, their challenge then is how do I only do value-added work? Incidentally, when we taught people what to do, we said, value-added work is probably only done 10 percent of the elapsed time of any process. You are not going to be able to get down there so don't set a target of 10 percent of the time because you will get too frustrated.

To help with this, we have put in the idea of entitlement. Entitlement in most processes is about a third of the elapsed time. It is about three times the value-added work. So if somebody was doing something in nine days, they would logically expect, when they got done with their analysis and developing a new process, that they would be able to do it in three days.

JH: *What role does Bossidy play in sustaining the effort?*

JS: Bossidy walks around a lot, I mean he's with business units a lot. He says he is out of his office 60 to 80 percent of the time and that's true. He has a wonderful, healthy disregard for the organization structure. It's wonderful! He goes any place that he wants to. I'd say it's healthy because he can do it without an enormous amount of fear in the organization, they expect that of him. He wants his managers to do the same thing. He handles it in a way that's not threatening to people. That's a unique skill!

JH: *He's a pretty big and imposing guy, isn't he?*

JS: Oh sure he is, he is. In many ways, he's bigger than life. He's got a great understanding of the value of symbolic acts. With this wonderful disregard for the organizational structure, people see him a lot. I was talking to Ernie, a new MBA, on the occasion of his first anniversary with the company. We got on to the subject of Bossidy and he says, you know this is amazing, I joined this company as a new MBA and I've talked to the chairman of the company twice in my first year. So Bossidy understands symbolic acts.

He's also publicly impatient. People see him. They write letters to him. He writes handwritten letters back. He's very visible and accessible. He sees customers a lot, talks about customers a lot. He's always encouraging people to simplify processes.

JH: *Has he been consistently the same guy or do you see him evolving?*

JS: Oh no, he's growing, he is growing. He has a steel trap for a memory. Josh, I'll have a conversation with him and he'll say, damn it, you didn't tell me that a year ago. Well I forgot what I said a year ago, but he didn't.

JH: *Wow!*

JS: He absorbs a lot of information. He learns details at every level. Josh, do you know what an elevator speech is?

JH: *Yes. But what's your definition?*

JS: If you get on an elevator on the bottom floor and someone turns to you and says, hey, what do you know about quality function deployment, you have to the thirtieth floor, about two minutes, to describe the subject thoroughly. Well, we have a glossary of terms, thirty of them, that senior management was asked to give elevator speeches on. Now the first time they took the quiz, most could do about six on the average. By the beginning of year three, they could answer twenty-five or twenty-six of them. Bossidy was among them.

We just put out another group of thirty. The average score was high, around nine or ten this time. This was an entirely new group of different terms, different concepts. Bossidy was well above the average and by this time next year he will have all thirty of them down pat. So the environment is such where Larry is continually learning from the organization, from outside people, from other CEOs, and from the challenge leading this organization.

JH: *So, does he walk, talk, and eat fast? Is he the personification of speed?*

JS: Oh absolutely. I mean I'm not a golfer. I would hate to be on the golf course with him. Hate to be! He's walked off the golf course when somebody slow in front of him won't move.

JH: *Does he make decisions fast?*

JS: No, not too fast. He has a great decision process. He's a wonderful listener. He makes the decision. He has opinions on everything. He doesn't believe in a consen-

Bossidy Boots

Bossidy gets his natural, no-nonsense feel for opportunities from a lifetime of running businesses and taking risks. From the time he was 12 years old, Bossidy . . . spent evenings and Saturdays selling boots and loafers in the family shoe store in Pittsfield, Massachusetts . . . If snowflakes started falling late Friday night, his father handed the teenager a thick wad of about $500. Larry would drive three hours to buy rubber footwear at a midnight auction in Ware, then return in time to catch a few hours' sleep before selling the galoshes to soggy-shoed patrons on Saturday morning. By the time he reached Colgate University, Bossidy was making the bets himself. He noticed that white buck shoes were the rage on campus. So Bossidy haggled with his father to buy boxes of them. He read the market perfectly. *In a single day* he unloaded every pair at a nice profit to the crew-cut Colgate preppies.

From an August 21, 1995 article in *Fortune* by Shawn Tully

sus process because it's too slow. But since he can listen so well, people accept decisions that he makes a lot more because they know they've been heard. If you have a strong view you must argue it with him. He doesn't respect people that have strong views that keep quiet. He does all kinds of things personally to encourage people to disagree with him, if they want to.

JH: *So what gets you up in the morning?*

JS: It's wonderful being part of a team. Larry has built a leadership team, you know the top ten people, that share the same values, that like each other, that drive the same degree of change. Josh, we are so aligned it's unbelievable. We try to help each other succeed; politics is zero.

JH: *There isn't time for it, right?*

JS: I think so, I think so.

JH: *Does this speed thing spill over into your personal life? I mean, do you take it home with you?*

JS: Ask my wife, she says I'm awful.

JH: *You picked up some "bad" habits here?*

JS: You got it. I think Larry allows us sixty seconds each morning to reflect upon the last five years and to feel good about it, but not more than sixty seconds. Then we have to attack again.

JH: *Wow!*

A Classical Look at Time

Jim Sierk and his colleagues at Allied Signal have no time to sit and wonder where this American sense of time came from, why it is a cultural force—they have just activated it and watched the corresponding transformation in this once-staid company. But for the rest of us, what follows is a quick (of course) overview of time theory and what we have done to it in America.

Now time is a particularly profound force because the concept of time is so pervasive. All political, business, social, and personal aspects of life revolve around time. Nothing occurs outside a reference of time, which is a core system for all cultures. The subject of time itself has generated some thoughtful study and analysis.

There are two detailed views of time that are particularly useful to our discussion: one, the classic, cross-cultural studies on time and space by anthropologist Edward T. Hall, and the other by economist and futurist Jeremy Rifkin, president of the Economic Policy Institute in Washington, D.C.

Hall has identified nine different kinds of time:*

biological (fixed, like the ebb and flow of the tides)
personal (subjective experience, such as "time flew by")
physical (Newton's absolute time, Einstein's relative time)
metaphysical (déjà vu)
micro (various periods of waiting)
sync (the rhythm of a place, like the hustle and bustle of a city)
sacred (Indian religious ceremony)
profane (immutable, like the day for Thanksgiving or Labor Day)
meta (the philosophy of time)

Hall complicates things a bit more by talking about monochronic time (being driven by schedules, and doing one thing at a time, as we tend to do in the United States) and polychronic time (doing many things at once, as folks tend to do in the Arab world). On top of that, Hall writes about past, present, and future time (found in most industrialized countries), and an American obsession, segmentation of time: on time, late, never, forever, one minute, five minutes, half-hour, hour, etc.

Rifkin takes a different perspective in his book *Time Wars: The Primary Conflicts in Human History.* He provides a somewhat simpler categorization, listing six "distinct temporal dimensions that are continually at play as individuals intersect with each other in a social context." These, Rifkin says, are present in all cultures: "Every thought, event, occurrence, or situation is definable in terms of: sequence, duration, planning, recurrence rate, synchronization, and temporal perspective." Here is an example of how Rifkin's mechanism plays out in a real-life situation, the car pool.

sequence: the order in which folks are picked up
duration: how long it will take to get to each pickup place and reach the plant
planning: making allowances for traffic, weather, and construction delays
recurrence: the car pool is suspended on holidays and on weekends
synchronization: everyone in the car pool having the same respect for or adherence to the rules (Let one pooler be a few minutes late once a week and he upsets not only the timing but also his fellow passengers.)
temporal perspective: how the changing needs of the individual are weighed against the more permanent needs of the group

Throughout this chapter we have drawn on Hall's research and insight, especially from his books, The Dance of Life and The Silent Language.

Ironically, the pressed-for-time American is not much given to car-pooling—more typically we choose to drive alone (it's a rare chance for solitude), creeping along the freeway as the car-poolers cruise on by in their (sometimes) express lane.

Rifkin goes on to write fascinating things about clocks, factory discipline, computer time, schedules, "time ghettos," and the democratization of time. It starts to get complicated again. But you get the idea: there's a lot more to time than what we see on a clock.

Although Hall's and Rifkin's dissection of time is fascinating, we know you are looking for something short and sweet. So what follows is our synthesis of how Americans think of time and use time. There are just two categories (remember, we like things simple): **GO TIME** and **DO TIME**.

To get a feel for the differences between the two categories, peruse the list on the following page for a moment and think about the differences. We'll draw some conclusions and practical business applications at the end.

In short, we *go* to work, we *go* to meetings, when we are finished we *go* on to something else (🖵). When our team is down and we're running out of time, we say GO TEAM! The coach says, "On your mark, get set, go!" And when we have run another crazy idea by someone who is all too familiar with our crazy ideas, she says, "*Go* for it." There is even a *Go To* command on our computer menus and a square on the Monopoly Board where you can get extra dough when you pass *GO*.

By contrast, we *Do time* (as in jail, with no place to *go*). We *do* chores, which normally don't have a rigid time frame—except when we procrastinate, and then our partner says *now* (urgency, schedule-driven, rules, impending consequences) and we promptly get up and just *do* it, as the commercial says. In Hollywood, they *do* lunch, which means they are working on the deal.

We *go* to church, but *do* missionary work; we *go* to school, but *do* homework, we *go* to the doctor, but we *do* our exercises (at least we are suppose to *do* them). You get the idea.

In America, Go time and Do time together define our notion of time. But in more mature cultures, Do time is more likely to be the norm; our Go time may strike them as rude or abrasive or simply incomprehensible. When we travel overseas, especially for business, it's wise to leave the Go time behind—it will be here when we get back.

The goal is not to be in one column or the other, or to move from one column to another; both approaches are valid. Our intention is to make us all more conscious of how we see, use, and activate the Now Force in America. This division of time, like everything in this book, is designed to make us aware of the forces that define us as Americans in order to tap our emotional roots, that wellspring of natural energy that can't be taught or bought—just unleashed. It is also our intention to make us aware of our own sense of time so that we can be more effective in other cultures, especially those that have a completely different sense of time.

Doing Time in Other Countries

As anyone who has tried to do business in another country knows, different cultures have the same watches but a different way of telling time. Here we mean more than just adopting the twenty-four-hour clock—the way the rest of the world tells time. We mean that different ways of perceiving time translate into different ways of taking action—some deliberately, some even-paced, some quickly, some slowly, some

GO TIME	DO TIME
scheduled	flexible
formal	informal
sequential	multiple
beginning, middle, end	open-ended
regulation-driven	needs-driven
necessary (with urgency)	necessary (less urgency)
process-focused	outcome-focused
time-driven	circumstance-driven
policies and procedures	principles
dictated	negotiated
facts	knowledge
make quota	develop relationship
selling	buying
immediate (time pressure)	takes time
do the part	see the whole
do what's told	do what's needed

EXAMPLES

lust	love
Cliff Notes	book
fax	letter
computer	calligraphy
turnpike	blue highways
crisis	contingency planning
TV commercial	TV series
American movies*	foreign movies
Fountain of Youth	Fountain of Wisdom
emergency room	preventive medicine
diets	exercise
sound-bite	white paper
Frederick Taylor	empowerment
work life	home life
1-800-FLOWERS	cutting garden

*Go time is the hallmark of contemporary American entertainment. For example, in movies there needs to be a beginning, middle, and (happy) ending in two hours or less. In TV movies there needs to be a dramatic climax every ten or twelve minutes in order to hold an audience, because of the commercial breaks.

circuitously. Not taking the time to appreciate, understand, or accommodate these differences, up front, can cause needless confusion and conflict.

As we travel or work abroad, anthropologist Edward Hall reminds all of us, "it is just as necessary to learn the language of time as it is to learn the spoken language."

For the spoken language we generally brush up on the language or memorize some key phrases and bring along a dual-language dictionary or one of those new, multilanguage electronic translators. But we do nothing comparable to prepare ourselves for understanding the concept of time in the culture we are visiting.

Hall reminds us that non-Western cultures, for instance, describe an amount of time by telling you what *kind* of time it is: for example, in Madagascar, as long as "rice cooking" is about a half-hour, and the time to "fry a locust" is a moment. In Labrador, they use fishing as one way to track time: cod in June-July, dog-fish in August, herring in September. As our colleague and part-time Southern folklorist Laurin Baker reminds us—at least in the South there is tobacco-settin' time (around Easter when tobacco plants were transplanted into the fields), dog days (the hottest days of summer when it was even too hot for the dogs to move), and hog-killin' time (late fall, generally from just before Thanksgiving to around Christmas when it was cool enough to butcher hogs without risking spoilage, but still warm enough to work outside).

Although we may cut out the small talk with our American business associates, it is definitely not advisable to try such *go* stuff across the borders or across the ponds, especially in Asian, Scandinavian, or Mediterranean countries. In those countries there is no such thing as small talk in the sense of conversation that wastes time. *All* talk is designed to build and maintain relationships, as is the presentation of a gift, etc.

Janusz L. Mucha, a Polish anthropologist whose primary field of interest is urban communities of Native Americans and Polish-Americans, studied at the University of Chicago and the University of Wisconsin about relationships and time in America. Writing in "An Outsider's View of American Culture" in *Distant Mirrors: America as a Foreign Culture*, he says:

> When I make new acquaintants, including the dental hygienist, everyone addresses me by my first name. . . . Very soon, I discover that I am learning many intimate details of the personal lives of the people I just met, I find myself a bit embarrassed, but I doubt that they are. They become my friends so quickly, and as quickly they begin to share their problems with me. There are, in the English language, the nouns colleague, and acquaintance, but I do not discover them to be in popular use. In America, when one meets someone, he or she immediately becomes a friend.

Mucha notes that Americans want to know and address everyone by their first name, be able to say "hello," and to ask how one is doing. But he has learned that Americans "prefer the answer to be brief and positive: 'I'm fine, thank you.'"

Anthropologist Rahel Wasserfall extends Jan's (of course, that is what we can call Mucha, now that he has been introduced to us) observations. She was born and raised in France, lived seventeen years in Israel, and as a Fulbright scholar studied in America for two years at Duke University. Writing in *Distant Mirrors: America as a Foreign Culture,* * she illustrates how our fragmented, *go*-driven culture makes ambiguity in relationships problematic for Americans. She corroborates Mucha's observations about *instant* friends and contrasts her American and French experiences:

---

* The chapter is entitled "Gender Encounters in America: An Outsider's View of Continuity and Ambivalence."

In France, people will "let things happen"; in America, there seems to be no time, no room for "letting things happen." From the very first encounter on, one has to know if this relationship could lead to something and what kind of potential there is. Very little room is left for ambiguity, to slowly find out about the person, to let your imagination wonder about what you do not yet know. I believe this ambiguous style is at the basis of any encounter between genders in France, whereas in the American context, ambiguity is not well coped with and is interpreted as an untrustworthy character trait.

To help illustrate the profoundly different approaches taken around time by different cultures, we have chosen three countries—Germany, Japan, and Norway—whose use of time we compare to our own. See Snapshot #13. To make it easier to remember the different cultural attitudes, we've turned the graphs into familiar objects they most resemble.

GERMANY: HOCKEY STICK (Question, question, question, act)
At the beginning of a group process, project, or work effort, the German business executive, manager, and worker will not proceed until he or she understands precisely what the objective is, what is required, and how the project will be evaluated or measured. This involves a lengthy (some would say endless or exasperatingly long) time of questioning, thinking, reflecting, questioning, and more questioning. When *all* the questions have been answered to their satisfaction, the ensuing action is precise, reliable, straightforward to the goal. No special energy is exerted at any particular place in the process. Performance standards are established and a direct course is set for reaching the objective.

JAPAN: FLIGHT OF STEPS (Question, act, question, act, question, act)
Like the Germans, the Japanese begin with a questioning process, but it isn't as exhaustive, and some initial steps are soon taken. The questioning process is continuous. Question, action. Question, action. Check. Question, action. This process is called *kaisen*, and it is the source of what American business calls continuous improvement. It is also the source of the notion of quality as a continuous journey—a hard concept to sell to *go*-time Americans. Several Japanese executives have pointed out that Americans use quality improvement or TQM to fix things; Japanese, by contrast, use it to discover things. Unlike the Germans, the Japanese appear to intensify their energy as they near the goal or objective.

NORWAY: RIGHT ANGLE (Postpone, postpone, act, act, act)
Americans don't know much about Norwegians, pre-Lillihammer. We tend to think of them as Scandinavian, which is like thinking of Mexicans, Canadians, and U.S. citizens as Americans. There is very little *go* time in Norway. Like the Japanese, indeed like everyone but the Americans, Norwegians greatly emphasize relationships and relationship-building as a prelude to the deal.

Not only are all Norwegians not blonde and blue-eyed, they are ruggedly independent, and unlike their Swedish neighbors who live in cities or small villages throughout Sweden, Norwegian homes and homesteads are strung along the fjords and valleys of Norway, occasionally clustered into hamlets and villages. Consequently, the Swedes work more naturally in groups or teams; the Norwegians, like the Americans, have a preference for individual effort.

Snapshot #13

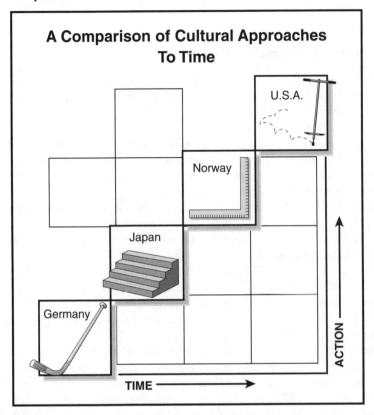

A Comparison of Cultural Approaches To Time

And unlike their Scandinavian neighbors, the Norwegians are driven by something called *skippertak*. If you're ever among a group of Norwegians, ask them what *skippertak* means. The first thing they will do is laugh. But the laughter is more likely to come from striking an emotional chord than your pronunciation. *Skippertak* is the word for immediate, focused action that comes at the end of a long procrastination period. Unlike the Germans or Japanese, the Norwegians aren't questioning anything, they just put it off for a while. Sooner or later, time runs out and the Norwegian worker is galvanized into immediate, focused attention. (The closest American equivalent is cramming for exams, waiting until April 14 to do your taxes, or putting off your Christmas shopping until the last minute). The origins of the word, as we understand it, after five or six different, but closely related explanations, comes from *when the skipper of a ship talks, or gives an order to act, everyone jumps to and the job is done instantly. But until the skipper or captain took charge, not much was going on.*

U.S.A.: POGO STICK (Act now, question later)
Here is the American bias for action at work: Let's spring to action NOW! and not get bogged down in planning. As the saying goes, we are frequently wrong, but never in doubt—act now, ask later, or "fire, ready, aim!" The downside is that too often we spend our time hopping around wanting to go *somewhere* but not sure where and indeed going nowhere in particular.

In Chapter 7, we'll say more about this sense of timing, this *go* time, because it is at the heart of Force #5, Oops, and it has implications for Force #6, Improvise.

The Origin of American Time

How did we end up with Go time and Do time? As we mentioned in Chapter 1, our cultural forces got locked-in at Plymouth Rock and during the formative days of the colonies. American time was no exception.

Before recorded history the Druids occupied England. They built a giant stone clock at Stonehenge. It is still there: a clock whose mechanism is the sun, stars, and moon. Together with the tides and seasons, it set the tempo of life on the islands, rhythms which were little changed by two thousand years of invasions by Romans, Normans, Franks, Saxons, Celts, and Norsemen.

By the fifteenth century there was a change in the way to keep time. Time was set by the time to milk, time to shear, time to butcher, time to harvest, time to go to market. Life was regulated by agricultural time, and what wasn't controlled by that cycle was dictated by the Church.

However, one group of Englishmen, called Separatists, didn't like the new encroachments of the Church, so they left for Holland, where they could be left alone. But over the next twenty years their restlessness continued, and on the eve of changing times in Holland, they decided it was time to leave, time to start over again, time to set a new clock—the American clock.

In the twenty years following the landing of the Pilgrims, fifty thousand English settlers arrived in America, bringing with them immediate needs for food, shelter, and comfort. With agriculture on a firm footing and the threat of starvation retreating in the face of bountiful harvests, the American economy flourished. By the end of the 1600s a European immigrant had a wide choice of destinations. One could choose from thirteen colonies, and an array of splendid new cities, and everywhere there was a need for houses to be built, streets paved, iron forged, ships launched, canals dug, and beer brewed. The pace was bustling, and it never slackened.

With the coming of the steam engine, the spinning mule, and the Industrial Revolution in the early 1800s, the tempo quickened even more. More hands were needed, because of steamboats, railroads, the telegraph, Alexander Graham Bell's bells, and much more.

McTime

McDonald's, where you can order and consume a Big Mac in five minutes or less in more than ninety-eight countries in the world, has made its own contribution to our Now time: fast food. (It has also spawned a whole string of McWords whose prefix indicates "quick and easy but less than completely satisfying": McJob, for example, is a job with no particular future that requires you simply to follow procedures without much thinking.)

In his book *Timelock*, Ralph Keyes has written a chapter on "The American Tempo," which includes the story of the creation of what we now know as McDonald's. The story is called (what else?) "McSpeed."

It's an oft-told tale of how two brothers operating a drive-in restaurant in San Bernardino, California, were experimenting with ways to turn sales over faster. The year was 1948. They fired their teenage car hops, revamped their kitchen floor plan and store, streamlined the menu, cut prices, prepared food in advance, and waited for customers to appear. They didn't. At least not at first.

Months went by, and many times the brothers were ready to quit, but gradually a new kind of customer began showing up. Whereas in the old days the restaurant had catered to the bobby-sox-teenager-after-the-movies crowd, the new speedy service was drawing a different clientele—cabbies in a hurry, shoe clerks, construction workers, and traveling men. The new pace caught on. Exploded, in fact. And within a year the McDonald's business had doubled. The rest is the story with which we're all familiar.

McDonald's has become a household name not only in America but also internationally. Part of the company's success in introducing fast food around the globe is due, ironically, to its sensitivity to cultural differences in time. In Russia, for instance, they discovered that while Russians had been growing potatoes for eons, they couldn't get them to market in a timely way, and they rotted en route. McDonald's spent five years teaching the Russians how to provide these raw materials for fries.

In the Japanese McDonald's, Big Macs are made to order. Each takes about ten minutes to prepare, the same amount of time it takes an American to polish off two.

Between the heyday of the old drive-in and the start of the speed-driven McDonald's, something had taken place in the American sense of time. That thing was World War II.

The war accelerated the tempi of all America. The very town of San Bernardino, which had been a sleepy backwater that shipped produce from the orange groves, became the home of a busy Air Force base. Kaiser Steel had a new plant just down the road. The war brought an influx of newcomers from all over the United States. After the war, America was a different place. More people had more cars and more money. And there was an impatience to spend and find gratification with this new-found wealth.

The McDonalds' changeover took place almost fifty years ago. The McDonald brothers' idea then was to bring 'em in and get 'em out fast . . . to turn over more customers and thereby prosper. Now, in 1995, McDonald's has installed McPlaygrounds for kids . . . to keep customers around longer. So, now McDonald's is more like the old drive-in. A place to relax and socialize. The more things change . . .

At the same time, there is a new fast-fast-food chain in the Midwest called Hot 'n' Now. You guessed it, sort of. Its purpose is to enable you to drive through *without* stopping and get served in thirty seconds or less. Each time a customer drives up, an electronic eye sets the big clock on the wall in motion and everyone inside is too busy to notice the countdown—they just scurry (in a process-choreographed way) to serve the customer on time. It is working so well that there may be one coming to your neighborhood—say, sometime tomorrow, maybe.

Not only do Americans eat fast, but you'll often see them trying to read the morning paper or book and eat at the same time. So it should come as no surprise that Americans have long since figured out how to shorten time around reading. It started a long time ago with an idea concocted by DeWitt Wallace and it ushered in digest time.

Reader's Digest Time

We don't know what your attention span is. We do know what Governor W. Averell Harriman said of President Kennedy's: If one could not engage his interest in the first *seven seconds* of dialogue, it was futile to keep trying.

That's a bit shorter than we would have guessed, and even though it is probably an exaggeration, it does illustrate how impatient Americans are.

Reader's Digest was conceived for just such impatient people, people who want to receive information quickly and succinctly. This very successful magazine, created around the Now Force, is also a one-stop, handy, pocket-sized package of the seven cultural forces that define Americans. For the past seventy-five years this little/big miracle has not changed in concept or structure; it still keeps its readers up-to-the-minute in Now time.

The Reader's Digest Association prints twenty-eight million copies of its magazine monthly in nineteen countries.* In doing so, it practically prints money as well—bushels of it—and has been doing so since 1922. It is by far the most successful publication ever to come off the presses, and until 1972 it was solely owned by just two people, the husband and wife team of DeWitt and Lila Wallace, who started the little periodical in a loft in New York's Greenwich Village back in the early twenties.

The definitive history of this remarkable American enterprise is a book by John Heidenry called *Theirs Was the Kingdom*.

> *From its very first issue the* Reader's Digest *established an editorial formula that it more or less faithfully adhered to for the next three quarters of a century: three pleasantly patronizing tributes to women, two to animals; an inspirational profile of one of DeWitt's heroes, Henry Ford, useful pointers on how to get ahead in life and work; and assurances that common sense and a grasp of facts were society's great equalizers.*

But there was more to the formulation than content. The magazine was designed to save the reader's time by culling the whole magazine world for only those articles of "lasting interest." Each article was a cut-down, shortened, bottom-lined, linear-flowing, non-highfalutin condensation of articles pinched from the leading magazines of the day. How Wallace got away with it for the first few years is another story. But what is of special interest is Wallace's clairvoyant hunch that Americans valued practical information prepared for quick study, and were willing to pay for both. The magazine sold for twenty-five cents at a time when the leading *Saturday Evening Post* went for a nickel.

Two other elements of the formula: It was a handy size that could fit in pocket or purse, and initially it carried no advertising. But to appreciate how the magazine came to be is to appreciate the seven forces at play, and how the intuitive genius of young Wallace came to arrive at the magic formulation.

Like all great success stories, this one leaves the reader astonished at the elegant simplicity of the idea. On the other hand, it was the quirkiness of the originator that sent him down a path that would intersect with success. Roy DeWitt Wallace was a preacher's son who found out about cigarettes, and whiskey, and wild, wild women

*If you want to inquire about or advertise in the Thai edition, call 914-244-5497 in New York.

CULTURAL FORCES PROFILE: Reader's Digest

CHOICE: no specific editorial focus, wide range of topics, from the quirks of science and the oddities of history to the secrets of beauty and the key to drug-abuse prevention.
IMPOSSIBLE DREAM: the first publication of its kind (now with hundreds of imitators).
BIG AND MORE: 16,261,968 subscribers worldwide, making it the largest magazine circulation in the world.
NOW: Condensed from books and longer articles; designed as a palm-size magazine for easy access and to be read fast.
OOPS: Steadfastly refused to write about Watergate, the biggest political scandal of the century and instead chose to continue to bash Washington bureaucrats. The *Digest* barely escaped being impaled in the cover-up.
IMPROVISE: Applied magazine concept to books; condensed books are now the biggest and most profitable part of the business.
WHATSNEW: Check out the next issue.

early on. And he loved 'em all. (How often has that been the case with single-minded and rebellious pathfinders? See the story of Bill Lear in Chapter 6.)

His wife, Lila, was a preacher's daughter. They called themselves "PKs"—preachers' kids. But long before Lila came on the scene, young Wally, as his friends called him, had been thrown out of schools and colleges three times and had held and been fired from a string of rinky-dink writing and editorial jobs. He had also spent a summer walking across Oregon selling illustrated calendars door to door.

In the good old days, a country doctor, plumber, or ice man would have a daily look-see into other folks' homes and might notice how they lived, and whom they lived with, and take in what they were cooking for supper and what magazines were on the table, whether they smoked, or if the wallpaper was peeling, and were there dirty dishes in the sink, or rats in the pantry, and whether they played the radio, and what they were tuned to. Today it is rare for even a near neighbor to gain access to the inside of another's home. Hence, pollsters are paid big fees to simulate the kitchen sinks, stove tops, and medicine chests with a set of stats, which are studied as pie and bar charts in skyscraper boardrooms by high priests in tasseled loafers.

In the summer of 1911, young Wally had the chance to do firsthand polling of what life was like as he hiked across the back roads of Oregon. He had people to talk to, and time to think about what they said. What he learned at age twenty-one, in the summer of a post–Teddy Roosevelt year, when the Wright boys were selling handmade airplanes and Ford was churning out Model T's, was that folks wanted to find out "what's new?" (🖳) right now (🕐).

Then, in the summer of 1915, having been canned from Webb Publications for suggesting ways to improve its magazines, Wally got together the money to print one hundred thousand copies of a publication of his own devising, a distillation of state and federal agricultural bulletins. He titled it *Getting the Most Out of Farming,* and he set out in his Model T to peddle the books, one at a time, farm to farm across the land.

Sales were satisfactory, and he was scraping by, and then one summer night he put up in the bunkhouse of a sheep ranch in Montana.

Heidenry tells the story:

> *. . . DeWitt was transported onto another plane by the most incredible idea of his life—in fact, one of the best ideas of the century. He wondered why, instead of digesting only the best of specialized information for farmers or tradespeople, he could not simply digest the best of all magazines and sell his product to everybody.*

Seven years would pass—Wally volunteered to go to France and was wounded in World War I—before he persisted relentlessly to make his idea unfold and pay its own way. It would be scorned by the intelligentsia and the round-table highbrows, but it had quietly taken root in the American social subsoil, and today, when other old newsstand standbys have long since vanished, it still beckons from checkout counters across the world headlining promises of impossible dreams, such as:

"FLATTEN YOUR TUMMY"
Doctors Tell You How, Page 17

How Much Time Should Elapse Before Things Change?

When you were a kid, how much time elapsed before you belted out that irrepressible American car refrain—"Are we there yet?" You may have been driving for less than an hour on that six-hour trip to Grandma's, or only a few minutes on the way to the park—whatever the case, that twitchy nerve took over, and out it blurped.

It's an expression that remains a part of us long after we get out of the backseat. Not a day passes at work when someone doesn't ask the same thing, only applied to a different kind of "getting there"—Is the report done yet? Is she here yet? Where do we stand on the final budget analysis? When will the training be complete? How far along are we on the revisions to our customer complaint resolution process?

This one ubiquitous question—"Are we there yet?"—is a sort of hallmark for America's impetuous culture. And no matter what we are doing, "soon" is not the answer we want to hear.

If we're not there yet, then how much time should elapse before we expect things to change? How people feel about change is an integral part of a culture's sense of time. It says a lot about people's frustration level, and how quick they are to take action. Ask yourself this question: When you think about making changes in your personal life or work life, would you consider yourself a *gradualist* (you believe change should come about slowly, through a gradual process) or a *suddenist* (you believe change should come about quickly, through a sudden process)? Which would you guess is true for most Americans?

One would expect Americans, with our strong Now Force, to want to make changes quickly, without dithering or waffling. However, it turns out that most Americans—55 percent, in fact— identify themselves as gradualists. Needless to write, we were surprised and disappointed in this finding, a result of our research for a training program. There went our assumption that Americans have a bias for action; that we shoot before we aim; that we put the cart before the horse; that we count our chickens before they hatch.

Then we remembered that how we see time is different from how we actually experience time. So next time we asked a question that would more accurately define the amount of time required for change to occur: Based on your experience, in your personal/business life, how much time does a change take? Check one and compare your sense of time and change with those of other Americans.*

❏ a few minutes   ❏ a few months
❏ a few hours   ❏ a few years
❏ a few days   ❏ several years
❏ a few weeks

It turns out that a majority of Americans say "a few months" or less, regardless of whether they see themselves as gradualists or suddenists. In fact, one in every five people who say they favor a "gradual" process for change define that as "a few weeks" or *less!* See Snapshot #14.

Fast Pedaling for Improvement

Here is what happened when this time frame was put into practice for a real business challenge. The report could easily be titled "Accounting for Time," because it was first activated by one of the Big Six accounting firms, Ernst & Young. E&Y's Richmond office experimented with this American time-change frame and got astounding results. What did they do?

John Daly, director of tax, led the charge, set the initial goal, and got out of the way—the essential three principles for any good leader. His department's business goal in 1992 was to generate six thousand new billable tax hours during the ninety-day period between September 30 and December 31.

To achieve this goal, Daly organized the office into three teams that loosely patterned themselves after the team structure of the classic twenty-three-day, 2,210-mile Tour de France bicycle race. The three teams were the Tax Pedalers (blue jerseys), Easy Money (green jerseys), and Refund Riders (red jerseys). At the end of each thirty-day stage, the team that won that stage got to wear yellow jerseys, just as docs the winner of each day's leg in the Tour de France.

Segmenting the contest into month-long stages offered an important psychological benefit, because a team can win a particular stage, even though it may be lagging in overall points. Each team thus has a strong incentive to keep going.

By the end of Stage One, four thousand new billable hours had been achieved; by mid-November, over six thousand hours, the original goal, had been reached. But there was still half the time remaining. A new goal was set—nine thousand hours, a 66 percent increase over the original goal.

That second goal was soon reached, and a third new goal was set at eleven thousand. By the end of Stage Three, when the ninety-day period was up, they had reached eleven thousand and fourty hours—nearly double their original goal.

In 1995 we saw the same approach to time and change taken by the newly in charge Republicans in the House of Representatives. As part of their so-called Contract with America, they had promised to vote on ten pieces of legislation within the first hundred days of the new Congress. This idea had come from Newt Gingrich, the newly elected Speaker of the House, who was a history professor prior to running for Congress. So it may not surprise you that the idea of a hundred days was

See Appendix for national survey details.

Snapshot #14

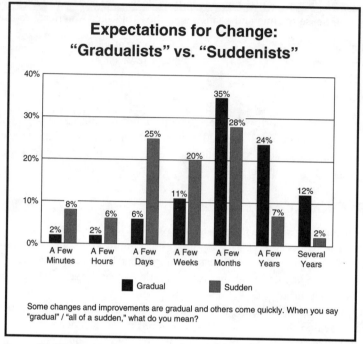

**Expectations for Change:
"Gradualists" vs. "Suddenists"**

Some changes and improvements are gradual and others come quickly. When you say "gradual" / "all of a sudden," what do you mean?

Source: The Wirthlin Group and ASQC

something he copied and modified, brilliantly we might add, to tap the American voter restlessness for change.

The First Hundred Days

For a future-focused culture, time went to hell in 1929. The Depression ruined everyone's sense of time.

But on the morning of March 4, 1933, a young kid named Jimmy Roosevelt helped his father straighten and lock the steel leg braces, tugged the trouser legs to conceal those pitiful spindles, and pulled the elder man into a standing position. He offered his arm to his father Franklin and felt first the grip, and then the weight, and with total concentration the two pretended to stroll out into the sun and the inauguration platform of the next president of the United States of America.

In no time the words would resound throughout the land: "the only thing we have to fear is fear itself." That phrase and Roosevelt's confidence made it seem as if at long last there was a ray of hope, the dawning of a new day.

It turned out that the new day was the very next day. It was a Sunday, yet President Roosevelt convened a cabinet meeting and called for a special session of Congress five days later. His immediate problem was to stop the run on banks and the hoarding of gold, and so he declared a three-day "bank holiday." When Congress convened on March 9, it was the beginning of a period of legislative hysteria and momentous change for the country.

The first bill passed was the Emergency Banking Act, which took the United States off the gold standard. Next came a bill reducing the salaries of federal employees, and another reducing military spending from $752 million to $531 million (today that would buy the Pentagon about half of one big bomber).

Then came legislation establishing the CCC, standing for Civilian Conservation Corps, a program to get young men off the streets and out in the wilderness in conservation projects. It was a joint effort by different departments working together. The Labor Department recruited, War Department equipped, sheltered, and supervised, Interior was in charge of fields and parks, and Agriculture directed fieldwork in national forests. Each corpsman got a dollar a day plus room and board and clothing. Within a few months there were over 250,000 young men enrolled. There were abuses, as indeed there are in most big undertakings, but on balance the "C's," as they were called, were a smashing success.

The Agricultural Adjustment Act was a bill passed to limit overproduction of commodities. That one is still around sixty years later and is still controversial. The Tennessee Valley Authority was a gigantic flood-control project that has changed the geography of several Southern states. The ERA or Emergency Relief Administration was a money giveaway operation run by Harry Hopkins, a social worker who eventually became Roosevelt's most trusted adviser. But one of the most significant laws passed was the National Industrial Relations Act, which had buried within it Section 7(a), the effect of which was to tie the big labor unions to the Democratic party and keep the Democrats in power for the next twenty years. Never before had Congress passed so much legislation so swiftly, and that session became known to history as "The Hundred Days."

Two years later there was another surge of legislation that some called the "Second Hundred Days," during which a revolutionary law called the Social Security Act was passed. The Works Progress Administration provided jobs building bridges, streets, parks, and other projects having long-range value. The National Labor Relations Act guaranteed to labor the right to organize.

Newt's Hundred Days

Regardless of one's views on the merits of the Contract with America, what resonated with people most was the time period, the urgency to get on with it, to do something, to break the gridlock. Republicans invited—dared—voters to hold them accountable for achieving change within a hundred days ("a few months"). While most politicians talk about accountability, the Republicans put a time limit on it and a ten-point agenda that made the accountability (at least numerically) easy.

Furthermore, they delivered, although the process wasn't pretty. It turned out that the ten items in the contract were a lot of process to process in a hundred days, the easy stuff going down the first day, the harder stuff taking longer. Impressive, but not the stuff the *first* hundred days were made of.

The mistake we feel that the Republicans made was in not having a second hundred-day contract, obviously with fewer items, but a hundred-day time frame nonetheless. Now the urgency is gone. It is back to politics as usual, in the time sense. One can't escape noticing what happened when there was no time frame to hold "them" responsible.

Now the Republicans will fall into the trap of reminding future-oriented voters of the past by saying, "Remember 1995? We delivered. Remember the contract? You can trust us again."

Unfortunately, that kind of posturing could relegate a fascinating American experience in time-politics to a gimmick. Beware the various promises—that are bound to come—to do this and that on day one, or in the first hours of taking office.

For the Democrats, who used to be the majority, their minority status now means delaying tactics and amendments; for the majority it means some confusion about what comes next. Obviously, Newt rules with an iron fist, and he and his lieutenants know the schedule, but the public doesn't—and that is the missed opportunity.

Time Is Money

The language of time in America is summed up in three words: time is money. In our eagerness to get things done right away—and make or save money—we naturally look for shortcuts. And this being America, there are people out there whose business, time management, is to help us do everything faster. Time management is also money, big money.

One 1994 time-management bibliography listed 184 books on the subject, about half of which had been written within the past five years. They all appeared to be geared to American notions of time, with little or no reference to other cultures or the vast differences in time between cultures. For example, the classic culture studies on time written by the venerable Edward T. Hall are seldom cited and rarely make even the bibliographies.

Alec Mackenzie, author of *The Time Trap* (make that 185 books), put the matter of time management in perspective for us by pointing out that time cannot be managed, like capital, physical resources, information, and human resources. In spite of how we refer to time—as wasted, spent, killed, saved, lost, etc.—you can't increase or decrease time, nor can you invest it as you can other resources. You've got to use it the instant it is available—not a moment sooner or a month later. Mackenzie's point: "The very notion of time management is a misnomer. . . . We can only manage *ourselves* in relation to time. . . . We cannot choose *whether* to spend it, but only how."

However, if time is money, then we need to find the quickest way to make it. As we have seen, Henry Ford had a process (the assembly line) but not the sense of timing that would be necessary to turn America into an industrial giant. Back then there were no time-management consultants, no Franklin calendars. Just-in-Time, the most important single innovation in manufacturing since Henry's mass production breakthrough, would not surface until the middle of the century in the pioneering work of Taiichi Ohno, a brilliant, self-taught engineer at Toyota. So where would one have turned?

Would You Hire This Guy as a Time-Management Consultant?

He won a U.S. doubles championship in tennis. In another favorite sport, croquet, he carefully plotted the angles of his strokes. When he walked he counted his steps to determine the most efficient stride. A victim of insomnia, he slept upright in bed or in a chair. He went to Harvard Law School but didn't practice law. He testified be-

fore the U.S. Congress on the "science of shoveling," which he invented. He got over one hundred patents in his lifetime. Who would this be?

❑ Thomas Edison   ❑ Eli Whitney
❑ Morris L. Cooke   ❑ Frederick W. Taylor

The godfather of scientific management was a time freak who profoundly impacted the course of business events in America. Though somewhat maligned these days, Frederick W. Taylor's legacy is still alive on shop floors and in boardrooms everywhere. He preached (for him, time management was the gospel) that asserting *complete control* over the time-related dimensions of work was the only way to optimize the output of each worker. His key principles were for management to (1) control knowledge, (2) plan and direct work on the shop floor, and (3) run things by a "work schedule." He called on managers to plan in detail and issue orders to workers that in Rifkin's words specified "not only what is to be done, but how it is to be done and the *exact time* [author's emphasis] for doing it."

Thanks to Taylor, American industry burgeoned into the giant it was, and arguably still is. Everything was done in Taylor time. It's the American way. It exemplifies the forces at work: new idea (🖳), everybody wants it now (🕐) in a big way (🕴) and that invariably results in an abuse of the idea (👓).

Jeremy Rifkin, writing in *Time Wars*, observes that Taylorism found its way into the rest of the culture, "changing the way we lived and interacted with each other in the modern world. The new man and woman were to be objectified, quantified, and redefined in clockwork and mechanistic language . . . their life and their time would be made to conform to the regimen of the clock, the prerequisites of the schedule, and the dictates of efficiency."

Today, the empowerment movement, in all its variations, is a direct challenge to the Taylor principles, in fact, the opposite of those principles. But his legacy of the "one best way" thinking still hobbles Americans at home and especially abroad where it is the antithesis to so many other cultures.

Ford Fast

Henry Ford is considered the father of mass production. He started out in 1911 producing about two cars a day, but he had a dream that he could produce one every minute! Here is Henry's fast track:

YEAR	TIME PER CAR
1911	12.5 hours
1913	1.33 hours
1920	60 seconds (dream fulfilled)
1925	10 seconds

How to Manage the Time-Managers

It is not our intention to provide a synthesis of ideas, strategies, gimmicks, reminders, schemes, old tricks and new, for making time an ally, not a master. But we won't hesitate to pass along a few tips that seem to work because they are particularly in sync with our Now Force.

At the heart of so-called time management is the control of how time is used. So tips abound on how to have shorter or more efficient telephone calls, for example. One expert says don't ask about the weather, the vacation, or the kids. Get to the point. Acknowledge that you are both busy people and ask the question directly, preferably indicating that the question is a quick one, presumably with a quick response.

This is very American advice, in *Go time*. What is particularly effective about it is that it fits the force. Many of us are not good at weather chitchat; it is a transparent crutch, and it's a waste of time in the sense that our heart isn't really into the warm-up stuff, and besides, we execute it poorly.

Wasted Executives*

Activity	Minutes Per Day	Days Per Year
on telephone hold	15	7.5
reading unnecessary mail	32	16
unnecessary meetings	72	36
Wasted Totals:	almost 2 hours	about 2 months

The 24/72-Hour Rule

Beginning in the mid- to late eighties, many managers began to seriously challenge Taylor and look for immediate ways to engage workers in quality improvement. Employee suggestion systems that had been around for years got a second wind. But in typical American bias-for-action style, few companies took the time to figure out what had inhibited the use of suggestion systems in the past.

Milliken and Company, the textile giant headquartered in Spartanburg, South Carolina, was one company that took the time to find out what makes the suggestion system work. They discovered two things: timeliness of response, and in W. Edwards Deming's words, constance of purpose. In other words, respond quickly and continue the effort, don't make it a "flavor-of-the-month" program. The first taps into the Now Force. The second taps into the Big and More Force.

In 1988 the company instituted the Opportunity for Improvement program (OFI, called Ohfee by one and all). In the first year the average was only one-half suggestion per associate (as an employee is termed at Milliken). Then they implemented the 24/72-hour rule: Within 24 hours the person who received an Ohfee had to acknowledge the receipt of the suggestion (facilitated by sending the first carbon from the suggestion form back to the employee). Then, within 72 hours—in just three short days—the second carbon from the form was sent to the associate, informing him/her of the action taken on the suggestion: adopted, modified, additional information requested, sent elsewhere for further consideration, rejected.

Rejection did not become a problem however. By 1990 over 88 percent of the suggestions were adopted. By then the number of suggestions per associate had climbed to more than nineteen for a total of 288,000. If that seems like a lot, says Chairman Roger Milliken, "It is sobering to know that the average Japanese company receives thirty such OFIs a year per employee. And the leading Japanese companies receive fifty to a hundred!"

*Based on a survey of 200 executives by Accountemps, a personnel agency.

Faster Time Is More Money

Not only has OFI proved profitable for Milliken, but the company has also turned time guarantees into money. Everyone shies away from the unconditional guarantee unless they can use a lot of small print.* Milliken, however, decided to put its delivery of carpets on a guarantee basis. It didn't used to be that way, but times have changed, not only for the textile industry, but for all business enterprises. The challenge was how to deliver on the guarantee and make it profitable in the process.

To back their guarantee Milliken needed to know the exact production time of their carpets, from start to finish. They then built in some additional time for slippage, about another 25 or 30 percent. Here is their genius. (For competitive reasons, the times in this write-up are illustrative only.)

Say the time from order through design to delivery is twenty days, including the slippage time. Milliken's guaranteed delivery date for customers is then set at thirty days. If a customer can live with that schedule, there's no problem for either party.

However, a lot of customers, probably most American customers, want it *now*— a rush order. So Milliken offers to deliver it in twenty-two or twenty-three days, but the company must charge a premium for the "rush" order. Result: The customer is happy and doesn't mind the premium charge; in fact, he appreciates the Milliken effort. Milliken is still well within the maximum time for delivery and its guarantee. The best part is that Milliken makes more money on the rush order and disrupts nothing in the process. When it first introduced this approach, 38 percent of the orders from one plant were rush orders.

Milliken is clearly a company that manages with a keen sense of the Now Force. They not only manage themselves by a conscious awareness of Now Force, but they helped turn the entire textile industry around in the mid-eighties by introducing Quick Response, now a highly imitated strategy that takes concurrent engineering to new breadths. Quick Response brings in business operations into a current time process, not just engineering. Sales, marketing, design, manufacturing, inventory, in short everyone is concurrently involved in the conception-to-delivery mode of the textile industry.

While there are companies like Milliken that have learned to leverage time, there are companies like Federal Express (now shortened to FedEx to save some time) that were born out of an intuitive awareness of the Now Force.

FedEx: The Now Time Company

You know you have hit the big time when the purple-and-orange-lettered FedEx truck driven by a smiling courier pulls into your driveway or walks up your stairwell and hands you the purple-and-orange envelope. First off, it's always a blessed relief to get what's inside, because it absolutely, positively had to get there.

Fred Smith, a twenty-year-old sophomore at Yale University, understood this characteristic of American culture when he thought up his topic for his business class project. We all know the legend, how he wrote a term paper describing his idea for overnight delivery of documents anywhere in the country by means of a fleet of airplanes flying to a hub system converging on Memphis of all places. Fred got a C on the paper, and most of his buddies thought he was lucky.

We don't know who said it, it's been around so long: "The large print giveth, the small print taketh away."

But it took more than full faith in a sophomore's brainchild to make FedEx what it is today. The company serves one of the most important aspects of American culture and business: the need for a Now response. And FedEx knows that the only thing it has to sell is NOW—without fail.

As you drive your car toward the executive offices on tree-lined FedEx Loop, passing Priority Road on your left and Urgent Avenue on your right, you experience the same kind of lazy, laid-back ambiance of a Southern back-roads drive. That's FedEx by day.

FedEx by night is something else again. Here's a company whose very heartbeat—the LIVE OR DIE nucleus of its existence—depends on part-timers working in the middle of the night! It's amazing to realize that this $10 billion business is really run in the wee hours of the night by people who are probably holding another job. Or going to school. Or looking after kids when the sun comes up.

These are the sorters who come to work at eleven o'clock on blistering summer nights in Memphis, ready for the planes that are coming in from all points carrying more than one million parcels and purple-and-orange envelopes. In the din and sweat and churn of conveyor belts, fork lifts, cargo nets, collecting bins, planes landing and taking off and tow tugs crisscrossing, the beeping and scurrying, these sorters must now spend the next four or five hours picking up and putting down, switching and redirecting, and making sure it's done right, because the only thing the company has to sell is that it "absolutely positively has to get there"—to Wall Street or a winding-way in Wyoming—in less than ten hours. But they do it and will do it again tomorrow night, and the night after, and the night after that. The routines don't change, just the routes.

What is just as amazing is that morale is Now time as well. Always up, always ready to go, always into it. How does it happen? It happens because, being a *now*-driven company, FedEx understands the power of *now*, and in its interactions with its employees it is fast and straightforward.

The energizer is instantaneous communication via a television network that puts the whole cadre worldwide in instant one-on-one contact with the folks in Memphis, and vice versa. Now, almost every megacompany in the U. S. has a television connection with its workforce; however, it's the content that takes the measure of the commitment. It's one thing to *tell* them, but how do you show them?

Even Feedback Is Fast at FedEx

FedEx does it through a clutch of employee nurturing programs whose acronyms would make a Beltway bureaucrat blush. There's the SFA program, which if implemented at General Motors would probably unglue that organization. SFA is the Survey-Feedback-Action program, wherein employees grade their superiors, including Fred Smith. The operative word in SFA is action, because there are processes in place that require that the feedback, good or bad, be acted upon—*now*.

When everything gets done extra well (doing things right is rote at FedEx), the fastest salute for special merit is the Bravo/Zulu Award—from the name of the flags that ships fly when they want to signal "job well done." It's a spontaneous, discretionary award given on the spot (☺) to front line people by their immediate supervisors in special recognition of their going beyond the call of duty (♦).

The Bravo/Zulu is usually a couple of tickets to a ball game, a small, very personal gift, or a cash handout to enable the recipient to take the family out to dinner in celebration. It must be working wonders because the costs of this simple lagniappe have been running over $1 million annually—cheap at twice the price.

Where does this all lead? In a narrowly focused service business, FedEx like all service organizations, must constantly create and establish new service opportunities. Powership is one of those ideas for FedEx and it's changing the way the other service companies do business.

How FedEx's Now Time has Changed American Retailing

There was a time when a farmer in Skowhegan, Maine, could look out across the valley in the Fall and spot a "sport" (deer hunter) who had no doubt come from Boston, and know that just hours earlier the hunter had no doubt climbed the stairs over the P.O. at two in the morning, walked right into L.L. Bean's factory/show room, and gotten himselfs covered in enough day-glo to prevent him from being mistaken for a 14-point buck.

In those days deer hunters, or anybody else passing through "Down East," the southeast part of Maine, could stop in Freeport, day or night, 24 hours a day, 365 days a year, and climb the stairs to Bean's. Most of this famed retailer's business was mail order. Therefore, it was handy being located over the P.O. because all Mr. Bean had to do to ship an order of long johns was to drop it in a hole in the floor.

Fifty years later they are the biggest cataloguer (10 million packages per year!), they've got a new showroom, and they are still open day and night year round, but no longer over the P.O. Now they've got something even faster. Its called Powership, and it was dreamed up by FedEx. Powership is an automated shipping system that enables a customer anywhere in the world to pick out something in the Bean catalogue, phone the 800-number and have it delivered the very next morning.

Powership automated shipping service started in 1986 and now accounts for 60 percent of FedEx's volume. The Powership method kicks in when a customer dials the 800-number and places an order. At the instant the order is taken the FedEx label is printed and FedEx billing is automatically tabulated.

In charge of this operation for FedEx is Leah DeSantis, a nine-year veteran in marketing. When we asked her what drives the folks who make FedEx a routine part of our life, Leah pours forth a cascade of perks and bennies. But Leah is quick to point out that the most powerful inducement to on-time perfection is the open invitation to all employees to advance, develop, and grow into new jobs. Job hopping within is seen as one of FedExers' biggest energizers. Leah said that she, even after nine years, is in almost constant retraining for something new.

All of this to keep the FedEx air cargo fleet aloft. That's 460 planes, with a lift capacity of 15 million pounds daily, flying nearly one half million miles in a 24-hour period. The FedEx couriers on the ground log 2.5 million miles a day, equivalent to 100 trips around the earth.

Take Five: How We Spend (Waste) Time at Work

At the beginning of this chapter, we described how Allied Signal is in the process of training everyone in how to get rid of their non-value-added work. They have targeted about 70 percent of each employee's time as non-valued work, knowing that it is closer to 90 percent. But 70 is a good starting point.

While this may seem extreme to you, there is some research to support the Allied Signal mandate and provides a powerful incentive for all of us to reassess our understanding and approach to time in today's competitive environment.

The first person to get us thinking about time efficiency in a serious way, back in the late eighties, was Tor Dahl, an economics professor at the University of Minnesota and chairman of the World Confederation of Productivity Science. Tor Dahl's research backed up a lot of talk about freeing resources at work and making everyone feel better in the process.

What we like about his approach is that he has five broad, simple, straightforward questions that set in motion the whole discovery process about time and productivity. The answers are astounding and they immediately identify the potential for improvement. This is not a process that must be sent to a lab or university for analysis; it doesn't require a committee or task force to process the data; and it doesn't require technology to do the tabulation. The results are immediate, personal, and, to repeat ourselves, astounding.

Paraphrased, these questions are:

1. How much time do you spend waiting?

2. How much time do you spend doing things that *should not be done by anybody*?

3. How much time do you spend doing things that should be done, *but not by you*?

4. How much time do you spend doing your thing *right*?

5. How much time do you devote to doing your thing *better*?

These questions are at the heart of productivity improvement for every kind of organization. They also ferret out the causes of job-related stress, and they point to where we should look for increased job satisfaction, both professionally and personally.

Question 1, "How much time do you spend waiting?" relates to occupancy, in Tor's words, "being fully occupied all the time." He points out that it is always possible to do something else while you are waiting, but that's not the point or purpose of this question. Tor has used his methodology on a wide range of businesses, including schools and other public-sector organizations. Because of all the business concerns about public education, we have chosen to include the responses of a school district as a specific example of this approach to identifying the opportunity for improvement.

For a schoolteacher, waiting time is represented by morning announcements that interrupt class periods, waiting to use the duplicating machine, or waiting to make a telephone call because there are only a couple phones in the building. For a run-of-the-office worker this time might include waiting for a signature, waiting for the repairperson to fix a critical piece of equipment or waiting for parts, waiting for the requisition or purchase order, waiting for the meeting to start.*

Questions 2, 3, and 4 relate to effectiveness, doing the right things, working on the right objective. Tor fine-tunes his evaluation of effectiveness by "ruling out" two things. The two rule-outs are *screening* (Question 2), "eliminating what *nobody* should be doing" and *delegation* (Question 3), "assigning what should be done by *someone, but not by you*." What remains are the things *you* should be doing that *planning* (Question 4), in Tor's model, would help you do better.

Examples of screening for teachers are: baby-sitting kids, walking someone to the principal's office, calling the vendor person to fix a machine; for an office or plant worker, screening may include the plethora of political games, rework,[†] attending unnecessary meetings, and filling out useless forms.

Examples of delegation for teachers are: disciplining kids who are late for class, hall duty, picking up trash, cleaning the classroom,[‡] parenting students. For office and plant workers, delegation is highly variable—it clearly relates to the existing job description and the things that creep in, soon take over. Delegating does not warrant or justify a "that's not my job" attitude, which is pernicious, but applies to those legitimate tasks that have snuck in and consumed the time you should be spending on the things you were hired and trained to do.

Examples of planning for teachers are: providing for the individual learning needs of students, updating curriculum, and improving existing lesson plans.

Question 5, "How much time do you devote to doing your thing *better*?" relates to efficiency and doing things right that have been identified in Question 4. For teachers, efficiency has to do with segmenting learning styles and individualized instruction, with alertness to shifts in mood, and recognizing and encouraging progress. For business, this would include learning a new software program, some cross-functional training, agenda-based meetings,[‡‡] cross-industry benchmarking, brainstorming.

Now those astounding results: More than two-thirds (68.1 percent) of a teacher's time could be rechanneled into more productive activities, like *teaching*, for example. So to all the education reformists among us, to industry executives who are frustrated with a "failed" education system that translates into an illiterate workforce, to the

---

*Milliken & Company has discovered that meetings scheduled to begin on the hour or half-hour never start on time. Somehow Americans think eight o'clock means around eight. So they now call an eight o'clock meeting for 8:03 or 7:58 and they report that more meetings now start punctually. We tried it at a conference too and it works.

†Management consultants generally agree that in an average manufacturing or highly processed company 25 percent of an average worker's time is spent in rework. The percentage gets up to 30 percent for service companies, and higher for government agencies. In companies that have sophisticated quality and process improvement programs, like the companies we are writing about in this book, those figures are often halved, but they are still not within striking distance of the best Japanese companies that have rework down into the middle and low single digits.

‡In Japanese schools students spend from fifteen minutes to a half-hour each day cleaning up the mess they made; cleaning is not left to janitors or teachers. Nicholas D. Kristof, writing for The New York Times, *"Japan's Schools: Safe, Clean, Not Much Fun," (July 18, 1995), noted that even some of their lessons have a practical spin to them. As an example he cites: "for every action, like sticking gum under a desk, there must be an equal and less pleasant reaction, like removing it."*

‡‡Only one company in the more than one hundred we have worked or met with used a detailed agenda for our meetings with them. That company was Corning, formerly Corning Glass Works, the specialty materials, consumer housewares, laboratory sciences, and telecommunications company. Hammond adopted the process for sponsor meetings of the American Quality Foundation and they worked extremely well. Each agenda item has a specifically stated purpose with a goal, process, and desired outcome. It takes time, but saves time in the end.

budget-hackers in Congress who think too much money is the problem, to the bean counters in public school administration, we say: It's not the teachers (or the kids), it's the way teachers are forced to spend their time.

Percentage of Time Allocated to Selected Current Activities

Activity	Teacher Average	Industry Average
Occupancy	6.7	23.4
Effectiveness		
Screening	8.3	19.7
Delegating	14.5	15.1
Planning	26.5	17.9
Efficiency	12.1	15.9
TOTAL	68.1	92.1

The implications could not be more apparent. For public education the consequences of ineffective use of time and lost productivity are staggering. And matters are not likely to get better. There isn't a public school district in the United States whose budget is not strained; most, in fact, are trimming costs wherever possible, which only exacerbates the problem. With the current state of affairs and the current state of blame-the-student or blame-the-teacher, teachers can expect no relief from the distractions in the classroom, hallways, cafeteria, and school grounds. Delegating, the activity that generates the most job stress, is unfortunately the area where the least improvement is likely. It's hard to delegate when there is no one available to pick up the task.

For industry, the misuse of time is significantly worse—92.1 percent.[†] However, this series of five questions clearly identifies the opportunity that exists now to free up resources, and in a downsizing environment, to reallocate those resources to more productive use.

There is no end to the strategies available to make better use of our time, and no shortage of consultants to show us how to do it. And, clearly, managing people so that they use time effectively (do the right things) and efficiently (do things right) is important to business and competitiveness.

American Insomnia

Up to this point we have stressed the urgency and immediacy of Now time, but in truth not everything happens quickly in America. How many times has someone at your company said, "Things take forever around here," or, "Nothing ever gets done at this place," or, "Not in my lifetime . . ."

The opposite of Now time in America is the Sleeping Giant. This expression has seeped into common usage—from where we're not sure. Some have attributed the expression "We have won the war because the sleeping giant has been awakened," to Churchill, who had dinner with Ambassador John Winant and W. Averell Harriman

---

†Averages based on 819 Tor Dahl and Associates studies.

on December 7, 1941, the day the Japanese attacked Pearl Harbor and America entered the war.

What is on record are the private thoughts of Japanese Admiral Isoroku Yamamoto, the man who planned the Pearl Harbor attack. He had always opposed a war with the United States, having spent a few years at Harvard and as a naval attaché in Washington, and had traveled extensively throughout the United States. He was one of the few leading figures in Japan who understood the size, the scale, and the immense resources of the United States. He knew in the long run that it would be impossible for Japan to defeat an awakened America. On the eve of Pearl Harbor he confided to his diary, "It is not unfair to assault one who is sleeping. This means a victory over a most careless enemy." It was an old Samurai principle of "win first and fight later."

By 1970 the script writers for the American movie *Tora, Tora, Tora* had Yamamoto with a line of dialogue that may have reflected his true misgivings: "I fear all we have done is awaken a sleeping giant and fill him with a terrible resolve."

We are not certain what it will take for American business to wake up to the tremendous power of activating the time force. A little more than a dozen years or so ago (eons for Americans), we were so busy with productivity, with bigger and more that a little time out for quality improvement was the last thing on our minds or on our factory floors.

This was the period of the American industrial colossus, nodding off in the comfort that big is best and the soporific notion that if we beat them on the battlefield, we need not worry about them in the marketplace. But this time, the sleeping giant woke up with a migraine, and, in Pogo's classic words, the enemy was us.

Between 1950 and 1980, the United States share of the worldwide automotive market had plunged from 76 percent to less than 21 percent. In 1955, 96 percent of all radios sold in America were made by Americans. By 1965 it was down to 30 percent, and by 1975, close to zero. In 1964 America was a net exporter of machines; today we import more than half of what we need.

It was another military expert, Douglas MacArthur, who called the disregarded American quality experts to Japan to fix the radios so that he could pull the country together and get Japan back on its industrial feet—so they could snatch the radio and electronics business right out from under our pillow. The quality gap was so profound that Americans rested in the comfort that productivity was the name of the game, built-in obsolescence the strategy, and brand loyalty the assurance.

As Hammond and Jerry Bowles noted in their book, *Beyond Quality*, while U.S. companies were basking in the glory of mass-production and marketing genius in the fifties and sixties, the Japanese were "chipping away at the house that Ford built."

In a country with few natural resources, where frugality has long been a way of life, a manufacturing and service revolution was taking shape. . . . In short, the Japanese believed—and history has verified—that a management-led, customer-focused movement toward a goal of continuous improvement is a strategic business issue and a source of competitive advantage. By the time American management got the message in the eighties, it was almost too late.

Unlike the spontaneous and practically unanimous American response to Pearl Harbor, the collective business reaction to the quality challenge was more of a yawn. Some, like Milliken, Xerox, Corning, Motorola, Hewlett-Packard, and Ford, bolted out of bed—no wonder they are the quality leaders today. The computer, banking, airline, automotive, insurance, and health care industries basically set the snooze alarm until the customer woke them up.

One danger of this American time dimension is implicit in the name given to it— sleeping giant. Clearly, we have too many corporate somnambulists out there. Quality improvement is about being alert all the time. The competition doesn't sleep.

Now Fake Sheet

Time is a common cultural force worldwide, but America is the most time-obsessed country in the world. We are uniquely impatient with time and live in the present/ future (NOW) with little or no regard for the past (yesterday is history). This Now Force drives our personal and business bias for action, that tendency to plunge in without first testing the waters, or even learning how to swim; it accounts for our impatience with planning; and it is primarily responsible for the fact that we make mistakes. It is manifest in every aspect of our behavior.

★ American time is primarily *Go time*. Although there are more formal or classic ways to organize time, Americans fundamentally divide everything into *Go time* and *Do time*. Go time is scheduled, sequential, urgent, and more formal. Do time is flexible, open-ended, less urgent, and informal. America is predominantly obsessed with Go time, while most other cultures, especially Asian cultures, are Do-time oriented. Go time in business is more concerned with the part instead of the whole; for example, with closing a sale rather than with developing a relationship. But it was this urgency with time that fueled the exploration of the frontier and the explosion of the industrial revolution that transformed America (see page 153).

★ Americans opt to plunge right in with little or no regard for planning (see page 158–9) in contrast to other cultures like Japan, Germany, and Norway. For example, many American companies have struggled with *kaisen*, the imported Japanese concept for continuous, incremental improvement. In more ways than one, this is a foreign concept to Americans, who look for, or are motivated by the search for, a breakthrough opportunity that is likely to come from trial and error, rather than patience and dedication to a deliberate planning and building process that fits the Japanese or German cultures.

★ On average, 92 percent of work is wasted. Research done by Tor Dahl and Associates documents that the average American business wastes or misdirects 92 percent of work time in the following ways: 23 percent waiting for approvals, material, or support; 20 percent doing things that shouldn't be done; 15 percent doing things that should be done by someone else; 18 percent by not doing things right (efficiency); and 16 percent not doing the right things (effectiveness). Similar studies in public schools show that teachers are wasting 68 percent of their time on average (see page 174). The challenge to all organizations is to do what Allied Signal and others are doing with regard to mandating that everyone get rid of non-value-added work. For schoolteachers this means freeing them up to do the things they were hired and trained to do, and therein may lie part of the answer to reversing the failure of public education.

★ Speed can accelerate quality, productivity, and profitability. In 1991 Larry Bossidy was greeted as the new CEO of Allied Signal with projections of a negative cash flow of $435 million. One year later, the company had posted a positive cash flow of $255 million. How did he do this? In one word: speed. Bossidy established speed as a corporate value, launched a training program for ninety-five thousand employees in record time for a company of this size, and redesigned all work processes in order to do things faster—and better. He, and all his managers, are required to give "elevator speeches" (a two-minute or less extemporaneous explanation of quality tools and management principles) to demonstrate their familiarity and competence with the processes that drive the increased quality and productivity at Allied Signal. Not one to rest on his laurels, Bossidy launched another training program in 1995 to reduce non-value-added work by up to 70 percent in each and every employee worldwide (see page 147).

★ A plurality of Americans expect things to change in a few months. National research by the Wirthlin Group documents that the ideal amount of time that should lapse before we expect things to change in America is a few months. This finding has major implications for business, which is used to annual plans and longer time-cycles. Companies like Ernst & Young that have broken down work into smaller time intervals have virtually doubled their original performance goals (see page 165). Matching goals and work processes to these shorter time intervals taps the need for Americans "to get on with it" and explains in part the success of the Republican's hundred-day time frame for the so-called "Contract with America."

Time is money, and for Americans there is never enough of both. Companies that can harness the American bias for action can significantly improve quality, productivity, and profitability. Shorter-term work cycles outperform more conventional work cycles.

Chapter 5

Fire, Ready, Blame
Trying to Do Things
Right the Second Time

Like that American kid at the beginning of the book with his box of Legos, Ameri-can adults are less focused on doing things right than on just doing things. We have seen already that Americans have impossible dreams and that we are in a big hurry to get them done. But when it comes to acting on them, we usually get caught up in the Oops Force. We prefer to "wing it" and go off "half-cocked." Even these expres-sions are purely American. But our mistakes allow us to improvise and that is often where we shine.

We Americans oops-it collectively as well as individually. Those oopses are also valued, and sometimes they are even money makers; customer loyalty is higher among those companies who have experienced an oops and then fixed it quickly than among those who have not experienced an oops.

Oops, the Trigger Force

There are two basic kinds of oopses: one that ends in total failure, such as the tragic disaster of the space shuttle *Challenger*, and the other that continues on in spite of the occasional oops—the oops rebound is what we call it. The overall American space program is an example of the latter. We'll examine both kinds in this chapter.

Unlike the other seven cultural forces, the Oops Force does not function on its own. It is the trigger or pivot force. Oopses are the result of many things gone awry, including wrong choices, unrealistic dreams, a mismatch on technology, not enough time to take on Big or finish More. Once you are in an oops situation, you have choices, but time is usually not on your side. So Oops triggers the Improvise Force and the Whatsnew Force that enable us to manage or fix the oops.

Because Americans take quality and improvement personally, fixing the problem is more productive than fixing the blame. But fixing the problem requires a systems-thinking approach that Americans are not very good at. This comes more naturally to Japanese and other cultures. It is hard for Americans, who want to do something immediately. Lashing out at someone is easier than taking time to provide analysis and identifying corrective action.

To tap our full business performance potential, American management has to figure out how to handle the Oops Force and channel it into constructive directions. If mistakes are denied, improvement is delayed. If improvement is delayed, time is lost. If time is lost, somebody else eats your lunch. Thus, American companies need to create environments in which mistakes can be quickly identified (☺) so that everyone can learn from them and move on. The responsibility of management is not to prevent mistakes from happening, but to keep mistakes from compounding into catastrophe for the customer—and there is a big difference! The former is impossible (and not necessarily a good idea); the latter is an imperative.

"A Telescope Built by Mr. Magoo"

That was the headline used by *U.S. News & World Report* to describe the $1.5 billion Hubble Telescope fiasco in 1990. After spending the money and sending the twenty-five-thousand-pound machine three hundred miles into space, the NASA folks found out the big eye had blurred vision.

The telescope's problem concerned one of the two reflecting mirrors that was not made right the first time. Testing the two mirrors together before launch would have caught the oops, but testing was rejected because it was "too expensive." Roger Angel of the University of Arizona, America's leading builder of advanced mirrors for terrestrial telescopes, told us that "NASA fell into the trap of thinking everything about optical telescopes was so well understood that no scientific innovation [or basic management practices] was necessary." Angel reports that the oops they found could have been uncovered "with elementary tests."

Of course, where there's an oops, there's blame and Hubble was no exception. Shortly after the flaw was discovered, *The New York Times* headline on June 29, 1990, read, "Nasa and Contractor Point Fingers at Each Other." This prompted the U.S. House and Senate to get in on the blame game and convene hearings on the defect. The debate roiled on and the controversy widened.

Meanwhile the company that made the mirror, Perkin-Elmer, had just been acquired by Hughes, which was part of General Motors. It denied that a manufacturing error was the source of the problem, but also declined to rule out any possible causes, including human error, in the setting up of testing apparatus. "We completed all of our testing to specifications, and the cause of the problem is still a mystery," said a spokesman for the manufacturer.

Thus as the fix-it team assembled to figure out how to correct Hubble's myopia, NASA's Edward Weiler was prompted to say, "This project is going into the history books as a national disgrace or as a great American comeback."*

"A Perfect Defect"

That's how a NASA official described the problem with the faulty mirror. Ironically, what made corrective action feasible was a contractor's oops—grinding the lens too flat at the edges by .000039 inch. Because it was this and not merely a flaw in the material, it was possible for physicists to search for an optical fix.

---

*Americans love comebacks, it is part of The American Oops Script. We'll say more about the power of comebacks later in this chapter.

It was James Crocker, of the Space Telescope Science Institute, who made the breakthrough. It started with an observation he made while taking a shower in a Munich hotel. As reported by Sharon Begley in "Optometrist in Orbit," (*Newsweek*, December 6, 1993), "He became intrigued by the shower head which slid vertically on a track and tilted 90 degrees." Out of this observation came the beginnings of a solution. (Only an engineer could see the connection; we certainly would not have.)

The corrective device turned out to be a six-hundred-pound package of optical goodies called COSTAR, standing for Corrective Optics Space Telescope Axial Replacement. In two words: contact lenses—at the cost of $26 million.

In January 1991, almost a year after the flaw was discovered, a crash (comeback) program was started to build COSTAR. Meanwhile, a good many other problems had been plaguing Hubble. Half her gyros had failed, a solar panel had fouled, and several measuring devices were flip-flopping.

The repair mission itself would cost $629 million. To make sure they got it right the second time, the seven astronauts rehearsed four hundred hours in a NASA space simulated water tank, flew in the "vomit comet" flight simulator, and used virtual-reality helmets to simulate repair tasks. The Hubble was fortunate in that it was the first satellite built with simple handholds, restraining bars, and footholds to accommodate spacewalking mechanics.*

The *Endeavour*/Hubble flight was the toughest assignment ever handed a shuttle crew, and the most complicated mission since the moon shots twenty years before. Five space walks were planned. Up they went into the sky—trained and eager.

Pulling within thirty-five feet of the telescope, they reached out with the mechanical arm and dragged it into the cargo bay. Now, remember, this telescope sits four stories high upright. The astronauts were wearing puffy pressure suits at zero gravity, and it was three hundred degrees below zero outside. The first few days were given over to the replacement of gyros, a new camera, and solar panel repairs.

The job of putting COSTAR in place fell to Kathryn Thornton. Tethered to the shuttle *Endeavour* and blinded by the size of the package, Thornton guided the six-hundred-pound refrigerator-sized COSTAR by the words of spacewalker Tom Akers. Akers slowly and cautiously directed her to shove it a few inches this way, now a little to the left, and down . . . and then . . . she finally felt the COSTAR click into place. Eureekaaaah!

Then in a classic American response—when you have been down, embarrassed by an oops, and roared back to fix it—flight director Milt Heflin exulted, "We slam-dunked this damn thing."

Now this thing was anything but a "slam dunk." A slam dunk is a crowd pleaser. But note two things about what Heflin said and one thing we said. Heflin used the collective pronoun we, which is inclusive and was his way of saying it was a team effort, even though it was Kathy who "slam-dunked" it. Second, Heflin said, "this damn thing," as though the lens just ground itself with no human intervention. As we will see throughout this chapter, it's very American to blame somebody or something else, much easier, though less effective than taking personal responsibility. The third thing to notice is that we used the word "exulted" instead of the routine word "said." We used this word because, as we mentioned earlier, Americans take

Thank God for "low tech."

improvement and fixing things very personally. Although we don't talk about it a lot, we do get emotional about these things, especially when we make a comeback from an oops.

The American Oops Script

The Hubble oops, although bigger and more expensive than most, is typical of the process. All oopses—big ones, small ones, corporate ones, and personal ones—tend to follow eight general steps that we have identified and called "The American Oops Script."

1. **Take on the impossible.** This often involves doing something that has never been done before (Chapter 2), usually something that is related to the Big and More Force (Chapter 3), invariably something that is being driven by the Now Force (Chapter 4).

   The Hubble telescope was obviously big, but even more, it was a first.

2. **Begin before we're prepared.** We fire before we aim, and we aim before we are ready. This is usually a result of poor or incomplete planning, acting before the necessary resources are in place, jumping in before everyone has been trained, starting off before the mission is clear.

   NASA skipped the elementary tests that would have caught the problem.

3. **Fail on the first attempt.** Given steps 1 and 2, it's hard not to arrive at 3. NASA got it up okay, but it obviously didn't work as it was supposed to—all the images were blurred—because they tried something so difficult without being 100 percent prepared.

4. **Begin pointing the finger.** The personal emotional response to failure is usually embarrassment, both for the actual failure and for letting others down. The usual response is defensive: we begin the blaming process.

   Everyone—government and industry officials alike—got into the blame and counterblame game.

5. **Prepare for another chance.** Through some form of mentoring and coaching, we (most of us) move beyond the negative feelings and take some specific steps to avoid failure (the negative approach) or succeed (the positive approach) on the second try. Often, brilliantly creative solutions are devised.

   Fix-it teams brainstormed ideas on how to repair the telescope and rehearsed extensively on how to make the repairs in space. Hubble's ingenious "contact lens" was devised.

6. **Try again.** This is the land of comeback opportunities. A critical part of the oops process is the opportunity to try again, regardless of the second outcome. Americans are not limited to one comeback—we get multiple chances. You get three strikes and as many foul balls as you want. In fact, we often get more than three "strikes" in business, politics, and personal pursuits.

   Almost three years later the shuttle Endeavour, *with the repair team on board, enables the comeback and the Hubble is repaired.*

7. **Celebrate.** This can be a ticker-tape parade down the avenue when the whole job is over or a pat on the back for progress being made. It continues the essential emotional dimension of the oops process.

> *In addition to flight director Heflin's "slam-dunk" pronouncement, there were celebrations from Perkin-Elmer to outer space.*

8. **Move on to something else.** Success triggers the need to move on; it kicks in the seventh force, Whatsnew. And moving on is important because it in turn starts the process all over again—another oops invariably comes because we don't stop long enough to master the who, what, why, when, and how.

> *NASA is on to other things now—space stations, Mars, and so on.*

Just because there is a script, don't count on every oops following it. For example, think of one at your company, and you will notice that some get stuck on 2. Many skip 4. Others can't get past 4 to reach 5. Many ignore 7 or don't move to 8. But let's take a look at the power that comes from knowing the script and following it when something goes wrong at work or at home.

It's Been This Way from the Beginning

Before we had a script, we had the Pilgrims. And while we all know how their story ended, we indulge our usual American propensity to forget the process and focus only on the end result by saying, since it worked out okay, there's nothing to learn. That is a misuse of this force; oopses may well be inevitable, but they also are important opportunities for learning.

We have talked already about how the forces got locked-in (Chapter 1), and about the Pilgrims in particular. But let's look more closely at the Pilgrims' planning, or lack thereof, in organizing their expedition.*

The Pilgrims have a plan: They are in Leyden and have decided to sail for the New World, in spite of the fact that they have neither money nor ship. Like most American plans, as soon as it is made, they begin to change it—more than once.†
While they are arguing about whether or not to set out for Guiana or Virginia, they receive an offer from the Dutch to settle at the mouth of the Hudson—a sweetheart deal offering free transportation, free cattle for each family, and best of all, freedom of religion and protection from the English king.

By early 1620, talks have been going on for a couple of years, the Dutch offer is on the table, when along comes Thomas Weston, just in from London, promising that, with his connections in London, he can put together an investment package that will deliver the Pilgrims to the New World. All they have to do is draw up a contract that he can take back to his investor friends in London. (It was probably the pull of that connection with what Shakespeare called "this sceptered Isle, this England" that turned them toward the Weston proposition.)

OOPS #1

Now, instead of an airtight package from the well-organized Dutch, some of the Pilgrims begin to take apart the plan and opt for the Weston deal. At this point, some

---

*It is all well documented in Bradford's Journals, but our source is George F. Willison's book, Saints and Strangers.

†This is a process our research identified as "deconstruction." Unlike the Japanese, who improve things by building on what exists, Americans improve things by taking them apart. This process starts right off with the plan, which we begin to deconstruct immediately after everyone has signed off on it.

Pilgrims back out, so the London investors have to make up the difference with so-called "Strangers," a random pick of people around London who want to go to the New World in search of a better life. That's okay, but they are not motivated by the same high-minded religious fervor as the "Saints."

What criteria do you use for making deals or accepting offers? Does everyone need to be on board or do just a few get to make the decision? On what basis do you choose your partners or traveling companions? Do you look for persons or organizations who share the same values or is it just whoever comes along for the ride?

OOPS #2

These Leyden Pilgrims decide they are going to become fishermen in the New World. They cash out their homes and buy a sixty-ton boat called the *Speedwell*. Their idea is to outfit it with new sails and new masts and sail alongside the chartered 180-ton *Mayflower* to the destination, then keep her there to ply the fishing trade. On July 21, 1620, the *Speedwell* sails from Delft amid tears and sighs and prayers. En route, the boat heels sharply as she sweeps past the cliffs of Dover, taking in water over the gunwales, but manages to drop anchor alongside the *Mayflower* in Southampton.

How many times have you teamed up with someone and headed into uncharted waters to do something that neither of you had ever tried before? And put all your money on the line?

OOPS #3

The Leyden Saints meet the London Strangers for the first time—the folks with whom they will sail with to the New World and entwine their lives for all the years to come. The relationship gets off to a rocky start. There is mighty wrangling about provisions for the ships, which the several agents have not coordinated. No single person is responsible for keeping the books. And two weeks are lost while the *Speedwell* is refitted in an attempt to stop the leaking.

Do all of your joint ventures, team efforts, or group activities, especially with strangers, have clear lines of responsibility?

OOPS #4

Finally the two ships sail out of Southampton. But after a few days at sea the *Speedwell* starts to leak again, this time so badly they have to put in at Dartmouth for repairs. Two more weeks lost. They set out again.

In the rush to get on with a new venture, do you always make sure that someone has been assigned to check up on all those things that were supposed to be taken care of before everyone set sail?

OOPS #5

Three hundred miles off Lands Ends, the Saints and the Strangers are forced to do a U-turn. The *Speedwell* skipper explains, "[she was] so leakie as he must bear up or sink at sea, for they could scarce free her with much pumping." So they put in at England's Plymouth, abandon the *Speedwell*, and pile everyone aboard the overloaded *Mayflower* to try again.

When you have to abandon an initial plan or your resources have been cut in half, do you review your plans, or does everyone just pile on board in order to get on with it—hoping for the best?

OOPS #6

They sail for the New World with an estimated time of arrival in late November. They have no idea that they will be blown off course and end up way north of their destination where the winters will be harsh—unlike anything they have experienced before.

Do all your new ventures have contingency plans? Have you at least considered the "what ifs?"

In the end, the voyage of the *Mayflower* and the settlement of the Pilgrims was counted a success. The oopses, each of which played a part in driving the project forward, were soon forgotten. But three centuries later we are still setting out on unplanned voyages in leaky ships, dealing with our oopses as they occur, rather than thinking ahead, ever confident that we will land triumphantly on our Plymouth Rock—wherever that may be.

Who's to Blame?

It's clear the Pilgrims went off half-cocked. But they didn't blame themselves for that mishap or for any of the misfortunes that would befall them in the days, months, and years ahead. They said about their leaky ship what they said about all of their misfortunes: It was the intervention of "divine providence." That was the alibi that let them off the hook, and it provided cover for them for years to come.

Alibi-making is a big-time occupation in America. Today, not much gets chalked up to divine providence (except by insurance companies, which have that disquieting exemption "an act of God," which seems to cover all the things you wanted the policy for in the first place). Still, like the folks aboard the *Speedwell*—we don't blame ourselves, we blame somebody else or something else. Today, we make excuses for our oopses, gaffes, slipups, and sheer stupidities by saying "The dog ate my homework," "I'm still waiting on legal," "Personnel hasn't approved it yet," "The computer is down," or, "I asked Chuck to count the votes." Just like the behavior that prompted the oops, our alibi-making is instinctive—it flies on automatic pilot. The person who hesitates in giving an alibi or fixing blame on someone or something else is presumed guilty on the spot.

No culture is immune from self-made oopses. However, different cultures handle them differently than we do. Shame, an unknown quality in America, is a powerful force in Japan. Executives quit over product failures. Politicians resign over scandals not necessarily of their own making, but for which they bear responsibility. And avoidance of shame accounts for much of the orderliness in Japanese society.

In his insightful book about the cultural differences between Americans and Japanese, *More Like Us,* James Fallows has a chapter titled, "The Japanese Talent for Order." The very next chapter is "The American Talent for Disorder." Fallows says, "Japan gets the most out of ordinary people by *organizing* them to adapt and succeed. America, by getting out of their way so that they can adjust individually, *allows* them to succeed."

This emphasis on the individual does allow us to succeed. But it also makes it difficult to identify, prevent, and fix mistakes. Because a mistake is made, we see the person not the process. Instead of seeing the broken fence, we go after the escaped goat. We point fingers instead of lending a helping hand. Some companies handle this knotty issue by going so far as to say, "We don't tolerate mistakes around here." But frankly, we've never heard of a successful company operating on that dictum.

How to Plan for an Oops (Buy Lots of Umbrellas)

In 1987 Disney World was the host of the International Chamber of Commerce meeting. It was the first time this important event was being held outside the capital of the host country. Former president Jimmy Carter, other heads of state, ambassadors, executives, and dignitaries were in attendance. This was a big deal for Disney (♦). (As we described in Chapter 2, Disney knows how to do big things in a big way.)

So Disney pulled out all the stops, including a champagne reception for three thousand in front of the Magic Kingdom, in spite of the fact that they knew there was a big chance of rain. (Disney has sophisticated rain-radar all around the property to help forecast and track severe thunder and lightning storms). Unlike the Pilgrims, they had a contingency plan.

Three seconds after President Carter finished speaking the heavens opened up (we don't think it was anything he said) and the rain came pouring down, in buckets. Six inches or more in less than an hour. Everything and everybody without some form of cover was about to be drenched.

When the first drops hit, Valerie Oberle, a seasoned Floridian and Disney executive, had radioed for the umbrellas. Within one minute, three thousand umbrellas showed up for the guests. As the guests scampered for cover, the Disney cast members, soon in water over their ankles, moved everything inside (✄) and carried on as though it had been planned that way. The show and the dinner went on!

Before you chalk this up to "that's show business," consider the real business impact on Disney's reputation if they had had only a hundred umbrellas, no radios, and employees also running for cover from the rain. Consider what would have happened if Disney had had no contingency plan and nobody had had an idea (general) about how to implement it.

This was more than simply show business—this was smart business planning around possible oopses. Although there was no way to prevent the rain, there were ways to prevent the event from being compounded by other oopses triggered by the rain and three thousand rain-soaked dignitaries scampering for shelter.

That evening the slightly inconvenienced but not wet guests, under cover of the umbrellas and the contingency plan, had nothing but praise for the ability of Disney to turn this oops into a positive experience. This quick (🕐) response by Disney went way beyond their expectations. The newspapers picked up the theme the next morning. And folks at Disney remember it to this day.

Dick Nunis bought all the cast members a new pair of shoes and folks sat down for a major debriefing on the event on what went right and what went wrong. This is a Disney business habit; after each major event they do a debriefing, congratulating themselves for things well done and well improvised, and making a list of things gone wrong—oopses: We should have communicated more clearly, we should have had the buses lined up here instead of there, we should have. . . . The oopses are all documented and go into a file, no doubt where all of us would put a list of oopses, if we kept one.

Four years later, for a similar event, an opening at EPCOT Center, Oberle was once more in charge of the (contingency) umbrellas, in case they needed them again. Of course it rained again. But this time, everyone was better prepared because the planners had been required to dig out the oops file, refresh their memories on things gone wrong at the last event, and ask "What have we learned?" and "How can we take steps to prevent those oopses from happening again?"

This successful oops management process has become so routine at Disney that Oberle, now in charge of professional development programs for Disney University, uses the same debriefing process at the end of each meeting in her division. Meetings start off with a clear agenda, including the objectives of the meeting. Each meeting designates someone as a facilitator, a time keeper, and a weed whacker to keep the meeting on track so that they can be more efficient. (A weed whacker is someone who keeps the focus on the agenda and alerts the group when someone goes off on a tangent by saying, "We are in the weeds, let's get back on focus.")

At the end of the meeting, the group takes a minute to review how well the session went: Did they stay on time? Did they meet their objectives? Were the necessary decisions made that would enable them to go forward? And were everyone's assignments clear? This process, Oberle reports, keeps the oopses down and makes the meetings more efficient.

Not everyone has an oops management process— remember, most of us like to wing it again and again and only *say* that we learned something along the way. There is nothing magical in Disney's process, the company saves that for its products and the Disney experience.

How Not to Plan for an Oops

Twenty-five years before Disney's rainy event, another big oops was being played out. This time in New York City, this time not so well-planned.

On a brisk September night in 1952, Broadway was host to a big, brassy movie premiere, complete with red carpet, celebrities, limousines, flashbulbs, searchlights, newsreel cameras, and most important, the drama critic from *The New York Times*.

The next morning (☺) it was right there in bold headlines, smack on page one of *The New York Times*,

THIS IS CINERAMA

This new technology was hailed as the way movies would be changed—forever. By noon, double lines at the box office reached around the block. And within a couple of years, fifty theaters around the world would be equipped to show it.

Cinerama was an entirely new cinema experience (▯) that exploited peripheral vision, that marvel of the human optical system that enables us to be acutely aware of 180 degrees of our surroundings, even while our eyes are sharply focused on an object close at hand.

The experience was visceral. Physical. Totally engaging. It was atmospheric, saturating the eyes with wonder, and the ears with magnificent sound. It was experiential theater. The first of its kind (⟿). It played not on the emotions, as conventional movies and stage plays do by means of actors portraying character and developing plot. Cinerama played on the senses.

This novel movie system was the invention of a special effects wizard named Fred Waller, who had set up an experimental theater in an indoor tennis court on one of those vast baronial estates on Long Island's North Shore. He had been tinkering with it for years, but the Hollywood moguls saw no future in it.

One day a man came along who did. He was world-famous at the time: Lowell Thomas, a broadcaster whose voice was familiar to listeners around the globe. Also, Thomas had "discovered" Lawrence of Arabia and had risen to instant celebrity with his illustrated lectures on the exploits of T. E. Lawrence in the Arabian deserts.

When Thomas saw Waller's laboratory demonstration of Cinerama for the first time, he instantly realized its commercial possibilities. Thomas was, after all, not just a mere reader of news, he was an extraordinary public personality, closely identified with high adventure in faraway places. And he was a born storyteller, who had a knack of making his own exotic travels accessible and fascinating to ordinary folks. He realized that whatever came out of that lab would make tales taller (▮).

And so a deal was struck, giving Thomas and his team the exclusive production rights in exchange for (1) the promised delivery of a completed film to play in a New York theater that would be modified for Cinerama and (2) the equipping of twenty-five additional theaters throughout the United States within one year of the opening. If Thomas did not open a show on New York's Broadway within the specified time, he would forfeit all rights to the system.

Learning from Other People's Mistakes

Now as you read on, we will pause several times to invite you to think through what you would do if you could walk a mile in Thomas's shoes? What steps would you take to prevent or minimize any oopses? Or, would you just wing it?

1. First Opportunity

Is this a deal you would have made? Why? Why not? How would you have modified it? Once you made the deal, what kind of system, if any, would you have put in place to deliver it? What would be the essential first steps in a deal like this? How would you manage this project? What would you do first? Which of the following do you think Thomas did first, and what next? Number your choices in order.

   ___A. put a creative team together

   ___B. developed a plan to make the movie and modify or build the twenty-five theaters

   ___C. came up with a big idea

   ___D. created a time line for the project

   ___E. designated a project manager

   ___F. established a fixed budget

   ___G. established a budget review process

   ___H. established a creative plan

   ___I. developed a contingency plan

   ___J. implemented the creative plan; authorized filming to begin

Thomas, of course, did very little of the above. Instead, with a bold idea for a sort-of* travelogue picture in mind, he and his manager, Frank Smith, set out to raise

---

Big ideas usually cover for poor plans. The bigger the idea, the more it suits us; the more that can go wrong, the more room there is for creative alibis when something does go wrong. Keep reading.

money to start production. As this story unfolds, you'll see that Thomas did three things on the above list, in this order: C, A, and the last part of J.

Thomas teamed up with Broadway impresario Mike Todd to make the first picture. Yes, the same Mike Todd who eventually married Elizabeth Taylor, and the same Mike Todd who made megabucks on a film called *Around the World in 80 Days*. The same Mike Todd who was to die in a plane crash on a mountainside at the pinnacle of his extraordinary career.

Generally speaking, Mike and Lowell were not of the same mind, except for one monumental American inclination. They both liked to go off and wing it—improvise —in this case, to make a picture, with everything riding on it, without a plan.

So Mike took what little money they had, flew to Europe with a small crew and the one and only Cinerama camera in existence, and began shooting. Before long, the crew arrived in Milan, home of the world-famous La Scala opera house. Here's what happened, as told by Lowell Thomas in his own words (look for some of the seven cultural forces at work!):

Never had a camera been permitted inside those sacrosanct halls. And even assuming we could overcome such a formidable obstacle, how much would it cost to film the world's most prestigious opera company? Where would we get the lights . . . and where would we get that kind of money? Enter Mike Todd, blue-eyed, five feet eight, and 160 pounds of sheer chutzpah,* requesting an interview with the managing director of La Scala opera. For the first twenty minutes he talks about the miracle of Cinerama, its spectacular newness, the smashing impact it is going to make on the entertainment world, the millions upon millions who will come and come again, to be enthralled by it.

Mike goes on. La Scala? Yes, well a marvelous opera company, perhaps the world's finest, and too bad it is so little appreciated in the United States because it is so little known. In New York and Chicago, perhaps Los Angeles, the cognoscenti know La Scala's reputation, yes, but they are a mere handful. Whereas the name of Cinerama will soon be on the lips of 200 million Americans. I can just see Mike hunching forward at this point, screwing up that marvelously expressive face in sudden thought. Perhaps a segment of La Scala opera would be a useful thing for the first Cinerama production, and in any case he would be willing to do it for the sake of spreading the fame of the great opera company. But, there were a few things: the opera must be the opulent Aïda; full provision would have to be made for the Cinerama crew and their equipment; and to make the occasion appropriately important, the audience—how many could La Scala hold? Two thousand? [Two thousand] would have to be specially invited and, of course, dressed in full evening regalia—gowns, white tie, tails.

Stupefied, bewitched, the managing director agreed. Not a word was said about a fee for La Scala—and indeed, no fee was ever paid—not a cent. And the half hour we shot of Aïda with its magnificent scenery and six hundred players became one of the highlights of our first production. It was a stunningly beautiful

---

**Though a Yiddish term meaning unmitigated effrontery or nerve, gall, audacity, it describes a typical American way of doing things, especially outside of the country. It doesn't work as effectively stateside, though that doesn't keep business people from trying.*

sequence, and some of the most stunning shots of all were of that elite, white-tie audience.

But good as it was, when I (Jim Morrison, one of your authors and then a Cinerama film editor) assembled Mike's footage, there wasn't enough of it to open on Broadway. More money was needed.

2. Second Opportunity

We've seen what happened to Thomas and crew when they went off half-cocked. Now with that experience, what are Thomas's options at this point? He can't fire the budget manager he didn't hire. He can't review the budget plan he didn't develop. He can't hold someone accountable for the project plan that didn't exist. What did Thomas do? Rank your guesses.

___A. fired everyone and started over again

___B. picked the best footage and staged a showing for investors

___C. created some alibis and asked for more money

___D. created a budget plan this time, at least to impress the investors

___E. made some staffing changes that were in the best interest of the project

___F. revised the time line because of the delay in the project

If you haven't caught on by now, Thomas took the American shortcut, if you want to call it that. At this stage, he only did C and E. Thomas went to Wall Street with an alibi or two, but the money men wouldn't budge as long as Mike Todd was still part of the project. Todd was already $6 million in the hole and bankrupt from earlier projects, and to keep Cinerama alive, he had to cash out.

Thomas then partnered with Merian C. Cooper, the man who brought us the first *King Kong*, and a lot of those John Wayne shoot-'em-ups. With a few short months to go before the deadline, Lowell and Cooper tried to figure out what to do next. They decided to do what Lowell did the first time around: Wing it, that's what.

They winged it quite literally—they hired a Hollywood stunt flier named Paul Mantz, who had a modified B-25 Mitchell bomber left over from World War II, installed the still-only-Cinerama-camera-in-the-world in its nose and had Mantz fly low over the Midwestern wheat fields, through mountain passes, deep into the gorges of Bryce Canyon, Utah, over the snow-capped Rockies, under the San Francisco bridges, and on and on across America.

When these spectacular shots were shown on the screen with the stereophonic recording of the Mormon Tabernacle Choir singing "The Battle Hymn of the Republic," "America the Beautiful," and "Come, Come Ye Saints," the effect was overpowering. We instantly knew we had a winner, if only we could get it done on time. The major question was did we have enough time to finish on time.

During the next few months, while we were editing and scoring the picture, Cooper was deep into the production of a John Wayne picture called *The Quiet Man*. He would work in Hollywood on the Wayne picture during the week, and on Friday nights he would take the red-eye to New York (twelve hours in those prop-plane days), work with us all day and night Saturday and Sunday, and then fly back to Los Angeles to devote himself to his other picture. Meanwhile, with the deadline drawing closer, the technical complexities brought the whole enterprise to the edge of disaster.

As of the night before opening on Broadway, the whole show had never had a complete run-through. The next twenty-four hours in this saga show how The American Oops Script that we outlined earlier in this chapter works; with less than a day to go before curtain time, the clean, new thousand-foot rolls of film began to arrive from the Technicolor Laboratories in Hollywood. We had to splice together forty thousand feet of film on eight huge reels in perfect synchronization (take on the impossible). Moreover, at dawn, it became apparent that the special Cinerama reels wouldn't hold enough film (failure). After some fulminating, an assistant editor (prepare for another try) with a mechanical bent made a smaller core and with a tighter wind (try again) was able to get all forty thousand feet on the eight reels (success).

The reels were raced to the Broadway theater. With four hours to spare, a rehearsal of the show was run for the first time ever. But we hadn't made it yet. If there was a break in the film or a broken splice, it would mean that the show would have to be stopped, and each of the four projectors would have to be rethreaded and synchronized before starting again. Thanks to divine providence, there were no glitches.

As the black-tie opening night audience took their seats, we grunts sat nervously in the balcony, kept awake, after thirty-six hours without sleep, by pure adrenaline. The lights dimmed, the curtain parted, and our show was on the big screen on Broadway. It was elegant, right up to the closing credits—and then the film broke. Fortunately, nobody in the audience knew—least of all the critic from *The New York Times*. He was out the door ahead of the crowd to write a glowing review.

Part one of the deal had been met—barely. Now the money was pouring in, but not fast enough to convert the twenty-five new theaters, part two of the deal that needed to be met in order to retain the exclusive production rights. So Lowell Thomas decided to sell his interest to folks who made brassieres. Not such a crazy idea, since they also owned a string of movie theaters.

Taking his winnings, Thomas and his business manager decided to buy a little low-watt UHF television station in upstate New York. They had a plan this time. They would elevate the station to VHF and increase its value by linking it up as an affiliate of CBS. They were confident this could be done, because Thomas had the highest rated radio broadcast five days a week on the CBS network.

3. Third Opportunity

The new Cinerama people asked Thomas to make another Cinerama picture—in a hurry (⏱). Based on Thomas's prior experience, plus what you know about the Now Force, what do you suspect (not hope) he did? Pick just one this time—you've got the point by now.* Once again rank your choice.

    ___A. made a list of mistakes learned from his first experience

    ___B. developed a detailed plan with rigid budget controls

    ___C. developed a tighter time line

    ___D. developed a contingency plan

*In general, the Now Force is so powerful that we think we can do something again and somehow, without planning and attending to the plan, avoid another oops. Observe in your company how many times this happens around the Now Force.

____E. worked with same crew so that earlier mistakes aren't repeated

____F. created a more manageable idea

____G. wrote out a detailed creative plan

____H. winged it

You guessed it: He winged it.

Thomas's idea for his second Cinerama film was *The Seven Wonders of the World*. It was to be a big, spectacular travelogue (⬧). The director he chose was a respected cameraman turned director (▢), whose only guidance came from a quiet dinner with Thomas, a booklet describing the ancient Seven Wonders, and a pat on the back. Again no script—not even a road map. In Thomas's own words, "I had decided in place of a fixed script, we would follow a kind of leapfrog system, shooting what most appealed to us as the opportunity presented itself. . . . I simply plotted a random zigzag course around the globe, ready to pick up where the Greeks of antiquity had left off, flying on to wherever the next marvel would beckon us."

Jim Morrison, now an assistant director and one of a film crew of eighteen, took off with their ponderous equipment (⬧) in a chartered Pan American DC-4 Clipper, with carte blanche to fly anywhere in the world and shoot anything. With Morrison and crew headed in one direction, Paul Mantz in his B-25 bomber with a camera in its nose took off for the African wilderness, shooting along the way.

Before long, a few million in bra company earnings had been spent. It was apparent that the picture was in trouble—surprise, surprise! The money had stopped, and the crews were stalled, living in a four-star hotel in Rome with a chartered plane parked at the Rome airport and a B-25 parked in Cyprus. *The Seven Wonders of the World* was at a crossroads.

The brassiere people had to decide whether to come up with more money, or cut their losses and close it down—a no-brainer, but not the stuff Americans are made of. To complicate matters (and provide further incentive for Thomas to pull another divine providence out of his hat), the brassiere company owned a television station adjacent to the one Thomas had bought in upstate New York. They were in a clear position to block his application for a UHF license. It was improvise time for Thomas.

Somehow Thomas persuaded His Holiness, Pope Pius XII, to make a special appearance in the film and also to allow the Cinerama cameras to film the Vatican and the vast interior of St. Peter's as one of the modern Seven Wonders of the world.* The sequences were shot, the backers relented, the production continued around the world, the picture was finished, and it became a hit. Lessons weren't necessarily learned, but everyone was happy and Thomas went back upstate.

There is an interesting epilogue to this story. Thomas was successful in converting his Albany UHF station and becoming a CBS affiliate. To run the station, Thomas put in charge a kid he'd watched grow up in his own backyard. The kid's name was Thomas S. Murphy (see Nice Guys Finish Big, page 127), a boyhood friend of Jim Morrison's. The corporate name of the company station was Capital Cities Broadcasting, which grew, prospered, and swallowed ABC, which last year was swallowed by Disney, making Tom Murphy one of the biggest co-deal makers of the century.

This was temporal divine providence—you take what you can get.

A FAILURE MUSEUM

The next time you are passing through Ithaca, New York, take time to check out the New Products Showcase and Learning Center. It contains over 60,000 products that have failed in the marketplace! There are over 2,300 shampoos, 600 coffees, four shelves of mustard and an equal number for barbecue sauces. Jalape-o soda is among the 5,500 beverages that consumers didn't swallow. You'll also find many short-lived celebrity products such as Billary beer (this is Bill & Hillary beer, of course, not to be confused with another former president's distillery gift to the nation, Billy Beer), Bush cologne, and Muhammad Ali potato chips.

According to James Dao who describes this only-in-America museum,* "The collection had been much larger, but raccoons broke into it several years ago and destroyed thousands of packages of candy, pet food and dried goods." The four-legged looters also got to a large portion of the curator's collection of laxatives that didn't cut it in the marketplace. Dao added that unfortunately the animals left behind "convincing evidence that the products' expiration dates hadn't been reached."

The Center's curator, Robert M. McMath, was a former marketing executive at Colgate-Palmolive. He has been collecting product failures for more than forty years and figures that eight out of every ten products are losers. For a fee of $1,500 he and his wife, Jean, will tell you all about the failures and facilitate a discussion on consumer packaging gone awry. There isn't much that hasn't been tried and failed in some form or another.

Redefining Failure

We were tempted to write the Cinerama story as a Keystone Kops comedy with a happy spin at the end—after all, Americans like happy endings. Besides, those of us who experienced Cinerama, experienced something way ahead of its time that may never be duplicated again.

There is something to be said for putting a happy spin on failure as a way of dealing with an oops, but that would miss the point of this force and leave us in fantasyland, if Disney will pardon the expression.

Let's face it, companies don't like to use the F word. You can get some executives to talk about mistakes from time to time and most will say, "Our people learn from their mistakes." But that's as far as it goes. By and large companies reported to us that who makes what kind of mistake determines management's response. Therein lies a compounding mistake: not having a plan to acknowledge, process, or learn from mistakes. We believe that American companies would greatly benefit from a more formal way to process mistakes and provide *real* learning from failure.

No company we talked with, or read about during the research for this book, except Disney, has a process for dealing with mistakes. Most don't even have the empathy that Johnson & Johnson has.

*James Dao, "From a Collector of Turkeys, A Tour of a Supermarket Zoo," The New York Times, September 24, 1995.

In Chapter 2 we introduced the idea of certain business words having both conventional and high-performance definitions. Failure is such a word. As you can see in the following table, the high-performance definition of failure is practically the opposite of the conventional meaning.

FAILURE
Conventional vs. High-Performance Meaning

Conventional	High Performance
breakdown	breakthrough
avoid them	expect (and plan) for them
delay action	act on them immediately
feel stupid	feel embarrassed
blame somebody	examine system
inhibits learning	enhances learning
slows things down	speeds things up
breeds more failure	breeds success

Business organizations tend to see mistakes, oopses, failures as breakdowns that delay action and slow things down. In this kind of environment, employees are made to—or simply do—feel stupid. The last thing they do is own up to their mistakes and take personal responsibility for them. The first thing they do is get into the blame game. This is all negative energy, like the gerbil on the treadmill, using up energy but getting nowhere. So much time is spent avoiding mistakes or covering them up that no wonder no one wants to talk about the F word. And in the process communications break down, and trust, essential to a learning environment, is eroded.

The high-performance definition of failure doesn't *welcome* mistakes but sees them as inevitable, something that ought to be anticipated and planned for—just like service or repair time for equipment, power outages, computer crashes, and other business delays that we view differently than human error. When you use the high-performance definition, you don't point fingers, you lend a helping hand. You fix the system, not the blame. And you act on the oops immediately, seeing it as a breakthrough opportunity.

This Isn't Business, This Is Personal

Unlike the American gangster movies where sooner or later someone who is about to blow your head off says, "This isn't personal, this is business," we take quality and improvement personally *and* it is serious business. Unlike the French who have perfected the art of making you feel as if it is your fault when you complain about something that has gone wrong, most Americans step right up to the plate and take the matter personally—and try to fix it.

(The Japanese take things personally as well, but in a different way. If you complain about an oops in Japan, the protocols immediately kick in—the instant appropriate bows, apologies, and rush to repair any damage. This is all rather obsequious and ritualized. It lacks the personal *and* emotional dimension you get from an American.)

As we have mentioned earlier, Americans have a somewhat adolescent culture; this is particularly true when we examine the process we use to repair or improve things. Although we'll cover this adolescent improvement process in detail in Chapter 6, suffice it to say here that what drives our initial adolescent response to an oops are the *emotions* we bring to bear on the oops as we work our way out of it.

Unfortunately, part of our cultural inclination has always been to deny our emotions or at least shun direct contact with them. Yet if we choose to deny emotions, the way out of oopses is simply harder and more time-consuming because the support is not there, and the steps that can be taken to reduce mistakes cannot be activated effectively. Emotions are a key part of the learning process; the research shows that Americans learn about quality when we fail to live up to someone's expectations and we feel *bad* or *embarrassed* about it. We also know from our research that Americans learn about improvement by tapping into a whole range of emotions from *pain* and *frustration* to *ecstasy* and *triumph*. If we deny these kinds of feelings, there is no complete opportunity for learning or improvement.

Clearly then, the word *emotion* is another in our series of important business words that has a high-performance definition, not commonly understood in organizations.

EMOTIONS
Conventional vs. High-Performance Meaning

Conventional	High Performance
sign of weakness	sign of strength
no place in business	essential in business
avoid emotions	emotions trigger learning
confuse	explicate
table them	integrate them
avoid emotional people	seek out emotional people
pay attention only to rational presentations	listen for the emotion in the idea or presentation
use of nonemotional words	use of emotional words

The differences between the conventional meaning and the high-performance meaning are mostly counterintuitive. Legitimizing emotions in the workplace gets to the heart of the oops learning process: Emotions don't confuse the issue, they explicate them. When we know a patient is upset, we treat him differently. When we know a customer is disappointed, we treat her differently.

If we stick to the conventional meaning, we lose the productivity momentum that can come from the high-performance definition approach. At the Disney World Port Orleans and Dixie Landing Resort for example, employees are trained to listen for the emotions of a customer.

Why, then, don't companies figure out a way to see emotions as a legitimate part of the improvement process and work to integrate emotions into the course of business? Rather than avoiding emotions, companies should look at the power of seeking them out. The next time there is a presentation on a work product or process, listen for the emotions in the idea or plan. If there are none, ask, "How does every-one *feel* about this plan or process?" If the now stunned group says nothing or sim-ply replies with the ubiquitous "fine," then probe by asking emotionally leading ques-tions, such as, "Is anyone apprehensive about going forward? How high are the per-sonal risks in meeting the objective? Is anyone afraid of failing? What is the worst thing that can happen and how would that make you feel?"

As part of this dialogue, ask the why questions. Rosemarie Greco, president and CEO of CoreStates Bank, says, "The why questions immediately get to the heart of the matter. They help you get below the surface of the initial response. I make it a habit to ask, 'Why is that?' and then probe further with another 'Why is that?' until I am satisfied that I have understood the apprehension or barrier to going forward."

Crises Are Like a Box of Chocolates

Forrest Gump is the role model for dealing with a crisis: Confront it immediately, engage it, and see it as an opportunity to move on. As you may recall, there was nothing that got in Gump's way, from the school kids who taunted him on the bus to the drill sergeant who cussed him up one side and down the other, from the terror in Vietnam to constant rejection by Jennie. There is nothing that he didn't confront head-on and deal with at the moment. The consequence is that Forrest Gump's life looked worry-free. Yet the deception was not one of Hollywood's making; this was not a special effect, it was the result of seeing big and small crises as opportunities instead of problems, and of handling them as such. It wasn't part of the script, but Gump was using the high-performance definition of crisis that follows.

CRISIS
Conventional vs. High-Performance Meaning

Conventional	High Performance
big problem	big opportunity
avoid at all costs	confront it
let it pass, if possible	engage it
wait for one	plan for one
slows things down	energizes everything
put it behind you	learn from it

The tendency, when a crisis hits, is to wait (provided that it is not a life-threatening crisis) to see if it will pass and what tomorrow will bring. The hope is that the problem will blow over and that there will be no need to dust off the crisis management plan that has been filed away someplace, if there is one.

In a now classic case of crisis management, the way Johnson & Johnson handled the Tylenol poisonings in the fall of 1982 is the stuff corporate legends are made of. At the outset, it's important to remind everyone that this crisis was not of J&J's doing—but they owned it nonetheless. Lawrence G. Foster, vice president of public relations for Johnson & Johnson in those years, said upon reflection on this crisis, "No crisis management plan would have been sufficient in the face of the Tylenol poisonings because not even the best managers could have planned for a tragedy of that proportion."

The crisis, as you may recall, involved an unknown criminal who poisoned pain-relief capsules with cyanide. As a result seven people in the Chicago area died. Within hours of the crisis, J&J acted—instantly, visibly, openly, and dramatically—there was no hesitation. They notified the public and medical professions immediately and pulled all Tylenol medications from the shelves in the area. Concurrently, they notified the Food and Drug Administration, cooperated with the FBI and local law enforcement agencies, and responded completely to all press inquiries.* Meanwhile, back at the plant, they halted the production of Tylenol just in case.

In the midst of this major crisis, another poisoning incident involving Tylenol surfaced in California. Without hesitating to check out the validity of the report—which turned out to be false—J&J pulled *all* Tylenol capsules from the marketplace—*nationwide*.

One dramatic result of this prompt action—which is often overlooked in the business implications of the story—is that two bottles of Tylenol capsules containing cyanide were recovered before they could claim more victims.

An Opportunity to Learn

The Tylenol story is also a good example of how the Oops Force acts as a trigger to activate the other forces we write about. The Improvise Force and the Whatsnew Force—the two forces we describe in the remaining chapters—got J&J back on track. Here's how.

Like Rocky, J&J was now in an underdog status, having lost so much market share, even though Tylenol still remained the number one pain reliever throughout the entire crisis. Sideline experts and second-guessers, outside of the J&J family, said they overreacted; many marketing experts predicted that Tylenol would never recover from the crisis or regain the market share it had held.

Time for an American comeback. In less than six weeks (⏱), McNeil Consumer Products Company, the J&J company that makes and manages Tylenol, was back on the market with a triple-seal (✂) tamper-resistant packaging. It was the first (🖥) in the industry to respond to the national mandate and new FDA regulations for the tamper-resistant packaging. Within another month, Tylenol was back to 80 percent of its pre-crisis sales level. Within approximately fifteen months it had regained all of the market share it had lost and picked up fully where it had left off.

Then another crisis—another Tylenol poisoning on February 8, 1986, approximately three and a half years after the first incident. This time it was a young woman who died in Westchester County, New York, from cyanide poisoning after ingesting an extra-strength Tylenol capsule.

The crisis was handled the same way, with two notable exceptions. Whereas the first crisis took several months to work through, this one was handled in less than

---

Tylenol quickly became the nation's number one story. J&J handled over 2,500 inquiries. Two news clipping services generated in excess of 125,000 clippings. And according to Foster, "One [clipping service] said the Tylenol story had resulted in the widest domestic coverage of any story since the assassination of President John F. Kennedy." It was ranked as the number two national impact story of 1982 by the Associated Press and United Press International.

two weeks time; by February 17 the problem had been resolved, and for all practical purposes, permanently fixed. And this gets us to the second exception: production improvisation (✀).

J&J fixed the problem, once and for all, by announcing that all Tylenol capsules, even the ones in the tamper-resistant packaging, were being discontinued: They would no longer be made or sold. Instead, J&J announced that it was introducing a new form of Tylenol, a solid caplet that was coated and shaped in order to make it easier to swallow. The company also announced that it would replace, free of charge, all capsules in the hands of consumers. A toll-free number was provided and the consumer had the choice (☑) of the replacement or a full refund. It has since become the analgesic dosage form of choice for many consumers and J&J was back in business, defining it, reinventing it, leading it, and setting an example for all of us on how to manage an oops of major proportions.

Not only had J&J responded to the crisis in benchmark terms, but it took one of the dimensions of the high-performance definition of crisis—plan for one—and did precisely that. The creation of the caplet was prompted by the first oops. J&J reasoned that if it happened once, it could happen again and no tamper-resistant package could prevent it.

The company planned right. By the time the next oops occurred, it was ready with a substitute product that proved more effective. In other words, J&J learned from its experience. Curiously, it did not codify the process or create a set of rules or procedures to follow, but it did provide an example for all of us to follow. Except for Exxon and the *Valdez* and Intel and its chip, which stuck with the conventional definition of a crisis and botched it accordingly.

In the Beginning There Almost Wasn't a 3M

While the Tylenol case provides an example of how a mature company can handle the Oops Force, what can be learned, or at least observed, about the Oops Force at the beginning of the creation of a company?

As a trigger, the Oops Force often pulls us up short and confronts us with a choice: We can try again until we get it right, or we can take a different approach to achieve the same end, or we can try something entirely new as we saw in the Tylenol case. A common American streak is to just keep plugging away at the original idea until there is success, as we saw earlier with Henry Ford. Perhaps, no group has tested and persisted in the Oops Force as much as a small group of risk takers in rural Minnesota in the year 1902. They thought they had struck a bonanza along the shores of Lake Superior when they found a deposit rich in corundum, which next to diamonds is the hardest pure mineral in the world. At the turn of the century, the machine age was well under way, and the kinds of machines that were being built required greater and greater tolerances. This meant that there was a greater need for abrasives to more closely hone machine parts. That was what prompted a butcher, a physician, two railroaders, and a lawyer (always need one of them) to chip in one thousand dollars each and form a company to mine it.

They named their company the Minnesota Mining and Manufacturing Company. Today it is known as 3M, one of the leading manufacturing companies in the world, consistently appearing on *Fortune*'s list of most admired companies. Back then they were something else.

It took a year to extract the first ton of the mineral. Then they discovered that it would cost as much to ship it out of the wilderness as it would sell for on the open market (☞). So two of the founders hitched up a team of horses (✂) and dragged it out themselves (once again, the oops triggers other forces).

Two years later, they made their first sale: one ton of the stuff for twenty dollars. This was not exactly the return they were expecting on their investment and effort, not that they had taken the time to put those expectations down or analyze why things had turned out the way they did. They should have been grateful, however, since it turned out to be the last sale they would make (☞).

Now keep in mind that these grown men had invested their own cold cash (not somebody else's, as in the case of Cinerama) and spent a lot of time in this mining venture bringing out stuff they couldn't sell. Yet instead of going back to their jobs, butcher shop or law office, they decided to go into the sandpaper business (🖥).

So to take full advantage of what they believed was valuable corundum up near Lake Superior, they raised more money (♦). By 1906, four years after the start-up, the investment exceeded two hundred thousand dollars. They hired a plant manager with twenty years' experience making sandpaper, and they were turning the product out by the ton. But they still couldn't seem to give it away (☞).

It turned out that there was a pretty good reason this corundum couldn't be given away. And if the 3M boys had taken a spoonful of the stuff they thought was corundum and given it to an undergraduate geology student to assay, they would have discovered why: What they were mining and turning into sand for paper was not the stuff sandpaper is made of. Not only was it not corundum, it was not even suitable for much more than growing weeds. On the other hand, if they had checked, there might be no 3M Company today. But they didn't, so there is.

Five years after forming their company, based on the certainty that they were mining corundum, they discovered that they were mining something else. Five years into a very big oops, and these guys were still plowing ahead.*

By now you know The American Oops Script, so you know that our entrepreneurs tried again. If ever there were five people more blessed with that American characteristic called "stick-to-it-ive-ness," it hasn't been recorded. Instead of quitting, they fired a lot of help, one of the investors pitched in working two jobs, and they hired two young men who were anxious to get off the family farm. Knowing nothing about selling, one of them would make sales calls in a most unconventional way (✂). Instead of going through a company's purchasing agent, he would wander onto the shop floor and talk to the people who actually used the product!†

Just as countless modern-day business books suggest, this unorthodox direct-to-the-user approach gave dramatic results. The gang who couldn't mine right was persuaded to switch to a different kind of abrasive and start a crude form of quality control, and lo and behold, twelve years after the start-up, the company was becoming profitable.

---

*At this point, you may have the same feelings that one of our outside readers had when she was reviewing this chapter. Her margin note said, "This is really hard to believe. Were they really not selling it? How could they keep it up? Did they really not know what they were taking out of the ground?" It's all true.

†Too many American companies still don't get it.

Common Ground

What do the following people have in common with President Clinton?

Richard Nixon

George Foreman

Elizabeth Taylor

Stacy Keach

Donald Trump

Marion Barry

Drew Barrymore

Michael Milken

Sergio Zyman

Your first response might be, who in the hell is Sergio Zyman? Elizabeth Taylor, Stacy Keach and Drew Barrymore are actors (a case could be made that George Foreman and Donald Trump are, too). Michael Milken, Stacy Keach, and Washington D.C. mayor Marion Barry spent time in the hooch-house (Nixon came close). But Zyman is the key. When we tell you who he is, you'll know what all of these folks have in common with the President of the United States, Bill Clinton.

Sergio was responsible for one of the biggest oopses in recent American business history. In 1984 he was the marketing man behind the disastrous launch of New Coke. Today, he is back as chief global marketing executive for Coca-Cola. So what everyone on the above list has in common is comebacks. So far, Clinton is the only one who has been given a title to go along with this American phenomenon, "The Comeback Kid," to go with all of his bounce-backs.

Sergio returned to Coca-Cola in 1993 as a result of what chairman Roberto Goizueta describes as a change in their corporate thinking. In a May 1, 1995 *Fortune* cover story on failure, Goizueta told reporter Patricia Sellers, "We became uncompetitive by not being tolerant of mistakes. The moment you let avoiding failure become your motivator, you're down the path to inactivity. You can stumble only if you're moving."

WOW! All that from one of America's most admired executives. Not too many years ago, the "F" word was left to the tabloids; it was not something you discussed in business. Today, failure may not be something you put on your resume, but increasingly top executives value someone who has failed or made mistakes. None other than Bill Gates, who has made a mistake or two himself, likes to hire people who have made mistakes (so maybe it should go on your resumé). Gates told Sellers "[a mistake] shows that they take risks. The way people deal with things that go wrong is an indicator of how they deal with change."

Comebacks—trying again—is an essential part of The American Oops Script, the business kind as well as the movie kind. Americans love comebacks. It explains the success of the initial movie *Rocky* not to mention *Rocky II* and *Rocky III* and *Rocky IV* and, yes, in case you missed it, *Rocky V* with the promising subtitle, *The Final Bell*.

Jack M. Brickman in his book, *Scene and Structure*, coaches would-be screenwriters to perpetuate this comeback idea which resonates so well with Americans. In his chapter, "Linking Your Scenes: The Structure of Sequel," he directs:

Disaster works (moves the story forward) by seeming to move the central figure further back from his goal, leaving him in worse trouble than he was before the scene started.

A sequel begins for your viewpoint character the moment a scene ends. Just struck by a new, unanticipated but logical disaster, he is plunged into a period of sheer emotion, followed sooner or later by a period of thought, which sooner or later results in the formation of a new, goal-oriented decision, which in turn results in some action toward the new goal just selected.

Comebacks are not limited to individuals or the movies. Companies, indeed whole industries, make comebacks. Besides Coca-Cola, there is the American automotive industry, and the airline industry is another perennial "comeback kid" industry. Apple used Macintosh to make a comeback and IBM is using every trick in the book and a few more up chairman Louis Gerstner's sleeve to make its comeback.

One way to identify forces in a given culture is to analyze its laws and regulations. Comebacks are an integral part of our American rules, regulations, and legal procedures. It is easier to file for bankruptcy and start over again in the U.S. than in any other country in the world. In 1994 there were 92,000 businesses that took advantage of these legal provisions to declare an oops and start all over again—count on most of them making a comeback.

Then there are some companies, like Going Out of Business and its subsidiary, Lost—Lease, Everything Must Go, that are in a permanent position of making the passerby think they are positioning for a comeback, when in reality "going out of business" is the business they are in.

The Problem with Do-It-Right-the-First-Time Exhortations

In two words, the problem with the popular management exhortation "Do It Right the First Time," is *we don't.* In the case of 3M, we see that they didn't get it right the second, third, fourth, or fifth times.

There are two significant dimensions to the research on why this is the case for Americans. First, as we discussed in Chapter 3, Americans are not motivated by perfection as other cultures are. Second, we feel mistakes make us better people.

When The Wirthlin Group asked Americans, "In general, would you be a better person if you did everything right the first time or occasonally made mistakes?" one in every four, unequivocally said occasional mistakes are preferrable. An additional 18 percent hedged ever so slightly, opting to rank themselves 8 or 9 on the 10-point scale. Less than 10 percent said they would be better off if they did things right the first time.*

The researchers then asked the respondents to focus specifically on mistakes they had made. The general question remained the same: Did mistakes make them a better person? The evidence weighed in even more strongly. Thirty-nine percent gave an unequivocal yes and an additional 25 percent hedged slightly, choosing to rank themselves an 8 or 9 on the same 10-point scale. This means that practically two thirds of all American workers see mistake-making as a positive contributing factor in their development.

*We've never met one of these folks. We suspect they are somehow angling for sainthood.

Snapshot #15

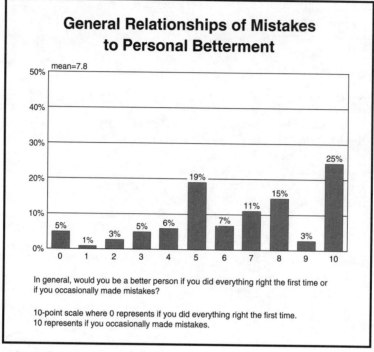

General Relationships of Mistakes to Personal Betterment

mean=7.8

In general, would you be a better person if you did everything right the first time or if you occasionally made mistakes?

10-point scale where 0 represents if you did everything right the first time. 10 represents if you occasionally made mistakes.

Source: The Wirthlin Group and ASQC

Dealing with Oopses

We can all laugh at the hapless 3M founders and second guess them at each step, but what course do we choose when there is an oops in our work life or personal life. Let's walk through the options for a moment or two.

"Oh no!" you mutter to yourself. "I've really done it this time!" In spite of the new quality improvement program telling everyone to "do it right the first time," you've messed up. You didn't measure twice, you skipped a couple of steps in the process, you tried something new without checking, you took too much on, what-ever—you've messed up again. Immediately, your stomach begins to churn, your palms sweat, and your brain races through the possible scenarios. You've been here before. The screw-up may be different than the last one, but the four core choices (☑) in stage one of the oops process are the same:

1. Ignore it
2. Create an alibi
3. Blame someone else
4. Tell someone

1. Ignore it

I never varied from the managerial rule that the worst possible thing we could do was to lie dead in the water with any problem. Solve it. Solve it quickly, solve it

Snapshot #16

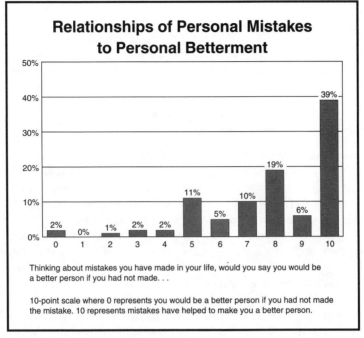

Relationships of Personal Mistakes to Personal Betterment

Thinking about mistakes you have made in your life, would you say you would be a better person if you had not made. . .

10-point scale where 0 represents you would be a better person if you had not made the mistake. 10 represents mistakes have helped to make you a better person.

Source: The Wirthlin Group and ASOC

right or wrong. If you solved it wrong, it would come back and slap you in the face and then you could solve it right. Lying dead in the water and doing nothing is a comfortable alternative because it is without risk, but it is an absolutely fatal way to manage a business.

Thomas J. Watson, Jr.,
Chairman, IBM

There are three primary ways to ignore an oops: the classic ignore (pretend nothing happened); simply hide (passive—wait until someone else finds out); cover up (active, do something—take steps to cover your tracks or try to patch it over or create a diversion).

Ignoring is usually the first line of defense. *No one needs to know. If I keep my mouth shut, no one will be the wiser. I'll act surprised if somebody says something. I'm being transferred anyway.*

Sound familiar? Any one of these, or a variation on the theme, is often what we think or say when we oops it. These thoughts and behaviors are often the result of fear—fear of being caught, looking stupid, being put down, getting yelled at, or being cut out of future activities. At the extreme end of fear, of course, is the fear of losing our job. So we take what appears, at first, to be the safe way out.

This approach may work once or twice, but it's very risky, it could make matters worse—it becomes more expensive to fix later on, trust in working relationships erodes, the emotional stress from not speaking up sooner begins to wear on you. And depending on the nature of the oops, such action may endanger someone else further down the line.

2. Create an alibi

I can't say, over the miles, that I had learned what I had wanted to know because I hadn't known what I wanted to know. But I did learn what I didn't know I wanted to know.

William Least Heat-Moon
Author, *Blue Highways*

Americans are the best alibi makers in the world—it is second nature to us. Alibis are those word mazes some call explanations and others call excuses. The choices are endless (☑). They range from simple declarations that masquerade as a statement of fact to elaborate, complex, interwoven excuses. *I was with a customer. Amal said he would supervise the installation. I was waiting for Charlene. The parts didn't arrive. Jack said that he had checked with Jackie about the new specifications that had come from corporate but there was a whole section missing that she said they would send next week if it didn't arrive with the courier who is on his way from Buffalo and should be here sometime this afternoon, Lord willin' and the creek don't rise . . .*

When all is said and alibied, this is just another form of "ignoring it." You'll notice that alibis cover everything except personal responsibility. Think of all the time and energy that goes into thinking up the excuse, rehearsing it so that it sounds believable, and then telling it. Imagine what would happen if the same amount of energy and creativity went into a solution!

3. Blame someone else

The search for a scapegoat is the easiest of all hunting expeditions.

President Dwight D. Eisenhower

It's Kareem's fault. That's what Captain O'Reilly told me to do. The manager didn't make it clear. Foreman did it. The customers are always changing their minds. Everyone else is doing it this way. Whoever was on duty last night forgot to mention it to me.

This approach takes panache. Don't hesitate if you opt to try this way out. And don't let your eyes wander after you've named someone—this lends some credence and buys you some time. You can bet that the person you blame will find out sooner or later, and that, in turn, will create the need for another alibi. It never ends. Of course, you can avoid a personal vendetta by saying "everyone" or "nobody."

4. Tell someone

You've got to have an atmosphere where people can make mistakes. If we're not making mistakes, we're not going anywhere.

Gordon Foward, President
Chaparral Steel

This is usually the last resort. It's not so much the telling that we dread, but the response we fear. No one wants to be put on the defensive, get blamed in turn, or be scolded. *Hey, don't get mad at me. What do you mean, I should have known better. No, this has never happened before. Yes, I told you as soon as I found out.*

According to the national survey conducted by The Wirthlin Group for the American Quality Foundation, the primary reason employees don't speak up when something is wrong and needs fixing is their perception (or the reality) that "no one cares" or "nothing will be done about it." Fully 30 percent of American workers feel this way. This attitude is evenly distributed across workers at all levels of the organization. It's pervasive and should serve as a wake-up call for management.

Another substantial number, 38 percent gave a *personal* reason for not speaking up when there was an oops and something needed to be fixed. Of this group, 21 percent said they didn't want to be embarrassed or "cause trouble" for somebody else; 13 percent said "it's not my place, not my job"; and 7 percent said they "don't want to get people mad" at them. An additional 5 percent had a great alibi—they said that they didn't know how to express themselves.

This big not-telling factor among American workers is disquieting because these numbers tend to remain constant over time when compared to similar questions in other national surveys. It appears to be a corporate chicken and employee egg situation. Employers want people to speak up, but employees, for the reasons cited, say why bother because nobody cares, and besides, I have personal reasons for not speaking up. Clearly the challenge is to create an environment or process in which employees can speak up quickly and freely without the fear of reprisals—of any kind.

These four basic approaches are pretty dismal choices, but they represent our typical reactions when things go wrong. We create a pattern that works for us and then get in the habit of using that approach every time something doesn't work out right. The research is also clear on the fact that we tend to follow the same pattern at home.

None of this makes us feel very good—at work or at home. Sooner or later, we'll feel guilty. Trust is destroyed and relationships go south. It is also a clear waste of time. Our mind is occupied for hours, even days, with weighing all the possible scenarios: *Is this alibi going to be convincing enough? Did I use that one the last time? Should I just come right out and own up to it? Whom should I tell? When? How much detail should I give?*

We fret and stew about oopses. Our delay in taking the Forrest Gump approach interferes with our concentration and the quality of our work. It prevents us from getting on with our lives. And most important, when we bury or overlook an oops we miss the opportunity to discover something about ourselves, the system, or the process that we are working on. We miss something we value: the opportunity to learn.

If, on the other hand, we are given the opportunity—or more likely, if we *create* the opportunity—to learn from our oopses, we get smarter in the process.

The Oops Values Ladder

Oopses are going to happen, period. However, as we saw in the Tylenol case, J&J took steps to prevent the oopses, at least the same ones, from recurring.

The most effective way to plan for oopses or minimize their impact and maximize the learning around them is to create a learning environment at work for this to happen. Some seminal work by The Wirthlin Group provides a way forward and up.

One of the most valuable experiences we have had over the past few years is working with an economist and political scientist looking at the issues of business performance from a different perspective. They set aside the engineering, TQM, and traditional business models and led us through a unique values identification process that shed some great light on what employees need for optimal work performance. The economist in the group was none other than Richard Wirthlin, and his protégé, Dee Allsop, was the political scientist. Wirthlin made his reputation as Ronald Reagan's pollster and communication strategist, starting with Reagan's successful years as governor of California through his years as one of America's most popular presidents.

Wirthlin's work as a taker of the American pulse enabled him to see the disconnection between what voters valued and what politicians offered. In response, Wirthlin created what he calls a "values ladder," which establishes a hierarchy of need, starting from general issues in the marketplace to specific personal (shared) values of the individual. Through its values work, The Wirthlin Group, as it is known, was able to identify the Reagan values that most deeply resonated with voters.*

The Wirthlin Group sees the same chasm in business: companies not connecting with what customers value, be they insurance companies, fast-food restaurants, car companies, or hotel chains—where the values ladder works equally as well.

But we are a little bit ahead of our background on the power of a values ladder. There are three main parts to the values ladder, each with a number of rungs (or steps) to get from the concrete specifics of the commodity marketplace to the intangible (but real) values of the individual. These three major parts are: attributes, consequences, values.

In political campaigns, in which this values ladder was perfected, **attributes** are the specific issues that candidates are addressing†—such as fair taxes, reduction of government spending, ERA (Equal Rights Amendment), abortion rights, balanced budget, Star Wars, MX missiles, economic recovery, improved education. What issues are addressed and how the candidate addresses them leads to the **consequences** voters attach to the candidate, e.g., he cares about people, he inspires confidence in the White House, or he has the ability to keep us out of war. The **values** that the voters expressed in the 1984 election and ultimately used to judge the candidates were a hope for a better America, the need to preserve world peace, and the desire to make the United States and the world a better place for future generations.

Here is one example of how Reagan used the values ladder in 1984. He took an issue like Star Wars (**attribute**) to move up the ladder to position himself as the candidate most likely to keep us out of war (**consequence**), and having cornered that position in the voters' minds, he positioned himself on top of the ladder (**values**) as the candidate most likely to make the United States and the world a better place for future generations. Mondale chose other issues (**attributes**) and argued against Star

---

*Reagan used this strategy successfully because he believed in the values he espoused. In other words, there was a match between Reagan's beliefs and voters' values (at least a substantial majority of voters' values). Political debates are less about values and more about means for reaching or addressing those values. The Republicans found that out in the election of 1992 when they latched on to "family values"—a universal value—but chose discordant ways of expressing those values. In short, they had the right song, but the wrong notes. They lacked the Reagan match. Watch elections for this discord.

†These are taken from the actual issues in August 1984 in the presidential race between Ronald Reagan (Republican) and Walter Mondale (Democrat).

Snapshot #17

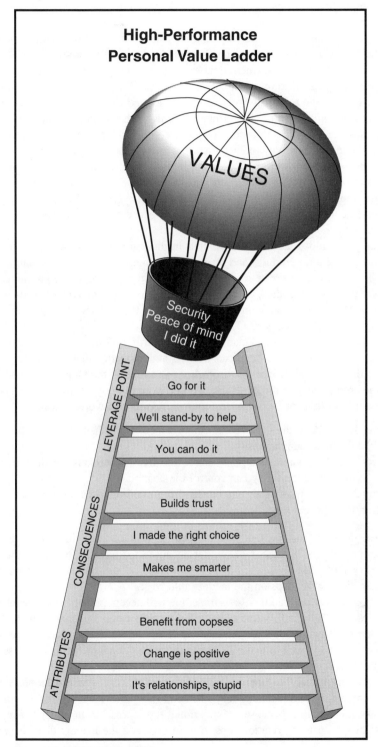

Source: The Wirthlin Group, ASOC

Wars. In the voters' minds, Mondale never got off the bottom rung of the ladder and the lopsided victory in the general election demonstrated the strength of the values ladder approach.

On the strength of this showing, the American Quality Foundation asked The Wirthlin Group to create a similar values ladder for quality products and services. Unlike political campaigns, where issues change from election to election, the issues for the consumer tend to remain relatively constant.

For example, the **attributes** related to product and service quality are issues like timeliness, reliability, value, performance, knowledge and attentiveness of the service person, and friendly attitude. **Consequences** included benefits like saves time, made right decision, got my money's worth, makes me feel smarter, and builds trust. The **values** expressed were personal satisfaction or fulfillment, peace of mind, and feelings of self-worth and self-esteem. In short, you can see how a salesperson with the right knowledge (an attribute) leads consumers to feel as if they made the right decision (a consequence) so that they can have peace of mind (a value) about their purchase.

Seeing the values ladder demonstrated in the political arena and applied to the consumer on general products and services, the American Quality Foundation asked The Wirthlin Group to create a specific values ladder for employee productivity. In other words, what attributes, consequences, and values get an American worker out of bed in the morning? What are the driving forces that enhance productivity? What is needed to tap those values?

Just as they do for political campaigns, The Wirthlin Group collected data from a random selection of typical American workers and converted them to a values ladder.

Here then is the ideal work environment to maximize the Oops Force and maximize the productivity of the American worker: your employees, to be more specific. At the attribute level of the work environment, American workers want:

Rung 1: a place where good relationships can be established and maintained (open and honest communications)
Rung 2: a place where change is seen as positive (Americans see change as positive to the degree that they can control the change.)
Rung 3: a place where they can benefit from their mistakes (oopses that lead on, rather than cause a stumble).

These three primary attributes of an ideal workplace have the following consequences or benefits: workers feel smarter because they have learned from their mistakes; they feel good about the control they have and the choices they have made; and these successive steps on the ladder build trust.

Then, and we would add, *only then,* people will accept personal responsibility for their oopses, because in this kind of environment they can learn, contribute, and make a difference. Why do they want this? As we discussed in Chapter 2, employees want to be valued—they want to make a difference but can't under existing business structures and processes.

The driving force, the American raison d'être for work, is the *personal* sense of fulfillment and accomplishment that is rooted in the knowledge that each individual can make a difference, because the individual has learned from his or her mistakes and established trusting relationships. And to give you the magnitude of how many

Americans believe this, 88 percent, virtually all workers, believe that they can make a difference in the quality of the products and services that their company provides. More than half (53 percent) of Americans say they can make *much more* difference, given the opportunity.*

This is more than a reflection of the eternal optimism of Americans; this is tangible evidence that, provided the right environment, employees are ready to learn, take responsibility, and make a difference. Now that is something you can sink your productivity teeth into.

Celebrations: Completing the American Oops Cycle

At the end of the values ladder comes the reward, the pot of gold at the end of the rainbow. Naturally, when we hear "reward," we think of some monetary or material gift, and there are times when this kind of recognition makes good sense (for example, FedEx's Bravo Zulu program as discussed in Chapter 4). But because Americans take their oopses and fixes so personally, there is another kind of reward that often makes more sense: celebration. Celebration is the high-performance definition of the proverbial pat on the back. And like that pat, it is one of the most powerful, and most neglected aspects of The American Oops Script. Unfortunately, celebrations are not an integral part of business. There are no regular high-fives, bear-hugs, end-zone rituals, head-butts, or Main Street parades in business to celebrate an improvement in a routine process, a breakthrough idea, a group achievement or a personal accomplishment—all the small, big, and incremental victories that go into making a business successful. This is unfortunate because celebrations serve two important functions in business: One, they complete the script and bring closure to an improvement process, and two, they provide energy to move forward and face the next challenge.

The lack of celebration in American culture is a function of several factors. First, the American work ethic has always expressed itself through some form of stoicism. Celebrations are too close to having fun and therefore should be avoided. Second, the Whatsnew Force (Chapter 7) may have kicked in so quickly that we are already on to something else before we have taken time to recognize the need for celebration. Remember, wrapping things up, finishing the job, is not high on the priority list for Americans—we'd just as soon leave the details to someone else and move on to something else.

The key problem is that we have defined celebration too formally. The conventional definition sees celebration as something that comes at the end of a process, usually the end of the year, when sales quotas have been met, or a "banner" year has been declared, or something big or "worth" celebrating has been identified. The celebration then needs to be formal and planned at great time and expense—a hall needs to be hired, entertainment gets booked, prizes are picked, etc.

The high-performance definition of celebration is spontaneous and in order to tap into the intrinsic values of Americans, it needs to be immediate and keyed to improvements as well as end results. Celebration is an important part of trying again; the courage to try again needs to be celebrated just as much as the end result. And we'd get to the end result faster if there were more process celebrations.

National Baseline Survey, 1992; The Wirthlin Group. (See Appendix)

CELEBRATIONS
Conventional vs. High-Performance Meaning

Conventional	High Performance
ceremony	party
emphasize results	emphasize process
tied to milestones	keyed to progress
large	any size
expensive	inexpensive
planned	spontaneous
set in time	anytime
selective	inclusive
impersonal	very personal
audience	congregation

Unlike conventional celebrations, the high-performance definition of celebration is not detached or distant. It accommodates the personal need for celebration that is often very emotional, not necessarily something to be exhibited in public.

No More Tombstones:
Getting the Most out of Reward and Recognition Programs

Closely related to celebrations are reward and recognition programs that most companies have in one form or another. A conventional celebration is explicitly for the purpose of giving individuals and groups rewards and recognition. However, most fail to connect with the cultural forces and consequently have little intrinsic value or motivation.

Most rewards in American business are delayed and look to the past. The result is a closed loop, loss of momentum and energy, and another wooden plaque, tombstone-like on the wall, a reminder of the past, of where we have been. All this in a culture that is obsessed with Now (Chapter 4) and New Potential Identities (Chapter 7). See Snapshot #18.

The most effective time to reward an American is as soon as possible after the goal has been met. The focus should be on the future, not the past, on a new potential identity, on new impossible dreams. The more immediate the reward, the less loss of energy.

What's in It for You

The reason for celebrating is obvious: Reward the employee(s)—make him/her/them feel their worth. Employees who feel their worth know their worth; employees who know their worth are more productive. But there is more than just the carrot and the stick here. Celebration is what makes The American Oops Script both final and worthwhile. It not only makes the process complete, but makes everyone eager to take chances and improvise the next time around. And improvising, as we'll see in the next chapter, is what Americans do best.

Snapshot #18

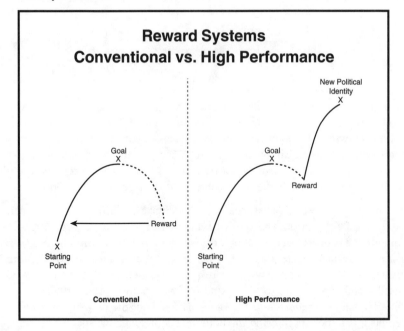

Oops Fake Sheet

Unlike the other cultural forces, the Oops Force does not function on its own. It is the trigger or pivot force. Oopses are the result of many things gone awry, including the result of wrong Choices, unrealistic Dreams, a mismatch on technology, not enough Time to take on Big or finish More. Once you are in an Oops situation, you have Choices, but Time is usually not on your side. So Oops triggers the Improvise Force and the Whatsnew Force that enable us to manage or fix the Oops.

★ By and large, most mistakes, the big ones anyway, follow a script we call The American Oops Script. The script begins by *taking on the impossible* or something that has never been done before. We *begin before we are prepared,* usually the result of inadequate planning or the lack of a clear mission. We *fail the first time and feel bad.* This emotional response is often overlooked or denied and usually ends up leading to some kind of finger pointing. Nevertheless, we *prepare for another chance and try again.* Throughout the preparation and new attempts it is important to *celebrate* both the learning and the success or triumph in the end. Succeeding enables us to *move on to something else,* thus completing the cycle. (See page 184.)

★ Conventional business terms inhibit performance. The conventional meaning of certain words limits the ability of American business to both understand and leverage them to increase quality and productivity. Based on the research done for *Stuff,* high-performance definitions, which tap into the cultural meanings of the words, are provided. These words include failure, emotions, crisis, and celebration (see page 196). In short, the high-performance definition is the opposite of the conventional meaning. For example, failure is not a breakdown, in the conventional sense of the word, but a breakthrough opportunity, in the high-performance definition.

★ Americans value mistakes as learning opportunities. Over 80 percent of Americans accept mistakes and say they are better people as a result of mistakes they have made. Mistakes are learning opportunities and they fly in the face of management exhortations to do things right the first time (see page 204).

★ Create a work environment that accepts mistakes. Based on work done by The Wirthlin Group, a values ladder has been created that can move us from the conscious and conspicuous level of competition, the work pit, through a process of identifying and understanding the consequences of those choices and activities in order to tap into the personal values we aspire to and that bring peace of mind and personal satisfaction. Not surprisingly, an environment that is tolerant of mistakes and enables people to learn from their mistakes is the first rung of the ladder (see page 209).

To tap their full business performance potential, American companies need to create environments in which mistakes can be quickly identified when they happen so that everyone can learn from them and move on. The responsibility of management is not to prevent mistakes from happening, but to keep mistakes from compounding into catastrophe for the customer—there is a big difference! The former is impossible (and not necessarily a good idea); the latter is an imperative.

Mistakes, and learning from mistakes, is a big part of the American improvement process. The challenge for American management is to figure out how to handle the Oops Force and channel it into constructive directions. If mistakes are denied, improvement is delayed. If improvement is delayed, time is lost. If time is lost, somebody else eats your lunch.

Interlude
Montezuma & Maple Leafs

"It has been two years since we met for the first time. Since then, a great deal of water has flowed beneath the bridges of the Rio Grande." An eloquent and poetic beginning of a speech by Mexico's President López Portillo on February 15, 1977, in Mexico City. The occasion for the speech was a visit by then-President Jimmy Carter, who had made the trip (from a Mexican's point of view) to exploit the Mexicans again. Carter was there (from an American's point of view) to explore the implications of a new discovery of significant oil and gas reserves in Mexico.

President López continued:

A great deal also has happened within our countries and between our countries, as it has in the world and to the world. Today, it is only fitting that we evaluate our objectives and face the facts that confront us. We know better now what each expects of the other, but I believe we also know that we have not yet put our friendship to the test, since we have not yet decided what we are willing to make of our relationship. . . . Among permanent, not casual neighbors, surprise moves and sudden deceit or abuse are poisonous fruits that sooner or later have a reverse effect. . . . Mexico has suddenly found itself the center of American attention, attention that is a surprising mixture of interest, disdain, and fear, much like the recurring vague fears you yourselves inspire in certain areas of our national subconscious. Let us seek only lasting solutions—good faith and fair play— nothing that would make us lose the respect of our children.

If you don't recall Carter's response, you won't believe what he said. On second thought, in the context of this book, you might. If ever there was an example of the adolescent American character, this is it—at the highest levels of government:

President López Portillo and I have, in the short time together on this visit, found that we have many things in common. We both represent great nations; we both have found an interest in archaeology; we both must deal with the difficult questions like energy and the control of inflation . . . we both have beautiful and interesting wives; and we both run several kilometers every day. As a matter of fact, I told President López Portillo that I acquired my habit of running here in Mexico City. My first running course was from the Palace of Fine Arts to the Majestic Hotel, where my family and I were staying. In the midst of the Folklórico performance, I discovered that I was afflicted with Montezuma's revenge.

According to Alan Riding of *The New York Times,* Mexican newspapers were ordered to ignore the insult. Not so in America, where one newspaper noted that Carter handled "an ultra-sensitive, enormously important diplomatic mission with beer-parlor bravado."*

Our history with Canada is different, and clearly American presidents are a little more comfortable in Canada than they are in Mexico. Although the symbols are different, we speak the same language (except for French Quebec, of course). We have a 5,527-mile-long border with Canada—the longest unpatrolled border between two countries in the world—and we export more to Canada than we do to Mexico, Japan, and Europe combined. Finally, with the exception of a few flights of acquisition fancy, a skirmish or two back in the eighteenth and nineteenth centuries, and occasional border disputes which we always settled in our favor, we have lived peacefully with Canada from the outset.

Not so with Mexico.

We not only do not speak the same language, but we have a much smaller border—only 750 miles—a border that we fence and patrol.[†] Our jokes, our movies, our stories about Mexico are loaded with derogatory stereotypes, clichés, and insults, manifestations of a condescending attitude toward our southern neighbor that is both ancient and pervasive. Our joint history, from the Mexican perspective, is one of murder, plunder, deceit, and blatant imperialism. From our perspective, it is one of "Manifest Destiny," in which we took ("paid" $15 million for) half their land in 1848 and from that time forward sugarcoated the experience with romantic legends, movies, a TV series, books, and stories about the Alamo.

As several international commentators have noted, Americans tend to see the rest of the world as undeveloped Americans. This arrogance is clearly at the source of cultural ignorance or naïveté. CNN has made the rest of the world a global village, but America remains above the clouds on electronic Mount Olympus, above the fray, subtleties, and knowledge about life "down below."

About all Norte Americanos know about Montezuma is Carter's tourista reference. Few know he was a king of the Aztecs, who had one of the most advanced civilizations of the world. And fewer still are aware that his fatal experience with another visitor to Mexico, Hernán Cortés, the Spanish explorer and conqueror, set the

*Carter made this "joke" in a departure from his prepared text. Starting speeches with jokes, regardless of how appropriate they are, is uniquely American. Other cultures simply do not do that. And American business people should curtail this practice as well as the constant use of sports metaphors, because the American language is difficult enough for others to understand, let alone the nuances, double entendres, and metaphors that simply don't translate. Joke-telling is part of the adolescent nature of Americans, but adolescents don't always play the fool.

†The current political vogue in some quarters is to urge more fences, more border patrols, and more barriers to solve everything that ails America.

expectation that Mexicans have—to this day—about meeting with visitors with "good" intentions. The Spanish came for gold, Carter came for liquid gold—oil.

To Mexicans, Montezuma is about reverence, not revenge. When Montezuma first learned that the Spanish armada had arrived at what is now Veracruz and a bearded white man (Cortés) had come ashore, clad in iron (armor), with strange beasts (horses), he thought that surely this was the legendary Aztec man-god who had died three hundred years before, with a promise to return—the mysterious Quetzalcoatl.

Although there was doubt in his mind about the intentions of the visiting man-god, Montezuma sent a hundred runners with gifts of gold. The favor was not returned. The Aztecs were sacked and co-opted and Montezuma was stoned, as the result of several acts of deception and usurpation. Montezuma's doubt exists to this day; it's a formative part of the history of Mexico, and it radically affects Mexicans' faith in the future—the gods may desert them again. Montezuma is as emotionally important to Mexicans as Lincoln is to Americans, probably more so.

In America some feigned disbelief and incredulity at Carter's remarks, others dismissed them as a Carterism or as no big deal, and still others exploited the gaffe for personal or political purposes. None of this ambiguity existed in Mexico, however: They all saw Carter's remarks as a disquieting reminder of a historical pattern of abuse, deceit, and exploitation from a neighbor who could not be trusted.*

~~Melting Pot~~ Melting Pot Metaphors

Our research into the cultural forces of Mexico and Canada got us to thinking about the constant reference to America as a "melting pot." Intending no offense to Israel Zangwill, author of the 1908 play entitled "The Melting Pot," this image is misleading. A character in Act I says, "America is God's crucible, the great melting pot where all races of Europe are melting and re-forming."†

As dramatic as the sentiment might have been at the time, there are a number of reasons why this theatrical overreaching no longer has any currency, if it ever did.

First, it implies a boiling-down process or a blending to the point of no distinction; the net result being hash, stew, gravy, or smoldering metal. The fact of the matter is, the only melting (melding) that has taken place has occurred among selected European nationalities that intermarried in subsequent generations in America. Ilana Harlow, a folklorist in Queens, has identified 120 separate nationalities living in the borough of New York City. She found them not because they had melted but, conversely, because they each have separate enclaves, specialty food stores, ethnic shops, and distinguishable cultural habits that remained intact—even among successive generations. What do they all have in common? They are proud to be living in Queens, proud to be New Yorkers, proud to be (or be in the process of becoming) American.

---

*This mistrust stems from the Mexican War in the mid–nineteenth century and the "purchase" of land that now constitutes Arizona, New Mexico, and California, from the disproportionate benefit of economic development in the late nineteenth century that resulted in the political unrest that led to the Mexican Revolution in 1910 to the continuing oil exploitations through the mid–twentieth century. Today we read about an American bailout of the monetary crisis in Mexico, and as Americans wonder about Mexico's stability, Mexicans wonder about the continuing price they will pay and what form the exploitation will take this time.

†A crucible is a container or hollow area in the bottom of a furnace in which melted metal collects.

Second, it is an elitist, racist metaphor that has no place in our vocabulary (we are not being in-vogue revisionists here). What were "all the races" in Europe that Zangwill referred to? Certainly not the Irish, who were viewed as dregs and were hard-pressed in the days Zangwill's play ran to find a furnace to keep warm by, let alone get melted in.*

Leaving God out of it for a moment, the crucible, apparently full of Europeans, didn't have room for or ignored Native Americans, Mexicans who were now "strangers in their own land" (the United States having appropriated half of Mexico's land), Chinese (we had an Exclusion Act for them in 1882), the Japanese, African-Americans, and others who bypassed Europe on their way here.

Third, "melting pot" doesn't capture the spirit, energy, or dynamics of being an American, or becoming an American.

Fourth, the population of the United States is becoming increasingly non-white. For example, by the turn of the century, the majority of Californians will be other than white. Twenty-five years later, the rest of the U.S. population will reflect the same dynamic shift in ethnic representation.

Here is an alternative to melting pots: **quilt or patchwork quilt.**

Why a quilt? As our sidebar details, quilts are common to most cultures, each with separate, identifiable patterns and other characteristics. Quilts are not made by making everything the same or by using identical materials, but by common threads that hold the pieces together. The whole is clearly greater than the sum of its parts— that's a more appropriate American metaphor.

Quilts, Mosaics, and Tapestries

At the outset there may appear to be no relevance in how a country sees itself in terms of a popular metaphor, that is, no practical, business relevance. But our research suggests that such metaphors are in fact a useful shorthand, way to think of ourselves and our neighbors.

Thoughtful metaphors are helpful, thoughtless ones are insulting and harmful. The intricacies of these metaphors continually manifest themselves in the ways people in each country go about their business at work, at home, and in their respective communities. Because ours is a shorthand culture, as we have already pointed out, these metaphors should assist us in our business dealings with our next-door neighbors.

To the best of our knowledge, Canada and Mexico don't have metaphorical equivalents that carry the same weight or presence as our "melting pot." So, if we think of America as a quilt, how can we extend the shorthand to our neighbors in a manner that has relevance for everyone? After thinking about it some and integrating what we have heard from colleagues in both countries, our proposal for Canada is "mosaic" and for Mexico "tapestry."

Over the years we have heard others talk about Canada as a mosaic, referring to the separate French- and English-speaking parts of Canada, or the six provinces and

---

Consider this from Professor Ronald Takaki in A Different Mirror: A History of Multicultural America: "America turned out to be a nightmare for many Irish immigrants . . . Irish immigrants found themselves pitted against workers of other races, including the Chinese" and "the pervasive presence of the Irish in railroad work produced the popular saying that there was 'an Irishman buried under every tie.'"

Patchwork Quilts: The American Metaphor

In Schnuppe von Gwinner's introduction to his wonderfully illustrated *The History of the Patchwork Quilt*, we were struck by his observation that his native German-language literature on quilts "concentrated on pure technique and left little room for history." By contrast, the American quilt story is full of lore, history, and social significance. Once again, we were reminded of the German emphasis on precision (the Lego kid at the beginning of the book and the other references to the German approach in advertising, training, and production) in contrast to the American emphasis on invention, variation, and doing your own thing.

While quilts have deep roots in European and Asian cultures, patchwork is found in most cultures. However, the term "patchwork quilt" is primarily associated with America, underscoring our spontaneous and improvisational approach to just about anything we do. (We write more about this Improvise Force in Chapter 6). By definition, patchwork quilts are pieces of fabric that have been sewn together and then quilted. This includes appliqué, sewing one piece on top of another, and sewing pieces side-by-side. Von Gwinner says:

> Though the patchwork tradition is at home in almost every culture, the American pioneer women of the nineteenth Century have won the fame of achieving its richest development. The origin of this textile art form that is so beloved today could not have been a single stroke of genius; rather the roots of this tradition are widely branched. They are found in the greatest variety of cultural, social and industrial development . . .

The same could be said about everything else American, hence the value of the metaphor. In contrasting quilts made in England to those made in the colonial days in America, von Gwinner says that American quilts had a very practical value and "speak of necessity." They were often made at communal gatherings, and for many quilting became synonymous with attending to the needs of others and celebration. Those quilting gatherings, also known as "bees," became important to the social function of the community, especially in rural areas of the country.

The American art of patchwork quilting continues to this day. And while quilting bees no longer serve the social fabric of a community as they once did, the history and significance of the bees is imbued in each and every quilt. While there is no exact count of quilt-makers in the United States, von Gwinner puts the number at about seven million.

two territories, or the Canadian polar population centers, the Toronto-Montreal-Quebec megalopolis in the east, or Vancouver metropolis in the west. For us, mosaic works: The parts are separate, substantial in their own right, and distinguishable, but they fit together in a classic art form, reflective of Canada's heritage.

The appropriate metaphor for Mexico is a tapestry. Mexico has the most integrated population. Over 60 percent of Mexico is mestizo; 29 percent is indigenous and virtually indistinguishable from the majority mestizo population.

Tapestry is an ancient art form, highly valued and treasured around the world—full of pageantry and lore. There is a certain nobility about tapestry as well as a certain mystery. Unlike a quilt or mosaic, in which the parts are distinguishable, the individual threads in a tapestry are not, but together they form a strong, almost impenetrable cloth of lasting value.

Beyond Metaphors: The Business of Neighbors

You can't run a business on metaphors. They can help us understand the macro dimensions of a culture but not the mechanics and mechanisms that make a business or economy work.

NAFTA* is the joint trade agreement that now defines the working relationships between and among the three neighboring countries in North America. It had its attractors and detractors in each country, with each side predicting a worse fate if the other side prevailed. In America the debate was much more acrimonious than in the other countries, but no more so than other contentious arguments about national and international relations. In the end it engendered incredible bipartisanship, with all the living past presidents in support, economists and executives in agreement, academics and anchorpersons in sync. The debate was all about change: How much? With what consequences? With what benefits? For whom?

Changes will come. Indeed they have already come. But they are changes in economic patterns, manufacturing alliances, trade barriers, living standards, regulations, jobs, commodities, and the like. What we are concerned with in this section are the things that *will not change—the forces in the respective countries that were operational before NAFTA and will outlive NAFTA.* Of these, we fear, we have little knowledge, or more accurately, little regard, especially in the United States.

Quality Improvement Study in Mexico

For help in shifting our perceptions about the things that NAFTA won't change, or at least getting us to think about the dynamics that will ultimately make or break the trade experiment, we are grateful to Groupe Schneider, North America–Square D Company (see sidebar on page 223) for letting us share this research with you. It is being discussed for the first time outside of Groupe Schneider, NA, with a mutual intention of sharing knowledge and expanding the dialogue about ourselves and the folks next door.

The following observations about Mexico in particular and Canada in general are based on the study† that was done for Groupe Schneider, North America–Square D, the Illinois-based subsidiary of a French company that does business in Mexico and Canada as well. Square D wanted to know if an overall North American strategy for quality improvement could be developed and, if so, how it should be created and implemented. The research was a comparative study or validation of two other

---

*The North American Free Trade Agreement was implemented January 1, 1994.

†A joint study of Archetype Studies and Culture Dynamics, Inc., commissioned and completed in late 1994. This Interlude includes material prepared for Square D Company and it is being used by permission of Square D Company.

studies done on quality and improvement in America and reported on in some detail in Chapters 5 and 6. In short, the Mexican research was a compare-and-contrast analysis of the American study.

Major Differences

The four major differences that the study discovered among the neighbors of North America are:

1. Source of Motivation

Mexicans, rooted in the past, know who they are. Americans are future-driven, constantly uprooting and questioning themselves; they use the past as a safe haven or home base from which to search continuously for new potential identities (discussed in greater detail in Chapter 7). Canadians, with an identity permeated by ambivalence about their past and anxiety about their future, thrive in the present. See Snapshot #19 on page 230 for additional details.

2. Purpose of Work

Mexicans work hard to keep or preserve what they have. Americans work "smarter" to get more. Mexicans do not respond positively to the American penchant for looking for the fastest or easiest way out. The Mexican search for total knowledge stands in sharp contrast to the anti-intellectual or don't-know-but-can-do attitude of Americans, who act first and think later. Canadians share the work-to-get-ahead drive of the Americans, but approach the work process much as the Mexicans do, from a knowledge and reasoning basis. Once this knowledge is understood, Canadians act more quickly than Mexicans.

3. Sense of Time

In Mexico there is an inverse relationship between position and on-time responsibility: the higher the title, the less punctuality. Mexico's reliance on passive resistance to process something conflicts with the U.S. bias for action; Canada's reliance on bureaucracy and process to get things accomplished also conflicts with American Now time (see Chapter 4).

4. Process Safeguards

Mexico's penchant for postponing things until *mañana* does for Mexico what reliance on process and bureaucracy does for Canada. Two corresponding dimensions in the U.S. are deconstruction (improving things by first taking them apart) and "the sleeping giant" (passivity or indifference until finally provoked to action), which we also discussed in an earlier chapter.

Not Boxed in at Square D

Square D is one of the organizations that comprise Groupe Schneider–North America, a division of Groupe Schneider, a $10.5 billion French global electronics company, a leading supplier of electrical distribution, automation, and industrial control products. Square D is a good example of practically all of the cultural forces we write about, so it could fit practically anywhere. But we have included the company in this Interlude because it has operations in Canada and Mexico and because the company's desire to understand business practices in Mexico better by examining national cultural forces led to the study we are reporting on.

Square D was founded in 1902 as McBride Manufacturing Company and was later renamed the Detroit Fuse and Manufacturing Company. Back in those days, it was common for factories to use open knife-blade electrical switches. These open switches were often hazardous, sometimes resulting in injury or death.

In 1915 the Detroit Fuse and Manufacturing Company created and began marketing an enclosed switch that addressed the safety hazards of the earlier models. The letter "D" was embossed on the square cover. The squared boxes with the stylized D became so popular that the company is now officially known as Square D.

Square D, maker of over twenty thousand separate and distinct products, is headquartered in Palatine, just outside of Chicago. There, more than sixteen thousand employees thrive on a tradition of breakthrough thinking and global leadership. The company is an innovative leader in the electrical industry with an impressive list of product breakthroughs (those leaps we wrote about Chapter 2). And this innovative tradition has earned it a "Best of the Best" listing in Robert Camp's 1995 industry bible, *Business Process Benchmarking—Finding and Implementing Best Practices*. It is cited by Camp as having particularly outstanding practices in technology transfer and training.

An independent panel of judges for the international consulting firm of Arthur D. Little also named Square D as one of its 1995 "Best of the Best Supply Chain Management" practitioners. And it was in good company, right up there with well-known consumer companies like Xerox, Volvo, Toyota, Texas Instruments, Procter & Gamble, Motorola, and Ford. Square D was cited for "their vision, foresight, and management qualities," the things we wrote about in Chapter 2.

On top of these coveted business recognitions, Groupe Schneider has been named by Xerox Corporation as its "first-ever" Global Certified Supplier, a recognition that is being publicized worldwide through full-page ads in *The Wall Street Journal* in early 1996. This award recognizes the highest performance standards for customer satisfaction provided by Xerox throughout the world. It bestows on Groupe Schneider–North America and Square D a preferential supplier status for all new Xerox product orders and service contracts. Xerox has also made them its "world standard for automation, industrial control and electrical distribution equipment."

To help us understand what makes Square D connect so forcefully with its customers and earn these kinds of recognitions, we revisited Rick G'Fellers, who had worked with us on the Mexico study. G'Fellers is part of Square D's vast training effort; he's manager of quality projects in its Quality and Customer Satisfaction group.

While it is technology and innovation that achieves the breakthroughs, it is Square D's substantial commitment to training that provides the on-going support to maintain these high levels of customer satisfaction and business performance. G'Fellers is one of more than thirty trainers that spend $7.5 million annually, on a hundred and twenty-five different training courses throughout the company. He says, "Without this sustained dedication to training, Square D would not be attracting the people it does, nor producing the results it has. There is nothing here but diversity in work, large-scale energy, ample challenges, and plenty of opportunity for growth and development. That's what connects for me. That's what makes Square D a great company to work for."

The Mexican Study

The Mexico study addresses essential nontechnical elements for a successful quality improvement strategy—identity, perceptions, motivation, behaviors, work habits, and rewards. The basic conclusion upends the usual American approach to global business: There is one way to do things, the American way, or more specifically, the American company way. The study concludes that no *effective single strategy* for improvement could be created to serve the three countries. Customizing—creating an improvement strategy in each country that activates its unique cultural forces—is the most effective way to go.

Business goals and objectives can be shared, but the processes for achieving those goals must be different in order to maximize the results. The operative word is *effective,* implying efficiency and maximum result. Companies like Motorola, Corning, Arthur Andersen, and McDonald's have universal business processes that work for them. But companies like Johnson & Johnson and Hewlett-Packard find their decentralization of international operations effective. We opt for the decentralized, culture-leveraged process improvement strategy, especially since we have seen this strategy take root in America as companies become more conscious of the seven cultural forces and activate them domestically. As the Square D study shows, the intrinsic culture-based motivators in each country are radically—not mildly—different. Any restriction or limitation on those forces results in less than a total commitment or total engagement of the individual. These national cultural forces should not be ignored, if optimizing output or finding a competitive advantage is the objective.

This research finding is supported by the work of Charles Hampden-Turner, management consultant and professor at Cambridge University's Judge Institute of Management, and Alfons Trompenaars, managing director of the Center for International Business Studies in the Netherlands. In their book, *The Seven Cultures of Capitalism*, they report on a major study of management value systems in Britain, France, Germany, Japan, the Netherlands, Sweden, and the United States. No surprise, Americans run their enterprises the way they see themselves—as individuals—

others would say imperialists imposing their way on everyone else, having given the matter no thought. But to Americans, if it works (obviously from their point of view), that is all that matters.

The tools and technology of most business operations are universal. A Pareto chart (used to determine which problems to work on and in which order), cause and effect diagrams (a tool for identifying, exploring, and displaying the possible causes of a problem or condition), and control charts (used to discover variation and measure statistical control) are all universal. Same tools, same process in all countries.

Everything else is *not* universal, especially when it relates to motivation, reward, meaning or value of work, loyalty, value systems, marketing, supplier relationships, and customer interactions. These dimensions of business are radically impacted by national cultures and, if we choose to ignore those cultural influences, we do so at considerable loss. So, to the degree that businesses operate internationally on the tool/technology dimension, universalism works. However, to the extent that businesses deal in process improvement, training, motivation, employee management, and customer relations, only "exceptionalism" or localizing the process, procedure, or relationship works.

En el lenguaje de los Mexicanos

While happily in the process of preparing the report for Square D Company we rediscovered Octavio Paz, the winner of the 1990 Nobel Prize for Literature.* And while we have read only translations of his essays, we admire his penetrating insights and commentary on Mexicans and Americans—in the (translated) language of the Mexicans. We have drawn from his *Labyrinth of Solitude* and other essays, translated by Lysander Kemp, to complement and support our findings about Mexico. Let's begin with an arresting, inward look at Mexico, which has major implications for our business dealings and relationships with that country:

> *The developed half of Mexico imposes its model on the other, without noticing that the model fails to correspond to our true historical, psychic, and cultural reality and is instead a mere copy (and a degraded copy) of the North American archetype. Again: we have not been able to create viable models of development, models that correspond to what we are. Up to now, development has been the opposite of what the word means: to open out that which is rolled up, to unfold, to grow freely and harmoniously. Indeed, development has been a straitjacket. It is a false liberation: if it has abolished many ancient, senseless prohibitions, it has also oppressed us with exigencies no less frightening and onerous.*

The cultural dynamics in Mexico that all nations who do business there need to pay attention to include the following:

1. Passive resistance

2. Hard work

3. Authenticity

*For those of you who are unfamiliar with Paz, he is author of more than twenty-five books of poetry and prose. He is a poet, essayist, playwright, philosopher, and social critic. He served as Mexico's ambassador to India and as a Mexican diplomat in France and Japan.

4. Paying attention to los rangos (hierarchy)

5. Being closed, circumspect

Dialogue with Octavio Paz

First we will summarize our research findings about each of these dynamics, then we will quote Octavio Paz, or let him speak through the translator. The reader should keep in mind that unlike the research for this book, which identifies the seven cultural forces that define Americans, the Mexican study we are reporting on had a narrow business focus. So these dynamics do not necessarily reflect the macro cultural forces of Mexico; such a study has yet to be done. However, the more we read and understand Octavio Paz and others, the more familiar we get with Mexico, the more we feel that these dynamics could indeed have the same weight and influence as the forces that define Americans.

1. Passive Resistance

This is the power to resist, oppose, or withstand something or somebody without relying on force or dramatic gestures. It is both the capacity to act and the act itself. Think of it as austere fortitude or the ability to endure incredible pain without complaining. This is not the equivalent of "no pain, no gain" in America, which Americans accept but complain about. Rather it is the *real* proof of strength and courage.

Octavio Paz: *Resignation is one of our most popular virtues. We admire fortitude in the face of adversity more than the most brilliant triumph. . . . Our sense of inferiority—real and imagined—might be explained at least partly by the reserve with which the Mexican faces other people and the unpredictable violence with which his repressed emotions break through his mask of impassivity.*

2. Hard Work

Mexicans don't live to work; they work to live. This is not working hard to get ahead, as it is in America, but working hard to keep what one has; it is an act of preservation. Work makes the fiesta possible, and the fiesta is a way to transcend work. The fiesta is the reward for work; in America, money is the reward, so the harder one works (with no fiesta and little or no vacation) the more money one gets.

Octavio Paz: *The modern [Mexican] worker lacks individuality. . . . He is a laborer, which is an abstract noun designating a mere function rather than a specific job . . . work is the precursor of the fiesta. The solitary Mexican loves fiestas and public gatherings. Any occasion for getting together will serve, any pretext to stop the flow of time and commemorate men and events with festivals and ceremonies. . . . During the days before and after the twelfth of December [Fiesta of the Virgin of Guadeloupe], time comes to a full stop, and instead of pushing us toward a deceptive tomorrow that is always beyond our reach, offers us a complete and perfect today of dancing and revelry, of communion with the most ancient and secret Mexico. Time is no longer succession, and becomes what it originally was and is: the present, in which past and future are reconciled.*

Findings: Comparison of Key Business Dynamics

MEXICO	U.S.A.
Dynamic 1 *Resist passively*	*Act now.* bias for action; jump right in; just do it.
Dynamic 2 *Work hard to live*	*Work hard* to discover who you are; to change; to actualize new potential identity; the Puritan ethic.
Dynamic 3 *Value authenticity*	*Value perception.* Appearance is reality, quality is perception. Knowledge is not that essential, for if you don't succeed the first time, try again.
Dynamic 4 *Accept* los rangos	*Equality.* Everyone is equal; equal opportunity; you are as good as your last deed.
Dynamic 5 *Be closed*	*Be open.* open-door policy; nothing to hide; question authority; advertise everything

3. Authenticity

In stark contrast to Americans, Mexicans reject appearances and search for origins that are supported by unquestionable evidence. Their quest is for the ideal conception, design, or strategy. Action is predicated on the certainty of a theory, verification of a strategy, assurance of completeness or thoroughness of a plan. While this often serves as an alibi for delaying action, it is the opposite of the low regard for adherence to plans and the bias for action that drives Americans. It is important to Mexicans to be genuine and real.

Octavio Paz: *The solitude of the Mexican, under the great stone night of the high plateau that is still inhabited by insatiable gods, is very different from that of the North American, who wanders in an abstract world of machines, fellow citizens and moral precepts. In the Valley of Mexico man feels himself suspended between heaven and earth, and he oscillates between contrary powers and forces, and petrified eyes, and devouring mouths. Reality—that is, the world that surrounds us—exists by itself here, has a life of its own, and was not invented by man as it was in the United States. . . . The North American wants to use reality rather than to know it.*

4. Paying Attention to *los Rangos*

There is no American word or experience for *los rangos.* The closest notion is hierarchy. To a Mexican this is the way the world is, and there is nothing that can be done about it. Whereas Americans question or challenge authority, or sound off about it, the Mexican accepts the order, which to them is given by destiny and by the gods. That is the way it has always been. The only escape is the fiesta.

Octavio Paz: *Order—juridical, social, religious or artistic—brings security and stability, and a person has only to adjust to the models and principles that regulate life; he can express himself without resorting to the perpetual inventiveness demanded by a free society. At the fiesta . . . the persons taking part cast off all human or social rank and become, for the moment, living images. . . . In certain fiestas the very notion of order disappears. Chaos comes back and license rules. Anything is permitted: the customary hierarchies vanish, along with all social, sex, caste, and trade distinctions. Men disguise themselves as women, gentlemen as slaves, the poor as the rich. The army, the clergy, and the law are ridiculed. . . . Respectable people put away the dignified expressions and conservative clothes that isolate them, dress up in gaudy colors, hide behind a mask, and escape from themselves.*

5. Being Closed, Circumspect

Mexicans do not show what they have inside; they don't open up. This hermetic quality is a defensive characteristic that keeps them authentic. It is rooted in the past, in the fear of upsetting the gods. This fear translates to all authority—the boss, the chief, the politician, the gods. It profoundly affects the Mexican's view of the future.

Octavio Paz: *The speech of our people reflects the extent to which we protect ourselves from the outside world: the ideal of manliness is never to "crack," never to back down. Those who "open themselves up" are cowards. Unlike other people, we believe that opening oneself up is a weakness or a betrayal. The Mexican can bend, can bow humbly, can even stoop, but he cannot back down, that is, he cannot allow the outside world to penetrate his privacy.*

Findings: Comparisons of the People

MEXICO	U.S.A.
Mexicans know their identity.	Americans are in a permanent search for identity.
Pessimistic	Optimistic
It is rewarding to show how strong you are, to be consistent with the past, to endure pain and suffering with dignity.	It is rewarding to make a breakthrough, create a better world for your children, change things, and discover new identities.
Mexican heroes are: People who are jailed, suffer and die with dignity, without opening up, without showing their suffering.	American heroes are: People who succeed, become rich and famous, often fail, and make a comeback!

North of the Border

The North Americans are credulous and we are believers; they love fairy tales and detective stories and we love myths and legends. The Mexican tells lies because he delights in fantasy, or because he is desperate, or because he wants to rise above the sordid facts of his life; the North American does not tell lies, but he substitutes social truth for the real truth, which is always disagreeable. We get drunk in order to confess; they get drunk in order to forget. They are optimists and we are nihilists—except that our nihilism is not intellectual but instinctive, and therefore irrefutable. We are suspicious and they are trusting. We are sorrowful and sarcastic and they are happy and full of jokes. North Americans want to understand and we want to contemplate. They are activists and we are quietists; we enjoy our wounds and they enjoy their inventions. They believe in hygiene, health, work and contentment, but perhaps they have never experienced true joy, which is an intoxication, a whirlwind. In the hubbub of a fiesta night our voices explode into brilliant lights, and life and death mingle together, while their vitality becomes a fixed smile that denies old age and death, but that changes life to motionless stone.

Octavio Paz
from *The Labyrinth of Solitude*

COMPARISON OF SOURCE OF MOTIVATION

The following snapshot is designed to provide an overview of the major differences in the source or locus of motivation among the countries in this study, as well as in France and Japan for additional comparison and contrast. Once we understand the primary source of motivation in a culture, we then have knowledge about its people and why they do the things they do the way they do them. The implications for business are profound; no area or activity of a business enterprise is—or should be—exempt from them.

Canada has two separate and distinct pasts (one British and one French) and an uncertain future, so it thrives in the present. Mexico is rooted in the past and is fearful or leery of the future because the gods may desert them again, as they did Montezuma, so they move cautiously forward in the present. The United States lives in the present for the future, where Americans see endless options and possibilities. The past is forgotten; it is like home base, a place to retreat to, if necessary. France had numerous ideal pasts, but struggles in the present with those pasts as it seeks to create an ideal future. Japan does not make the distinction between the past and the future as other cultures do; the present is an extension of the past into the future.

This summary chart then helps us understand why *kaisen*, the Japanese word for continuous improvement, may have more application in Mexico and Canada than in the United States, where breakthrough thinking to create the future, rather than improve the past, is the primary motivator. The use of quality improvement tools will

Snapshot #19

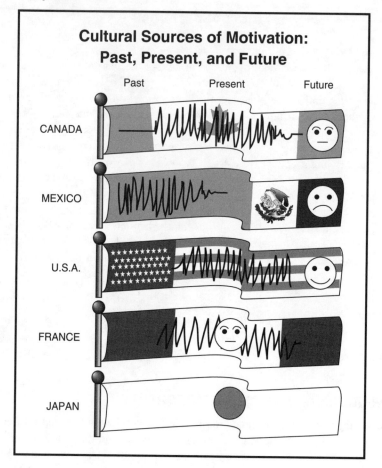

Cultural Sources of Motivation:
Past, Present, and Future

resonate in Mexico, where the search for knowledge is a primary motivator. Mexicans will need a context for improvement, while the Canadians will need a process. The Mexicans and French will be able to reason together, while the Americans will jump right in before thinking too much about it. The Canadians will seek rewards based on the present, while Americans will be more motivated by a new potential identity or doing the next thing.

We can't change culture, but we can change the way we do things and the assumptions we make about our policies, procedures, and practices in light of cultural forces and business dynamics. Each culture possesses its own wisdom; we simply need to tap the forces or dynamics of that wisdom in order to support the best improvement process.

Businesses can and do define their internal culture in universal terms to create policies and procedures that seek a common goal, but that is not where competition is headed. Mexicans do not check their culture at the corporate gate in the morning, nor do the Canadians pick theirs up at day's end. Not surprisingly then, the American improvement process that works so well for the United States is not only perceived negatively elsewhere, it is resisted.

Study Conclusions

1. There can be no single *effective* North American strategy for quality improvement, nor can there be an effective single *global* strategy. There can be common goals and some of the tools and technology can be the same, but these do not a strategy make. There must be different implementation strategies in each country if any company or organization wishes to maximize the leverage of its cultural forces. It is not enough to ask another country to simply translate goals and materials.

There is much to the common business slogan, "Think Global, Act Local," if indeed, "act local" means align the cultures or adapt the strategy to fit the forces in a particular country. Too often, "act local" simply means implement a strategy conceived at global headquarters, with little or no understanding for culture. Corporate culture and national culture are not the same thing. The "think global" implementation strategy should be to require the sponsoring or parent country to ask, "*How* can we achieve this [program or objective] in your culture?" This question should not be perceived as political or a courtesy with no intended consequences. It must be received as a serious management concern.

2. Mexico needs a Mexican empowerment strategy, not an American adaptation. Americans are more comfortable taking personal initiative, expressing themselves, doing things differently, challenging procedures, and inventing new approaches—the process and outcome of empowerment. Mexicans are not; there the dynamics around empowerment are completely different. In Mexico the motivation needs to respect the past, accommodate *los rangos* and proceed on the basis of knowledge rather than intuition. A casual, let-your-hair-down, let's-talk-it-over approach that is at the heart of the American empowerment strategy will not work in Mexico. The process needs to be more rigid, focused, structured, with clear objectives. Results will be slower in coming, but more reliable, more authentic.

3. Martin W. G. King is a Canadian who lives in Washington, D.C., and frequently writes about culture and politics. In a *Washington Post* op-ed, aptly titled "Uh Oh, Canada!," he reviews how Canada's ambivalent past has created anxiety about the future, thereby corroborating our observations. He concludes:

> Canada may well carry on as a state for some time, but only with major changes (or ruptures) in its structure. It all depends on the point of view, English or French, federalist or secessionist. Each sees a different way to the future in its own crystal ball. One thing is certain: Canada is a nation sick at heart, tormented by its identity crisis. Despite their sophisticated welfare state, their outward civility, their great modern cities and their struggling culture, always competing with America's mass media and airwaves (and losing more often than not), most Canadians can't really tell you what they are, although they are quick to point out what they are not: "American."

Americans need to tell Canadians that they know that they (the Canadians) are different and then treat them differently. Canadians are not lined up at the border waiting to become American. While many live in the shadow of the border, especially within the reach of our television and telecommunications, this is no invitation to assume that Canadians have become Americanized. This simple gesture, some would say courtesy, is the most basic principle of communication, relationship development, and process improvement in Canada.

Chapter 6

America's Urge to Improvise
and All That Jazz

Think about classical music for a moment. Who gets to call the shots?

No, if you said the conductor.

No, if you said the concertmaster.

No, if you said the first violin.

No, if you said anybody else but the composer.

Look closely at the musical score at left.* This is just one out of 189 pages of explicit written instructions from the composer Ludwig von Beethoven[†] to whomever may want to conduct his *Ninth Symphony*. There is no ambiguity here, no guesswork. These are directions—orders, really—on how the piece is to be played. He divides it into two parts, specifies *every* note for *every* player, and tells the conductor precisely how each set of notes should be played by what musicians. Beethoven even specifies the instruments: flutes, oboes, clarinets (in B), horns and bass horns in B, two violin voices, violas, and so on. Finally, he expects the piece to be over and done with in a little over an hour.

Despite some discretionary interpretation, the basic job of the conductor is to execute this set of directions as precisely as possible, making sure that each player is on cue, in tempo (also set by Beethoven), in mood, and generally hits each note as Ludwig intended. The critics and the audience—during and after the concert—will judge the conductor by how well this was done. The judgments here are about degrees of interpretation of the score—usually subtle nuances that most of us miss. The individual orchestra members don't even have this small degree of latitude: Their job is to follow the leader.

What we have here is the traditional way a company runs its affairs. The composer is the CEO who sets the goals, calls the shots, and lays down the rules. The conductor is middle management, executing a carefully delineated plan—telling folks

---

*If you are a classical musician, musicologist, patron of the hometown symphony, or proud alumn of your school orchestra days, please bear with us for a minute or two on this analogy. Both authors love classical music and as they say in mafia movies, "We mean no disrespect."

†This is not just because Beethoven was especially autocratic—all composers do this.

what to do, directing by the book, conforming to specifications, making sure every-one is doing their job (a Frederick Taylor score)—in short, calling the tune. The players (employees) do as they are trained, instructed, and rehearsed.

Now think of *jazz* for a moment.

Same question, different idiom: Who gets to call the shots?

No, not the composer.

No, there is no conductor.

No, not necessarily the band leader or ensemble head.

In the case of jazz all the players get to participate. In fact, there is music (the product or service) only when there is agreement by the participants (the employees) on the following:

1. Who will lead

2. The tune to be played

3. The key it will be played in

4. The tempo

5. The order in which they can solo

Look closely at the music score on the opposite page. This is it: a key structure, a few notes, and a few chord changes. This is all that is necessary to make music the American jazz way. In particular, this is *all* any group of musicians needs to play John Coltrane's "Giant Steps,"* for as long as they agree that they want to play it—no time requirements, no obligation to finish in thirty-three minutes, no specifica-tions on the number of players or the kind of instruments, no specific instructions of any kind, except the discipline of the basic melody.

The American Idiom

We may not be as comfortable in a blues bar as we are a concert hall. To many of us, jam may be something we put on toast and riff may be the sound a small dog makes, but jazz is uniquely American. In short, we may not fully understand it, but jazz is *the* cultural idiom of America.[†]

Max Lerner in *America as Civilization* said, "Every civilization finds the musical instruments that express its idiom." Unlike the violins and harpsichords of classical music, the American music form is about brass and percussion. These and the other instruments of jazz express melancholy moans and triumphant shouts—the core of the American experience. Thus Armstrong, Beiderbecke, and Coltrane are as representa-tive of American culture as Adams, Brandeis, and Carnegie. Duke Ellington, Coleman Hawkins, and Thelonious Monk were as inventive and innovative as Eli Whitney,

---

*The sheet of music shown on the previous page is actually a "fake sheet," a pared-down, one-page version of the original score. (How very American: a shortcut for an already simple process.) The original score runs a page longer and, yes, there is a bit more structure to it. But this fake sheet is all that is required to play "Giant Steps" and it (or any similar versions), not the actual score, is what is most often used by musicians. This version was provided courtesy of our resident jazz coach and Morrison's neighbor, Richard Donahue.

†The best books we found on understanding this American idiom are Albert Murray's The Omni-Americans: Black Experience and American Culture *and* Stomping the Blues, *also by Murray.*

Thomas Edison, or William Lear. And Wynton Marsalis has as much insight (though not the specifications) on management as Peter Drucker or Tom Peters.

If you're singing and forget the words or drop the music, just *scat*—not as in "get out of here," but as in invent or mumble and create something new, as Louis Armstrong reportedly did.* And if somebody steps on your horn as happened to Dizzy Gillespie in 1953 you keep it that way, bends and all (🎺), because as he said, "I hear the sound quicker (🕐)."

Management by Jazzing Around

If American executives could adapt one management style that has been overlooked in our search for competitiveness, increased productivity, and higher quality, it would be one based on the lessons from jazz. The most basic and insightful are:

★ In jazz, you do not get expelled from a group for failure to hit the high notes (doing things right the first time), but for failure to pay attention—a canon not part of contemporary American management.

★ In jazz, each player is given the opportunity to solo. The player can change the key, the pace, and even wander afield, but soloing is essential—it's the umbilical cord to the result.

In this chapter we examine the basic rhythms of American teamwork and provide a new high-performance definition for teams. We introduce a new beat for the American improvement process and rediscover the requirements for innovation. We visit 3M and see how its "take five" (they actually take fifteen) has resulted in sixty thousand product innovations over the years. And to see some famous and not so famous Americans solo, we visit inventors (improvisers) like Ray Heyer, Bill Lear, and Gene Kranz. Finally, we'll show how the other cultural forces form a tight combo with improvisation and innovation.

The First Improvisers

You've heard it from us before, but the impulse to improvise as a cultural force was also conceived on board the *Mayflower*. You'll recall that the Saints and Strangers† were chartered to land in Virginia. When they realized they were off-course, they did what Americans do to this day when they are in a jam—they improvised. Before going ashore—wherever that was going to be (destination is not a prerequisite for improvising, getting out of the mess is)—they held an impromptu conference on board and sketched a melody, known as the Mayflower Compact. The signing of the Compact was an answer to an emergency. The Strangers were near mutiny, but the Saints were in charge. However, this was not a contract between king and nobles, but rather a social contract among equals hurriedly improvised during a crisis on the high seas. Later, this contract would be embellished a great deal, but the chord it struck is the American tune.

The audience didn't know the difference when this first happened—the improvising was so effective they thought it was part of the plan.

†*This would make a great name for a jazz group.*

Thinking on Your Feet

Driving to Wal-Mart to buy some fax paper, I (Morrison) was stopped at a traffic light when along came fourth-grader Jeremy Bickert, the runt of a litter of six, riding a hand-me-down bike. Jeremy was late for school and looking wobbly as he pumped his bike across the intersection. The weight of his backpack caused the wobble. He was pumping hard with both feet, steering with one hand and holding the broken end of a brake cable with the other. The night before, Jeremy's older brother had snapped the cable while doing wheelies and neglected to tell anyone (☜).

Jeremy shot like a rocket down the hill. No brakes.

I followed cautiously behind, knowing Jeremy was heading for a nasty spill when he would have to take a sharp turn into the school yard. Just as that moment arrived Jeremy Bickert stood upright on one pedal, swung the other leg up over the seat and pushed his Reeboked foot between the spinning back wheel and the bike frame, bringing bike and boy to a smooth safe landing by the school door at the very instant the first-period bell rang.

Jeremy had improvised in the most elegant way. Like most improvisations, his actions were spontaneous and inspired, and they used the technology at hand.

The Twins

We have heard claims that the Mayflower Compact was really an innovation. We see more improvisation, but certainly accede that there was an element of innovation. To be sure, *improvisation* and *innovation* are twins—not identical, but closely related. They behave in much the same way but are curiously different in their personalities. Webster defines *improvisation* as something extemporaneous: creating or arranging something offhand, or fabricating what is conveniently at hand. Improvisation has a quality of spontaneity that is not readily apparent in innovation.

Innovation is more formal—improvisation in a three-piece business suit. Its process is structured, orderly. It is more about the introduction of something new, a new method or device or idea. It is arrived at by a more systematic and reflective process.* Innovation is generally lacking in the urgency, sometimes desperation, that so often surrounds improvisation.

The inherent informality of improvisation makes it accessible to almost everyone in an organization; there isn't the intimidation that often precedes the more formal process of innovation. Improvising opens doors to innovation. When we improvise we use what we have—something that is second nature—whereas innovation requires more exacting materials, more time, more deliberation, more patience.

Management Improvisation: Lessons from on High

The supreme achievement of American technology had broken down utterly. All that was left was a spacecraft whose very complexity made it harder to handle, plus a group of flight controllers and three astronauts who were themselves products of

---

The local library lists one-hundred-thirty-eight books under "improvisation," and all of them deal with some form of the arts—drama, music, sculpture, poetry, etc. It has a like number of books listed under "innovation," and most of them deal with managing situations in business.

the vast bureaucratic machine that had produced the malfunctioning spacecraft. . . . However, the accident had also demolished most of the technological appurtenances, such as checklists, and flight plans . . . and also much of the automatic equipment aboard the spacecraft which performed tasks that earlier mariners would have performed for themselves.

This is how Henry S. F. Cooper described the *Apollo 13* mission in his book, *13: The Flight That Failed.* This was the flight that stood the world on its ear. This was the flight that never made it to the moon, and barely, just barely, made it safely back.

Cooper concluded: "Now the flight controllers and the astronauts were no different from any other sailors facing disaster at sea. They would do a lot better by themselves than their elaborate paraphernalia had done by them."

Analysis of the accident would later prove, as in the case of Jeremy's bike, there had been a breakdown in communication and process. Five years earlier, when *Apollo 13*'s service module was under construction, there had been a change of specification in the wiring of the oxygen cylinders, and the changes were made without taking into consideration the effect of the change on one other component. It was an accident that waited five years to happen.

In case you haven't seen the movie (or read the books), the routine liftoff occurred at 2:13 P.M. EST, April 11, 1970.* It was followed by fifty-five hours and fifty-five minutes of textbook flight. Then suddenly a sharp bang rocked the spaceship.

Tom Hanks, playing the part of astronaut Jim Lovell, the *Apollo 13* flight commander, feels a jolt and notes the array of blinking warning lights on his dashboard. In a now classic understatement, he says, "Houston, we have a problem." At that moment, the flight surgeon on the ground noted that the pulse rates of all three astronauts had jumped from 70 to over 130—up where it should be toward the middle of a twenty-minute aerobic exercise program, or ten minutes into a contested squash game.

Gene Kranz, flight director in Houston at Mission Control, did not know what had happened, if anything, because the NASA teams had such complete faith in the redundancy built into the space systems.

Thirteen minutes after the bang, Lovell looked out the window and saw something he was not suppose to see—a thin sheet of vapor. "It looks to me that we are venting something," he understated. "We are venting something out into space," he repeated. At this point it became clear to Lovell and Krantz that they were in big trouble.

A Trio in Space with a Backup Band on Earth

From this point on, the astronauts and Mission Control would need to improvise;† from this point on they were all Jeremy Bickerts. But they were a little more than

---

We highly recommend the movie, not to just see it, but to study and analyze it. The release of the movie Apollo 13 *on the twenty-fifth anniversary of the crisis and the overwhelming public response to it is about more than good filmmaking—it's about America's perpetual love affair with frontiers and unexplored space. Show it in your corporate training programs or at your next executive retreat. Join your staff in drawing the parallels between this crisis and how it was handled and the last time there was a crisis in your organization. What are the things that you would do differently? Why? Make a list of things that are new to you and set up a plan to implement those in your organization. And don't forget the popcorn!*

†*Their improvisations were highly technical, so we'll deal with the technology only to the degree necessary to understand the improvisations.*

late for school. At stake was a $400 million expedition and the precious lives of three human beings.

With the command module losing power, Kranz ordered it shut down to conserve what little power was left: That was the only way to buy some time. The *Apollo* crew moved into the LEM, the moon landing module, which was to act as a "lifeboat." It was designed to support the life of two men for two days, now it would be required to sustain three men for four days.

Although it was not intended as such, the Mission Control communications setup was ideally configured to deal with the improvisation that would ensue. The Mission Control system allowed the various flight controllers to talk directly among themselves without interrupting the main loop of the flight director. It enabled a free-flow of ideas for discussion, for weighing alternatives, for reconciling conflict, without overloading Flight Director Kranz's attention.

Managing the Improvisers

Although there were thirty or forty of the best space engineers in that room, they were all looking at less than two days before the spacecraft would smack into the earth's atmosphere, and nobody had any idea where to begin. "Suddenly I realized it all had to begin with *me,*" were the words later spoken by twenty-seven-year-old John Aaron, who would be in charge of the power-up of the command module. Knowing he could not create a coherent plan with so large a group, he picked out the six or eight key people he would need to improvise what he called a "strawman timeline" for a rough outline of what had to be done. "A strawman is something you can throw rocks at," he later explained. "Things always overwhelm you until you have a plan."

Four different control teams rotated throughout Mission Control. Kranz, as chief of flight control and leader of the "White" team, had spent a lot of time training the controllers to achieve what he called "uniformity of decision" from one shift to the next. This system also assured consistency in speaking with the astronauts.

Remember the point made in Chapter 2 about the essential need for everyone in an organization to understand the plan, the details, the goal? Improvisation is not a do-as-you-are-told; it's about intuition and judgment calls based on knowledge, training, and experience. In this case it isn't about getting to Jerusalem by the end of the year, but getting back to earth before you run out of oxygen.

When the Black Team took over, astronaut Fred Haise was trying to get the LEM running. To run the simplest checklist would take two hours that they didn't have. It had never been done before (⚙)—even in simulation—but Haise, working with Mission Control, was able to improvise, eliminating a number of steps that were intended for a moon landing, and get the LEM running in just fifteen minutes (🕐)!

This situation illustrates how the Now Force is linked to the Improvise Force: In Chapter 4 we saw how Allied Signal is using time to invent, innovate, and improvise on strategies and techniques to enhance its productivity and quality. As you may recall, Allied Signal, incidentally a major supplier to NASA, chose to streamline its processes before there was a crisis or requirement to do so.

Meanwhile, Kranz took his White Team to a control room that had an exact duplicate of the spacecraft. They spent several hours trying to figure out what happened and exploring ways to bring the ship down safely. They stuck to it until they came upon a sequence for organizing an action plan. Like any effective leader, Kranz knew

The Management of a Crisis: "It was all improvisation." A Conversation with Gene Krantz

JM: *How'd you like the movie?*

GK: It was reasonably good. They had to exaggerate a few things. A spacecraft out of control has to look like a spacecraft out of control. As I look back on my log after twenty-five years I'm really amazed at the composure that everybody had. That's point one. Point two, I'm amazed at how our leaders gave us the responsibility and let us exercise it. They didn't get in our way. In fact they even did blocking for us. They facilitated us doing the job. I'd say it was a triumph of leadership at a very high level, as well as leadership at the mid-level, the flight director's leadership.

JM: *How did you get everyone working together?*

GK: I think I let too many people in the room than were necessary to get the job done. I guess there were in the order of fifty or sixty, and we needed half that number. But I didn't really know who were going to be contributors. But I did know who my lead people were by that time, so it was really a question of what needed to be done. Within a few hours we broke down into small teams. We had short-term actions and long-term things we had to do.

JM: *Wasn't there a moment when you knew it was deadly serious?*

GK: I think that was later on in the mission. I think the principal impression I had was that when I got there the mood of the room was relatively somber, because these were young kids. They really needed to be pumped up and made to believe that they were going to get the crew home. So, I think that was the real turning point. I had to give 'em the words. So I said, "Hey, we've been in tough times before. And there's no surrender." It was all improvisation, it sure as hell was. It was just scratching my head to figure out how we would do things; we knew we couldn't do it the normal way. John Aaron, I think, said it right. "We actually did everything the reverse from the way we normally do." Normally we would power up the less significant systems first and that provides the opportunity to evaluate the more significant systems. This time we did it the other way round. We were power critical and what we wanted to do was get the important things up first.

JM: *You never gave up, did you?*

GK: See that's the product of the training we had. The simulation team has all the same skills that the flight control teams have. Their objective is to train us. To seek out [weaknesses] in planning, procedures, techniques, personal relationships, that type stuff, and then, punch holes in 'em. And in the early part of the training they are generally capable of beating us up. But as time goes on we hold our own, and pretty soon we are operating as a team. And so what they do is start loading us up with problems to find out the point at which we break. And by the time you finish that your attitude is so positive you never surrender. The press called me arrogantly confident throughout the whole mission. And you do develop an arrogance in the sense that you're never going to be defeated.

the limits of human effort; he didn't want to compound the crisis. So he sent his people off to bed. He knew they would function better with rested minds.

Every company, both large and small, has stories, legends, and even myths of that indefatigable commitment and stick-to-it-iveness that was required to get the proposal done, the equipment recalibrated, the customer request filled, the show to go on. However, when burning the midnight oil, the weekend blitz, or the marathon effort become the norm, people burn out and judgment is impaired. Not surprising then, the only thing a jazz group will not forgive is failure to pay attention; a missed note is one thing, failure to pay attention is grounds for dismissal. Paying attention is the discipline of jazz. Too often it is a missing element in business performance.

Out of the crisis grew an orderly sequence of decisions—an order we dare say is applicable to any business crisis or emergency situation.*

1. Take no action that might make matters worse.
2. Keep the astronauts alive.
3. Take no irreversible actions until necessary.
4. Conserve resources.
5. Provide as much flexibility as possible.

When the rested Kranz team met again, the priority was to create (improvise) a checklist and action plan for the safe return of the astronauts. Checklists establish order and create a certain reality. They are like recipes for cooking or any process for that matter. In driving a car the checklist is made up of the basics we do automatically: (1) Close door. (2) Put key in ignition switch. (3) Put shift in neutral or park. (4) Turn ignition, etc.

Sometimes we can afford to mess with the recipe, change the order and still get the same result. This often happens in business when a customer is pressing for a product or service and exceptions have to be made to normal procedures. It happens all the time in a hospital where the nature of an emergency dictates the intervention. It happens on Capitol Hill when a stop-gap measure needs to be passed to remedy a national security problem.

Not so in space. A spacecraft is so complicated, it is imperative that each step be taken in precise sequence to preclude a serious accident.

What normally would take months and months to prepare and ends up looking like a big-city telephone book would now have to be written and compiled in less than three days (°⚷◝◔)! But according to astronaut Jack Swigert, they could never have gotten back to earth without the White Team's checklist.

Some Common Sense

Everyone knows how the story ends—with sighs of joy, a big splash in the Pacific, and a ticker-tape parade.

But most of us don't remember or know about the commission formed by NASA administrator Thomas Paine to determine what had happened and *how we could learn*

The list is quite reminiscent of Johnson & Johnson's handling of the classic Tylenol tampering crisis we described in Chapter 5.

from our mistakes. The commission, which included moonwalker Neil Armstrong, released its findings in short order (⏱) and went a long way toward restoring the nation's faith in the space program.

Of course, in writing this story, we are reminded of another Thomas Paine, who wrote in *The American Crisis* that "these are the times that try men's souls." We'd modify that poignant phrase and say that these are the kinds of circumstances that try men's wits and test their improvisational spirit.

Drucker Calls the Innovation Tune

Not surprisingly, Peter Drucker has already codified and bona fided the improvise/ innovate equations in clear, concise language. Of course, he has expanded on his listing with illuminating examples in a book called *Innovation and Entrepreneurship*. The chapter that we reference is "Purposeful Innovation and the Seven Sources for Innovative Opportunity."

We won't try to improve on Mr. Drucker's work. Nor dare improvise with it. However, we feel obliged to present a summation of his observations. We also took to the field, in this case a trip to 3M in St. Paul, to validate this stuff and see if we couldn't learn something more about how those folks have come up with sixty thousand new products in ninety years. Innovation, after all, is 3M's motto.

Let's start with Drucker. He made it easy to find the thesis of his book: he put it in italics (a writer's fake sheet to simplify things for the reader). He says, *Systematic innovation therefore consists in the purposeful and organized search for changes, and the systematic analysis of the opportunities such changes might offer for economic or social innovation.*

Drucker asserts that systematic innovation requires the monitoring of *seven sources* of innovative opportunity. Here are the seven with an example of ours in parentheses, which we explain next.

1. **The unexpected** (NutraSweet)
2. **Incongruity** (Scotch Brite soap pads)
3. **Process need** (Eli's Gin and Tonic)
4. **Changes in industry structure or market structure** (credit cards)
5. **Demographics** (telemarketing diversity)
6. **Changes in perception, mood, and meaning** (health care)
7. **New knowledge** (microreplication)

1. The Lucky Finger Lick: An Example of The Unexpected

Back in 1965 James Schlatter was mixing amino acids one day in a G. D. Searle & Company lab trying to come up with a test for an ulcer drug. The mix bubbled over and dripped down the outside of his flask (💬). Later in the day he happened to lick his finger. He was startled at the taste—it was sweet.

Schlatter is now retired. But when we asked him to recount the moment of the unexpected, he told the story as if it happened yesterday. He said that the instant he tasted that sweet stuff on his finger, he "*ran* out of the lab and right down to the office of my supervisor. I was disappointed that he wasn't in, so I left word with his assistant that I wanted to show him something right away. Well, he showed up an hour later, and tasted the stuff, and he got excited too. I was beside myself."

He tells how they retraced his steps, trying to figure out where the sweetness had come from. Finally, they discovered that it was from the flask where the amino acids had spilled. The unexpected discovery turned out to be the artificial sweetener *aspartame*, a simple combination of two amino acids. These days it can be found in everything from soft drinks to puddings.

It took sixteen years to bring NutraSweet to market.* Today it generates well over $500 million in sales—not bad for an unexpected taste on a finger. And yes, James Schlatter says he got a raise, eventually. He retired from Searle at age fifty-five when Searle was bought out by Monsanto.

2. Never Rust Soap Pads: An Example of Incongruity

He came in the room carrying a shopping bag from which he produced just two things: a plastic pop bottle and one of those scrubbing pads used to clean pots and pans. Ray Heyer has the look of a lean, left-handed, side-arm relief pitcher coming in in the last of the ninth to put the fire out. In fact, he's an engineer at 3M and he told us, "We had to get from this (holding up the plastic bottle) to this" (holding up the soap pad)—an incongruity if we ever saw one.

Heyer came to 3M right off the farm, having gotten an engineering degree along the way. He says that 3M has found over the years that in hiring ex–farm boys they get a frame of mind that is always ready to improvise, something you have to do every day when your manure spreader freezes up, you birth a calf, or you get a leak in the silo roof.

There is a kind of glow that comes over Ray's face as he talks about his "baby"—Scotch Brite Never Rust Soap Pads, now a head-to-head competitor to Brillo and S.O.S. steel wool. For the last seventy-five years those two products were a market segment that had been asleep in the soap dish. Yet there was certainly room for improvement; a look at your kitchen sink reminds you that steel wool begins to rust as soon as it gets wet. The steel slivers impale delicate hands and are tough to remove.

For several years 3M had been on the lookout for a way to fix the rust, but studies showed that the cost of raw materials (plastic) was prohibitive. Then in the late eighties with the introduction of plastic bottles in the soda pop business, a cost-effective source for plastic was evident in recycled bottles.

Heyer and his team took it on. However, their early experiments with the bottle dross turned out pancake flat. The team was stumped and their innovation DOA.

All the to-ing and fro-ing at the mighty 3M labs and engineering interfaces could not figure out how to plump-up and firm-up the pads so that they could absorb and hold detergent while at the same time provide what they call in the abrasives trade an "aggressive abrasion."

But it just so happened that at one time, twenty-five years before, Ray had noticed that at a certain point in the refining process recycled plastic went through a kind of "ropy" stage. So what if they stopped the process at this stage and tried to make a puffy pad? EUREKA! That's all it took.

---

*Much of what accounts for this long process in getting an innovation to the marketplace is the lack of innovation *in the government bureaucracy that approves new substances for the marketplace.*

Within months after 3M brought the Scotch Brite product to market, it captured 20 percent of the scouring-pad market in just 36 weeks! 3M loves those incongruities.

3. Eli's Gin and Tonic: An Example of Process Need

In their biography of Eli Whitney, Jeannette Mirsky and Allan Nevins tell how Whitney, on his way to take a tutoring job in South Carolina, stopped by the plantation home of Mrs. Nathaniel Greene, widow of the famous Revolutionary War general. Having just graduated from Yale's class of 1792, he was deeply in debt and still reeling from a trip that found his ship crashing into the rocks at Hell's Gate. He caught smallpox in New York and spent six seasick days at the rails aboard a packed boat down from New York. To cap it off he learned upon his arrival in Savannah that the tutoring job for which he expected to be paid a hundred guineas a year paid only fifty. Eli was in trouble. Should he accept the fifty guineas or spend another week at the rails all the way back up North?

As always, talk at Catherine Greene's table turned to what was uppermost in the minds of Southern plantation owners: Rice and indigo were no longer cash crops; tobacco prices had not only fallen, but that same weed exhausted the soil of their land. Their only hope was to grow cotton.

Alas, black-seed long-staple cotton, the kind preferred by the English mills, could not be grown inland. Green-seed short-strand cotton, which did flourish inland, was seriously flawed. It took a whole day to pick the green seeds out of just a pound of cotton—the numbers just weren't there.

Now Eli had grown up on a farm in Massachusetts and, as a teenager during the Revolution, he turned a quick buck making iron nails in his father's tool shed. He was handy with a lathe, and understood mechanics and metalcraft. Thus with a little urging from the Widow Greene he turned his attention to the green cotton seeds and how to extract them from the bolls.

Eli's Gin: It was a perfect meeting of need and nimble mind and after only six months Eli had a working model. Fired with enthusiasm, Eli set out for the nation's capital (then in Philadelphia) to see Secretary of State Thomas Jefferson and obtain a patent. Whitney got his patent, and made a friend of the future President.

But he was no match for the sharpies who found a hundred ways to avoid paying him royalties. While the patent was pending, the machine had been exhibited to groups of Georgia planters, and before long the knockoffs were ginning all over the South (the unfortunate story of thousands of inventions and innovations to this day).

The speed of ginning now made cotton planting economically possible in the South. Within sixteen years of the introduction of the cotton gin, annual production of raw cotton in the United States rose from two million to eighty-five million pounds. Ironically, the whole experience left Whitney near poverty, but once an innovator always an improviser.

Eli's Tonic: About this time, a war with France was thought to be imminent, and the muskets that had won the Revolution had come from France. With that source gone, Whitney proposed to manufacture ten thousand muskets in two years for the United States Government, using a precision system of interchangeable parts he had invented and wanted to test. Until then, each musket had been handmade, one at a time, and thus, no two were exactly alike.

Whitney was never able to keep up with the demand for his cotton gins and knockoffs were popping up everywhere. It is likely that this drove him to devise what he called the "uniformity system," a method employing power-driven tools that would make parts of sufficiently close tolerances that they could be interchangeable without filing and fitting.

Eli was late in the delivery of the weapons, but amazed the government investigators when he selected parts from random piles and assembled a musket on the spot. The order for ten thousand muskets was finally filled nine years later. This was the beginning of the machine tool industry in the United States, which stood world leader at the end of the Second World War. However, today the United States stands number four in machine tools, behind Japan, Germany, and Sweden.

4. Charge It: An Example of Change in Industry Structure

"America began to change on a mid-September day in 1958, when the Bank of America dropped its first 60,000 credit cards on the unassuming city of Fresno, California," according to Joseph Nocera, in his book *A Piece of the Action: How the Middle Class Joined the Money Class.* Over the course of the next twelve years, before mass mailings of credit cards were outlawed, over 100 million of these now common plastic cards would fall from the heavens right into your mailbox.

All prior attempts to create and launch a general-purpose credit card had failed. But we know from the Oops Force (Chapter 5) that failure is an opportunity to try again. And that's precisely what Joe Williams and his gang of six at Bank of America did. Nocera says, "Nothing about how credit cards should work was obvious. The credit card trailblazers like Joe Williams were making it up as they went along, groping for answers that didn't yet exist, learning a business as they were inventing it"— the Improvise Force at its best.

Nocera's book makes great reading and it's full of opportunities to learn from other people's mistakes. He describes what made the card work for Bank of America:* choice. For the first time, the consumer had control over all key decisions related to the card—buy things, arrange payment plans—all the things we take for granted today.

Unfortunately, the Fresno drop precipitated premature drops in San Francisco and Los Angeles. Like *Apollo 13,* the bank was quickly venting a lot of things; everything that could go wrong did. It was a big oops.

Then bank chief Clark Beise chaired the meeting that could have pulled the plug on the entire enterprise. However, instead of pulling the plug, they concluded that the concept was indeed right and they had already made all the mistakes—there were none left to be made. So they brought in some new players, changed the approach, got some experts (installment credit folks), and the rest is credit history.

5. Telemarketing in Tongues: An Example of Demographics

Marty Shih, a Taiwanese-born American, has hit it big in the U.S. in the world of telemarketing. You might do the same if you spoke Chinese, or Spanish, or Korean, or any other language that reaches segmented populations in America. What Marty has going for him is a thorough knowledge of cultures, language, and the buying habits of recently arrived Asians. *Business Week* reports that Marty also has a staff of

Prior to 1958 there had been gas cards, airline charge cards, a half-dozen major department store charge cards, and Diners Club, which had the first card that could be used at more than one establishment. But there was nothing that did what cards do today or what Joseph Williams had up his sleeve for Bank of America.

two hundred telemarketers in his Asian Business Connection based in Rosemead, California. They are hawking everything imaginable, including specialty foods and other goods—from the homeland. It all adds up to some $40 million in sales.

One thing that drives Shih's success is the simple fact that fewer new arrivals have been hit by mainstream telemarketers, and newcomers (as well as the rest of us) welcome a call in our native-born language. Ethnic telemarketing is the fastest-growing segment of the market and, recognizing this, MCI is calling in nineteen languages, and getting responses two to three time greater than calls made in English—what *Business Week* calls "speaking in tongues."

6. Health: An Example of Change in Perception, Mood, and Meaning

As Drucker notes, mathematically there is no difference between a glass being "half full" or "half empty." But in terms of perception the two views are often a litmus test to sort optimists from pessimists, risk takers from more cautious people, leaders from followers, health nuts from hypochondriacs.*

Health is a clear example of how changes in perceptions over the past ten years or so have led to innovations. Practically all health indicators in America are up.

The glass is half full: People are living longer, cure rates for cancer keep getting better, advances in surgical technology have shortened hospital stays, culprit genes have been isolated, and everyone seems to be more conscious of health than at any time before.

No, the glass is half empty: three-fourths of the nation is overweight, practically everything causes cancer, we lag behind other industrial nations in terms of infant mortality rates, suicide rates are up for younger people, the fear of old age is an obsession in America, and the cost of health care is a sickness itself, sending temperatures rising on Capitol Hill and getting the budget surgeons cutting away at time-honored federal programs of Medicare and Medicaid.

Both perceptions have created vast opportunities for innovation. Pharmaceutical companies, medical specialists, technologists, HMOs, insurance companies, aerobic instructors, TV programmers, equipment manufacturers, and countless others have all jumped in to take advantage of both sides of the equation. There is now a plethora of new books, health care book clubs, newsletters, and magazines. Virtually every network has a TV doc and special segments devoted to causes and cures. The vitamin business has grown exponentially and new food products with health care claims clamor for shelf space in both traditional food markets and new specialty shops that cater to the health prevention appetites of Americans.

Much of the increase in the sale of sporting goods can be attributed to the increased health awareness among Americans. Specialty clubs, jogging equipment, exercise rooms, mountain biking, rock climbing, Nordic Tracks, and indoor everything are all innovations in response to the change in perception about health care. Within ten years the industry has grown from $15.7 to over $44.6 billion in sales.

*In the latest business joke going around, you've probably already heard that a reengineering consultant will tell you that the glass is neither half full nor half empty—you simply have too much glass.

From Oops to Improvise to Gold Medal

In fifth grade this gangly, awkward kid tried every event in track and field without success (✺). By the time he got to high school he made third team football, and sat on the bench in basketball. But he retained a keen interest in track.

Although he ran high hurdles, the high jump was his destiny. Even so, he couldn't master the classic "straddle" form that was the way the big winners were taking prizes. He had a little more success with the "scissors" method, which gave him a best jump of five feet four inches.

Then at age sixteen, Dick Fosbury tried something different (✂). Something urged him on. He reasoned that with so much weight in his upper body he might be able to jump higher if he could figure out how to throw his upper body over the bar first. He tried and it seemed to work pretty well, but the landing in those days was in sawdust. It was hard, and Fosbury was risking serious injury, but he persisted. Eventually, the sawdust would be replaced by cushy foam, and with that Fosbury improved remarkably.

That was the beginning of the now famous "Fosbury Flop." Before long he had passed his personal best and was jumping five feet ten inches and his high school coach wisely allowed him to develop this new technique (🖳).

In his senior year in high school, Dick Fosbury won the National Junior Olympics with a jump of six feet seven inches. But no college coach gave serious thought to Fosbury as championship material except for Oregon State coach Berny Wagner, who took a chance and offered Fosbury a scholarship.

Wagner tried to switch Fosbury back to the straddle jump (✺), but Fosbury balked. "The roll is so complicated," he said. "I just never had the coordination for jumping that way."

By 1968 the year of the nineteenth Olympic Games in Mexico City, Fosbury had mastered his "flop" technique and in the Olympic team trials he jumped seven feet three inches and made the team. The high-jump competition was on October 14, 1968. Late in the afternoon, all competitors were eliminated save two Americans, Edward Carruthers and Dick Fosbury. The bar went to seven feet four and a half inches. Carruthers missed three times and was eliminated. And now it was up to Fosbury. He missed the first (✺), and the second (✺), but on the third try he cleared the bar a full one and one half inches above his personal best (✺).

He went home to a ticker tape parade, got his degree in engineering, and never again found the need to compete in track and field. But the Fosbury Flop is the only high-jump method used in world-class competition today—a method that bears his name and is forever associated with improvising and innovation.

Even companies have begun to emphasize exercise, diet, massage, naps, and "balance" between work and life programs as a direct benefit to both the employee and to the company's bottom line through increased productivity and lower health care costs. And as long as the perceptions exist, the innovation opportunities will continue.

7. Reflector Lights: An Example of New Knowledge

Microreplication is an innovation technology that involves "creating precise, microscopic, three-dimensional patterns on surfaces such as plastic film," according to Roger Appledorn, a forty-year veteran conjurer at 3M, whose title at the Optics Technology Center is corporate scientist. Next time you drive down a country road on a dark night and your headlights suddenly catch a brilliant yellow triangle warning you of a dangerous curve, you can thank Roger Appledorn and all the rest in the 3M labs concerned with innovations in reflecting technology.

Appledorn told us that the commercial applications of this new knowledge are enabling 3M to create products that "retro-reflect the light striking surfaces, transport light from one place to another, speed up the flow of fluids inside a pipe, serve as a new-generation abrasive, polish plastic eyewear, and finish metal."

INTERPLAY OF THE SEVEN CULTURAL FORCES

FORCE	IMPROVISE	INNOVATE
Choice (☑)	More practical	More theoretical
Dream (☁)	Search for solution	Focus on unknown
Big & More (❗)	Focus on smaller things	Leads to bigger things
Now time (⏱)	Urgent time pressures	Long-term
Oops (👓)	Responds to them	Part of process
Whatsnew (💾)	Results expected	Creates new

America's King Lear

It is an object of almost obscene beauty—a dagger slicing the rarest air, teasing gravity, and kneeling only to the earth's curvature. It's a Learjet.

The Learjet was the brainchild of a most unlikely American genius, one who tracks all the seven cultural forces. His name is Bill Lear, and he had more oopses than a dozen cats have lives. His middle initial could easily have been "I" for improviser extraordinaire. No other culture in the world could bring forth a creative talent with a personality so reckless, bombastic, irresponsible, charming, flamboyant, opinionated, fun-loving, vain, cruel, thoughtless, libidinous, or self-assured. And he got away with it.

Bill Lear was:

★ a high school dropout at fifteen

★ jailed for adultery at twenty-one (how times have changed)

★ married four times

★ inventor of the first car radio

★ inventor of the airplane autopilot

★ creator of aircraft that taunted the borders of catastrophe

★ the founder of a company called Motorola

★ a millionaire at twenty-eight

At the end of his life he bet and lost his millions on the technology of a bygone century—a steam engine, of all things. In this quick retrospective, we see how Bill activated all of the forces and wouldn't let an oops or twenty keep him down.

The first flight of the Learjet took place in 1963, but its origins went back to an evening thirty-eight years before, when Bill was twenty-four and a radio repairman in Tulsa, Oklahoma.

Bill's Improv, Part I

That night a truck pulled up in front of Grandma Lear's home and unloaded a crate containing a mail-order airplane kit for a one-seater Lincoln Sport. At last the unasked question about where Bill was spending his money was answered.

In his spare time, Bill and a friend, working in Grandma Lear's backyard, cut, pasted, sawed, wired, and welded into the night as their airplane gradually began to take shape. The plane came with a three-cylinder Anazani thirty-five-horsepower engine, but Bill, hearing about an old six-cylinder Anazani in town, thought he had a better idea (✀). Why not put the six-cylinder engine into his Lincoln Sport?

(If this starts to remind you of the American kid with his Lego set at the beginning of the book, something is working. The only real difference here is age and size of the parts.)

When the engine arrived it was in terrible shape. Bill tore it down, cleaned it up, put in new bearings, and began to mount it on his airplane. Finally, with winter closing in, the project was completed. Bill took it apart, loaded it on a truck, and drove it out to a nearby airport, hoping that a pilot friend, Woody Woodring, would take it for a spin the next time he came through Tulsa.

With Woody at the controls, the Lincoln Sport groaned and grunted and lifted off. It rose a few feet and bounced back to earth. *(Failure; try again.)* Woody made a few more runs at it, but soon gave up. A dispirited Bill Lear tore down his plane, dragged it back to Grandma's, stored it in her shed, and looked about for a new interest (💾).

Hello, Madeline.

Bill Lear, age twenty-two, husband and father of two small children, fell in love. Again. Even in his personal life, Bill seemed unusually driven by the seven forces. In the next two years he would divorce (*fail*), run off to Texas with Madeline (*improvise*), be chased by the FBI (*now time*), be jailed for violation of the Mann Act (*fail*), marry Madeline (*try again*), become flat broke (*fail*), and land in Chicago determined to make it big in radio (*try again*)—car radios.

Soon after the Wall Street crash of 1929 there was a sudden interest in car radios; only the new models had them and folks driving around in the older models, which they now had to hold on to, wanted one. So Bill Lear came up with an inexpensive design (✀) that solved most of the maddening problems of the cheap radios that others were installing. He formed a partnership with Paul Galvin to manufacture car radios; they decided to call their new company Motorola.

Motorola prospered,* but not with Bill Lear. He got interested in aviation and aviation navigation aids (💾). Actually, he got reinterested in aviation. Just on the crest of a highly profitable venture, Lear decided to bring to life his impossible dream—the one he had left back in Grandma's garage in Tulsa.

Motorola made crummy radios, went into TV, and lost business to the Japanese (one of the big oopses in American industry), who had been taught by Americans how to make better radios. Now, of course, Motorola, which failed and tried again, is into different electronics and has become one of the most respected corporations in the world—the first company to win the Malcolm Baldrige Award.

Bill's Improv, Part II

Lear was bound and determined to produce a small jet for the private aviation market—it was his impossible dream. Now it was time to try again.

By now you shouldn't be surprised to find out what Bill is about to do. It's predictable: He's an American. The only way Lear could stretch the $12 million he had on hand (from the Motorola deal) and get his dream jet into production was to skip the first step of building a prototype, flying it, certifying the design, and then doing the expensive tooling for mass production. In a word, Bill had to *improvise*. He started right off with production tooling. As he himself said, "With this approach you're either very right or very wrong."

This time Bill Lear was very right. Being driven by a vision of beauty and simplicity in which every component sang harmony, he created an airplane that looked and felt good to passenger and pilot alike. And it worked the first time around!

In 1966, at the age of sixty-four, Bill started over again (▤). Mindful of the pressure on the auto industry to address the pollution problems posed by the gasoline engine, Lear thought the answer was not incremental improvement but a radical approach (◌◌). He believed he could master the problems of the steam turbine and thereby revolutionize transportation throughout the world.

Unfortunately for us, he didn't pull this one off. Nevertheless, Bill leaves a legacy of how the seven cultural forces work at a personal level. In addition, he mirrors the entrepreneurial spirit that inspires the other Bills and Billys who are out there trying to get their ideas to fly.

Bill's Crew's Improv

Jim Taylor, former head of sales for Cessna, tells of the time the Learjet came up for FAA certification. As part of the test, they were required to fire a dead bird at the windshield. Lear was so confident that his windshield would sustain the assault, he vowed to sit in the pilot's seat when the bird was fired.

When everything was set, with Lear seated in place, his engineers, who were fearing for his safety, told him the president of the United States was on the phone. When Lear left to take the call, they fired the bird, which not only penetrated the windshield but went clear through the metal cockpit bulkhead.*

Sales were good for a while, but when a recession hit and a change in the tax code struck private aviation, Lear was in financial trouble once again. He sold his shares to Gates Aviation for $21 million. Bill was out of the jet business, but his dream still flies.†

---

*At the outset of this test, FAA shot frozen birds at the windshield with predicable devastation. Someone soon pointed out that frozen birds don't fly and the test was unfair. So live birds were used until the ASPCA got wind of it, so to speak. Now the test uses dead birds.

†You, too, can own one of these graces, the top-of-the-line Learjet model 60. Call 1-800-289-5327 and ask for Marj. They go for $9,650,000 a pop.

Go Team, Whoa!

Forget all the swooning over teams for a moment. Listen carefully and you'll sense a growing unease, a worry that these things are more hassle than their fans let on— that they might even turn around and bite you. . . . The most common trouble with teams: many companies rush out and form the wrong kind for the job. . . . To com- pound the problem, teams often get launched in a vacuum. . . . The reengineering craze is also taking its toll on teams. . . . So you've created the right types of teams, built an atmosphere of trust, and changed your organizational structure—and your teams still seem to be misfiring. What's the rub?

These are not pretty words. There is something downright un-American about them. Something treasonous. Even mean-spirited and spiteful. They might call to mind Big Daddy's words in Tennessee Williams's *Cat on a Hot Tin Roof,* "a pale and ordorous smell of mendacity."

As disquieting as they are, these are the observations of Brian Dumaine, a senior editor at *Fortune* and one of the most distinguished business analysts and writers, a specialist in the people side of business. Strung between these conclusions are mini testimonials and reports from the field, on the successes and failures of American business's current love affair with teams.

Dumaine's article, "The Trouble With Teams" (September 5, 1994, wonderfully and inventively illustrated by Rodica Prato) should be required business reading. The only exception we take to the article is Dumaine's conclusion that "There's no secret or magic formula" to changing things. We disagree. It may not be magic, but there is a new approach, based on a recent study* that can reverse the conclusions Dumaine has reached. As a way to introduce you to the thrust of the study, ask yourself if there is anything fundamentally missing from the following criteria or questions in order to have a successful team:

1. What's the mission or goal?
2. Who's the customer?
3. Who's the leader?
4. Who else is on the team?
5. What resources are available?
6. What are the time constraints?
7. Are there any other constraints?
8. Has this been done before?
9. What are the success criteria?

In our workshops, we elicit a list of similar questions from the participants. There are usually one or two things added or several of these are restated in some form or another. On *no* occasion has the group identified the *two* essential criteria or

The study was commissioned by the American Society for Quality Control (ASQC) and the corpo- rate sponsors of the study, Disney, Eastman Kodak, General Motors, and Kellogg. It was completed in 1995.

questions that need to be addressed in order to optimize a team in America. These two questions do not come to mind because they are not asked by management, they are in the recesses of *our* minds, and it might be un-company to ask them.

The two questions are:

1. What's in it for me?

2. What will I have to sacrifice (give up) in order to participate?

Invariably as soon as these two questions are identified in our workshops, the response is a variation of the same theme: "WOW! You're right!" "Absolutely!" "Yes, now that you mention it!" Or just a smile or slight nod of the head.

Our proposition to you and our response to Brian Dumaine is this: Next time, add these two questions to your list and what you've learned about the cultural forces. Here is a hypothetical script for how you might do it:

Thanks for adjusting your schedule on such short notice to make time for this meeting. *[When was the last time someone acknowledged that they were disrupting your work with an unscheduled meeting?]* I know you are all busy. I appreciate your commitment and continuous effort on behalf of the division. We are making a lot of progress, none of which could have been possible without your individual contributions. *[Perfect time to single out two or three examples from the group. Make them current contributions, not something that was done a while back.]*

A crisis *[remember this is a positive trigger for action as we described in Chapter 5]* has developed with one of our best customers, Customer A, and we want to fix the problem quickly *[activate the Now Force]* and strengthen our relationship *[emphasis on the human side, not the product or process side]* with them. Now as I outline the challenge before us, I want each of you to be asking yourself two important questions. We've never asked these questions before, but we know they are important to you. I've already asked them of myself. *[It is very important to serve as a role model and show you are not asking something of them that you have not asked of yourself.]* And before we proceed on this project, we all *[include yourself]* need to share our individual responses and have a clear understanding of them before getting started.

The questions are: One, What's in it for me? Two, What do I have to give up or sacrifice in order to be part of this effort? The first one is very personal and we want to know your personal desires, hopes, and expectations. That way, we may be able to structure things in a different way and judge the success of the effort on a broader basis. This may not be possible, but we won't know that until we know what's on your mind.

The answer to the second question will enable us to manage everything more efficiently and provide some support and backup for you if that is necessary and required. We'll know what's not going to get done or postponed because you have been pulled away from your work to be part of this effort.

We've never done this before *[activate the Dream Force, Chapter 2]*, but our challenge is . . .

In order to meet this urgent need of the customer—quite frankly, I think we can surpass it *[activate the Big and More Force, Chapter 3]*—we need a group to improvise, invent, create, fix, do whatever it takes to get the impossible done.

As I lay out the challenge, think about our two questions. As you can see, I've posted them on the wall to my right so that they are in plain view. *[A symbolic gesture that shows you are serious.]* After we've gone over the challenge and clarified some of the basics, let's take a break and come back and have an open discussion about the two new questions.

That's the basic melody. You can play it in any key, any tempo, and any time frame you choose. The members of the group will give you the direction on where they want to solo and why. Pick a leader—even more of an improvisation, let them pick a leader and then set them loose.

"Giant Steps"

So much for the theory. What follows, to paraphrase moonwalker Armstrong, are small steps for management, but a giant step for this new thought process.

Does it work? Yes. Here is one example.

Snap, Crackle, and Pop! "Their Faces Just Light Up!"

The Kellogg Company says good morning to more people in more different ways than anyone we know. In fact, we grew up with them and raised a bunch of kids the same way. Kellogg, of course, is the world's leading producer of ready-to-eat cereal products (Corn Flakes, Frosted Flakes, Rice Krispies, Fruit Loops, Pop-Tarts, and Eggo Waffles). Their anecdotal experience with three pilot teams has created a strong demand within this global manufacturing company for more training on the *Stuff* project. Ken Tabor, director of quality at Kellogg, reports that whenever he presents the research (over thirty internal presentations and counting), people's "faces just light up." Even the international staff that works in the United States reports that the *Stuff* information invariably results in someone saying, "Now we understand why you Americans behave the way you do."

Tabor and his colleagues have tracked the results of the *Stuff* research through three early-on team experiences at Kellogg. They found that the *Stuff* research works and that it can make a substantial difference in teamwork, if the new process is applied properly. Based on the success of these efforts, Kellogg is continuing to activate the cultural forces and encourage all other teams to try it as well.

Following are excerpts from an interview we had with Tabor about his experiences with the *Stuff* research and its application to teamwork:

> *Throughout my career in quality, something told me that the Japanese way would never really work in America. More importantly, I knew it wouldn't work*

at Kellogg. The Japanese had some things that you could take and use, but their actual concepts and programs, I always knew they wouldn't work. I didn't know why. The few I had tried failed for some unknown reason.

But when I heard about the Stuff research, I got pretty excited and said this makes sense, there may be something here. I could see how I could take it and make it work in our own company. I was able to tailor a presentation on this information and present it to our senior management group as part of our quality strategy plan.

Our management people got pretty excited about it; they said, you know, this makes sense, what you are telling us about quality and America versus other cultures. We can see how we might use it at Kellogg. So I received permission to take off with it, and I did.

I began to give the strategic quality plan to the people of Kellogg North America. And every time I gave it, the first half was always interesting, but when I gave the findings of The Stuff Americans Are Made Of in the plan and how it could be used at Kellogg, people just got excited. Their eyes lit up. They could instantly relate to those findings about bias for action, catch a new potential identity, learning from mistakes, I mean you could tell that 89.9 percent of them, every one of them was like wow, now I understand why we do things the way we do. This makes sense.

When I put the team piece on it, which was just a nice third leg,* once again our people's faces just lit up. They could instantly relate to the findings about bias for action [Chapter 4], potential new identity [Chapter 7], learning from mistakes [Chapter 5], etc.

When I put the team findings into the Stuff presentation at a later date, once again our people's faces just lit up. They got excited about it: this is great, it makes sense, how can we use it?

A couple of my sponsors, the vice president of human resources and the vice president of product development and research, said they would like to try and use the Stuff and see if it works.

So, we developed a one-day training program and commissioned three pilot teams to follow the Stuff findings. Here is what we learned. One pilot team, Team A, decided they knew how to do it better, or at least thought they knew how to do it better. They did not do well at all. The results were not what the person in charge (the lawgiver) wanted. The leadership was poor, not in keeping with the Stuff recommendations. The team did not function well and the people did not feel good about their experience of being on a team.

The second team, Team B, basically tried to follow the Stuff recommendations, but could not completely due to travel schedules. They did okay, but not as well as you would expect if the Stuff findings had been followed completely.

---

*A reminder: There are three cultural studies, one each on quality, improvement, and teamwork, that constitute the core of the Stuff research. For more details, see the Appendix.

> The third team, Team C, followed the Stuff findings. There was a good leader, they all understood their objective clearly, achieved excellent results, and felt great about their experience of being on a team. They came to the lawgiver and myself throughout the process for additional consulting and direction and ended up doing a great job.
>
> What is interesting is that this exact same team, Team C, failed with the same mission earlier in the year. Thus, we were able to measure the differences in their two team experiences. To say the least, they were pleased significantly more with their results the second time through the project, as well as with the individual recognition they received.
>
> This information has gone like wildfire throughout the company. People started talking to other people about it, and all by word of mouth. I have been asked to give the presentation over thirty times to more than a thousand people. They call me and want me to give it to their department. People say that Stuff just makes sense—it works.

"I Got Rhythm"

What we, along with Ken Tabor, noticed about the words improvise, innovate, invent, imagine, and impossible is the obvious. They all begin with the letter *i*, as does the imprimatur of America—individual. It is what's missing in teams. This does not equate to individualism run amok with everybody doing their own thing, but the opportunity to contribute on a personal basis as we wrote about in the Imagineering process at Disney in Chapter 2.

What then, you may wonder, happens to all those team metaphors floating around that the boss likes? You can still use them. However, with your "I" glasses on listen carefully the next time to the announcer of your favorite *team* sport and take note of how many times the announcer says the word "team" compared to singling out individuals by name, and talking about them as individuals.

You'll likely note what we have observed: Announcers and sportscasters call the group a team, but they report the progress of the game through individuals. The team doesn't tackle, an individual does. The team doesn't catch the ball, an individual does. The team doesn't advance the ball, a couple of individuals do while some other individuals are running a fake play to confuse the individuals on the other side. You'll also note that the commentators say, so-and-so has made a difference since coming to this team, or so-and-so has been shifted to such-and-such a position and now he is a standout, etc.

This focus on the role and contribution of the individual *within* a group is the salient point. It's what made Team C at Kellogg work when it had failed earlier. But unlike Team A, which went its own way, with individuals exercising their own prerogatives, and Team B, where certain individuals did all the work for the group, Team C linked the contribution of each individual to the goals of the group.

Clearly, teams that have individuals doing their own thing end up in disarray. At the other extreme are teams that totally ignore the individual and participants are expected to subject themselves, unilaterally, to the group with no outlet for addressing or meeting their personal needs. Not surprisingly, the productive teams function in the middle, with respect for the individual and clarity among participants about one another's expectations. Once this plateau of understanding has been achieved, the individuals can then move forward more effectively as a group.

That's the magic formula for high-performance teamwork in America.

TEAMWORK
Conventional vs. High-Performance Meaning

Conventional	High Performance
group	individual
pull together	what's in it for me
contribute	sacrifice
share	what's in it for me
big goal	personal goals
advance the cause	what's in it for me

The "I" in Improvement

How do Americans improve things, make them better? What are the basic models for improvement? What assumptions do we make about how people improve? What drives improvement? Is it working the way we had hoped? Can we improve the improvement process?

Like the other management practices we have been writing about, improvement is best done quickly with the individual in mind. Not surprisingly, the high-performance definition of improvement runs counter to conventional business wisdom and practice. Our improvements leave the station before we know where we are going, but heading on down the track beats sitting around the station waiting for someone to say, "All aboard."

In a wonderfully illustrated, clearly and concisely written book called simply, *Jazz*, John Fordham tells two pertinent stories about John Coltrane, whose fake sheet we saw at the beginning of this chapter. Among Trane's personal contributions to jazz were extending the upper ranges of the saxophone and, in Fordham's words, "deepening the scope of bebop harmonies [and] developing unprecedented speed and facility to playing two lines at once." Fordham notes:

> To make the onrush of sound ever more urgent, he experimented by substituting even more chords than bebop had, at times shifting the harmony virtually every beat. He [Trane] told Wayne Shorter [composer] that his aim was to start in the middle of a sentence and progress to its beginning and end at the same time.

The second story Fordham tells is based on a famous exchange between Coltrane and Miles Davis. Fordham writes:

> Coltrane told his boss that, once immersed in a solo, he didn't know how to stop. "Try taking the saxophone out of your mouth," Davis said.

The majority of American workers have a little (maybe a lot of) Trane in them. They prefer to start in the middle and often don't know when to stop. Starting at the beginning is too boring and picking up where someone else left off is not as much fun, or rewarding, as doing your own thing. They know that in business, like jazz, improvement is not necessarily orderly or about making things better by taking what exists and building on it. Rather, improvements are the result of innovations, improvisations, breakthroughs, and experimentations of the kind Coltrane exhibited.

Going Around in Circles

The basic improvement model in America is known as PDCA or Plan, Do, Check, Act. It comes to us by way of philosopher/educator John Dewey, but is better know in management circles as the Shewhart or Deming Circle.* (See Snapshot #20). It's a perfect circle that is being taught in most industry training courses and quality improvement seminars. And therein lies the problem—it's about orderliness and perfection, two disconnects for Americans that we discussed in Chapter 2.

As desirable as the intent and purpose of this model are, it just doesn't jibe with the way Americans do things—it's the wrong melody and has no beat. There are four principal reasons why the Deming circle does not connect with Americans: first, perfection is not a motivator for Americans (Chapter 2); second, the Now Force keeps us from doing things in an orderly way (Chapter 4); third, we don't really learn anything unless it connects to our experience (Chapter 1). In the next chapter, we talk about the fourth reason, the fixation on whatsnew.

How then, can we realistically expect Americans to go around in circles, in an orderly way, planning (the starting point, collecting data, listening to the customer, thinking through the procedures), doing (implementing the plan, creating prototypes, testing), checking (feedback, adjustments, improvements), and acting (standardizing, getting the rhythm down), which becomes the starting point again for planning.

One of our associates who did some research for us on the book is Doug Park, a systems expert and quality management specialist based in Boise, Idaho. In his work with companies he is often asked to get folks back on track with PDCA. He says, "By the time I get there, they are doing it in reverse. They go counterclockwise, starting with act—we got this down, they say (with no data, no customer input). Then they move quickly to check. Sometimes, they just bounce back and forth between the two. Act, check, act, check."

The last image the actual American improvement process would conjure up is a circle—a squished egg is more like it. Even scrambled eggs would do. (See Snapshot #20). There is order here, but this is the American version of order—same notes, different arrangement. We may not recognize disorder as order, but that is what it is.

This should not come as a surprise; we laid the groundwork for this conclusion in earlier chapters. The improvement process for Americans is more improvisational, more about fixing things and moving on, than careful planning, adherence to the plan, and an orderly stepped process that incorporates feedback and leads to a continuous improvement process.

---

*Walter A. Shewhart, known as the father of statistical process control, worked with W. Edward Deming, the prophet of quality control (now known as TQM), at Bell Labs in the late 1920s. This chart is interchangeably credited to both.

Snapshot #20

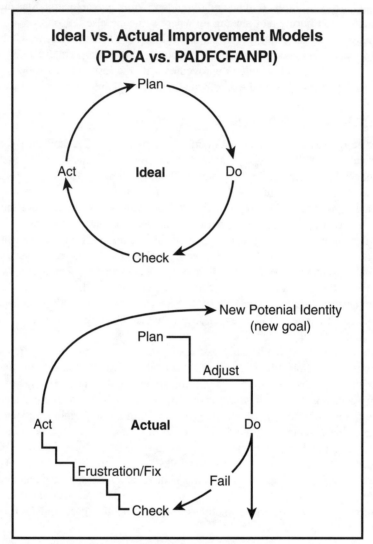

Ideal vs. Actual Improvement Models
(PDCA vs. PADFCFANPI)

Source: Adapted from American Quality Foundation

The fundamental problem with PDCA, in the words of Duke Ellington is, "It ain't got that swing." For it to mean something, it has to have the swing, the emotional dimensions of improvement, the rhythm we groove to behind the counter, on the assembly line, in the kitchen, in the lab, in boardrooms, on trading floors, up in space, out on the plain.

We know that planning is something that doesn't get most Americans up out of bed in the morning and that most of us rarely stick to the plan. So why start there? We know we don't do things right the first time and we don't have formal systems for learning from our mistakes. So where does that fit in? Once we own up to the mistakes, the fixing (improvement) process is not a pretty one—it's downright painful at times. And when we fix something, the last thing we want to do is go to another planning meeting; we want to know whatsnew? How is that accommodated?

As we have illustrated in Snapshot #20, the process of incorporating these essential operation components of improvement is all over the place—lots going on, lots of improvising. As it should be for Americans.

Let's walk through the model. What's going on here? What resonates with you? What have you observed at your company? Where have we missed the beat? Is the rhythm right?

You'll note that it starts with the objective. (No, we haven't backed off "impossible dream," we're just trying to put this in immediate terms for you—activating the Dream Force can come later). Then the plan. Depending on the complexity of the objective, planning could be as simple as that checklist that runs through your mind in the shower or the notes on the back of a barroom napkin or as formal as the sophisticated group planning process most organizations have that sometimes "goes on forever."

More important than the type of plan is this: When was the last time you stuck to the plan, or more precisely, how much time lapsed before you started to tear apart the plan you had just signed off on? According to The Wirthlin Group survey we have cited in previous chapters, about two-thirds of Americans (64 percent) lean toward starting off by "questioning things and taking them apart" compared with the rest who "take things as they are and add to them." One-fifth of all Americans (21 percent) insist on immediately improving things by starting with questions and taking things apart, not the orderly let's-improve-what's-already-here. The rest are shades of let's take it apart until you get to the hard-core 12 percent at the other end of the continuum who wouldn't think of taking anything apart and are totally at home with the idea of building on what exists without feeling their style cramped at all. That is their style and thank God for the balance in most corporations.

Regardless of where we are on the continuum most of us invariably break the plan down into manageable parts that fit us, finding our way through with our personal MAP (the Motivated Ability Pattern that we described in Chapter 1). It's also a variation of the what's in it for me question that we raised earlier in this chapter. The plan doesn't say anything about how I am going to tackle it: I've got to figure that out on my own.

This is also something we do in an unacknowledged, unstructured way within our organizations. Allowances are not made for "taking the plan apart" once the process has been agreed to. It's an unspoken, unconscious thing we do. Our observation and recommendation is that awareness of this process would get everyone on track quicker and the results would be better if we made allowances for this personal need.

When the planning (and adjustments) is complete, we get to the "do" stage. We learned in Chapter 5, "Fire, Ready, Blame," that we don't do things right the first time and we don't have open enough, supportive environments to enable us to acknowledge mistakes promptly, actually learning from them quickly and moving on. So this model could get stuck at this point without a process for catching mistakes and moving on to the check stage.

The next step in the ideal model, check, enables you to look back and see how you are doing. This is adjustment time. Often in a real crisis, this is where the Improvise Force kicks in. Both models allow for this adjustment. However, the real model acknowledges the frustration that is associated with the fixing process, with the improvement process.

Of course, we hate frustration, yet it is often what we need to move us through a crisis, find a solution, improvise, and get done what needs to get done. Ironically, we are often at our best when most frustrated. And research at the University of Chicago and elsewhere supports the idea that frustration is essential to breakthrough thinking—the stuff Americans are made of. So Ben Franklin had it right all along—*no pain, no gain.*

Once we get the breakthrough and the process standardizes the improvisation or innovation, the *ideal* model calls for using this point as a benchmark to start the process all over again. The *real model* says, "Hey, been there, done that. Whatsnew?"

Improvise Fake Sheet

Jazz is *the* cultural idiom of America. Even if we are not as comfortable in a blues bar as we are a concert hall, we cannot deny that jazz is uniquely American. Unlike European-rooted classical music, the jazz group values improvisation and provides each individual with an opportunity to solo, to make a visible contribution. The priority in jazz is to master your own instrument (to make the sound yours) and to pay attention in the group, not do as you are told and get it right the first time. Consequently, jazz is a strong metaphor for American management.

★ Improvisation and innovation are twins. They are not identical, to be sure, but closely related. They behave in much the same way but are curiously different in their personalities. Improvisation has a quality of spontaneity and urgency that is not readily apparent in innovation. Innovation is more formal—improvisation in a business suit. Its process is structured, orderly. It is more about the introduction of something new, a new method or device or idea. It is arrived at more systematically and by a more reflective process. The inherent informality of improvisation makes it accessible to almost everyone in an organization; there isn't the intimidation that often precedes the more formal process of innovation. Improvising opens doors to innovation. When we improvise we use what we have—something that is second nature to the American worker—whereas innovation requires more exacting materials, more time, more deliberation, more patience.

★ Management guru Peter Drucker asserts that systematic innovation requires the monitoring of *seven sources* of innovative opportunity. The seven, with examples we describe in some detail beginning on page 242, are: the unexpected (Nutra-Sweet); incongruity (Scotch Brite soap pads); process need (Eli's Gin and Tonic); changes in industry structure or market structure (credit cards); demographics (telemarketing diversity); changes in perception, mood, and meaning (health care); and new knowledge (microreplication).

★ The individual is missing in teamwork. Although teams are the most popular way for companies to organize their employees, there are two fundamental questions the *Stuff* research identified that are at the heart of team performance, but are rarely raised, let alone answered. The answers to these two questions can dramatically enhance the performance of teams in America. These two questions are: (1) What's in it for me? and (2) What will I have to sacrifice (give up) in order to participate? The Kellogg Company has validated this new research and discovered that the team that closely followed the recommendations of the study outperformed the other two teams that didn't (see page 253).

★ The classic Plan-Do-Check-Act model is incomplete. It is missing the key emotional elements that are so fundamental to Americans and integral to performance improvement. The classic circle model suggests a process that moves in orderly fashion from planning to testing, to improving, to implementation. This model belies the real process of performance improvement—a *dis*orderly process that often discards or modifies plans, immediately leaps into action that frequently results in often unchecked failure. Improvement comes more through improvisation and fixing after the fact than in doing things right the first time. And rather than repeating the cycle as the classic model suggests, Americans are more interested in spiraling upward and onward than getting "stuck" in a perceived vicious circle (see page 257).

Americans covet the opportunity to improvise, to fix things. This ability to improvise enables us to show we are human, to make a personal contribution as the jazz metaphor suggests, and then to move on to create, innovate, or invent something else.

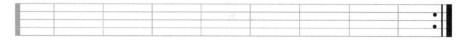

A REPRISE

Marsalis Metaphors on Management

We now know what Dan Morgenstern, director of the Institute of Jazz Studies at Rutgers University, meant when he said, "Wynton [Marsalis] is someone who can guide us. He's one of the shepherds of this music."

When we saw Marsalis's highly instructive four-part PBS television series (and book), *Marsalis on Music,* we watched as he artfully blended and used nonmusic examples to explain the basic elements of jazz to a group of children. He dribbled a basketball to illustrate rhythms, accents, and rests in jazz and he walked the audience through different functions of floors in a skyscraper model to illustrate the variety of character in a chorus. Through that simplicity he illuminated the meaning and structure of music in general and jazz in particular.

We were certain that given the chance he could just as effectively shed some light on the pressing issues of American business. (Maybe there is another series here!) In the meantime, we culled some of Marsalis's press clippings at his Lincoln Center office in New York and found some powerful metaphors, some crossover analyses, and some compelling insights that can "shepherd" us in our further understanding of the cultural forces, the jazz metaphor, and the challenges of engaging others in quality and productivity. Here, from some excerpts of interviews that Marsalis has given over the past few years, are a few correlations to the challenges facing management today.

On the responsibility of leaders:

"When you lead a band, you're leading a group of cats that know more about everything they do than you do. That's the one great thing I learned from Art Blakely. He's one of the greatest leaders in the world, and the reason is that he doesn't try to pretend that he knows stuff that he doesn't know. But he's the leader of the band, and when you are in his band, you never get the impression that he's leading it. Yet,

I knew all the time that he was the leader. He didn't have to tell me that. He's that kind of man. When Miles [Davis] had the band with Herbie [Hancock] and them, do you think he told them what to do? He was struggling to figure out what *they* were doing. He had never had cats like that, but he was wise enough to let them decide what was going to happen. He didn't make them play just what he could play. But they always knew he was the leader, and you can listen to the records and know he's the leader." (James Liska, "Wynton & Branford Marsalis: A Common Understanding," *Down Beat*, December 1982.)

On diversity:

"I don't like the term [black classical music] because music is not either. The reason that they use the term 'black' or 'white' is a reaction to the prejudice that black people have been subjected to in this country and in the music industry. That term doesn't describe music: that means what Beethoven was writing was 'white classical music,' and Beethoven's music don't have nothin' to do with white or black. He was trying to deal with getting out from under the aristocracy. Louis Armstrong was trying to deal with getting out from under white people. If you're talking about Elvis Presley, you can call that 'white music'—that's cool—because it became white. Not because Elvis Presley made it white, but because the media made it white. They pushed him because he was white.

"I would say . . . all American forms grow out of the blues. The blues is an entity. The blues is a heavy aesthetic achievement. The greatest thing for any culture is to create an art form. I think the blues is the basis of American music." (Kevin White, "Trumpeter Wynton Marsalis: Sounding Like Himself," *Digital Audio*, April 1985.)

On delegation:

"A lot of times when I write for this band, I try to highlight what each member can do. If you have something to improvise on with strange time signatures or really difficult chord changes, you give that to Todd Williams. If you need something played with a certain type of real melodic purity and beauty, you give it to Wes. Reginald Veal, he has a true imagination. He can create a lot of different moods, and plays with real episodic conception. And Herlin really knows how to groove. He really understands that concept.

"Whether it's New Orleans music or more modern, post-bebop forms of jazz, everyone in the band has a responsibility to know where they fit in each one of those styles. Every night on the bandstand we're reminded to listen, concentrate, and always be able to interact with the other players." (Andrew Jones, "Wynton: Outstanding in His Field,"*JAZZIZ*, September 1991.)

On the need for improvement:

"Jazz is about elevation and improvement. Jazz music always improves pop music. What Louis Armstrong did, singing songs by Gershwin and Irving Berlin, was improve them. Bird improved 'I'll Remember April.' The biggest honor I ever had is to play with the musicians I've played with. To stand on stage with Ron, Herbie, and Tony, Sonny Rollins, Dizzy Gillespie, to have the opportunity to talk with them and have them teach me stuff.

"Work on your sound. Understand that the control and the production of expressive sound is the highest aspect of music. Study the noble level of thematic development in Louis Armstrong, Lester Young, Charlie Parker, Thelonious Monk. Know that all musicians have to have good sounds no matter what instrument they play. Learn how to hear your place in a band when you're improvising." (Howard Mandel, "Wynton Marsalis: The Interview," *Down Beat*, July 1984.)

On teamwork:

"Jazz is democracy, because jazz is, number one, the willingness to swing. And swinging is a matter of coordination, and the coordination means that you are willing to communicate with other people. That's how swinging is—you get three or four people together, and the only way they can swing is if they work together. And that's what democracy is—freedom of expression that elevates everyone. And that's why the people are ready for this music. Everyone wants it, they're ready to start trying to get together. They're ready for a positive change, and they're ready to start trying to get together. They're tired of fighting each other. They're tired of being white and black. People are ready to be Americans, and that's why it's time for jazz." (Creating a Cannon," *Down Beat*, December 1992.)

On empowerment:

"What a kid learns from playing jazz is how to express his individuality without stepping on somebody else's. The first thing I tell kids is, "Play anything you want but make it sound like you." The next step is learning to control that self-expression. Don't just blurt something out. Adapt it to what the other guy is doing. Being a good neighbor—that's what jazz is about. Jazz is democracy in action." (Tony Scherman, Wynton Marsalis: The Professor of Swing," *Life* Magazine, August 1993.)

Wynton Marsalis is Artistic Director of Jazz at Lincoln Center, part of the Lincoln Center for the Performing Arts. If you would like to support the center, contact the Planning and Development Department at 212-875-5420.

Chapter 7

Whatsnew?
The American Fixation

From the new-and-improved-again-Tide, which you may glance at a second time in the supermarket, to tomorrow's hippest Web page, not a day passes in America that something new isn't being concocted, hatched, or foisted on eager eyes. Evening broadcasters, newspapers, and magazines battle to lay claim to the newest whatsnew. It is hard to believe, but over twelve thousand articles are published *each day* trying to keep engineers, executives, educators, ecologists, economists, eggheads, eschatologists, and etceteras up-to-date.

Every culture is interested, to some degree, in whatsnew, but in America it is an obsession. To keep up with the latest of anything, to be *first* to know something, or to have the latest gadget is conspicuously American.

Whatsnew is the last of the seven cultural forces but it is closely related to the other forces: it is the end result and goal even of improvisation(✀); it is all about what is happening now (🕐); it gives us more choices (☑) from which to dream and scheme (°⟨⟩); and things that are bigger (▮) and faster (🕐) are by definition new.

In this chapter, we'll show how this force defines the way a company conceives of itself and constantly reinvents its business processes (the *re*discovery of what was new yesterday may be a whatsnew for tomorrow, with an improvisation or two). Because of the pressing need for organizations to be vigilant about customer satisfaction, we provide an overview of the evolution of customer satisfaction and describe whatsnew there. We'll introduce you to a national training program at Disney University that takes the cultural forces we have written about and translates them into practical, hard-nosed business applications. We'll introduce you to Harley Earl, a premier creator of whatsnew in auto styling and design for more than three decades, hear from Lester Thurow, stop by a school in Tucson, and see whatsnew through the experiences of a former nun, now the highest-ranking woman in American banking.

Whatsnew, Mr. Earl?

Up and down the street it made heads turn. Pedestrians raced to the curb as it moseyed past the White House in that sleepy Southern town that was Washington, D.C. in 1939. The car was long and low and had a grill that was shaped like a dumdum bullet. It was a convertible, sort of. It had a sweeping rear deck sloping aft that gave it the look of icy metal being poured.

Harley Earl was at the wheel of his car and his wife Sue beside him. This wasn't just "his" car, it was *his* car. Earl had designed it himself along with an entire line of GM automobiles. Back in Detroit, Mr. Earl's custom-made car, the "Y-Job," as it was called, was a familiar sight. But not in the nation's capital.

Mr. Earl was driving slowly through the streets of Washington, because it was time to take it easy. His new 1940 line of cars were in the dealer showrooms across the country, and in a kind of annual fall ritual, millions were pouring out to see them.

For a nation gripped by a withering economic catastrophe, the chance to eye a dream for a few fantastic moments was irresistible. Americans were trooping into showrooms in droves to stare in wonder at the whatsnew on wheels. In fact, every fall for the next thirty years Americans would come by the millions to kick tires, push buttons, toot horns, roll windows, open hoods, slam doors, dial radios, wiggle gear-shifts, adjust seats, and tell junior to keep his dirty feet off the new upholstery.

Why? To find out whatsnew.

However, on this day, the guy who made whatsnew new had an old problem—a flat tire. He hobbled into a D.C. Buick dealer for a tire change, but nobody there could figure out how to remove the fender skirt to get at the wheel on the Y-Job. Mr. Earl's creation was suffering from a classic whatsnew problem: unfamiliarity. But after wiring his office in Detroit for instructions, some sketches were hastily made and sent by courier to Washington, and a few days later Mr. and Mrs. Earl were back on their way to Florida for a vacation.

Up-to-Dateness

When Alfred P. Sloan took over the management of the unwieldy General Motors empire, he knew he would need to find someone with a fresh eye for style and de-sign. In the mid-1920s he heard about a thirty-year-old fellow named Harley Earl, who was born and raised in Hollywood, where he built custom bodies for the auto-mobiles of movie stars.

Mr. Earl would take the chassis of an ordinary car—its frame, wheels, and engine—and build a custom body to the client's taste and specifications. Soon moneyed gents wearing two-tone wing tips and plus fours would be seen driving Mr. Earl's cars to golf at Piping Rock or to polo fields on Long Island's North Shore. Tom Mix, the famous cowboy actor, was pictured in the newspapers and magazines driving bizarre Mr. Earl machinery that looked like no other critter on the face of the earth.

Meanwhile it was dawning on the carmakers that there was a force out there that could be activated and ridden to profitability—America's fixation on whatsnew. Alfred Sloan's technical adviser, Henry Crane, addressing a gathering of the Society of Automotive Engineers in the twenties said, ". . . a continual modification of ap-pearance is equally important. The tag of up-to-dateness is practically essential . . . . I think you will realize from the foregoing remarks that I believe wholeheartedly in change for the sake of change . . . ."

In Sloan's autobiography, *My Years with General Motors,* he wrote, "The degree to which styling changes should be made in any one model run presents a particularly delicate problem. The changes in the new model should be so novel and attractive as to create a demand for the new value and, so to speak, create a certain amount of dissatisfaction with past models as compared with the new one." Sloan saw in Earl the man who would provide those novel, attractive changes. Indeed Earl's lifetime of employment with GM transformed the way Americans would perceive the automobile and helped to make it the engine that drove the economy for half a century.

The Earl Era

Until Mr. Earl came along, the job of styling cars was pretty much left to engineers and people who worked in what was then called the "art and color department." Earl's first assignment was to come up with a design for a car to be called the LaSalle. It was to be a less expensive and sportier Cadillac to compete with the Packard Eight.

He worked tirelessly with a team of clay modelers for three months, and when it was shown to boss Sloan it was an instant hit. It went on to become a best seller in 1927, the year Charles Lindbergh flew across the Atlantic.

Earl's styling department quickly grew in size and influence through the thirties, and his flamboyant personal style soon became as well known in Grosse Pointe as the rolling stock that bore his imprint.

Earl's biographer, Michael Lamms, says, he "had a profound appreciation of the entertainment value of glitter and chrome. Earl developed a theory of 'light value' of chrome trim; that it should capture the maximum brightness and throw it directly into the eye of the beholder. To make this happen, Earl constantly urged his designers to bevel or tilt chrome trim at 45 degrees to the horizon so that reflections would bounce up in the viewer's face." Or as veteran car designer Strother MacMinn put it, "Harley Earl designed so you could walk around a car and be entertained the whole trip."

The World War II twin bomb P-38 fighter plane was the inspiration for the most notorious and contagious of Harley Earl's flights of whatsnew fancy—the infamous tail fin. The first fin started out as nothing more than a bump at the end of the rear fender of a forties Cadillac but in the next ten years tail fins grew and were sharpened, tattooed, chrome-tipped, bejeweled, impaled with stoplights, then splayed, flayed, and parlayed across all models and all brands. On one Cadillac model the gasoline cap was sequestered beneath the hinged stoplight on a knifelike tail fin.

Whence and Wither Goeth Whatsnew

The American fixation on Whatsnew was not invented by Mr. Earl, nor did it die out with him.* Remember that $100 million rollout of Windows 95 and those midnight lines outside the doors of computer software shops on August 23, 1995, to be the first to buy a copy? Ford spent $200 million on advertising its whatsnew Taurus, although perhaps not with the same results. Times have changed since the days when folks lined up every fall just to get a glimpse of whatsnew.

---

*A good case could be made that this all started on August 17, 1807, the day Robert Fulton sailed the steamboat Clermont 154 miles up the Hudson, while all those silken dandies were looking on from the shore. The boat created such a stir that the New York legislature passed a bill making it a crime for anyone to mess around with it. Others may see Ben Franklin as the originator of whatsnew in America, from bifocals and flippers to stoves and lightning rods. But by now you know you should be looking even further back, way back in fact, to Plymouth Rock where the Whatsnew Force was locked-in with the Pilgrims. What was new in Plymouth? Everything.

Whatsnew today is the information age and what changes will be wrought by the intellectual energy it is generating is anybody's guess. The 1800s changed a world that was driven by muscle to a world driven by machines. The world that is now upon us is one that will no longer be driven by machines but by brains.

Managing in New Times

Harvard Business School professor Shoshana Zuboff has brought some new thinking and analysis to the questions raised by this shift from a machine- to a brain-driven economy. In particular, she has concentrated on the need to shift away from enormously successful hierarchical management systems put in place at the turn of the century. She notes that their purpose then was to standardize and control industry. They were (are) systems that rested on the premise that complex decisions needed to be removed from lower level jobs and passed upward to the management ranks.

As Professor Zuboff writes in *Scientific American* (September 1995), in the new world of the information age, this age-old system cannot hold. Zuboff believes "It is more efficient to handle complexity wherever and whenever it first enters the organization—whether during a sale, during delivery or in production." The idea being that the computer gives a comprehensive view of the entire business to any employee in great detail, thereby increasing the intellectual content of that employee's work at all levels.

What Professor Zuboff is suggesting is that the day will come when the all-knowing hierarchy, with which we are familiar, will be radically different. There is widespread agreement on this among management gurus, including Drucker, who writes in *The New Realities*, ". . . a large business or government agency twenty years hence . . . is far more likely to resemble organizations that neither the practicing manager nor the student of management pays much attention to today: the hospital, and the university. For like them . . . they will be knowledge-based, composed largely of specialists who direct and discipline their own performance through organized feedback from colleagues and customers."

Zuboff also holds that with the computer providing access to an abundance of information of a kind hitherto available to just a few, the role of supervisor will increasingly become that of teacher, whose role is to show operators how to interpret data, thereby increasing productivity. We are beginning to see this applied in such forward-looking organizations as FedEx (a company we visited in Chapter 4), which gives customer service representative wide-ranging discretion in handling customer complaints.

Fads vs. Whatsnew

Zuboff is not a faddist, nor should she be confused with one. Business faddists, though they would never call themselves that, tend to focus on or promote a technique or special process; you usually know them by their acronyms. Zuboff, by contrast, has identified a fundamental shift in business practices that are now, of course, subjected to a range of fads or techniques.

Sometimes the technique comes first and leads to a fundamental shift in business philosophy or practice. For example, total quality management grew from its humble statistical process control (SPC) techniques in the 1920s to a full-fledged management movement in the 1980s.

However, often whatsnew in business is mistaken for and derisively called the "flavor of the month" program. Now we have no problem with new flavors on a hot summer's night at our neighborhood ice-cream stand, why do we in business?

We suspect that has more to do with the perception that management's whatsnew is a substitute for clear direction and what W. Edwards Deming called the "constancy of purpose." If Whatsnew is a force for innovation, change, and renewal, then no company or organization should shun it. If it is a bullet for a management hunting expedition, it will not work.

In a real sense, everything we do in business was a whatsnew at one time or another. Since 1970, American business has been MBOed, JITed, QFDed, Xed and Yed and Zed, CATed, CSIed, PITed, TQCed, QWLed, SBUed, MBWAed, TQPed, MDQed, VAMed and CAMed, SPCed, Q1ed, MAPed, and TQMed. Of all of these, TQM has survived, endured, proven itself, and by anybody's definition taken the fad-test and passed it.

Why TQM and not the others? TQM focuses on systemic matters and it has a self-renewing process. It seemingly has a built-in whatsnew attitude. In Chapter 4 we provided one example of the breadth of whatsnew in TQM in which we showed how Allied Signal injected speed into the traditional management process and has had runaway success with it. We also showed in Chapter 2 how the *actual* and systematized process of empowerment works at the Ritz-Carlton Hotel Company. And in this chapter we will see how whatsnew at Hewlett-Packard is reinventing their management process—a baker's dozen years since one of its joint ventures won the coveted Deming Prize in Japan.

For many people, TQM is synonymous with customer satisfaction, or vice versa. We think of them as one and the same. Customer satisfaction is clearly more fluid and therefore has led much of the innovation within the traditional quality control community and created much of whatsnew in business management.

W³: Women, Words, and Work

We are not as surefooted on this one as we have been throughout the book. But no one is fully grounded when it comes to whatsnew. In fact, that's how we often get to whatsnew.

We know for certain that what we are about to propose here is firmly grounded in our culture. Like everything in this book, this analysis draws from the broader dimensions of American culture and the recommendations are based on the need to take these factors into account as we seek to improve our business performance and extend our global competition.

Our proposition is this: Women become more fully engaged in the design, development, and management of all aspects of any businesses that are relationship-based, especially those that focus on the external customer.

This is not a gender thing, but a cultural reality in American life. American men, in general, are more *transaction-oriented*; American women, in general, are more *relationship-oriented*. By contrast, European and Asian men are much more relationship-oriented than American men—by a long shot. So in that sense, it is not so much a question of gender as it is culture. We also hasten to add that no value judgments are intended or implied; this is not a matter of right or wrong, but of cultural reality. As we said in the beginning of the book, all cultures have wisdom.

It is clear to anyone who has done business overseas or over the borders, that women have not penetrated the management and executive ranks in Europe, Asia, or the rest of the American continent as they have in the United States. Despite the prominence of women in the highest elected positions of government in some European countries (not yet the case in America), women are less visible in overseas corporations than in the United States. In fact, there is still a general abiding prejudice against women managers and executives in most countries.

Arguably, America is in the forefront of opening up opportunities for women in business. But the expression "glass ceiling" is an instant reminder that progress is not what it should be. This is not a sidebar on the glass ceiling, but an opportunity to point out where the competitive advantage lies for Americans.

We identified some of the factors that influence America's transaction-oriented culture in Chapter 4: our bias for action and impatience with time (🕐) gets in the way of the long-term demands of relationships. Remember, we showed how we are more *go*-oriented than *do*-oriented. Anthropologist Edward T. Hall, whose work we cited in that chapter, writes a lot about "context" in cultures. In fact, this is one of his strongest contributions to our understanding of how cultures communicate.

By context, Hall means the full environment—the entire stimuli—in which a message is communicated *and* understood. Language, words, are the essential element. But context also includes listening, reading between the lines, interpreting silences, measuring tone, reading a hand gesture, empathy, intuition, and other nonword dimensions of communication. Another word for context is emotional literacy—the degree to which we are literate about what's said and what's not said. This is also right-brain, left-brain stuff.

Cultures vary on the amount of context that is integrated or accepted in the communication process. High-context cultures assign a lot of meaning to the nonword aspects of a specific message. In fact, these nonword factors define the meaning of the words. That is why it is so difficult for Americans, a low-context culture, to understand what the Japanese, a high-context culture, mean when they say yes, no, and maybe.

In low-context cultures, the words themselves define the meaning. The focus is more on the communication itself, the exact word, the specific gesture. Examples of high-context cultures are the Japanese, Chinese, and Mexicans, which we discussed in the second Interlude, "Montezuma and Mapleleafs." For these cultures, history, status, family, tone, and timing are important and contribute to the meaning of the communication. Examples of low-context cultures are the Scandinavian countries, Germany, and the United States. Canadians, especially the English-speaking Canadians, are more low-context than high. Here history and status are not important, rather the communication is understood in a narrow range of external influences.

As we've noted, American women are more high-context than American men. Women have a higher tolerance for ambiguity, open-endedness, listening, and processing words and context. Men have a narrower focus, are more time-driven, and bring logic and precision to the process. For example, any husband who has ever argued with his wife knows that she is apt to suddenly disengage from the conversation and become totally silent, driving the husband crazy and prompting him to ask, "Is it something I said?" The answer is not *what* he said, but *how* he said it. Or it may be what he didn't say—the context, in other words, that triggered the silence.

Men try to recoup from these entanglements by saying more words, not less, only making matters worse.

Herein lies a powerful competitive advantage for an American corporation. Rather than starting with a culturally conditioned, transaction-oriented man and expecting that "some training" will unschool his patterns of communication and interaction, begin instead with women, who automatically function at the high-context level. The investment of "some training" here will reinforce desirable patterns of communication, rather than try to change them.

A good and complete reference on the business applications of context is *Global Work* by Mary O'Hara-Devereaux and Robert Johansen. They have taken this idea and Hall's work one practical step further. They have applied the high- and low-context characteristics to specific professions and jobs. See Snapshot #21.

Snapshot #21

High Context	Human Resources
	Marketing/Sales
	Management
	Manufacturing
	Products
	R&D
	Technical
	Information
	Systems
	Engineers
Low Context	Finance

Source: Institute for the Future

As an example of the differences, O'Hara-Devereaux and Johansen have made the following comparison between a high-context marketing person and a low-context engineer:

> *The marketing culture is driven by rapport-building practices that attach high values to relationships. The best marketing people are good at understanding, accepting, and blending with the views of their customers. They are always selling—either themselves or their products or their clients. Engineers, on the other hand, tend to be driven by analytical thinking. They value precision and skepticism. To the engineer, the marketing people look fuzzy and even unprincipled: "They'll do anything to get a sale—including promising what we can't deliver." But from the marketing perspective, engineers often seem insensitive and rigidly boorish.*

There is a lot of merit to these kinds of considerations, especially because they activate the Whatsnew Force. The attention that needs to be paid to this new level of relationships in business cannot be overstated. We've been successful in the past with the transaction-based model (where engineers and others ensure that the product measures up), so some would argue there is no need for change, as provocative as it might be. Until recently, American business could afford this position because we were the dominant player in the business world. But take a look around today: With the notable exception of Germany, the other countries in the high-stakes business world, Japan, China, Korea, and Brazil, are predominately high-context cultures where the relationship-based model is second nature. If American companies want to remain competitive in the high-stakes global marketplace they cannot do it on a mere transaction-based model. Those days are gone forever.

But where would we find the role models for the relationship-based model? The current ranks of CEOs are mostly drawn from finance (the bottom of the low-context continuum) or marketing (the near top end of high-context continuum). It is rare to find a CEO in an American corporation who has come from the highest end of the continuum, human resources. We could only think of one, the woman in the profile that follows.

A Trailblazer for Women: Something Men Can Bank On

Today, her 29th floor office is a cross between a small SoHo gallery and an Upper East side working studio. Four years ago it was a male's mess when she moved in, but one of the first things that the staff at CoreStates Bank in Philadelphia asked her was how she wanted her office remodeled—that's the first thing new executives are supposed to do. They assured her that the walnut paneling, leather chairs, and formal portraits could be replaced in no time and she could have her pick of furnishings. She said no. And her staff quickly learned that when Rosemarie B. Greco says "no," she doesn't mean, "not right now, check with me later, I'll think about it," but simply, "no, now let's get back to work."

Now why wouldn't the first woman president and CEO of CoreStates Bank and one of the highest ranking women in banking in the world want to make a bold and brash statement at the outset, establish her turf, and throw some weight around? She did, but not in the conventional way. Simply put, she told us, "I could not justify spending one penny for a new office when the profitability and performance of the bank was down and I was brought in to help turn things around. My office was not a priority or even a remote consideration for me." By eschewing the traditional trappings and perks of a bank executive, she sent out more signals about her management priorities on day one than a month of memos ever could.

Today the office is bright, airy, and orderly. The paintings are hers—reminders of personal places that renew her energy and inner strength. One, by a local artist, is a watercolor painting of the corner grocery store that she lived above while growing up in a working-class neighborhood in South Philadelphia. The other is a mystic beach painting that could be anywhere, but is most likely the New Jersey shoreline where Rosemarie escapes whenever she can. Tucked to one side is a working executive's desk. All of this came three years later, *after* she had accomplished what she had initially set out to do, and the earnings and growth rate were turned around ahead of schedule.

Rose*marie* (only strangers call her Ms. Greco or slip-up and mispronounce her first name as Rose-mary) personifies the seven cultural forces and exemplifies the relationship-based model of management discussed above. She is the youngest in a family that struggled to make ends meet for its six children. She said, "In my household, adults prevailed. We had limited space. My youngest sister was thirteen and my oldest brother was twenty-one. There was just no way for me to get my way by being competitive. So, I learned to win through managing relationships, through negotiation and facilitation (✂)." As far back as she can remember, Rosemarie dreamed of being a school teacher (🐌). However, her father died when she was a teenager and her hopes of being the first family member to graduate from college were dashed (🐞). In order to help out the family, she transferred out of her college-prep courses and enrolled in the secretarial program (☑). But when offered a government-paid typist job for $60 a week, she consulted with her mother and siblings, and with their support and encouragement, took a job at seventeen for $37 a week teaching sixty-seven third graders at Our Lady of Mt. Carmel in the heart of South Philadelphia (💻).

Two years later she joined a convent (💻), the Convent of the Sister Servants of the Immaculate Heart of Mary at Immaculata College, one of the most accomplished teacher orders in the country. Writing for *The Harvard Business Review*'s "First Person" (a popular management profile of an experienced manager written in the first person), she said that she expected to learn the science of teaching, but actually learned the art of management. Her early jobs were all New Potential Identities, stuff legends are made of: valet, secretary, and chauffeur for the Mother General (CEO) of the Order. Everywhere the Mother General went Rosemarie wasn't far behind— with her notebook in hand. Everything she observed she wrote down, and before long, she had her first management manual. She writes, "I didn't know it at the time, but walking beside her, scribbling notes furiously, I experienced the connections between teaching and managing that would serve me so well later in my career."

Three years later, after leaving the convent, her twenty-seven-year career in banking began where a lot of women's careers ended in those days—as a secretary—at a branch office at Fidelity Bank in Philadelphia. There her career was one New Potential Identity after another. She drew on the family-negotiation skills that she had learned growing up and the attention to detail that she had noted in the convent. Exemplifying the Whatsnew Force, she recalls that, "Every day I asked someone to teach me something new." And everything she learned went into a three-ring binder that eventually became the bank's first training manual. Rosemarie's "First Person" account, "From the Classroom to the Corner Office," is instructive as a tutorial on personal development and a chronicle of the corporate days before diversity.

In 1991, Rosemarie left Fidelity Bank, where she was President and CEO, and came to CoreStates as President and CEO of First Pennsylvania Bank. In 1994, she was promoted to President and CEO of all of CoreStates' banks. She is now responsible for all CoreStates' domestic and international banking activities and is the only woman on a five-person executive-management committee. She supervises over four thousand six hundred employees, is responsible for two-thirds of the bank's deposits, one-quarter of its loans, and one-third of its net income. And she's got the newly decorated corner office, across from City Hall.

We visited her in the middle of the big bank merger frenzy of 1995, which included an abortive one between CoreStates and the Bank of Boston. She provides an interesting perspective on bigness and banks (remember Chapter 3). She talked about the "Pac-man mentality in banking" where everything is reduced to numbers and crunching the competition. "Big," she reflected, "is defined today in terms that quantify *reduction*. Mergers are measured by how much we can *squeeze* out of a relationship, not by how much we can put into it. Every merger announcement is about staff reductions, fewer sites, reduction in equipment, and the like. It seems that all the analysis discount growth and only emphasize opportunities in mergers for reducing expenses. Then they want it both ways and start to push, push, push, earnings, earnings, earnings."

She worries that the younger generations are too thing-oriented to know how to relate others. "From their earliest years, kids today are absorbed in things and haven't the foggiest idea about relationships or how to relate to others," she says. "They grow up treating relationships like commodities, like just another thing to conquer or manipulate as though this were all some kind of game where the winner takes all."

However, after nearly three decades of banking experience, you'll still hear her say, "I haven't quite figured it all out yet"—a whatsnew attitude, if there ever was one. She has learned to live with ambivalence; and uncertainty is part of her daily routine—something she readily admits. Don't misread. Her strength comes from her integrity, fairness, and consistency, not from her authority to boss people around. Just ask the people who report to her. We didn't, but she reports that men in particular, initially misread her. "When they would come to me for a decision, I would say, yes, no, or what you rarely hear in banks at the executive level—I don't know. If it wasn't the answer they were looking for, they would try again. Soon they learned that in this office, yes means yes and no means no, and no time should be wasted circumventing the final decision." She digressed for a minute, looked out the window on her old neighborhood, and said, "It's amazing how much time goes into revisiting decisions that have already been made . . . . Such a waste of time . . . . The most troubling part for them was not the yes or no, but the I don't know. They were not comfortable with uncertainty, ambiguity, and my need for reflection. They were also uneasy when I asked why, not just once, but why, why, why. They weren't used to someone wanting to get to the bottom of the decision."

Easy to Say, Hard to Do

Rosemarie has perfected (she would deny the attribution) the art of managing by visiting around. It's a habit of hers to visit with customers on *their* turf and with all branch offices. It's a practice she instills in others, but not by edict. When she is out visiting a customer, *everyone* knows it and the message is modeled.

Her observations about management conventions are equally straightforward: "easy to talk about, hard to do." She cited empowerment as one example and said, "If you really want to be empowered, you have to put yourself at risk. People forget that, and its my job to teach this discipline. When someone comes to my office and says, 'I don't feel empowered,' I say, 'Tell me why not?' They'll say, 'Because I can't make this or that decision.' 'Why?' I ask. 'Is there a policy that inhibits you? What would happen if you made the decision?' Invariably it comes down to someone finally admitting that *I* might be upset with the decision *they make*. At this juncture, it is important to make sure they are certain that they know that they are making the right decision? I always ask, 'Do you *believe enough in your decision* to do it, to see it through? Do you know the real risks? Have you assessed those risks?' If the answer is yes, then what I might think doesn't matter—that's empowerment, and it's hard to do, hard to teach."

Rosemarie has what she calls "passion for business" (as well as making a mean lasagna, playing the bass, and tending to family and various demanding civic responsibilities). She says, "You can't be passionate if you don't have emotions—good, bad, joy, or pain. Does this mean you should go into a rage? No, but you do need to express *how you feel*. (In her earlier days she was know for her temper. On one occasion she banged her door "so hard that the pictures in the adjoining office went askew." "That's when I was younger," she quickly adds. "Now, I just say, 'That makes me very angry. I'm going to tell you how ticked off I am. And I'm going to get over it. But I want you to know how I feel right now.' " This openness and candor about feelings is clearly a whatsnew in that it is consistently practiced at CoreStates, at least in Rosemarie's office.

When the Bank of Boston deal fell through, an analyst made a public statement that was blatantly not true. Rosemarie was furious, "absolutely furious," in her recall, and she did not hesitate to let her fury be known to her colleagues on the executive committee, the press, the analyst's boss, and, most importantly, her staff. Coming from a former nun, cum secretary, cum VP of personnel, cum President, cum CEO—everyone took note. Maybe there is another secretary at CoreStates writing it all down in a three-ring binder, and a few years from now, she, or he, will be chairman of CoreStates, or any other organization for that matter. Meanwhile, keep an eye on Rosemarie B. Greco; she is only forty-nine and is still taking notes.

New Potential Identity: The Inherent Whatsnew in Americans

Americans are not a contented lot: We are restless, constantly on the move, always working on something new, or busy redefining ourselves. In Chapter 6, we described how Americans work their way through an improvement process with the idea of "let's fix it" so that we can *go on to something else*. We described this perpetual invention process that drives Disney in Chapter 2. And the whole philosophy of becoming could not be better structured at a corporate level than at Levi Strauss & Co. with its Aspirations Statement—in full view, but just out of reach.

The whatsnew process is not limited to just the things that are around us or to the things we create, but to ourselves as well. New Potential Identities (please don't say NPI) is the name the *Stuff* research gives to this perpetual renewal phenomenon in America.

In most other cultures, individual identity is fixed early in life as a result of one's family heritage, class, money, or status. Once set, it doesn't change easily or at all. Not so in America.

Executives, managers, teachers, parents, and other authority figures should take special note that the dimension of the Whatsnew Force is inextricably linked to personal improvement for Americans. New Potential Identities are an untapped emotional well-spring for Americans and they have major implications for how companies should reward employees as we discussed in Chapter 5. And they get at the heart of the American improvement process that we discussed in the preceding chapter.

A New Potential Identity in the context of the Whatsnew Force should not be confused with career counseling or moving up the corporate ladder, or step stool, as may be the case in new horizontally "flattened" organizations. New Potential Identities, like so much else that defines Americans, are spontaneous, often out-of-the-blue possibilities, usually an expansion of current reality. Although you are most likely to see them for yourself (once you open yourself up to the possibilities), they can be pointed out or suggested to you by others.

Unlike an orchestrated career path, the New Potential Identity is general in nature, without a specific plan to make it happen (see why it's so American!). It doesn't have to be pursued, but it pulls us forward, inextricably. On the other hand, it can linger, change, vanish, or come back as an impossible dream.

Snapshot #22

What Are New Potential Identities?	
ARE	*ARE NOT*
spontaneous	planned
new	more of the same
created	given
a pulling force *(a magnet)*	a driving force *(more money)*
about the future	about past and present
vague	developed
options	fixed ideas
personally controlled	imposed by others
spirals	closed loops

Anyone can turn his existing skills into a New Potential Identity if he just gives himself permission to do so. Remember, New Potential Identities are spontaneous—those what-ifs that float through your mind from time to time. So if you are a carpenter in the middle of a roofing job and you suddenly think about how much fun it would be to be a woodshop instructor—congratulations, you've found a New Potential Identity. Similarly for a union representative who decides to take her organizing skills and run for city council. The whole field of computer programming and software development is driven by people searching for New Potential Identities and making them a reality. In fact, New Potential Identities may be most prevalent here because the programmer has a technology basis from which to realize the identity.

A strong majority of us (59 percent) report that we are "*always* in the process of becoming" what we want to be. And while you may expect that of younger Americans (71 percent), fully 39 percent of Americans fifty-five and older are equally restless, attesting to this undying notion that we can become anything we want to in this country. Conversely, a correspondingly smaller percent of Americans feel that they have arrived, that they have reached the end of the road or are simply content with where they are. As we get older, this arrived category becomes more pronounced. (See Snapshot #23).

The national survey was ambiguous about why people choose the third option, "I'm not what I could be." As design participants in this study, we feel that this is the group that is most pessimistic, the least sanguine. African-Americans and the unemployed lead this category with 23 percent in each group saying they are not what

Snapshot #23

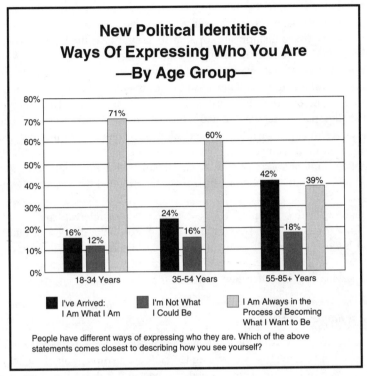

New Political Identities
Ways Of Expressing Who You Are
—By Age Group—

	I've Arrived: I Am What I Am	I'm Not What I Could Be	I Am Always in the Process of Becoming What I Want to Be
18-34 Years	16%	12%	71%
35-54 Years	24%	16%	60%
55-85+ Years	42%	18%	39%

People have different ways of expressing who they are. Which of the above statements comes closest to describing how you see yourself?

Source: The Wirthlin Group and ASQC.

they could be. Spanish Americans are the least downtrodden of all subgroups: Only 10 percent hold this view compared to 15 percent of Caucasians who do.

Those with total optimism, who see the future with seemingly endless possibilities, are, not surprisingly, more apt to be students (83 percent—virtually all), college graduates, professionals/technical workers, those with incomes of $75,000 or more, part-time workers, and those who live in the West. The close seconds are those with technical educations or some college, with incomes between $35,000 and $75,000, white-collar workers, and Spanish Americans.

So the New Potential Identity is a dynamic of the Whatsnew Force that is widely in play in America. It is not only a personal manifestation of whatsnew, but the force is equally active in groups, communities, and companies.

Hewlett-Packard: The Whatsnew Company

Any big established company that generates more than two-thirds of its $31.5 billion annual revenues from products and services introduced within the past two years can only be thought of as a whatsnew company. That's Hewlett-Packard, a diversified manufacturing and services company with over 23,000 products, operating at 600 locations in over 100 countries around the world. This is a company that is perpetually reinventing itself.

HP dominates the laser and inkjet printer business. In 1994, just ten years after introducing their first printers, they shipped their 30-millionth printer—not bad for two young guys, Bill and Dave, who started their company out of their garage.

That garage is now a historic site (or altar for some) near the HP campus in Palo Alto, California. Continuously inventing and reinventing itself (playing the Whatsnew Force for all its power and leverage from its inception in 1939) is HP's signature. From its start in the audio oscillator business to inventing the first scientific hand-held calculator and creating the world's first major commercial RISC (reduced instruction set computer) architecture and a host of products and services in between, HP rides the technology wave like nobody else can. They can do that because they are always mindful of their roots and the HP way, defined by cofounder Bill Hewlett as "the policies and actions that flow from the belief that men and women want to do a good job, a creative job, and that if they are provided the proper environment they will do so."

We caught up with one typical HPer who captured our interest from the first day we met him a few years ago. He's Richard LeVitt, corporate director of quality. Richard and his team have just completed a global benchmarking study to discover whatsnew in quality management.* In his inimitable fashion, he covered a lot of ground in a wide-ranging interview. Here are the highlights:

JH: *I get the sense from listening to you that the obsession with the future and whatsnew is not new at HP.*

RL: The intensity of focus on the future has always been here. In the early days it was an excitement about rapidly changing technology, the invention of the transistor and the invention of integrated circuits and the spectacular shrinkage of components and lowering of costs that led to the explosion of what's possible with technology. And so there is an *obsession* about the future that exists because the future has so much promise. The technology is changing so rapidly and so spectacularly, it literally creates business opportunities overnight. You have to be really fast and really nimble to see these opportunities first.

JH: *Does HP train its people to be future-oriented?*

RL: Our education program for general managers is *not* about how to run business operations, it's not about making a profit this quarter. All those things are important, but the key message is about creating the future. So we talk about scanning the environment, anticipating, positioning strategically into the future, analyzing scenarios, and being able to see ahead farther than other people can. All this enables us to make better choices about what course of action to take, what business, what industry, what technology to pursue. That's our orientation. It is so powerful it can cause us occasionally to neglect the real-time operational issues, the daily routine of running a business.

JH: *What do you mean by scanning?*

RL: Scanning is an obsession with what's going on out there, what is happening in universities, changing demographics, changing conditions of society, what is

*Look for a "White Paper" on whatsnew in quality to be issued in the fall of 1996 as part of the HP's sponsorship of the annual National Quality Month Campaign.

happening as the world becomes a smaller place and globalization increases. Scanning enables us to get glimpses, to have an understanding that we can create some new product or service that fits the possible future. Scanning is standing on a hill and using your hand as a visor, looking in all directions as far as you can see. That's scanning.

JH: *Do you have a scanning department or vice president of scanning?*

RL: Scanning isn't managed by a department; it is established more by culture than by creating functions. We are encouraging all senior managers and all technologists to have better scanning skills so that they have that ability to stand taller, and see farther than they might be able to do otherwise. So it's not a matter of creating a scanning department, it's a matter of creating *a scanning competency in the organization*. This is taught in a week-long seminar called, "Creating the Future."

JH: *What's an example of how scanning helped HP?*

RL: A few years ago the growth in one of our major businesses started to slow down to single-digit growth and in our environment that's a slow pace. So the leader of that organization, Ned Barnholt, instituted a change project they call Project TMO (Test and Measurement Organization). This project was focusing on the specific challenge of identifying new businesses, new ventures, new things that they could do to accelerate their growth. For example, they had been dependent on the defense industry; testing requirements of defense contractors made up a large part of their business. We didn't see the end coming as dramatically as it did. Now we see more clearly where those shocks might occur in the future. We've developed some alternate strategies to anticipate which scenario might be in play. We have a strategy that is tailored to each situation so that we are not casting about blindly in response to being caught by surprise. As a result, in the last several years TMO has gone from single-digit growth back to nice healthy double-digit growth that is consistent with the overall growth rate of the company. It's a really nice turnaround story, a real success story.

JH: *Some think the computer industry is going to hit a brick wall within ten years. What does your scanning tell you?*

RL: Actually there is a strong awareness of that possible scenario. It's an awareness from what's called a technology S-curve that we use in planning. That is you have an early phase where you are exploring options and the needs of the market. The real performance capability of the technology is unclear. If you are onto something that customers like, it starts taking off exponentially. We experienced that most recently with the ink jet printers, which went from nowhere to a multibillion-dollar business in the span of about eight years or so. Eventually you reach the point where a particular technology can't take you very much further. Then you need a technology paradigm shift in order to jump on another S-curve. So we are literally looking for these technology life cycles, understanding where we are in the life cycle and where is the next big curve to jump onto. Some people believe that the evolution of computer technology will slow down as silicon services encounter fundamental physical limits in size and speed. There is another school of thought that believes that we're on the threshold of discovering entirely new technologies, not even based on silicon, but perhaps based on optical processing or even biology. So people are busy building massively parallel computers out of DNA. Other people are building massively parallel computers out of beams of light. There are a lot of possibilities out in the future for entirely new ways of building intelligent machines that are far beyond the capabilities of current machines.

JH: *HP has a high-quality reputation. So what is this we hear that you are now reinventing quality? What's that all about?*

RL: At HP we are constantly *dissatisfied* with the way things are. We are always changing, always looking for some better way. The better we get at something, the better we are able to see how it can be changed even further. The curious phenomenon then is this: the things that we spend the most time improving tend not to be the things that we're the worst at; they tend to be the things that we're the best at. Because we are worried about them, we are focused on them; we develop a skill and understanding about those issues and the more we learn about the issues, the more we see what's possible, the more we work to make that better. As you may know, *Fortune* magazine, in their annual corporate reputation survey of business leaders, ranked HP number one in quality management and number one in the quality of products and services. So this means that we need to stay out in front on quality, go on to the next thing, *re*invent quality. One of the most visible and consistent messages from our CEO, Lew Platt, is to be aware of the danger of complacency: Don't rest, don't go to sleep, don't become like IBM or DEC (which once became too comfortable with success and lost their edge). Another issue is that, as we go into consumer markets, we are really trying to satisfy entirely different customers than we are accustomed to. There is a growing sense that our traditional ways of managing quality, our traditional skills and competencies that we have in managing quality, aren't necessarily well matched to the needs of that marketplace.

JH: *What have you learned or discovered?*

RL: Through our research we didn't see *anyone* that really had the whole thing together. So we chewed on that notion until we realized that there was a possibility to synthesize a new way of thinking about quality inside a firm, of a way of managing quality that was profoundly different, and better than what we have seen in other places, anywhere. It looked like a real opportunity; that's why we call it *reinventing quality,* to define it as a significant shift.

This is the key element to the shift. Everyone talks about customer satisfaction, but it's always from the producer's stance. No one is genuinely *inside the mind* of the consumer, knowing the consumers' experience. What are they feeling? How are our actions, our decisions, and our internal operations affecting the customer's whole experience? The more we explored that, the more we realized that an understanding of the total experience is missing. And so our ability to really prioritize what we work on, what we change, what we do, what we don't do, is constrained by that lack of understanding. Now we want to understand the life cycle of the customer's experience as the customer goes through it.

So that's the core of the revolution: To understand those issues and then design systematically a quality system that addresses those things that should change to improve the customer's experience so that at the end of the day we have the ability to attract more customers, to keep customers that we have won because we perform well for them and to enhance the relationship we have with customers so that they are willing to do business in other ways with Hewlett-Packard. And so the ultimate result of all this is that quality becomes the strategy for growing the business.

JH: *You keep using the expression customer experience. Are you talking about what the customer is thinking before she makes a decision, what is going on while she is making a decision, what is going on while she is using it, what is going on afterward—really a lifelong relationship with a customer? For most companies, customer satisfaction is often thought of as a transaction, you know, in a shorter time frame. But you are saying that you want to move toward the total customer experience whatever that might be and wherever that might take you?*

RL: Yes.

JH: *Where does this total customer experience focus lead to from a management perspective?*

RL: The thing that is new, for us at least, is greater attention to the whole value chain. Our traditional approach to managing quality has been heavily influenced by the Japanese and there you take a team of people that own a process and you give them a responsibility for improving the process and they are instructed to change the things that they have control over and trust that everyone else will be doing the same thing. If everyone treats the people downstream as customers then it will all come out well at the end.

   The difficulty with that view is that you may end up having each team working on things which may be the biggest item to them but when you look at the performance of the whole system, as seen by a customer, it may be far from what it could be. So what we are moving to is a view of the whole value chain and thinking about a quality system that spans suppliers, our operations, technology partners, and sales channels—all to serve the customer.

JH: *How are you going about this? Where is the starting point?*

RL: In our initial research and benchmarking, we found pretty much the same stuff. We found that the fundamental intellectual ideas, the foundations of the quality field, hadn't changed much in a decade or so. As you think of technology and how rapidly it changes and if you think there is a technology to quality, you would expect it to be also rapidly evolving. But it doesn't look like it has been, and that was a big surprise at how stuck it seems to be. So what we have been doing is going outside the conventional boundaries of quality, looking particularly in the consumer marketing field, in psychology, in the cognitive sciences, looking at areas that are really out-of-the-box. To understand quality as the customer truly does, we need to understand emotions. We need to *feel* what they experience. We need to tell stories about customer experiences, and use these stories to engage employees in making change happen.

JH: *What gets you up in the morning?*

RL: I'm the kind of person that is drawn to big visionary things, big ideas. When I see something in a new way or understand something that I feel I could do something about, I get excited. Reinventing quality at HP is one such thing. You might have seen this cartoon from the "Far Side": there is this group of sheep munching grass in a field. One of them picks his head up and says, "Wait a minute, wait a minute, we don't have to be just sheep."

JH: *You're not going to believe this! It's right here in front of me. Honestly, it's right here. I've been collecting a couple of these to use them in my speeches!*

The Learning Attraction at Disney

What could be a better excuse for a visit to Disney World than a learning trip?

Business Week just made it easier to sell your boss on the idea. In its cover story of September 18, 1995, the editors of *Business Week* named Disney University in Orlando as one of the "Management Meccas" in the United States. A decade ago Americans searched everywhere but their own backyard for the key to productivity and the secret to engaging workers in the improvement process. Treks to Japan were commonplace. But by and large the copious notes taken there did not translate here.

On these global benchmarking tours, American executives confused the *why* with the *how.* The note-taking was on how the Japanese do this, that, or the other. Lost in the translation was the why they were engaged in the practice, and that all the difference makes.

Executives, from Tokyo to Toledo, Osaka to Oslo, are constantly looking for ways to engage their workers, to introduce change into processes, to enhance productivity. That is a transnational management need. *How* that should achieved should be culture specific, as we have described throughout the book.

For example, as we outlined in Chapters 2 and 4, the locus of American motivation is completely different from that of the Japanese. So a technique or practice that fits culturally in Japan will misconnect or backfire in America. For example, the discipline and collaboration necessary to make quality circles work effectively fit Japanese culture: Collaboration is endemic to their way of doing things. Americans, on the other hand, have no patience for this kind of deliberation and exploration. Lunging right in with individual initiatives—knowing they can improvise later if things go wrong—is patented Americanism.

As we have already said, an effective teaming process in America has a call-out, a "what's in it for me" component, that would never surface in Japan. In America this personal dimension not only needs to be addressed up front, but it should be leveraged throughout the life of the project.

So quality circles failed in America, as did a host of other transplanted strategies and notions. They failed for the same reason that some American management ideas, like zero defects and reengineering, also fail; the *how,* the human side of quality and productivity, is misunderstood, treated the same old way, or simply ignored. Up to 70 percent of the failure rate, noted by Michael Hammer and James Champy in their reengineering work, is due to the failure of companies to address the people side of the product/process equation.

In the appropriately never-ending cycle of whatsnew for American managers, "growing the business" is the latest in thing, the latest buzz phrase. An October 1995 study conducted by Opinion Research Corporation for the international management consulting firm of Arthur D. Little found that 63 percent of three hundred executives interviewed at a cross-section of manufacturing and service companies saw a silver (maybe platinum) lining in the reengineering fray. They concluded that reengineering, with all its problems "was necessary in order to experience growth again." Unfortunately, the study showed that the same personnel pit that was present in the preceding practices was still there: 79 percent of the participants in the study identified "the difficulty in hiring and retaining talent" as one of three primary factors that are impeding growth—the ignored people side of the equation. Again!

A Focus on the How

The Disney Professional Development Programs in Orlando has a solution, one that is beginning to take hold in corporations throughout America. They offer a training program that focuses on the *how,* not the what—precisely what the innovative leadership companies like Aetna Health Plans, AT&T, FedEx, Hewlett-Packard, Intel, and others are looking for. It is a training program that incorporates much of what we write about in this book, and, conveniently it is also called *The Stuff Americans Are Made Of* *

Disney's Professional Development Program has an exclusive agreement with ASQC† to develop and to market the *Stuff* program, as we will refer to it throughout the rest of this book. It is well suited for the task for several reasons. First, the Walt Disney Company was one of the principal sponsors of the initial research project. Second, the company has intuitively been doing a lot of this stuff from the earliest of Walt's days (see Chapter 2). Third, the Disney people have tried it themselves and it works for them. Fourth, the company has world-renowned professional trainers who deliver a memorable and lasting training experience.

The *Stuff* training program is basically a two-day, facilitated workshop that provides participants with three new integrated business basics:

1. The role of national culture in performance improvement

2. Tools for personalizing quality and productivity

3. A process for aligning people *and* process

While most training programs make claims that they do number 3, the alignment process, it is inconceivable how effective or lasting the alignment can be if it ignores the unconscious national cultural forces that go untapped or unheeded. Stuff *takes the guess-work out of the alignment process.*

Most training programs also make claims about the importance of the individual, number 2 above. Some in fact make an attempt to ferret out personality traits and preferences, but none identify and match motivated abilities to work processes as this

---

The training program predates this book. Although the Stuff *training program was initially created by Josh Hammond when he was president of the American Quality Foundation, neither author is affiliated with the training program.*

†ASQC *is the largest professional and educational association in quality. It was the parent organization that started and supported the research of the American Quality Foundation in the formative years of the* Stuff *training program and now works with Disney's Professional Development Programs in the marketing of the training program. ASQC recently completed the teamwork study that AQF had begun and continues to provide research support to the* Stuff *program. It is the source for the latest information on quality and the quality-related sciences. For more information, call 1-800-248-1946 or 414-272-8575.*

program does. *This step alone virtually guarantees increased job satisfaction and increased productivity.* (See Chapter 1, page 48, for a discussion of this process.)

Finally, to point to number 1, there are countless training programs about how Americans can sell in Singapore, market in Mexico, diversify in Denmark, negotiate in Norway, and build in Brazil, but there are none with an in-depth focus on what makes us American and how critical it is to know our culture before we can effectively deal with other cultures.

Check it out!*

Stuff *in Action: Finding a Cure!*

> *We gotta change our culture.*
> *We gotta change our culture.*
> *We gotta change our culture.*
> *No!*
> *We gotta understand our culture*
> *And work it!*

This is where the day-long give-and-take about how to step-up the high performance of the company ended up—on flip-chart paper, taped to the wall, with all the other strategies and details, where everyone in the room could focus on it. You've been there before, though the outcome may have been different. It's the end of the day: you are frustrated, new data has your mind spinning, some key assumptions have been challenged, you don't know exactly how this new stuff is going to fit, you are running out of time, then it all comes together. And you hope someone is taking good notes.

In this case someone was. So the day-long meeting between the facilitators from the *Stuff* project and the senior staff from Aetna Health Plans, the strategic business unit of Aetna Life & Casualty Company ended with a clear understanding of what comes next. Kevin Hickey, vice president in charge of operations at the innovative and hard-charging AHP, was leading the exploration about how the *Stuff* training can help them stay on top of the rapid changes in their industry and respond more effectively to their 19 million customers throughout the country.

Hickey describes Aetna Health Plans as a "national company doing business locally." They are one of the largest health care organizations in the U.S. operating concurrently in three businesses—health, specialty health (mental health, employee assistance programs, pharmacy and dental plans), and group insurance. In 1994 alone, they processed 88 million claims with total payments in excess of $17 billion.

The challenge is how to engage AHP's 21,000 employees in the growth of the company and, according to Hickey, "to establish an operating environment that supports our employees to create and deliver best value products and services to our customers." Hickey adds, "We are faced with the prospect of continuous change. It's part of being a major player in today's highly competitive managed care field. By relentlessly focusing on the customer, we are constantly changing the shape of our future." With

---

**For information about the* Stuff *training program, call 407-828-5611, or write to* THE STUFF AMERICANS ARE MADE OF, *P.O. Box 10094, Lake Buena Vista, FL 32830-0094. For information on the Disney Professional Development Programs, call 407-824-4855, or write Disney University, P.O. Box 10093, Lake Buena Vista, FL 32830-0093.*

AHP 2000 (their stretch goal for the turn of the millennium) they are defining and delivering AHP's future operating environment today. In other words, AHP is redefining managed health care and transforming itself at the same time—that's six of the seven cultural forces all in play at once: choice, doing the seemingly impossible, in a big and innovative way, now, with the process and outcome a constant whatsnew. (Naturally, there may be a few oopses along the way, but no one is hoping for them!)

Hickey says that in order to accomplish this, "We need to bring our people along this rapidly moving continuum, and that is where I think this broader cultural thinking can do us the most good." Intuitively they have already been connecting to some of the cultural forces. Now they want to do it consciously.

Like many other companies, Aetna Health Plans has been through a variety of business activities such as reengineering and streamlining for productivity gains. Not only was the cure worse than the illness, but there was no connecting with the people. DeAnn Anderson, vice president of AHP quality management, working with ASQC in the *Stuff* program, saw the missing link. Anderson said, "*Stuff* gives us the ability to tap into our unique strengths and bring out the best in our people. We saw a methodology that could align the hearts and minds of our employees and allow them to be successful as teams and as individuals. It provides a process for getting people on board naturally."

Now Aetna has embraced the notion that its corporate culture should align more with the national cultural forces. Hickey says, "We have been so obsessed with this idea of our own corporate culture that we completely overlooked the obvious. We are now making a conscious effort to bring this broader cultural awareness into play internally, rather than unknowingly struggling against them."

The cure? A dose of *Stuff* starting at the top. Hickey says, "There is no we-versus-them here. That kind of thinking hurts companies. We are all in this together." Last we heard, a plan was being put in place to start with the top 140 executives at Aetna Health Plans and put everyone through the *Stuff* training. Hickey said, "We are now on track to understand and activate the broader cultural leverages. Our goal is to optimize our most valuable resource—our people."

Stuff *in Action: Government as* Unusual

The *Stuff* training also has started taking root in government, largely through the efforts of Deborah Hopen, president of the Center for Strategic Business Solutions, now affiliated with Xerox Quality Services. She is one of the whatsnew professionals in America: multidisciplined,* equally as skilled in journalism and finance as she is in engineering and human resource management. She is a gifted trainer and systems thinker. And she is currently serving as the president of the ASQC.

For much of the past fifteen years, Hopen has devoted a lot of her time to working with teams. Of late she helped fine-tune the *Stuff* training program, linking hard-nosed business practices and engineering sciences to the human and emotional components of the program, and also helped bring it on-line in several companies.

We caught up with her just as she was coming from one of her pet projects, the city of Tacoma, WA. There, under the leadership of the city manager, Ray Corpuz,

---

The day of the generalist is back. Cross-functional competenance is the order of the day. The basics of business are arguably more important than a specialty or technical skill.

The Magic in Management
How Disney Does It

Disney has put together a series of thought-provoking executive management training programs that offer a rare behind-the-scenes understanding of the magic in Disney's management. Over seventy years of Disney business expertise provide the foundation for these intense two-and-a-half- to three-and-a-half-day programs. And they have turned the forty-five-square-mile resort at the Walt Disney World into a living classroom.

Specifically, they offer four tailored programs on The Disney Approach to People Management, Quality Service, Creative Leadership, and Orientation. Each program delineates and dissects Disney's management practices and enables participants to learn the whats and the whys of their successful approaches to employees (cast members, they call them), customer satisfaction, product innovation, quality service, and leadership. Participants in the Creative Leadership course get an insider's look at the Disney storytelling process, learn how to communicate a vision, and how to turn ideas into reality. The course on Quality Service is down-to-earth stuff on how to evaluate your service philosophy (indeed, it's a four-step plan), deliver superior service, and how to turn complaints into "service victories." The People Management course gets at the heart of the Disney magic, from employee hiring and selection to training and job satisfaction. And the Orientation course will send you home with more ideas than you'll know what to do with. Actually, they'll send you home with practical ideas that make a performance difference. This course is not about technology and capital investment, rather it's about the no-cost investment strategies that make a world of difference in people management.

All this and fireworks every night!

the city is putting in a total quality management system. Their plan calls for training eighteen-hundred city employees in the principles and practice of TQM and its allied sciences. Hopen is part of a team that has been hired by the city to coach them through the process and help do the team training. Through a series of talks and watching her in action, here is what she had to say on a range of topics:

The word "team player" is ambiguous: *I have heard a lot of complaining over the years about the phrase 'team player.' A lot of people don't like that phrase and yet it keeps coming up in performance appraisals with most of the companies I work with. A lot of people would say to me, "If I'm the team player then I'm not allowed to have my own ideas." I would try to facilitate the process and say, "No, no, you are allowed to have your own ideas, but you must learn to work together." Not surprisingly, I found out that managers talked out of both sides of their mouth: they talked about the need for diversity on the one hand, and then when you got put on the team they expected everybody to go with the flow.*

Insist on clarification early on: *One of the things we're learning in Tacoma is that if people express what they are looking for early in the process, then you can do* *more things faster. You start to learn about each other, so it's easy for me to turn around to the fire chief now in Tacoma and understand what his needs are. In Tacoma we have a Task Agreement form that we use. We now clarify all expectations up front and then take the time to say to each person, what do you individually want to get out [of this effort].*

No clash between empowerment and "getting the job done": *In Tacoma we went through a significant amount of training with the leadership team (all of the department directors that report to the city manager). We had them experience the process first and form their own teams so they could get a full sense of this* Stuff *process. We did a lot of training on understanding, when it's appropriate to control the situation, and when it's appropriate to let go, to empower. Just saying you are being empowering is like cutting the boat loose with nobody at the helm. So we worked through some scenarios and case studies, and did some real serious talking. Then over the next two months we had every one of the managers work on a team with a real tight deadline. They did their own Task Agreements, so they actually got to experience it. Through this process, they learned some real valuable things that they would not have learned through traditional training approaches.*

The Stuff ***research is foundational:*** *We took the Tacoma teams through what I call, "Phase-0," which is pumping up the leadership team and developing an implementation plan. We used the* Stuff *research significantly during this preparation period. It is foundational and we reference it all the time. When we hit a snag, we'll go back to the* Stuff *research and check ourselves. We'll ask ourselves, what does the* Stuff *research tell us to expect? How does the research tell us we might want to deal with it? It's very helpful. I mean it's an incredible tool for a facilitator-coach!*

Break things down into manageable chunks: *The first team in Tacoma had too many people on it—twenty to twenty-five people. It also lasted too long—it wasn't moving quickly. By the time we came in the people on the team were ready for something new. They were saying, "Why don't we just get going?"—the impatience you often see in a large task force. When we put the implementation plan together, we decided to break the work down as the* Stuff *research had identified. [See Chapter 4]. We did things in smaller pieces because we wanted to rotate people more often, give them a manageable task that they could see the end of so that they could say I'm going to be able to do this and move onto what's new. That's a real profound finding in the research.*

Faster results the new way: *Now here are the results: normally, resolving an implementation problem like the one we took on would take most companies somewhere in the six months to a year [time frame] based on my experience. I've checked with other people and I haven't found anybody yet that said that their organization was able to do a total quality implementation plan in less than six months. These teams did it in five weeks. It was phenomenal!*

Whatsnew can polarize people: *Well, first of all just the concept of the* Stuff *research is new for most people. And generally when you explain it they buy into it very easily. I would say that at the beginning a majority of the people start nodding* *their heads, they start saying, "Oh, gosh, yes I've seen it; oh, my gosh, I can't believe you've figured that out." But there are other people, a smaller percentage, that feel trapped and initially think it's too stereotypical, too general, I'm not like that. I found that you have to work through this. Some people react to whatsnew saying, "Wow! I got something new to learn, I can't wait to get into it." And some people react to new as, "What is this going to make me have to do?" They are kind of fearful of it because they say, "What am I going to have to do different? Am I going to be able to measure up?" I think it's that. You know I think it comes back to whether your tendency is to leap forward, be fairly intuitive, or whether you tend to have to touch it, see it, feel it, or try it on for size.*

Stop the dichotomy between hard and soft: *One of the things that's different for me is that most people in the quality profession talk about the soft side and the hard side of management. As long as we continue to talk about them as two sides we've got a problem. For me they are integrated. For example, I'll be talking about doing a statistical analysis, the "hard side," and at the same time ask a team how are they going to explain that to everybody else, "the soft side." Because I can't separate them in my mind, they are intrinsically tied together. When we try and divide up the two pieces, we do a disservice to everyone.*

Coping with Whatsnew

As various levels of the government experiment with process improvements and adapt TQM principles that have been tested in industry—seemingly old stuff by now—no one is exempt from new technologies, from scanners in grocery stores to global shopping on the Web. Whatsnew is now the increasing intensity and rapid pace of the knowledge age.

The $64,000 (not adjusted for inflation) question is how are we as a culture, a nation, coping with these seismic shifts in information and technology. Generally when we ask this question, we ask it of ourselves, our contemporaries. But these shifts will take place over a generation or more. So once again, we need to look to the future. The real question is whether our children are prepared; whether, as a culture, we are prepared educationally. Walter Kiechel III, former managing editor of *Fortune*, was fond of saying that the only problem with the 3Rs in American education is that we spell two of them wrong(writing and arithmetic). While the content of learning is debated, American business and government are reawakening to the need for cataclysmic revival in public education.

This attention needs to be turned into action, because at the moment, our own young people, compared to their contemporaries in the rest of the world, are not in good standing. Among those awed by the deepening crisis is Walter Wriston, retired chairman of Citicorp. He shares his concerns in his book, *The Twilight of Sovereignty*:

It dawned on me that information, in the words of Leon Martel, was "rapidly replacing energy as society's main transforming resource." Information technology is fundamentally different from industrial technology in that it can be programmed to do the required task and, if necessary, can be continuously adjusted. Industrial technology is just the opposite: the task must be adapted to the technology.

Wriston explains what this means to young people entering the workforce or to parents stashing away money for the kid's college education:

> *There is an abundance of highly trained and talented college graduates in faraway lands where there are few jobs. Geography no longer confines intellectual skills to underuse. Several U.S.-based Big Six accounting firms . . . now perform computer-assisted audits for American firms via satellite using customized software programs written by Filipino programmers. The audits are then zapped to the U.S. via satellite. American Express does the same kind of data processing using Indian programmers half a world away. Information now moves freely with the speed of light, all of which could start a train of events of immense political consequence.*

This idea of the marketplace moving to where the brains are is something new. It used to be the other way around. A person would graduate from school or college and go to the city to seek his fortune: brains going into the marketplace. But the idea of the marketplace going to where the brains are is something that calls for close scrutiny, because recent indications show that the brains, i.e., educated young people, are one of the resources that are in increasingly short supply in America. This was not always so.

What Was New in the Fifties

Those boom days of the fifties, the Eisenhower years, are looked upon with nostalgia. All those studly young veterans back home, tooling around in high-finned automobiles designed by Mr. Earl, living in Levitt-built "ranch" houses, and breeding with reckless abandon.

The boom was not what Congress had anticipated as World War II drew to a close. Some twelve million service personnel, mostly men, were about to be suddenly turned out on the streets in just a matter of months and there was a genuine fear of angry veterans standing in breadlines, selling apples on street corners, and the possibility of rampant inflation. Maybe even riots.

Always a whatsnew president, Franklin Delano Roosevelt had a remedy. Lobbied by the American Legion, Roosevelt got Congress to throw big money (♦) at the problem! They called the legislation the Servicemen's Readjustment Act of 1944. Everybody else called it the "G.I. Bill." It provided for tuition and modest living expenses for up to four years of college. Free!

The academic community was not happy. The president of the University of Chicago, Robert Maynard Hutchins, said of the G.I. Bill, "Colleges and universities will find themselves converted into hobo jungles . . . education is not a device for coping with mass unemployment." James B. Conant, president of Harvard was no more enthusiastic. He found the bill "distressing" because it failed "to distinguish between those who can profit most by advanced education and those who cannot."*

In spite of the protests of large segments of the academic world, by 1946 the veterans were going to college in record numbers. Instead of hobo jungles as feared by the learned Hutchins, quite the opposite occurred.

*Keith W. Olson, The G.I. Bill: The Veterans and the Colleges.

An article in *Life* by C.J.V. Murphy (June 17, 1946) about G.I.s at Harvard concluded that "for seriousness, perceptiveness, steadiness, and all the other undergraduate virtues, the veteran students were the best in Harvard's history." Benjamin Fine, education editor of *The New York Times* wrote in November 1947, ". . . here is the most astonishing fact in the history of American higher education . . . the G.I.s are hogging the honor rolls and Deans lists; they are walking away with the top marks in all of their courses. . . . Far from being an educational problem, the veteran has become an asset to higher education."

Ancient Bowdoin College on Maine's coast commandeered the barracks of a closed-down naval air station and housed its surplus students there, including Jim Morrison, one of your authors. Returning to Bowdoin from the war were old prep-school buddies who had since seen much of the world. Wooly Bermingham was still carrying some shrapnel picked up in the Battle of the Bulge. Jimmy Pierce was back out of the Navy and skating first team hockey. His sister Barbara had been a war bride who married a Yale sophomore cum Navy flier. The kid was shot down over the Pacific and through some miracle got picked up by a submarine. After the war he finished Yale on the G.I. Bill and moved Barbara and the kids to Texas. Some forty years later Jimmy Pierce was seated beside his sister Barbara when his brother-in-law, George, took the oath of office of president of the United States.

Ten years after the end of the war, 5,537,000 veterans had attended college under the G.I. Bill. And that number does not include the millions who opted for instruction in sheet metal, tool and die, steam fitting, auto mechanics, tire retreading, and tap dancing.

The ROI

At (distressed) Conant's Harvard, an ex-Army staff sergeant enrolled in the class of 1950. As a child, he had fled with his family from Nazi Germany to America in the early thirties and had gone to public school in New York City. Once out of the Army, and with Uncle and Aunt Sam footing the bill, he had decided to give fair Harvard a shot. He graduated *summa cum laude* in 1950 and in 1973 became Secretary of State of the United States of America. His name, of course, is Henry Kissinger. When Kissinger's brother was asked why he, Walter, had lost his German accent and Henry had not, Walter replied, "Because I'm the Kissinger who listens."

There were many other hotshots in the Harvard class of 1950, including James Schlesinger, later CIA director and secretary of defense, and Emory Houghton, president of Corning. They all entered the workforce at a moment in history when three-fourths of the world's GNP was generated by the United States.

The foregoing is not to suggest that this phenomenal economic power was generated entirely by the brains trained by the G.I. Bill. But it does suggest that there is a close correlation between learning and prosperity. It also suggests that when the government throws money at education—book learning, not "social engineering"—it is making a capital investment.

Moreover it gets its money back. In spades. The G.I. Bill is the intellectual Homestead Act of America. It did for our brains what the Homestead Act did for our brawn.

So, what's new about this? Whatsnew is that we have forgotten what was new.

Forget Whatsnew?

Ironically, the decade of the G.I. Bill is Newt Gingrich's favorite decade. If ever there was a time that money made a difference in the lives of individuals and in the vitality of the nation—this is it. Now the Gingrich-led strategy is to dismantle the role of government in education, to make it tougher for kids to secure college loans, to handicap the future. Why, based on the indisputable impact of the G.I. Bill, doesn't Dr. Gingrich propose a constitutional amendment guaranteeing every young American the right to a free government-financed education, or will a prayer amendment take care of everything?

There's nothing like a sudden plunge into the icy waters of an autumn pond to jump-start a sleepy body, and nothing like a half-hour with Lester Thurow to energize a flaccid mind. Thurow, of course, is the famed professor, economist, and former dean of MIT's Sloan School of Management, a Rhodes Scholar, and former staff member of the Council of Economic Advisers. Big time. But most of all he is seemingly free of ideological warp.

His December 1994 speech at Morningside College, in Sioux City, Iowa, the heartland of America, was a reality check for its students, and playing on C-Span offered cable viewers a rare chance to learn what we don't know about life in the coming century, and to contemplate the consequences of our present mind-set if we don't wise up. And quick!

Thurow said, "Every social system does some things well and some things badly. The communists ran lousy economies, but they ran very good education systems." He pointed out that the old Soviet Union turned out more scientists and engineers than the United States and that "many were [still are] world-class." He also hastened to add that in 1906 Massachusetts had the first universal compulsory public school system in the nation with the longest school year in the world. Like so much in American education, that is no longer true.

Thurow asked rhetorically: "What's the chance that if you're running a factory and you didn't change your quality standard for a hundred years you could still be world competitive?"

Retired Citicorp Chairman Walter Wriston echoes Thurow: "If we are to compete in a global marketplace we must constantly build and renew our intellectual capital. We have little or no control over the natural resources within our borders, but we do have control over our educational and cultural environment. The quality of education may be the most important way government can address productivity." And as long as we are throwing some heavy names around, none other than Peter Drucker has called information education the "primary material" of the new information-based economy.

Economists and globalists who take the broad view don't give us much wiggle room. In backyard American terms the picture is not as rosy as we would like. By 1994, the average working guy, with his wife bringing in a second income, had seen his income go down 23 percent in real terms, about 1 percent a year since 1973. At this rate, by the turn of the century it will be down close to a third. With the exception of the top 20 percent of American workers and college-educated females, wages are now falling for all groups, including graduate students. Thurow says that "Those

Russian scientists and engineers are putting pressure at the top on wages of the well educated, just the way the Chinese are putting pressure at the bottom on the wages of the not so well educated."

No one expects, political rhetoric aside, the conditions to change in favor of the average American in the immediate future. Yet it is clear as a mountain-spring stream that the skills that were sufficient to maintain a good wage twenty years ago are no longer adequate today. A renaissance in public education is an economic imperative!

Euripides warned long ago that "who neglects learning in his youth, loses the past and is dead for the future." So that's not new; whatsnew is our indifference as a nation, that "sleeping giant" indifference we talked about in Chapter 4. In this case, the alarm went off a generation ago and we've slept right through it.

However, there is some stirring in a growing number of communities and schools across the country. The whatsnew thinking that caught our attention is the systems dynamics approach being nurtured in Tucson, Arizona. Business readers may know this process as "systems thinking" or "the learning organization."

It is a method with a following in companies from Apple to Zenith. In the classroom version, it is a method and way of instruction that goes far beyond "content" to teach, coach, and facilitate learning by exploring the relevance of the content in the context of problem solving. It works equally as well in kindergarten as it does for twelfth-graders. But we are ahead of ourselves in the unfolding of this story—that often happens from the excitement that comes from whatsnew!

From Astronaut to Authority

The agent for the implementation of Jay Forrester's concept turned out to be one of his former students at MIT Peter Senge who had come to MIT intending to become an astronaut. Those dreams evaporated once he understood Professor Forrester's systems dynamics and the possibilities that discipline held for the guidance of troubled management.

Where Forrester's concept of systems dynamics embraced an analysis of highly complex systems through computer modeling, Senge would adopt a more informal mental-modeling method he came to call "systems thinking." Senge went on to write about this in his best selling book, *The Fifth Discipline*.

Senge and systems dynamics is a big whatsnew, especially in the salvation of our public schools. Ron Zarara of the Wilson High School in Portland, Oregon, told us that "There isn't a teacher I've met, who's learned this approach and tried it, who isn't enthusiastic. The level of retention, the ability of kids to carry the systems learning methods across the disciplines, their ability to take in more content, their level of problem solving and ability to construct mental models is powerful and effective."

If you have not read Senge's work, you may be asking, what is systems dynamics? To explain it in reductive terms and compress Senge's 424 pages into a phrase, it is "the discipline of seeing wholes." It applies equally to processes and people. This definition, then, casts any operational unit as a system, whether the system be a corporation, government, anthill, classroom, or a family trying to get along with one another. *Each* individual within the system, given an understanding of the system as a whole, is able to maximize his or her contribution to whatever the purpose of the system happens to be, whether that purpose be harmony, profits, learning, design, putting dinner on the table, or taking the garbage out.

Don't Die Disgraced, Part 1

"Well, one of my heroes is Andrew Carnegie. And Carnegie said, 'If I die wealthy I die disgraced.' So I've got a bit of a problem. I want to put it to good use, and if I can put it to as good use as Carnegie did by helping develop the library system in America, that would be very good." Stirring words spoken by Jim Waters, who has done in the field of chromatography what Andy Carnegie did in steel. Waters has made a good living by starting a company that manufactures liquid chromatographs, instruments used in the analysis of chemical mixtures.

Waters started his first company near Boston when he was twenty-two. Soon he became active on a local school board where he came to the simple belief that, if we did a good job educating youngsters, society would advance faster than if we did poor job of it. That is not a profound thought in itself, but how to go about it has seemingly stumped everyone.

Waters vowed that if he ever made enough money he would do something to help people in education. After a few false starts he became acquainted with MIT's Jay Forrester, whose pioneer work in systems dynamics he found intriguing. Waters was hooked. He told us, "Jay's work in systems dynamics is a technique for really understanding the enormous complexity of most problems. And I felt that in education we tend to simplify problems and to regard problems as simple cause and simple effect, all of which misleads children into thinking that is the way the world works."

Waters's original idea was to try to introduce systems dynamics at the college level, but he was dissuaded by Forrester, who made it clear that college is not a leading level for changing educational methods. It was Forrester's idea that a secondary school would be the best place to start.

Clearly, understanding the system as a whole is a *learning process*, and therein lies the connection between managing a global enterprise, a small business, or an entrepreneurial venture and learning seventh-grade science. This connection never became clearer than when I (Morrison) was scouting the location for a film I was about to shoot at the Orange Grove Middle School in Tucson, Arizona. The principal had let me into a noisy classroom where twenty or so seventh-graders were grouped in twos around an array of computers. I had been encouraged to ask any pair what they were doing, and the twelve-year-old towhead and the girl "partner" he was working with seemed somewhat irked that I was breaking their concentration. It turned out they had the assignment to find that ideal place in the four Southwestern states to locate a nuclear power plant, given the needs of the plant for water, distance from cities, requirements of terrain, workforce, seismic fault lines, emergency escape routes, and several other variables.

Hey! This was seventh grade! To arrive at an answer they were not just gathering facts, or what teachers call content. They were gathering and manipulating those facts to give meaning to the data. Meaning in their lives. These kids were thinking systematically and in doing so were finding that learning was an exciting experience.

The Orange Grove Experiment

The Orange Grove Experiment, for which I was about to start filming, had been underway for some years by the time I got there. What new principal Mary Scheetz
had found on her arrival a few years before was a typical junior high school in a
middle-class neighborhood with all the attendant problems of middle-class life in the
nineties. Orange Grove was also in the midst of bringing in sixth-graders and becoming a middle school, which meant creating a clearer definition of developmen-
tally appropriate instruction for eleven-, twelve-, and thirteen-year-old kids.

Word soon got out that change was fermenting at Orange Grove, which excited
the interest of a nearby neighbor of the school. He thereby presented himself to Mary
Sheetz with an offer to help as a self-described "citizen champion." The staff was
quick to recognize that here was a precious resource and Gordon Stanley Brown
quickly endeared himself to the entire staff. He was a gent in his young eighties,
borne by a cane and a will of steel, wearing the wisp of a white beard, speaking with
a sparkling clarity of mind and just a trace of his Australian origins. He had retired
to Tucson from Boston, well, Cambridge, where a building had been named in his
honor at MIT.

Brown's fame originated as one of the pioneers in feedback and servomechanisms,
those electromechanical gizmos that control autopilots and automatic devices. The
advances he made in that arcane science enabled our Navy in World War II to take
aim with uncanny accuracy. But the aim of taking aim was not the thing that fasci-
nated Gordon Brown or one of his prize pupils, one Jay Forrester. Yes, the same Jay
Forrester, one of whose prize pupils was Peter Senge of *The Fifth Discipline* systems
thinking fame. With the arrival of the computer in the fifties, and with the "what if"
simulations they could perform thereon, they could begin to understand for the first
time how complex systems worked *over time.*

How complex systems behave over time is a little-understood discipline, but
Brown and his MIT colleagues thought it might be a powerful way for young people
to learn. They realized that we live in a world of systems and that the basic operating
principles of a battleship gun's aiming system, given all of its maddening variables,
was little different from the social systems involved in operating a corporation or
classroom.

Twenty years after his encounter with Professor Forrester, Senge would author the
best seller that would send shock waves through many a Fortune 500 and government bureaucracy. As Senge has written:

> *Jay [Forrester] maintained that the causes of many pressing public issues, from
> urban decay to global ecological threat, lay in the very well intentioned policies
> designed to alleviate them. These problems were "actually systems" that lured policy
> makers into interventions that focused on obvious symptoms, not underlying causes,
> which produced short term benefit, but long term malaise, and fostered the need for
> still more symptomatic interventions.*

So when Brown introduced Forrester and Senge to the Orange Grove group, a
yeasty intellectual ferment began. It was first of all collegial, voluntary, all-inclusive,
and void of dogma, excepting that the school would be viewed by faculty, staff, and
students as a system whose function was—get this—*not to teach, but to learn how
to learn.*

But Can I Chew Gum in Class?

The staff was open and ready for a new vision for their school. But first, a particular concern for the new principal was the number of youngsters in "detention" on any given day—those youngsters being punished for any number of school regulations by the loss of their freedom during the lunch hour. Before a new system could work, new approaches to management were required to deal with old problems.

She attacked the problem with a method she called "walking and talking," by which she meant that most of her working hours were spent doing just that—walking and talking. Principal Scheetz spent little time in her office shuffling papers or summoning subordinates. The Orange Grove staff approached the problem by paying close attention to the systemic causes of behavioral problems and went about restructuring classroom and campus situations in ways that were likely to produce positive behavior.

They threw out a lot of the old rules, finding that the enforcement of petty prohibitions tended to sap a teacher's energy, which would otherwise be focused on teaching and learning. For example, the prohibition against chewing gum was tossed out. However, a kind of "contract" between staff and students was worked out to replace the old rule, creating a situation likely to produce positive behavior. Kids came to understand that chewing gum was a privilege and that enjoying the privilege required acceptance of responsibility for it. This included properly disposing of the gum when it became used up. So, if you happen to be in sixth grade science class when a kid decided to rid himself of worn-out Juicy Fruit, instead of a furtive under-the-desk disposal, there was apt to be a florid display of the wad being wrapped in paper and slam-dunked into the wastebasket.

The behavioral result? The detention problem that existed at the outset gradually subsided. And the process created a "creed" that addressed these matters on an ongoing basis. The creed is one simple rule: "Show respect for yourself and others."

This simple idea had power: Ask any sixth-grader at Orange Grove. Or better still, ask any kid's parent. The transformation didn't happen overnight, but happen it did. It continues today, seven years later.

A Yeasty Intellectual Ferment

Scheetz was lucky in that most of the staff was made up of many dedicated teaching professionals who were open to experiment, change, radical ideas—whatsnew. School boards are apt to be power centers with conflicting agendas and a passion for micromanagement, but members were kept informed, involved, and contributing. What was even more powerful was the attitude of kids whose parents were school-board members: Their own children were walking proof that something exciting was going on at Orange Grove School. Whoever heard of sixth-graders who couldn't wait to get to school.

How is Orange Grove different from the P.S. 38 we're more familiar with?

It is not apparent. At first, anyway. Noisier than most perhaps. You see the usual smiling braces, florid zits, fuzz mustaches, and bobbing heads topped by billed caps. They're American kids.

It's not until you corner a youngster and get one to open up about the science, math, or English class that you realize these young people are learning how to assemble factual information and fit it into the world they are living in. They learn by working with computer models and becoming involved in simulations of the real world. They often work in pairs, partners, so that they help each other learn, while at the same time they sharpen their listening skills. This is based on the belief that learning is a social phenomenon and that learning takes place as kids learn to cooperate with each other in problem solving.

Here is another example of structuring the system to enhance a learning environment. In a seventh-grade math class, a boy and girl might be partners who are given a hypothetical credit card with a credit limit. They then must "live" on the budget, buying whatever their imagined needs are, and maintain a payment schedule, using percentages, adding and subtracting decimals, prorating compound interest, and paying penalties. They even "get fired" and are faced with the dilemma of maintaining good credit in view of that adversity.

It's fun to watch. One has only to imagine how much fun it is to learn.

Learning Respect

The nicest thing about cooperative learning

is that it begins to instill respect of one

child to another child. They begin to learn

how to criticize ideas and not people.

Frank Draper, science teacher

Walk into any classroom and sooner or later you were bound to hear kids "dialoguing" (a Senge word you'll hear in corporate rooms as well) with one another about the causal loop, which is the new phrase for "cycles in nature," or negative and positive feedback. One class I caught took on the task of making a computer model of the plot of the novel *Animal Farm*, doing "what if" simulations of how George Orwell's story would be changed by introducing varying interventions. In another class you could watch students use computer models of how the body system works, about predator/prey relationships.

The class we used to call "civics" held mock jury trials or town meetings to discuss raising the mill levy to rebuild city hall. And it played the "soda game," which is the suds-free variation on the "beer game," a famous teaching exercise used at MIT's Sloan School of management.

But all of these devices would be mere gloss if it were not for the institution's bedrock social contract with itself: show respect for yourself and others. This simple rule does not invite mere compliance. It insists on a deep commitment by teachers, staff, and students alike, who have created an environment for the development of what they call their "shared vision"—a systemic view of the whole institution, and the role of each individual in making it function properly.

Don't ask what the vision is: It is still evolving. It consists of an ongoing dialogue in a special room lined with butcher paper. At least once a month the gang sort of gathers in this room around a brown-bag lunch and to an outsider it sounds like a lot of jabbering back and forth. But what is happening in all this jawboning is an ongoing process of clarification of the vision that the Orange Grove people share. When a nifty idea emerges

Don't Die Disgraced, Part 2

It is strange how like minds find each other, even across that vast distance between the skyscrapers of Boston and the saguaro cactus of Tucson, Arizona. For it happened at that moment, Gordon Brown, former Dean of Engineering at MIT, now in his eighties and retired in Tucson, told Frank Draper, a smart young teacher at a nearby middle school, about a new computer programming language called STELLA; a computer program based on systems dynamics which allows students to create models of real life situations on the computer.

Draper tried the program in his classroom, found that it helped kids learn, and Jim Waters was there with a modest grant to expand the program, add mentors, and help teachers at the Orange Grove school to learn to apply systems dynamics. Waters's contributions have gradually increased over the years, and programs have expanded to now include Tucson high schools and other middle and elementary schools.

As Waters says, "We like to jump on a moving train. When someone is already doing something, and we can help them with a little money and advice, then we become catalysts to see if the train can be made to move further and faster."

somebody gets up and Magic-Markers it on the butcher-papered wall. Gordon Brown might show up, or a parent, plus the secretaries, the nurse, and most of the faculty. The janitor floats in and out and all understand they are important participants in a learning system and are striving to improve, clarify, and refine the system.

Mary Scheetz is there. Always. She does not preside. She is merely first among equals.

You seldom hear derisive laughter or cynical retorts in classrooms. Mindful of the "show respect" rule, kids are continually made aware that derision adversely affects systems dynamics. The put-down or the abrupt dismissal of another's idea is not tolerated. Even the shy kid ventures forth with a contribution because it's a setting where all understand that success depends upon an appreciation of the value of everyone in the system.

Even Art Caldwell's job as janitor is clear. He and the principal have often worked side by side serving kids in the lunchroom. Because the students understand the importance of his job in keeping the place clean and orderly, the liberal chewing gum rule has been successful, out of respect for Mr. Caldwell.

Teaming to Learn

What they call "teaming" is of special importance at Orange Grove. By teaming, they mean that teachers meet frequently and exchange information to exploit opportunities for cross-discipline learning. Thus if the science teacher is about to approach the solar system, the history teacher might assign some work on Kepler or Copernicus. And while they are meeting, the teams take note of problems that might beset one or another student: a divorce in the offing, a child's cat gets run over, or a worry about having to move away.

Finally, there's a thing called "advisor base." It takes the place of the old "home room" idea. Under this system, a new sixth-grader coming into school is met by his adviser, a teacher who will be his "home room" adviser for the three years he will be at Orange Grove. So, when the kid arrives at his "home room" he meets not only new kids like himself, but old-timers; that is, seventh- and eighth-graders who are in the same adviser base. It's their job to look after the younger kids. Know them, respect them. It's part of the systematic effort at Orange Grove to break down age barriers. "We know that kids who do not make a contribution every single day begin to lose any reason for going to school. An adviser base is one more way for kids to make a meaningful contribution," says Frank Draper.

The daily adviser base period is a time for any and everyone in the base to have something to say about whatsnew in school, at home, or in the outside world. Some days it's good for a lot of laughs. Some days it's an insight into world events that would make a congressman sit up and take note. Other days they must deal with sadness of one kind or another—the loss of a pet, a calamity in the neighborhood, a sudden death in a family. By the time a student walks across the stage to graduate, each adviser will have seen him or her through three years of growth, change, and maturity.

As Jim Waters might say, "That's a train worth jumping on!"

The Endless Pursuit of Whatsnew

Now we come full circle, back to Jim Waters's role model, Andrew Carnegie, who in 1905 founded the Carnegie Foundation for the Advancement of Teaching as a national policy center devoted to the strengthening of America's colleges and schools. A year after it was founded, it was incorporated by an act of Congress.

The seventh and current president of the Foundation is Dr. Ernest L. Boyer, Commissioner of Education in the Carter administration and former Chancellor of the State University of New York. He has directed some of the foundation's landmark studies on education, including the alarming report on the deteriorating quality of high schools in America published in 1983, and the more recent report in 1991 called, *Ready to Learn: A Mandate for the Nation*, which focuses on childhood learning from prebirth to kindergarten and the critical necessity to focus on children's physical, social, emotional, and moral development.

A companion report, *The Basic School: A Community for Learning,* was issued in 1992. What struck us about the report is that many of its recommendations are operational in Tucson and a growing number of other school systems around the country, including a dozen or so pilot schools that are directly associated with the Carnegie Foundation's Basic Schools program. So our biggest fear about a lot of whatsnew reports—that they simply get shelved or put on the back-burner—has not materialized. That in itself is a significant whatsnew!

Here from the report's Introduction, is the context for *The Basic School* report:

> *The world has changed and schools must change, too. The lives of children who enroll in school today will span a new century. If, in the days ahead, educators cannot help students to become literate and well informed, if the coming generation cannot be helped to see beyond the confines of their own lives, the nation's prospects for the future will be dangerously diminished.*

The concept of a "basic school" is what we saw in operation in Tucson: it is based in the community (not just teacher-dependent), based on the fundamentals (language and core knowledge), and based on learning techniques that work (best practices). In basic schools teachers are leaders (Draper and colleagues), parents are partners, and the school operates off a shared comprehensive vision that includes everyone (Sheetz's priority).

We talked with Dale Coye, a fellow at the Carnegie Foundation, about the value and meaning of education, the burden that education carries—to solve *all* the problems of the world—the relationship of learning to living, and the expectations for the future competitiveness of the nation. Coye is not only a fellow at the foundation, but a parent with teenagers. So he is reminded daily about the need to connect theory to reality.

Coye talked some about "empty exercises" and the misdirected content of much of the learning in schools. (It reminded us of the study we described in Chapter 4, in which the Minnesota Public School System identified 68 percent of a teacher's time being spent on activities unrelated to learning.) However, his enthusiasm for the "basic school" concept was contagious and he, in turn, was equally excited about learning about the stuff in Tucson. We both got excited about whatsnew! As we inquired about how to get the Carnegie Foundation's full report,* he caught our attention when he underscored the Whatsnew Force by pointing out that education is, in the final analysis, the pursuit of the ideal. That, he said, "is something that we are always working toward."

---

*All Carnegie Foundation reports are available by writing them at 5 Ivy Lane, Princeton, New Jersey 08540

Whatsnew Fake Sheet

Whatsnew is the last of the seven cultural forces and it is closely related to the other forces: It is all about what is happening now (🕐); it generates more choices (☑) from which to dream and scheme (⤳); and things that are bigger (▮) and faster (🕐) are by definition new. The magnitude of the force, once defined by machines, is now measured by information. For example, in 1950, 73 percent of the American workforce was in manufacturing; today, only 15 percent is. Each day, over twelve thousand articles are generated to keep us all informed of something new and not too long ago there were only three TV channels and fifteen minutes of national news. Today there are hundreds of channels and entire networks devoted to bringing us the news—twenty-four hours a day with more on the way.

★ Constant search for New Potential Identities. New Potential Identities, like so much else that defines Americans, are usually self-generated, spontaneous, often out-of-the-blue possibilities or an expansion of current reality. They propel us forward and enable us constantly to renew ourselves. Unlike an orchestrated career path, the New Potential Identity is general in nature, without a specific plan how to make it happen. It doesn't have to be pursued, but it pulls us forward, inextricably. On the other hand, it can linger, change, vanish, or come back as an impossible dream. New Potential Identities apply equally to individuals and companies (see page 276).

★ Fads are part of whatsnew. While fads, often referred to as "flavor-of-the-month" programs, are, by definition, something new, they should not be confused with fundamental shifts in management. The shift from brawn to brain competitiveness is one such shift that we have been undergoing for the past decade or so. Today, the average consumer wears more computing power on his wrist than existed in the entire world before 1961. TQM, or Total Quality Management, is another fundamental shift. Though once labeled a fad, TQM and its derivative acronyms, are the foundational givens of any successful enterprise (see page 268).

★ Relationship management comes easier to women. Women should be more fully engaged in the design, development, and management of all aspects of any business that is relationship-based. This is not a gender thing, but a cultural reality in American life. American men, in general, are more *transaction-oriented*; American women, in general, are more *relationship-oriented*. By contrast, European and Asian men are much more relationship-oriented than American men—by a long shot. American women have a higher tolerance for ambiguity, open-endedness, listening, and processing words and context. Men have a narrower focus, are more time-driven, and bring logic and precision to the process (see page 269). Herein lies a powerful competitive advantage for an American corporation. Rather than starting with a culturally conditioned, transaction-oriented man and expecting that "some training" will unschool his patterns of communication and interaction, begin instead with women, who automatically function at the higher-context level.

The investment of "some training" here will reinforce desirable patterns of communication, rather than try to change them.

★ Training on American cultural forces is available at Disney University. A training program that incorporates much of what we write about in this book, and, conveniently called THE STUFF AMERICANS ARE MADE OF, is being taught at Disney University in Orlando. The *Stuff* training program is basically a two-day, facilitated workshop that provides participants with three new integrated business basics: the role of national culture in performance improvement; tools for personalizing quality and productivity; and a process for aligning people *and* process. Companies like General Motors, FedEx, AT&T, Aetna Health Plans, Kellogg, Hewlett-Packard, and the Walt Disney Company itself have started using the programs and designing ways to integrate the cultural forces into their process improvement efforts, with compelling results.

America is the land of whatsnew and perpetual renewal. No one is held back by class or status and individuals and corporations can become anything they want to at any time. With the transformation of work from brawn to brain, new potential identities are endless for everyone.

The American Lego
Kid Revisited

Business books aren't like novels: The plot doesn't thicken and you don't have to wait until the end to find out whodunit. As far as we are concerned, the Pilgrims gave it all away in Chapter 1: The seven cultural forces that define Americans took root in the years and decades following 1620. They got locked-in and here we are today, more or less following the same script.

A few years back, when Joel Barker and others were introducing the idea of paradigms, we were in attendance at a general business conference and everyone seemed to be saying "paradigm shift" about as frequently as some speakers say, "and ah." During a break, the fellow next to us reached into his pocket, pulled out some change, selected two dimes and put them on our worktable. He said, "Do you know what this is?" In short order, one of us said, "Two dimes," then catching his drift, added, "A-pair-a-dimes."

He grinned as he moved them around a bit and then asked, "Now what do I have?" "A-pair-a-dimes-that-you-have-moved-around?" I said. Then with a sudden slight grin, which Hammond's son gets when he's about to deliver one of his endless puns, the fellow said, "A-pair-a-dimes-shift."

What this lacks in sophistication it makes up for in simplicity. Our observation is that we have complicated too many things in business. There are too many principles, procedures, processes, policies, and pair-a-dimes. Volumes of personnel and customer procedure manuals exist, when one rule would suffice: Treat your employees the way you want them to treat the customer. Quality improvement, the most important competitive business strategy, has fourteen steps (Deming, et al.). Yet on average most of us can only remember seven of anything.* We are like the jazz musicians in Chapter 6, looking for a fake sheet, anything that will boil it down to just a few things we really need to focus on, so that we can improvise from there on out.

So we'll try to keep this simple, and under seven points.

1. Cultural forces aren't going to change. As the venerable Walter Cronkite used to say at the end of each day's TV newscast, "And that's the way it is." Unlike the tree in the forest that may or may not make a sound if no one is there to hear it, the seven cultural forces are present whether we activate them or not. Unlike the volatility of opinions, the cultural forces are not going to change. So use them with confidence and assurance—they will be around for a very long time.

We didn't plan it that way, honest. But that is why there are seven digits to a telephone number and virtually all advertising themes or slogans are seven words or less.

Throughout the book we have tried to show how activating these forces can substantially increase quality, productivity, and profitability. We admit that CEOs don't stand up and say, "Okay, let's now use, Cultural Force #4" (and probably still wouldn't even if this book were read in every executive suite in America). However, when Larry Bossidy, CEO at Allied Signal chose speed—#4, the Now Force—as a corporate value, the company was able to train 95,000 employees in 18 months— half the time it took Xerox, the benchmark company in corporate training, to accomplish the same thing. And Allied Signal is now undergoing a second training process to cut out 70 percent of *each* employee's non-value-added work!

Numerous other examples abound, including Disney's ability to link technology to the Dream Force (Chapter 2) and Hewlett-Packard's activating the Whatsnew Force (Chapter 7) to generate two-thirds of its $30 billion annual revenue from products made within the past two years. And we've described how other companies like Home Depot, 3M, FedEx, Levi Strauss & Co., the Ritz-Carlton Hotel Company, Johnson & Johnson, and others have connected business strategy and growth to one or more of the seven cultural forces.

Conscious use of the cultural forces works; they produce astounding business results.

2. Americans are improvisers, first. There is nothing we can or should change about that American kid we described at the beginning of the book. That wanton disregard for the instruction booklet, that inventive mind, that improvising spirit, and that patented impatience with time makes us uniquely American. That's what produced Thomas Edison, Frederick Douglass, Elizabeth Peabody, Henry Ford, Maya Angelou, Andrew Carnegie, Upton Sinclair, Sandra Day O'Connor, Dick Fosbury, George Lucas, Jonas Salk, Alfred P. Sloan, Fred Smith, and you and me.

The American Lego–kid attitude is in us and never goes away. As Americans, we are not rule followers. We have, in the words of James Fallows, "a talent for *disor-*der." Our Constitution, the oldest written one in the world, is about principle, leaving us to argue, negotiate, fight, and compromise about interpretation and application. And argue we do.

Like the Lego kid, we see beyond the constraints of others; we want to create by stretching the rules and improvise by changing the object of the game. Through our impatient impatience, we discover whatsnew. For better and worse, it is part of our nature. It is what has given us a century of unprecedented progress to stand on as we plunge headlong into the next millennium.

This stuff is uniquely American, and it works equally as well for personnel training, corporate communications, planning, marketing, sales, and manufacturing, as it does for R&D, customer relationship development, and quality improvement.

3. Narrow the gap between culture and business. About one in four readers of this book will have concluded by now that this American culture stuff is maybe interesting, but not relevant. In a group or in a company, we call this general reaction to any new idea, the *drag*-factor. We don't take this reaction personally—this *drag*-factor shows up in most of the survey work we have done, especially around employees and their attitude toward new ideas and procedures. As consultants and communicators, we have come to expect this. Nevertheless, it has a profound *drag* on a business and major implications for productivity.

As best we can tell, every new work strategy or process, every training program or lecture has this dimension. Approximately 25 percent of a given group—workers, customers, managers, suppliers—see no value to what is being said or proposed. Any company that can get that figure down into single digits has unleashed an enormous source of energy and reduced the *drag* on the organization. The *Stuff* pilot training program at Packard Electric was able to get the *drag* factor down from 22 percent prior to the training program to just 9 percent afterward. And, as we reported earlier, productivity tripled for one critical activity and quality increased twofold over the conventional improvement practice in the company.

We often end many of our workshops with the following table. See Snapshot #24. It is a contrast between ideal business expectations and the broader cultural realities that often hamper or adversely impact expectations. This is not a list of value judgments, but an overview of the clash between two competing realities—narrower business expectations butting up against unconscious cultural dynamics.

The challenge is to begin to think about how to reconcile conventional expectations and practices with the reality of the cultural forces at play in American society at large. For starters, just acknowledging the differences and consciously managing with these competing dynamics in mind will result in new approaches, new strategies, new ways of doing things. How can the popular executive notion of quality as a "journey" be turned into a series of short, exciting trips, ideally of a few month intervals? What would reengineering look like with an emphasis on people rather than on process? How can variations can be introduced into process to engage workers?

Cultural forces are not checked at factory doors or executive offices: they imbue everything we do. Therefore, they should be activated to enhance, rather than inhibit, business performance.

4. Engage employees. American executives are looking for a silver bullet management strategy that can get the job done quickly. The urgency is understandable—it's one of the forces. However, there is a serious problem with the metaphor. This silver bullet expectation is no doubt a generational hangover from the days when one masked guy (on a white horse, of course) and his Indian sidekick could solve a town's problems in twenty-seven minutes in your living room to the tune of Rossini's *William Tell Overture*.

As choice-insistent as Americans are, it is surprising how single-minded executives and managers tend to be when it comes to choices about how to engage American workers. "One-way" thinking, "no-way" responses to alternative strategies, and "my-way" execution is a deadly silver bullet strategy—pun intended.

What is the best way to motivate people to increase quality and productivity? What strategies have you tried? What success have you had? And what approach do you think most American workers would prefer, given a choice? If you were to guess, what percentage of your employees would choose each of the four ideas listed below? And what breakdown would you expect in the American workforce as a whole? Rank, in order, your personal choices and mark what you think most Americans choose.

❏ Let employees do more
❏ Pay them more
❏ Give them more recognition
❏ Listen to their ideas

Snapshot #24

Comparison of Business
Expectations with Cultural Reality

Conventional Business Practice	American Culture Dynamics
do it right the first time	fail, try again
zero defects	fix it
reduce variation	increase variation
conformance to specifications	improvise
continuous improvement	breakthrough
customer is right	I'm right
A+ (excellence)	C+ (average, get by)
team	individual
process improvement	personal improvement
journey	now!
extrinsic values	intrinsic values

How certain are you about the choices you made for your employees and direct reports? Are they specific to your industry? How much variation is there when you think of the nation as a whole? On what basis did you make your choices? Experience? Intuition? Personal preference? Existing management and compensation practices? All of the preceding?

Too many questions for a chapter that is suppose to have answers—quick answers? Here are the results from a national survey conducted by Gallup for ASQC a few years back. Half the American workforce chose either the first or last option: 33 percent said, "let me do more to put my ideas in action," and an additional 17 percent said, "listen to my ideas for improvement." In other words, what half the workers in America are really saying is, "Value me as a person; give me an opportunity to do more, to contribute. I can make a difference."

Remember our values ladder in Chapter 5: employees connect "making a difference" with their highest personal values—"personal fulfillment, accomplishment, peace of mind."

Less than a third, 27 percent, said, "pay me more." But as numerous companies that have gone down this pay-me-more trail have discovered, there is no lasting satisfaction in this approach. More is never enough (see Chapter 3).

The balance of workers, 19 percent, said "give me more recognition."* One could safely combine them with the "value me" group, because in effect they are saying, "I have already made an effort, and if you simply recognized it, I would do more on that basis alone." Positive feedback and celebration beget more improvement.

Note what is not *on the list.* No one said buy new equipment, provide more training, improve working conditions, update processes, or other options that would

---

If you are one of those who takes nothing at face value, you'll have noticed in adding up these numbers that the total comes to just 96 percent: 4 percent did not respond to the survey.

require technology or capital outlays. With the exception of those who wanted more money, practically three out of every four chose an option that simply says, "Pay attention to me as an individual and let me at it." This individual focus, this need to make a difference, this personalization of quality and improvement, are unique to Americans. Imagine what could happen if we managed our businesses to take advantage of these American strengths.

Engage your employees through the cultural forces. Americans are intrinsically motivated; they want to make a difference personally—that is something they treasure and when you tap into those personal beliefs and values, you strengthen your company, community, and country.

5. Within three months, things can change. As we documented in Chapter 4, the majority of Americans expect things to change within a few months. Remember how an Ernst & Young office, with a goal of 6,000 new billable tax hours, reached 11,040 within three months by combining stretch goal thinking (the Dream Force) with the Now Force?

The key was personal control and participation. As we have outlined above in point 4, the majority of American workers are set to go and want to make a personal difference. What are you waiting for?

There are two ways to get started. One is to call 407-828-5611 and inquire about the Disney University offering of the *Stuff* training program. Or pretend the models in Snapshots #25 and 26 are Lego instructions and *have at them!*

We ran across it in a useful book, with practical advice on how to deal with different cultures, called *GlobalWork: Bridging Distance, Culture & Time.** It contained a useful model that is applicable here.

Snapshot #25 is the model as we saw it in *GlobalWork*. This model is known as the seven-step "arc" model or "sky-to-ground-to-sky" metaphor. Snapshot #26 is our adaptation of this model to the seven cultural forces—in other words, we "Lego-ized" it.

These models say something you may already know, but bear reviewing. They are the progression of logical steps for the adaptation of a new process or idea. One is the theory, the other a LEAP map for the seven cultural forces. Hopefully, like the folks at Kellogg (Chapter 6) or Aetna Health Plans (in Chapter 7), the cultural forces idea resonates with you and now you want to try them—on your own. The authors of *GlobalWork* point out that this seven-step model is the "simplest way" to show the process. They say, "People have to get their heads out of the clouds and their feet on the ground before they can leap into action—let alone be creative enough to build a plane that actually allows them to fly."

The Lego-ized version starts with either the Dream Force (Chapter 2) and/or the New Potential Identity (Chapter 7). Get a general idea in mind about where you want to land.[†] Remember you are going to want to engage others in the process (item 3 above) and they will have important contributions to make. Then make choices about which of the seven cultural forces you want to activate—*improvise* to fix or invent

---

*The authors, Mary O'Hara-Devereaux and Robert Johansen, cite the work of David Sibbet, who has had more than twenty-five years adapting the process model work of cosmologist and inventor Arthur M. Young to organizations. Sibbet's book, Graphic Guide to Facilitation, Principles and Practice, spells it all out further.

†Remember that "Where do you want to land" is the "L" in the LEAP model in Chapter 2.

Snapshot #25

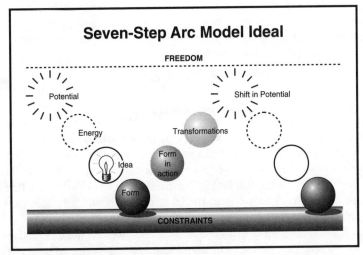

Source: Adapted from *Global Work: Bridging Distance, Culture and Time*, Institute for the Future.

Snapshot #26

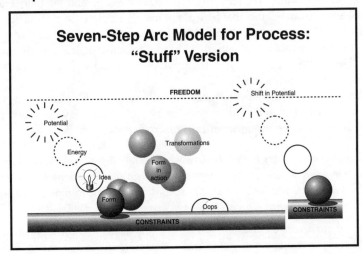

something, *now* to do it faster, *big* to grow the business, *oops* to learn from a mistake, and *whatsnew* to keep it going.

Keep in mind that most Americans expect things to move along quickly—three months is the optimum time. And remember that bias for action is likely to kick in just before you start checking to make sure the t's have been crossed. Unlike the seven-arc model, multiple tries are in order and the pace quickens for Americans; we want that breakthrough, that home run that clears the fence with miles to spare.

Americans will also break the mold of the model and see potential in another idea or process before the work is done. Like all the companies that we have written about in this book, keep that goal (dream, target, obsession) moving as well.

Do as the American Lego kid does: Follow your *American* instincts—get impatient. Take all the ideas, examples, and resources in this book, dream something up, mess with them a little, then invent something to your own liking, and add it. Don't be too concerned with it coming out right the first time. Try again. Remember, Americans love to improvise!

SOME FIRST WORDS

We made a conscious choice to not de Tocqueville the book. We also decided to wait until the end of our writing to revisit him and see how closely our research converged with his observations. He spent *only* nine months visiting America (from May 11, 1831, to February 20, 1832), and then in less than a year he published the first of his two volumes, *Democracy in America*. He did this all on his own without the conveniences and technology we have as observers and cowriters today.

Although working at other tasks and assignments, we, the authors, gathered our research over a five-year period of time and took about the same amount of time as de Tocqueville to get this book written and published. Would that it would endure as long.

Author and historian Daniel J. Boorstin, writing in an introduction to *Democracy in America* in 1990 said, "Tocqueville's distinctive message and the unique appeal of his book came from the fact that he was not merely an alert traveler, an acute student of politics and society. His book endures because he had the vision of a historian for the history-making events of his time, which still leave their mark on ours. . . . The enduring popularity of Tocqueville's book is itself an omen of the vitality of democracy in America."

The convergence of Tocqueville's insights with our analysis of the seven cultural forces is a happy and ennobling discovery for us, and a great way, we think, to end our book. Here are some examples of the numerous convergences:

> *I think that in no country in the civilized world is less attention paid to philosophy than in the United States. The Americans have no philosophical school of their own, and they care but little for all the schools into which Europe is divided, the very names of which are scarcely known to them.*
>
> *Yet it is easy to perceive that almost all the inhabitants of the United States use their minds in the same manner, and direct them according to the same rules; they have a philosophical method common to the whole person. . . . The Americans, then, have found no need of drawing philosophical method out of books; they have found it in themselves . . .*
>
> *Democratic people do not bother at all about the past, but they gladly start dreaming about the future, and in that direction their imagination knows no bounds, but spreads and grows beyond measure . . .*
>
> *The American lives in a land of wonders; everything around him is in constant movement, and every movement seems an advance. Consequently, in his mind the idea of newness is closely linked with that of improvement. Nowhere does he see any limit placed by nature to human endeavor; in his eyes something which does not exist is just something that has not been tried yet . . .*

The universal movement prevailing in the United States, the frequent reversals of fortune, and the unexpected shifts in public and private wealth all unite to keep the mind in a sort of feverish agitation which wonderfully disposes it toward every type of exertion and keeps it, so to say, above the common level of humanity. For an American the whole of life is treated like a game of chance, a time of revolution, or the day of a battle . . .

These same causes working simultaneously on every individual finally give an irresistible impulse to the national character. Choose any American at random, and he should be a man of burning desires, enterprising, adventurous, and, above all, an innovator. The same bent affects all he does; it plays a part in his politics, his religious doctrines, his theories of social economy, and his domestic occupations; he carries it with him into the depths of the backwoods as well as into the city's business . . .

Every man see changes continually taking place. Some make things worse, and he understands only too well that no people and no individual, however enlightened he be, is ever infallible. Others improve his lot, and he concludes that man in general is endowed with an indefinite capacity for improvement. His setbacks teach him that no one has discovered absolute good; his successes inspire him to seek it without slackening. Thus, searching always, falling, picking himself up again, often disappointed, never discouraged, he is ever striving toward that immense grandeur glimpsed indistinctly at the end of the long track humanity must follow . . .

Appendix: Background Information & Research Methodologies

This appendix is for the research curious, for those more interested in the how's than the what's, and for those who may be contemplating similar studies. It provides background information on some of the new research that we report on in this book, describes some of the methodologies that were used, and provides additional research findings to help illustrate the reach of a particular methodology.

As indicated at the outset, this book carries the same title as a training program being offered nationwide by the American Society for Quality Control (ASQC) through Disney University's Professional Development Programs in Orlando, Florida. The *Stuff* training program (as we will refer to it for clarification throughout this Appendix) deals with American culture and its application to quality and process improvement. It rests largely on the work of Clotaire Rapaille at Archetype Studies, Inc., and the work of Art Miller at People Management, Inc. By contrast, *The Stuff Americans Are Made Of* book is broader in its research scope, and we address a wider range of business issues. It is inclusive of other research, commentary, and analysis. The book also draws heavily on the authors' own independent research and extensive experience in government, business, advertising, and education.

Background

The *Stuff* training program was one of three primary initiatives of the American Quality Foundation (AQF), the first think tank on quality management, founded by ASQC in 1987. Robert Stempel, president of General Motors Corporation at the time of the formation of AQF, served as the organizing and permanent chairman of this independent, executive-directed foundation. Josh Hammond served as the founding president and managed the research activities of AQF.

The other two primary initiatives of AQF were the International Quality Study with Ernst & Young (see *Business Week*'s cover story on quality, November 30, 1992, that features the study, and *The Wall Street Journal*, May 14, 1992) and the American Customer Satisfaction Index with the University of Michigan Business School (see *Fortune*'s double-feature story on the ACSI, December 11, 1995).* After the foundation had completed the initial research and development of its chartered programs, AQF's operations where folded into ASQC in 1994.

*A six-part report on the IQS and details on the ACSI are available directly from ASQC by calling 800-248-1946 or 414-272-8575 or writing ASQC, 611 East Wisconsin Avenue, P. O. Box 3005, Milwaukee, WI 53201-3005.

The research and development programs of AQF were each sponsored by various corporations or a consortium of corporations. The formative research for the *Stuff* program was made possible by a challenge grant from General Motors Corporation and the following corporate partners: AT&T, The Walt Disney Company, Ernst & Young, MBNA America, Met Life, and NYNEX. The following corporate sponsors also contributed to and participated in the development of the program: Hyatt Hotels & Resorts, Intel Corporation, 3M, New York Life, Star Enterprise, and U.S. Healthcare. A follow-on study, launched by AQF, was completed by ASQC and sponsored by The Walt Disney Company, General Motors, Kellogg Company, and Eastman Kodak.

Research & Methodology

The research for the *Stuff* program consists primarily of four qualitative studies, three quantitative surveys, two formal pilot projects, and several informal project applications. Most of the qualitative studies were conducted by Archetype Studies, Inc., an international marketing firm that specializes in cultural archetype research. They conducted studies on "what quality means to Americans," in 1986 for AT&T,* on "what improvement means to Americans," in 1991 for AQF, and on "what teamwork means to Americans," in 1995 for ASQC. The Wirthlin Group, a strategic opinion research firm, also conducted a qualitative study on quality and improvement in 1992 for AQF. The quantitative surveys were conducted by the Gallup Organization in 1990 and 1993 for ASQC and by The Wirthlin Group in 1992 for AQF. All the quantitative surveys have the industry standard margin of error (plus or minus three or four percentage points) attributable to sampling and other random effects. (Josh Hammond participated in the design and management of all but the AT&T studies).

Clotaire Rapaille, founder and chairman of Archetype Studies, Inc., was the principal investigator for the formative research (archetype) studies. He is a French-born and -educated cultural anthropologist, a student of Carl Jung, Konrad Lorenz, and Jean Piaget. Rapaille uses a sophisticated focus group methodology that relies on a highly structured, three-hour session he calls an "imprinting" session. In these sessions he and his associates are not interested in what is said, per se (see the opinion level of the chart on page 12), but in the formative and reinforcing emotional experiences with the subject being studied. (We described one such study on page 18, the sidebar about doors and what security means to Americans.) Rapaille's studies focus primarily on each participant's first, most important, and most recent experience with the subject being studied. These three experiences are written down and analyzed later for content and structure.

The content, which can essentially be identified by the nouns in the stories, is disregarded: It is not important to the final analysis. For example, it doesn't matter if the first experience with a door was in a house at the end of a cul-de-sac in the suburbs, on a farm, or in a mid-town high-rise. Nor does it matter if your most recent experience with quality was with a toy, at a plant, or on a Friday afternoon. Those are content issues and highly variable.

What remains in the written experiences is the structure—the feelings, the nature of the experience. The structure is found primarily in the verbs, adjectives, adverbs

---

For details on the AT&T study and additional background on the archetype research and methodology, read Incredibly American: Releasing the Heart of Quality, by Marilyn R. Zuckerman and Lewis J. Hatala.

used to describe the event. It is found in the sequence of activities and the description of the emotions that were felt throughout the stages of the experience. For example, feeling *trapped* or *abandoned* behind a *closed* door or, with respect to quality, *failing* to live up to someone's expectations and being *embarrassed* about it. The structure provides the framework from which the discoveries of cultural archetypes are drawn. Unlike most focus groups that rely on what people say, imprinting groups uncover the emotional and unconscious dimensions of the subject being studied.

Each study is conducted through a minimum of ten separate sessions with approximately twenty-five people who must meet three rigid criteria: (1) be born in the country that is being studied (U.S.A. in the case of the studies referenced above); (2) the mother that raised the participant must speak the primary language of the country (English in this case); and (3) the participant must have lived continuously in that country for the first fifteen years of his or her life (continental U.S.A. in this case). In others words, if a participant was born in Canada to English speaking parents and moved to the U.S. at the age of one, the person would *not* qualify for the study by virtue of the fact that he or she was born in Canada.

In each of the studies listed earlier, approximately 250 adults participated. So, by the end of the study, there was a database of approximately 750 scripts available for analysis. This is substantially more than most conventional focus group work done by advertising agencies and marketing managers.

Once the content of the stories is analyzed, a "code" and "recipe" (critical path) emerges that crystallizes the emotional experiences of most participants. This code becomes a shorthand way to describe the archetype study. For example, for the door study, the code is "closed from inside," for quality, it is "fail, try again" (See Chapter 5), and for teamwork it is "launch the individual" (See Chapter 6). These codes are not communicated directly, but they enable an executive or manager to reduce the code and recipe to its bare essence. The recipe for quality, for example, is similar to the oops script that we described in Chapter 5.

Independent Validation

The primary limitations of archetype studies are twofold. First, because the findings are often counterintuitive, it is difficult to find a practical place in conventional business practices to apply them. For example, we now know that the word quality has high negative emotional connotations—most of our first and most important experiences with quality involve *failure*. Therefore, simply put, we should not use the word as we do in TQM programs. However, the use of the word is so ingrained in business that most companies continue to talk about quality with total disregard for the cognitive dissonance it creates with employees. (Herein lies a major part of the reason why most quality programs are short-lived or fail to meet the expectations of American executives).

Second, such studies do not quantify the findings by conventional demographics which make traditional managers more comfortable. This second point is compounded by the bias in business for quantitative research, for big sample sizes (that force again). Most political polls and public opionion surveys are based on national random samples of approximately twelve hundred people.

AQF addressed this concern of its corporate sponsors by commissioning The Wirthlin Group to independently validate the archetype studies on quality and improvement using conventional research methodologies. For example, on the subject of New Potential Identities (part of the improvement recipe in America), The Wirthlin Group was able to quantify the dimensions of this cultural dynamic, not only by age as we reported in Chapter 7, but also by education, income, and race. Thus a direct correlation between income and New Potential Identities was confirmed: Americans making less than $15,000 annually are less likely (46 percent) to be optimistic about their future options than are those making $75,000 or more annually (71 percent).* Similarly, Hispanics are slightly more optimistic (63 percent) about what they can become in America than are Caucasians (60 percent) or African Americans (52 percent). And unemployed Americans retain their hope in the future: more than half, 53 percent say they are still in the process of becoming what they want to be.

In addition, The Wirthlin Group was also able to put its research into a communications framework that resonated with AQF and its corporate research sponsors. Some of that research is described in Chapter 5 around the Personal Value Ladder.

Blending Methodologies

Using a different methodology to verify the conclusions of a study is complex. As a general rule this is not done in business. Nevertheless, while there wasn't convergence on all research findings, as one might expect, there was substantial agreement on the major conclusions. By blending the two research approaches, AQF was able to gain some value insight into the ways Americans think that would not otherwise have been possible. For example, when The Wirthlin Group asked a national random sample of twelve hundred Americans if they believed in gradual or sudden change—getting at the bias for action in Americans—55 percent (a substantial majority in polling terms) said they believed in gradual change. This was a major disappointment to AQF because it did not confirm the bias for action they had assumed was true. In reviewing the findings, Rapaille noted that this was the right answer to the wrong question. The right question was to determine how much time should lapse before people expected things to change. Framing the question in this manner made the words "gradual" and "sudden" irrelevant and confirmed the American bias for action. We report on this key finding in Chapter 4, page 164.

The Gallup Surveys

From 1985 through 1994, the Gallup Organization has conducted annual surveys for ASQC on three alternating populations in order to track change in attitudes, perceptions, and behaviors related to a wide range of quality improvement ideas. The groups surveyed were executives, workers, and the general public.

In 1993, the Gallup Survey of American workers confirmed the obvious about teams in business: they are very common. Eight out of ten workers report having some form of team activity at work. Nearly two out of every three full-time employees participate in these team activities with 84 percent involved in more than one team. Approximately 66 percent of these employees report that this is their regular or normal working group.

But the survey also confirmed the less obvious or hidden dimension of teamwork in America. Gallup found that fully two-thirds of American workers get more

---

One surprise finding in the Wirthlin data is that the percent of Americans who are content with their status in life or who have basically given up on becoming something else is relatively constant across all income groups at approximately 22 percent.

satisfaction out of *individual* work than teamwork, confirming the major conclusion of the study on teamwork that we reported on in Chapter 6.

Pilot testing

As Americans we have come to expect, even demand, pilot testing of programs related to public policy issues—Head Start, welfare, minority business set-asides, drug abuse prevention, health intervention programs, traffic control patterns, etc. Some may argue that this is all the government does—pilot test things to death. With respect to new drugs, the protocols are rigorous and demanding, requiring elaborate control studies. Not so in business.

In business, anyone can conduct and promote a study (usually a survey) with questionable methodology and limited analysis and use it as a basis for a new training program or a revised business improvement strategy. In most cases, the study is limited, poorly drawn, methodologically weak, and selectively analyzed. The program benefits are usually anecdotal. The best way to make a consultant who is touting a "research" report nervous is to ask for program documentation and a look at their research and methodology. As a general rule, avoid those who talk around the issue or quote some funny or disjointed numbers.

AQF made a valiant effort to establish a new research benchmark for business; however, the vicissitudes of the workplace complicated the process and limited the best of intentions. A rigorous research design by The Wirthlin Group was applied to the pilot-testing of the *Stuff* program at Packard Electric, a division of General Motors in Warren, Ohio (representing the manufacturing sector), and at an Atlanta-based business unit of New York Life (representing the service sector). The research design called for three groups at each test center: one to serve as the test group and the other two to serve as control groups. The first of these control groups received the pre-test and the post-test. The second group only received the post-test as a way to control for the Hawthorne effect.* The research design incorporated pre/post-test quantitative measurements, focus groups, and one-on-one interviews. The pre and post surveys provided for a comparison among the test and control groups on nearly 150 items covering eleven major areas of work and personal life.

There is no such thing as a perfect experimental design and this pilot testing was no exception. Both companies underwent significant unforeseen management and organizational changes *during* the course of the study. The researchers were not able to control for the impact of these changes on the test group. For these reasons, the comparisons among all three groups at each site did not fully materialize. Nevertheless, the researchers report that the *Stuff* program had three key overall impacts. One, a "significant and immediate positive change at the personal level at home." Two, a "significant, immediate, and lasting impact on interpersonal relationships at work." And three, a "significant positive impact on work processes and quality."

---

*The term "Hawthorne effect" is used to describe a positive change in the performance of a group of people taking part in an experiment or study that is due solely to their perception that they are being singled out for special consideration by management. The name comes from the industry site where these observations were first noted in the 1960s—the Hawthorne Works plant of Western Electric Company in Cicero, Illinois. We've often wondered why the term is used so dismissively by managers and consultants who say "that's only the Hawthorne effect," as though there was something inherently wrong with chalking up positive changes in workers to caring and attentive management.

While much of this change was reported in personal interviews and discussion groups, objective workplace measurements of error prevention and detection were used to show "significant improvement in areas where *Stuff* program principles were applied and supported." As we reported in the opening chapter of this book, Packard Electric's pilot test group significantly out-performed the control groups on two key measures—red-tags (an internal rework designation) were down by 42 percent and the number of days between failures in set-ups and change-overs tripled for the test group from twenty-nine days to over ninety days.

After All Was Said and Measured

While AQF and ASQC did not fully achieve their research intentions with the pilot testing, enough was learned through the process to redesign key elements of the program. These elements drew heavily on the benchmarked training and development experience of the Walt Disney Company, one of the original sponsors of the research effort. The Professional Development Programs at Disney University is now marketing and delivering the revised training program and ancillary services throughout the United States. The *Stuff* program is now substantially improved as a result of the pilot testing and incorporates several new Disney innovations that were not part of the test program. One such innovation is the MAP that is depicted on page 50–51.

The initial premise of the *Stuff* program was to design a training program that addressed the intrinsic needs of Americans and turned that process into a competitive advantage for American companies. It was hoped that much the way the Japanese have a seamless process for integrating work habits and personal values, so too could Americans bring their cultural dynamics to bear more effectively on the workplace. Through our research at AQF and the observations of others, we noted how company training efforts are almost exclusively focused on extrinsic values and objectives. Although there are some signs of change, in general, little, if any regard is given to the benefit of a training program on the *whole* person. In fact, some industries with high turnover in personnel, such as the investment community in the heyday of the 1980s, put little effort into training because it was perceived that that investment would only accrue to the competition!

AQF dreamed of the day when American companies would see training as a way to make their employees better people and thereby have better workers, rather than simply training for higher productivity and quality improvement with no regard for the development needs of the individual. The popularity of training programs like those offered by the Covey Leadership Center attest to the value of seeing the individual and personal improvement as the starting point. The *Stuff* program goes one step further, by providing a national, culturally based context for all training efforts that resonates with individuals and improves the person as well as the work process and company's performance. As author, administrator, and social-commentator John Gardner warns us, "If we don't value our plumbers as well as our philosophers, neither our pipes nor our arguments will hold much water."

BIBLIOGRAPHY

On Culture

Beckerman, Michael. "Dvořak Loved Pigeons and Trains, Not Ideology." *The New York Times*, January 23, 1994.

Beckerman, Michael. "It's Time to Play Ball, and Stretch and Sing," *The New York Times*, April 3, 1994.

Belch, Howard. "Creating a Canon," *Down Beat*, December, 1992.

Boorstin, Daniel J., editor. *An American Primer*. New York: Meridian Classic, 1966.*

Bradford, William. *Of Plymouth Plantation 1620–1647*. New York: Alfred A. Knopf, 1959.

Burnet, Dana. *Poems*. New York: Harper, 1915.

Conway, J. North. *American Literacy: Fifty Books That Define Our Culture and Ourselves*. New York: William Morrow and Company, Inc., 1993.*

Crouch, Stanley. "The Wynton Marsalis Interview, 1987," *Down Beat*, November, 1987.

DeVita, Philip R. and James D. Armstrong, eds. *Distant Mirrors: America as a Foreign Culture*. Belmont, CA: Wadsworth Publishing Company, 1993.*

DuPont, Robert L. *The Selfish Brain: Learning from Addiction*. (To be published). Washington, D.C.: American Psychiatric Press, 1996

Eichenwald, Kurt. "Mismanaged Care: The Perils of Dialysis," *The New York Times*, December 4, 1995.

Eliot, Marc. *Walt Disney: Hollywood's Dark Prince*. Secaucus, NJ: Carol Publishing Group, 1993.

Fallows, James. *More Life Us: Putting America's Native Strengths and Traditional Values to Work to Overcome the Asian Challenge*. Boston: Houghton Mifflin Company, 1989.*

Gross, Edward. *Rocky and the Films of Sylvester Stallone*. Las Vegas: Pioneer Books, Inc., 1990.

von Gwinner, Schnuppe. *The History of the Patchwork Quilt*. West Chester, PA: Schiffer Publishing Ltd., 1988.

Hall, Edward T. *Beyond Culture*. New York: Anchor Books/Doubleday, 1976.

———. *The Dance of Life*. New York: Anchor Books/Doubleday, 1983.*

———. *The Hidden Dimension*. New York: Anchor Books/Doubleday, 1966.

———. *The Silent Language*. New York: Anchor Books/Doubleday, 1959.*

Jones, Andrew. "Wynton: Outstanding in His Field," JAZZIZ, September, 1991.

Kern, Stephen. *The Culture of Time and Space*. Cambridge, MA: Harvard University Press, 1983.

Keyes, Ralph. *Timelock*. New York: Harper & Row, 1973.*

Lamb, David. *A Sense of Place: Listening to Americans*. New York: Times Books, 1993.

*highly recommend

Lerner, Max. *America As A Civilization: Life and Thought in the United States Today.* New York: Simon & Schuster, 1957.*

Liska, James. "Wynton & Branford Marsalis: A Common Understanding," *Down Beat,* December, 1982.

Loewen, James W. *Lies My Teacher Told Me: Everything Your American History Textbook Got Wrong.* New York: The New Press, 1995.*

Mackenzie, Alec. *The Time Trap.* New York: AMACOM, 1990.

Malitz, Nancy. "Wynton Marsalis: Crossover Trumpeter at the Crossroads," *Ovation,* October, 1985.

Murphy, C. J. V. "GI's at Harvard: Best Students in College's History," *Life Magazine,* June 17, 1946.

Murray, Albert. *Stomping The Blues.* New York: Da Capo Press, 1976.

———. *The Omni Americans: Black Experience & American Culture.* New York: Da Capo Press, 1970.*

Musto, David F. *The American Disease: Origins of Narcotic Control.* New York: Oxford Press, 1973.

Olson, Keith W. *The G. I. Bill: The Veterans and The Colleges.* Lexington, KY: University of Kentucky Press, 1974.

Payer, Lynn. *Medicine and Culture.* New York: Penguin Books, 1988.*

Paz, Octavio. *The Labyrinth of Solitude and Other Writings.* New York: Grove Press, 1985.*

Perin, Constance. *Belonging in America: Reading Between the Lines.* Madison, Wisconsin: The University of Wisconsin Press, 1988.

Reis, Al and Jack Trout. *Positioning: The Battle for Your Mind.* New York: McGraw Hill Book Company, 1972.

Rifkin, Jeremy. *Time Wars: The Primary Conflict in Human History.* New York: Henry Holt, 1987.*

Sancton, Thomas. "Horns of Plenty," Cover Story, *Time,* October 22, 1990.

Scherman, Tony. "Wynton Marsalis: The Professor of Swing," *Life,* August, 1993.

Solomon, Charles. *Enchanted Drawings: The History of Animation.* New York: Alfred A. Knopf, 1989.

Takaki, Ronald. *A Different Mirror: A History of Multicultural America.* Boston: Little, Brown and Company, 1993.*

Thomas, Lowell. *So Long Until Tomorrow.* Boston: G. K. Hall, 1987.

de Tocqueville, Alexis. *Democracy in America.* New York: Vintage Classics, 1990.*

Ward, Geoffrey C. and Ken Burns. *Baseball: An Illustrated History.* New York: Alfred A. Knopf, 1994.

White, Kevin. "Trumpeter Wynton Marsalis: Sounding Like Himself," *Digital Audio,* April, 1985.

Willison, George F. *Saints and Strangers.* New York: Reynal & Hitchcock, 1945.*

Zimmerman, Kent. "Wynton Marsalis: Leading the Revolt Against Ignorance in America," *The Gavin Report,* August 28, 1992.

On Culture and Business

American Quality Foundation. "Research Report: The Personal Quality Improvement Process of the American Quality Foundation." ASQC, 1994.

Baida, Peter. *Poor Richard's Legacy: American Business Values From Benjamin Franklin to Donald Trump.* New York: William Morrow, 1990.*

Browning, E. S. "Computer Chip Project Brings Rivals Together, But the Cultures Clash." *The Wall Street Journal,* May 3, 1994.*

Cole, Robert E. *Strategies for Learning: Small Group Activities in American, Japanese, and Swedish Industry.* Berkeley: University of California Press, 1989.

O'Hara-Devereaux, Mary and Robert Johansen. *GlobalWork: Bridging Distance, Culture & Time*. San Francisco: Jossey-Bass, 1994.*

Hampden-Turner, Charles and Alfons Trompenaars. *The Seven Cultures of Capitalism*. New York: Doubleday, 1993.*

Moran, Robert T. and Jeffrey Abbott. NAFTA: *Managing the Cultural Differences*. Houston: Gulf Publishing Company, 1994.

Trompenaars, Fons. *Riding The Waves of Culture: Understanding Cultural Diversity in Business*. London: The Economist Books, 1993.

Zuckerman, Marilyn R. and Lewis J. Hatala. *Incredibly American: Releasing the Heart of Quality*. Milwaukee, WI: Quality Press, 1992.*

On Business & Management

Bowles, Jerry and Joshua Hammond. *Beyond Quality*. New York: G. P. Putnam's Son, 1991.*

Burgelman, Robert and Leonard R. Sayles. *Inside Corporate Innovation*. New York: Free Press, 1986.

Cathcart, W. A. "Return on Quality: New Frontiers of Measurement at Avis." Speech, Fortune World-Class Quality Roundtable, London, 1995. New York: Basic Books, 1977.

Collins, James C. and Jerry I. Porras. *Built to Last: Successful Habits of Visionary Companies*. New York: HarperCollins, 1994.*

Cooper, Henry S. F., Jr. *13: The Flight That Failed*. New York: Dial Press, 1973.

Drucker, Peter F. *Innovation and Entrepreneurship: Practice and Principles*. New York: Harper & Row, 1985.*

———. *The New Realities: In Government and Politics/In Economics and Business/In Society and World View*. New York: Harper & Row, 1989.

DuPont, Robert L. *Drug-Related Impairment in the Workplace: A Practical Guide*. Rockville, MD: Bensinger, DuPont Associates, 1991.

Greco, Rosemarie B. "From the Classroom to the Corner Office," *Harvard Business Review*, September–October, 1992.

Gustin, Lawrence. *Billy Durant, Creator of General Motors*. Flushing, MI: Craneshaw Publishers, 1984.

Heidenry, John. *Theirs Was The Kingdom*. New York: W. W. Norton, 1993.

Howard, Robert. "Values Make the Company: An Interview with Robert Haas." *Harvard Business Review*, September-October, 1990.

Keidel, Robert W. *Corporate Players: Designs for Working and Winning Together*. New York: Wiley & Sons, 1988.

Krooss, Herman E. and Charles Gilbert. *American Business History*. Englewood Cliffs, NJ: Prentice-Hall, 1972.

Rogers, Everett M. *Diffusion of Innovation*. New York: Free Press, 1995.

Rashke, Richard. *Stormy Genius*. Boston: Houghton Mifflin, 1985.

Rifkin, Jeremy. *The End of Work: The Decline of the Global Labor Force and the Dawn of the Post-Market Era*. New York: Putnam Publishing Group, 1994.

Senge, Peter. *The Fifth Discipline*. New York: Doubleday, 1990.

Serwer, Andrew E. "Charlotte's Battling Bankers Are Scoring Big." *Fortune*, July 24, 1995.

Simison, Robert L. and Oscar Suris. "Alex Trotman's Goal: To Make Ford No. 1 In World Auto Sales." *The Wall Street Journal*, July 18, 1995.

Sloan, Alfred P. *My Years with General Motors*. Garden City, NY: Doubleday, 1964.

Shook, Robert L. *Turnaround: The New Ford Company*. New York: Prentice Hall Press, 1990.

Wriston, Walter. *The Twilight of Sovereignty*. New York: Scribner, 1992.

Zuboff, Shoshana. *In The Age of The Smart Machine*. New York: Basic Books, 1988.

———. "The Emperor's New Workplace," *Scientific American*, September, 1995.

Index